The Celestial Web

The Celestial Web

Buddhism and Christianity
A Different Comparison

Perry Schmidt-Leukel

Translated
by David West

Maryknoll, New York 10545

Founded in 1970, Orbis Books endeavors to publish works that enlighten the mind, nourish the spirit, and challenge the conscience. The publishing arm of the Maryknoll Fathers and Brothers, Orbis seeks to explore the global dimensions of the Christian faith and mission, to invite dialogue with diverse cultures and religious traditions, and to serve the cause of reconciliation and peace. The books published reflect the views of their authors and do not represent the official position of the Maryknoll Society. To learn more about Maryknoll and Orbis Books, please visit our website at www.orbisbooks.com.

Copyright © 2024 by Perry Schmidt-Leukel

English translation published by Orbis Books, P.O. Box 302, Maryknoll, NY 10545-0302.

Translated from the German, *Das himmlische Geflecht: Buddhismus und Christentum—ein anderer Vergleich,* copyright © 2022 by Gütersloher Verlagshaus, Gütersloh, Munich, Germany.

All rights reserved.

No part of this publication may be reproduced or transmitted in any form or by any means, electronic or mechanical, including photocopying, recording, or any information storage or retrieval system, without prior permission in writing from the publisher.

Queries regarding rights and permissions should be addressed to: Orbis Books, P.O. Box 302, Maryknoll, NY 10545-0302.

Manufactured in the United States of America

Library of Congress Cataloging-in-Publication Data

Names: Schmidt-Leukel, Perry, author. | West, David, translator.
Title: The celestial web : Buddhism and Christianity—a different comparison / Perry Schmidt-Leukel ; translated by David West.
Other titles: Das Himmlische Geflecht. English.
Description: Maryknoll, NY : Orbis Books, 2024. | Translation of: Das himmlische Geflecht : Buddhismus und Christentum—ein anderer Vergleich.
| Includes bibliographical references and index. | Summary: "A comparison of Buddhism and Christianity that treats the varieties and the various points of similarities in both traditions"—Provided by publisher.
Identifiers: LCCN 2024012701 (print) | LCCN 2024012702 (ebook) | ISBN 9781626985933 (trade paperback) | ISBN 9798888660492 (epub)
Subjects: LCSH: Buddhism—Relations—Christianity. | Christianity and other religions—Buddhism.
Classification: LCC BR128.B8 S32613 2024 (print) | LCC BR128.B8 (ebook) | DDC 294.3/352—dc23/eng/20240402
LC record available at https://lccn.loc.gov/2024012701
LC ebook record available at https://lccn.loc.gov/2024012702

For Paul F. Knitter
Pioneer of Religious Pluralism,
Buddhist and Christian,
Friend

Contents

Preface   *ix*

Introduction: The Celestial Web: Indra's Net   *xiii*

1 Comparing Religions: Why and What For?   1
   1.1 Comparing Religions in Religious Studies   1
   1.2 Comparing Religions in Theology   13

2 The Discovery of Fractal Structures: New Perspectives for the Comparison of Religions   23
   2.1 Perspectives from Cultural and Religious Studies   23
   2.2 Perspectives from Interreligious Theology   33

3 In the World   51
   3.1 Renouncing the World or Affirming the World?   51
   3.2 Renouncing the World and Affirming the World in Buddhism   58
   3.3 Affirming the World and Renouncing the World in Christianity   68
   3.4 Nonattachment and Loving Involvement   76

4 Ultimate Reality   85
   4.1 Impersonal Absolute or Personal God?   85
   4.2 Impersonal and Personal Notions of Transcendence in Buddhism   94
   4.3 Personal and Impersonal Notions of Transcendence in Christianity   101
   4.4 Speaking of the Ineffable   106

5 What Is Wrong with Us?   120
   5.1 Delusion or Sin?   120
   5.2 Delusion and Sinful Self-Attachment in Buddhism   124
   5.3 Sinful Self-Attachment and Delusion in Christianity   132
   5.4 Insight and Trust   138

6 Bearers of Hope — 142
  6.1 Awakened Teacher or Son of God Incarnate? 142
  6.2 Awakening, Proclamation, and Incarnation 147
  6.3 Disentanglement and Entanglement 157

7 The Path — 167
  7.1 Salvation: Self-Help or Other-Help? 167
  7.2 Salvation by Self-Help and Other-Help in Buddhism 173
  7.3 Salvation by Other-Help and Self-Help in Christianity 179
  7.4 Salvation of the Self from the Self 181

8 Beyond the Horizon ... — 189
  8.1 Blissful Cessation or Blissful Communion? 189
  8.2 Individual and Social Facets in Buddhist Concepts of Salvation 195
  8.3 Salvation as Union with God and as Perfected Society in Christianity 210
  8.4 On the Complementarity of Eschatological Images 225

9 Buddhism and Christianity: A New Understanding— A New Relationship — 232
  9.1 In the Eye of the Beholder? 233
  9.2 Fractal Structures as a Basis for Interreligious Learning 237

References — 245

Index of Names — 279

Preface

"The fourth book in the Hitch-Hiker trilogy" is how Douglas Adams prefaced his *So Long, and Thanks for All the Fish*. Something similar could be said about this book, since it brings together threads from three previous works: *God Beyond Boundaries*,[1] *Understanding Buddhism*,[2] and *Religious Pluralism and Interreligious Theology*.[3]

In *God Beyond Boundaries*, I outline a Christian and pluralistic theology of religions—that is, a theology that no longer implies that Christianity is the only true or at least best religion, but instead sees a genuine value in the diversity of religions. In *Understanding Buddhism*, I show how Buddhism fits into such a perspective—that is, how in Buddhism, experiences of transcendence have been conceptualized in specific ways and been made the key factor in ways of living that strive to combine wisdom and compassion. Finally, *Religious Pluralism and Interreligious Theology* describes in its first part how today, in all major religious traditions, pluralistic conceptions are developing that value other religions as alternative but nonetheless equally valid paths to salvation and liberation. The second part of the book then shows how a new form of theology emerges from such shifts: namely, an interreligious theology that people of different religions advance together. Such a theology still confronts the great issues of humanity: those questions that life itself poses to humanity and to each one of us, and that religions take up, reflect upon in ever new ways, respond to with greater or lesser caution, and translate into concrete practice. To this end, interreligious theology, guided as it is by the notion that religious diversity reflects religiously significant truth, no longer draws only on the tradition of its own specific religion, but also on the testimony of religious experiences and their intellectual presence within humanity as a whole.

Religious Pluralism and Interreligious Theology ends with the observation that this notion is true not only for the global history of religion, but also for each individual religious tradition. No religion is homogeneous,

---

[1] German original: Schmidt-Leukel 2005; English edition: Schmidt-Leukel 2017a.
[2] English original: Schmidt-Leukel 2006a; German edition: Schmidt-Leukel 2020a [1st ed. 2017].
[3] English original: Schmidt-Leukel 2017b; German edition: 2019a.

but instead incorporates an immense diversity of forms of expression. What is more, there are many astonishing parallels between the diversity within religions and religious diversity globally. These are even reflected in the diversity of religious attitudes that an individual person can harbor, either simultaneously or over the course of their life. Building on this insight, the present volume offers a different, novel comparison of Christianity and Buddhism, one that does not treat them as if they were more or less homogeneous entities. Rather, it accounts for the inner diversity of both religions in such a way as to reveal how the differences within both traditions are parallel. Although Buddhism and Christianity clearly differ from each other, they also resemble one another precisely in the structural patterns of their internal diversity.

Grasping this more clearly has far-reaching consequences for how we understand religious diversity and what it means theologically and religiously—consequences that point toward theological pluralism. For example, if we do not wish to interpret such diversity in an atheistic sense as a diversity of human illusion, it becomes possible to provide tentative answers to the question of why there is such a diversity of religious manifestations in the first place. In other words, we can answer the question of why religious truth appears in diverse forms. This is the subject of the present book.

Writing a *different* comparison also involves scrutinizing previous comparisons of Buddhism and Christianity, which is what I also do in this book. I was able to draw here partly on my own earlier research,[4] which has now been supplemented by considering and analyzing further and more recent comparative studies. I developed the underlying concept for the present book in the course of a series of lectures that I gave in October 2017 at the invitation of Professor You Bin at Minzu University in Beijing.[5] Once again, my sincere thanks go to my Chinese colleague for this opportunity. I would also like to thank Reinhard Achenbach, Karl Baier, Eve-Marie Becker, Albrecht Beutel, Lutz Doering, Christina Högen-Rohls, Assaad Elias Kattan, Hermut Löhr, Mathias Schneider, and Holger Strutwolf, who provided me with numerous helpful suggestions based on their own expertise. I am grateful for the many hours that my secretary, Martina Forstmann, and my wife, Doris, invested in carefully proofreading the various chapter drafts of the German edition. All remaining errors are, of course, solely due to my own carelessness. I would also like to thank the German Research Foundation,

---

[4]Schmidt-Leukel 1992.
[5]These lectures were published as *To See a World in a Flower* in a bilingual edition (English-Chinese) by Zong jiao wen hua chu ban she (Religious Culture Publishing House) in Beijing in 2019. The concept of *To See a World in a Flower* has been revised and considerably expanded in *The Celestial Web*—not merely in relation to individual chapters, but also by the addition of four new chapters so that the current version has now grown to three times the original size.

Preface xi

which, through funding from the Cluster of Excellence "Religion and Politics," made it possible for me to take two research sabbaticals during which I wrote the bulk of the original manuscript. It also provided the funds for the translation of the German book into English. My main gratitude for this is to David West, who took this task into his experienced hands.[6] Further, I would like to thank Robert Ellsberg of Orbis Books for his willingness to publish the present work as a sequel to *Religious Pluralism and Interreligious Theology*. And, of course, everyone at Orbis who put their time and effort into producing the book.[7]

Not least, I thank all those with whom I have been able to discuss my ideas regarding a fractal interpretation of religious diversity since I first presented them at my Gifford Lectures in 2015. The positive feedback and critical questions that I have received from numerous colleagues around the world; from participants at congresses, conferences, and guest lectures; and from my students—these helped me greatly in my own reflections. A very special role was played here by my conversations, over many years, with Paul Knitter, to whom I therefore dedicate this book.

---

[6] I discussed and checked the translation with David so that it is an "authorized" translation.
[7] Compared to the German version, the U.S. edition contains some minor revisions, corrections, and literature updates.

Introduction

The Celestial Web: Indra's Net

There is a common image in Mahayana Buddhism, the so-called Great or Eminent Vehicle, that equates reality with a celestial web: the jeweled net of the god Indra. The very influential *Avataṃsaka-Sūtra*,[1] in particular, alludes many times to this,[2] although nowhere does the text directly explain the image itself, assuming that it is already familiar among Buddhists. The Chinese Buddhist master Dushun (Tu-shun and also Fa-shun, sixth to seventh century CE) explains the image as follows, saying that it

> illustrates how the many things interpenetrate like the realm of Indra's net of jewels. . . . This imperial net is made all of jewels: because the jewels are clear, they reflect each other's images, appearing in each other's reflections upon reflections, ad infinitum, all appearing at once in one jewel, and in each one it is so.[3]

Thus, Indra's net is a web spreading throughout the sky, its nodes holding clear jewels, each reflecting the whole net in its own way. Master Dushun is considered to be the first patriarch of the Huayan school of Chinese Buddhism. This school draws especially on the teachings of the Indian *Avatataṃsaka-Sūtra*,[4] which probably dates in its later form from the fourth century CE and is an extensive compilation of even older texts of Mahayana Buddhism. Thus, the first Chinese translations of individual parts of the *Avataṃsaka-Sūtra* date back to the second century.

However, the idea of the world as a vast net belonging to the god Indra is much older, and indeed goes back to ideas already found in Vedic texts

---

[1] I have omitted diacritical marks for all names of persons and for all terms used as English words (such as nirvana, samsara, sangha, etc.) but retained them for titles of scriptures or references to the original terms and, of course, when they were used in citations.
[2] Especially in books 4, 5, 12, 21, 25, 33, 34, 39.
[3] As in his tract *Cessation and Contemplation in the Five Teachings of the Hua-yen*, quoted here from the English translation by Thomas Cleary (1983, 66).
[4] See Schmidt-Leukel 2006a, 141–43.

xiii

(*Atharva Veda* 8.8.8). But Mahayana Buddhism gives the image the special nuance of the clarity of the individual jewels, these symbolizing the "emptiness" or insubstantiality of all things that make up a world, indeed all worlds as a whole. This in turn leads to the idea of their mutual reflection, and finally to the idea that the entire web is reflected and refracted in each of its parts. The celestial web thus corresponds to a "fractal" pattern—that is, a pattern in which the structure's individual components repeat basic features of the whole structure.

According to the *Avataṃsaka-Sūtra*, the image of Indra's net is not connected with the idea of an amorphous mass. Even if the ultimate reality hidden in and behind everything transcends every material or conceptual form, and in this sense is "formless" or "amorphous" (Sanskrit: *arupya*), it is nevertheless manifested in countless forms, precisely as a myriad web of diversity and difference. Thus, the twenty-fifth book of the *Sūtra* says: even if all worlds interpenetrate each other infinitely, they can still be distinguished from one another. Those who can recognize the whole in each part do so "without destroying the features of their structures, causing all to be clearly seen."[5]

It is in this respect especially that the ancient metaphor of "Indra's" or "God's" net is suitable for the novel comparison of Buddhism and Christianity presented here, since I regard Buddhism and Christianity not as homogeneous entities, but as complex, multilayered, and sometimes heterogeneous structures. Scrutinizing the internal diversity of both religions reveals fractal structural patterns, which means that obvious differences *between* the two religions can also be seen *within* each of them. Structurally, a quasi-reciprocal interpenetration of both religions becomes visible; their relationship resembles the celestial web.

However, in the spirit of the *Avataṃsaka-Sūtra*, this does not mean blurring the differences, which will still "be clearly seen," but as part of a far more differentiated—indeed, fractal—structure. This, I hope, can help us recognize and understand better the structural patterns of religious diversity as a whole, including and especially in terms of their theological significance. The fact that some of the differences embedded in the fractal patterns turn out to be complementary makes clear how far such complex traditions are related to each other and can therefore enrich but also correct one another.

The first two chapters are devoted to the methodology of this new form of comparative religion. Chapter 1 addresses the significance and the crisis of the comparative method within religious studies and theology, but also the attempts to rehabilitate and reconceptualize comparative religion. Chapter

---

[5] According to Thomas Cleary's English translation (1993, 656).

Introduction xv

2 develops the thesis that religious diversity displays fractal patterns, and discusses the significance of this thesis for the understanding of religion and the comparison of religions from the perspective of religious studies and theology.

After these introductory reflections, I turn in the following chapters to the actual comparison of Buddhism and Christianity. Any comparison is of course selective, since, as Oliver Freiberger has noted, "one can only compare *in view of something*."[6] I take for my points of comparison how both religions relate to the world (chapter 3), how they understand ultimate reality (chapter 4), what their view is of the dark side of human existence (chapter 5), as well as how they see salvation/liberation in terms of the figures mediating it (chapter 6), the paths leading to it (chapter 7), and finally its goals (chapter 8).

The real point of comparison (*tertium comparationis*), however, is a second-order point of comparison. Each of chapters 3 to 8 begins from the different contrasts between both religions, which are often seen as opposites. Then I bring in the fractal perspective. That is, I show by means of prominent highlights that the different positions with regard to the respective thematic field (the *tertium comparationis* of the first order) can also be found in each of the two religions. *Comparing these intrareligious differences* thus forms my true point of comparison.

Each of these chapters also addresses the question of why, despite their different emphases and accents, both religions have developed such parallel intrareligious differences. Mutual historical influences play only a minor role at most,[7] and I therefore pursue a different line of inquiry: namely, whether each of the parallel differences can be understood as complementary—for it would then be conceivable that both, and presumably all major, religions contain something like an inner dynamic to synthesize opposing currents. Given the specific and thus inevitably partial emphases of each religious tradition, such a dynamic aims at a greater wholeness. An entelechy toward greater wholeness could at least partially explain the parallel occurrence of complementary differences. "The study of fractals in the natural world," says William Jackson, "reveals hidden implicit wholeness, orders hitherto undiscerned."[8] The mathematician Benoît Mandelbrot derived the noun "the fractal" and the adjective "fractal" from the Latin *frangere/fractus* (to break, broken),[9] the fractal fragment therefore implicitly referring to the larger wholeness of a fractal order. If we add the temporal dimension of

---

[6]Freiberger 2019, 31.
[7]On the issue of historical dependencies between Buddhism and Christianity, see Schmidt-Leukel 1992, 21–35; Winter 2008.
[8]Jackson, W. 2004, 60.
[9]Mandelbrot 1983, 4.

fractal orders, then we can agree with William Jackson: "Fractals involve holism in dynamic ways."[10] That is, individual complex entities that, like religions, are subject to progressive growth tend toward a kind of wholeness by forming more and more substructures, thereby integrating an ever-increasing diversity. Identifying such dynamic interconnections within both intrareligious and interreligious diversity is very significant theologically, since it can provide a new basis for how theology interprets the relationship between the great religions of humankind, and open up space for interreligious learning. I elaborate on this in the concluding chapter 9.

---

[10]Jackson W. 2004, 69.

1

Comparing Religions

Why and What For

1.1 COMPARING RELIGIONS IN RELIGIOUS STUDIES

Knowledge through Comparison

A new discipline gradually emerged in Europe toward the end of the nineteenth century: the science of religions, now mostly called "religious studies."[1] Many of its pioneers regarded one of the most important tasks of this new "science" as being the comparison of religions. Friedrich Max Müller (1823–1900) is widely seen as one of its "fathers." He was convinced that a comparative study of religions would yield similarly important insights as the "Science of Language" (comparative linguistics), which was a young but already very successful discipline at the time. By comparing different languages, the latter had succeeded in discerning and understanding better the historical development of individual languages as well as their differentiation into either related or unrelated language families. For Müller, it was now the task of the comparative study of religions to accomplish something similar. Only by doing so would it finally become possible to understand the actual point and purpose of religion as a human phenomenon.[2]

Many of the pioneers of religious studies were, like Müller himself, Christians. For them, the goal of understanding religion and religions better was linked to another hope: an unprejudiced and quasi-objective comparison of religions would finally be able to prove scientifically and without theological bias that Christianity is the highest and most perfect of all religions. The idea of the superiority or even the sole truth of Christianity had been taken for granted in the West for more than one and a half millennia, but clear

---
[1]See Tworuschka 2015.
[2]On this, see Müller 1868, xix.

doubts had been voiced since the Enlightenment at the latest. Not a few enlightened atheists used arguments from comparative religion to demonstrate the implausibility of Christianity and indeed of all other religions. In 1757, for example, David Hume wrote in his epochal *The Natural History of Religion* that an examination of actual religious ideas in the world barely allows any other conclusion than that they are "sick men's dreams,"[3] and that the study of religious history shows that religion is a source of constant conflict, violence, and other evils. "If the religious spirit be ever mentioned in any historical narration, we are sure to meet afterwards with a detail of the miseries, which attend it." Therefore, Hume continued, "no period of time can be happier or more prosperous, than those in which it is never regarded, or heard of."[4] In contrast to such views, which soon became commonplace among Enlightenment atheists, scholars such as Müller, Nathan Söderblom (1866–1931), Rudolf Otto (1869–1937), and Friedrich Heiler (1892–1967) counted on the hope that comparing religions could demonstrate the elements of truth and positive commonalities in all religions, while at the same time revealing Christianity as their actual fulfillment. "In order to understand fully the position of Christianity in the history of the world, and its true place among the religions of mankind," says Müller, "we must compare it."[5] It is not surprising that, with such an objective, the "Science of Religion" was also labeled "Comparative Theology" at the time.[6] Müller himself insisted on it as the correct name for the new discipline.[7]

Particularly popular and widespread among the early comparisons of religions were those comparing Christianity and Buddhism, and their two central figures, Christ and Buddha. Not only Christian authors, but also Buddhist sympathizers in the West and Buddhist activists and reformers in Asia made use of the comparative genre to pursue their apologetic interests and to demonstrate the superiority of their own religion. In Germany, for example, Georg Grimm (1868–1945), in his large-scale comparison *Buddha and Christ* (1928), contrasted what he considered to be the unsurpassed philosophical insights of Gautama Buddha with a Jesus who had become "the victim of the great delusion of his people," by which he meant the belief in a personal God and the expectation of a Messiah.[8] For Grimm, a bridge to the teaching of the Buddha could only be found in Christian mysticism.[9] In Sri Lanka, then Ceylon, Anagarika Dharmapala (1864–1933) wrote a number

---

[3] Section 15 "General corollary." See Hume 1757 (1777), N. 16.6.
[4] *Dialogues concerning Natural Religion*, Part XII. See Hume 1779, D. 12.11.
[5] Müller 1868, xxviii.
[6] See Nicholson 2009, 611–16.
[7] Müller 1874, 19. See also Masuzawa 2003, 317.
[8] Grimm 1928, 167.
[9] Ibid., 210.

of shorter essays that compared Buddhism with other religions, especially with Christianity and Hinduism, and he presented Buddhism as the most morally perfect religion and the one most conducive to a modern scientific attitude.[10] In China, the Buddhist reformer Taixu (T'ai-hsü, 1890–1947) was certainly open to being inspired by the social and charitable side of Christianity, but nevertheless used comparisons in his popular writings to emphasize Buddhism's ethical and philosophical superiority.[11]

A whole series of stereotypical contrasts emerged and took root with regard to the relationship between Buddhism and Christianity both in openly confrontational and apologetic comparisons, as well as in the supposedly neutral and unbiased comparisons of the young discipline of religious studies. These comparisons saw Buddhism as world-renouncing, pessimistic, and passive, and Christianity as world-affirming, optimistic, and active. They contrasted the Buddhist denial of a personal God with the Christian belief in a benign creator. While Buddhism understands the human predicament as delusion and thus as a cognitive problem, Christianity regards human misery as sin and thus in terms more of ethics. In contrast to the Christian belief in a savior sent by God, Buddhism draws on the teachings of an enlightened human being. As far as the path to salvation/liberation is concerned, Buddhism counts on the ability of humans to redeem themselves, whereas Christianity stresses divine grace. And while Buddhism sees the final salvation/liberation in a nihilistic manner as liberation from all existence, Christianity hopes for an eternal life in blissful community.[12]

While such clichéd juxtapositions have always also been modified to some extent, what becomes clear in the course of this book is that they nevertheless often continue to have an effect into the present. The strongest critical inquiries into the common stereotypes of Christian-Buddhist relations, however, have come less from religious studies than from the philologies and Christian-Buddhist dialogue. This is also due to the fact that the comparison of religions within religious studies has been increasingly criticized since the 1970s, and has thus become less important. In contrast, Christian theology has developed at about the same time an understanding of dialogue that sees other religions as a possible source of theologically relevant truth that should be recognized and explored. Comparative and interreligious forms of theology have since developed from this. However, let us first stay with religious studies.

Comparing religions was considered for decades one of the most important, if not *the* most important, methods of religious studies, often even

---
[10]Guruge 1965, 1–74, 347–477.
[11]Pittman 2001, 242–54.
[12]See Schmidt-Leukel 1992, 9–141.

giving the discipline as a whole its name ("Comparative Religion" or "Vergleichende Religionswissenschaft"). Influenced not least by Joachim Wach's reflections from 1924 on the theoretical foundations of religious studies,[13] many scholars accepted that comparisons in the discipline should be kept free of ideological and theological intentions, serving neither openly nor covertly Christian-theological or analogous religious as well as nonreligious objectives. Rather, according to Wach, such comparisons should serve the "exploration and representation of the empirical religions"[14] without normative points of view.[15] However, for Wach, religious studies certainly also pursues its own systematic goals, working out inductively the common, the organizational principle, the inner "framework" of religions.[16] And for this the method of comparison takes center stage.[17] According to Wach, comparative religion is "substantial, essential" for the development of a formal systematics in religious studies.[18]

Problems with Comparing Religions

However, Joachim Wach already drew attention to some "dangers" associated with the method of comparison. For example, there was the problem of tearing the phenomena compared from their original context and thus "not allowing the peculiarity of the phenomenon in question to come into its own,"[19] as well as the problem of choosing the right comparative viewpoint, the so-called *tertium comparationis*.[20] Nevertheless, he considered comparison to be indispensable, since only this could reveal structures, i.e., "regularities" and "patterns" ("Gesetzmäßigkeiten"), in the religions and their development.[21]

Diachronic comparisons of religious sources within a single religious tradition prove to be somewhat unproblematic and illuminating. Without such comparisons, it would be impossible to discern certain lines of development within a religion. Diachronic reconstructions always work with a perspective that compares the different stages of development. Yet precisely this form of comparison also allows for and even triggers synchronic comparisons—as, for example, when certain developments within a religious tradition branch

---

[13] Wach (1924) 2001. The following quotations are directly translated from this reprint of the German original and deliberately not taken from the English translation of the same work in Wach 1988, 1–150.
[14] Wach (1924) 2001, 68.
[15] Ibid., 61.
[16] Ibid., 178.
[17] Ibid., 179–80.
[18] Ibid., 182.
[19] Ibid., 183.
[20] Ibid., 184–85.
[21] Ibid., 186.

out and thus make discernible different manifestations of historical processes. The affinity to linguistics becomes particularly evident here,[22] since, as with the identification of related language families, it is also possible to identify religious families in this way—i.e., religions that are undeniably related to one another within a particular context of historical transmission, but that nevertheless differ from each other, with each producing its own process of further development and differentiation. But it is also possible to compare singular religions or families of religions with one another that are not related to one another by looking at their respective developments and characteristics synchronically. As with the comparison of different language families, this method allows for the differences between various religions or groups of religions to be characterized and thus classified or typologized. In so doing, religious studies used to be concerned with "the recording of their respective typical features, their dominant characteristics," which "should then form the principle of a grouping and division of religions," such as into monotheistic and polytheistic religions, natural and historical religions, or the widespread division into prophetic and mystical religions.[23]

However, classification and typologization were aimed not only at religions or families of religions but also at the individual elements or phenomena within them, the guiding assumption here being that the defining features of a particular type of religion can also be related to the elements within the respective religion or religious family. In other words, religious leaders, beliefs, narratives, cults, places of worship, ideals, ethics, aesthetics, feelings, etc., were thought to take on a characteristic form and hue corresponding to the different type of religion. But this never quite worked out, since the number and kind of parallels between the religions—also between religions of different families or types—were simply too great. Almost all the elements that can be named in a major religious tradition seem to be found in one way or another in other traditions, too. These findings could not be sufficiently explained by pointing to historical mixtures, dependencies, and crossovers, as Friedrich Heiler had still tried to do.[24] Rather, religions, especially when they reach a certain size and age, are too internally heterogeneous to allow themselves to be fixed to the form and characteristics of a certain type. They are not simply one specific part within the religious diversity of humankind, but form within themselves as living traditions their own diversity of diverging manifestations. A central thesis of this book is that there is a structural parallelism and presumably a substantial connection between the two: interreligious and intrareligious diversity.

---

[22]Similarly, Hock 2006, 71.
[23]Lanczkowski 1980, 53.
[24]See Heiler (1919) 1921, 233–34.

No Essentialization of Religion

Although religious studies has been aware of intrareligious diversity from the very beginning, this long played no major role in its systematic reflections. This has increasingly changed since the 1960s, and today there is no dispute in religious studies that there is no such thing as "Christianity" or "Buddhism" in the sense of constituting homogeneous entities. A first milestone in this development was Wilfred Cantwell Smith's epochal work *The Meaning and End of Religion*,[25] which was first published in 1963. Smith pointed out in this study on the evolution and function of the concept of "religion" that the essentialization connected to this concept since the modern period contradicts the historical reality of religions:

> Obviously, I am not suggesting that what men have called the religions do not exist. The point is rather that, as every historian of them knows almost to his bewilderment, they exist all too copiously. It is the richness, the radical diversity, the unceasing shift and change, the ramification and complex involvement, of the historical phenomena of "religion" or any one "religion" that create the difficulty. What has been called Christianity is, so far as history is concerned, not one thing but millions of things, and hundreds of millions of persons.[26]

In the end, Smith says, "There are as many religions in the world as there are people."[27] To avoid any essentialization of "religion," Smith suggested replacing the term "religion" with the pair of terms "faith" and "cumulative tradition." The former denotes here the inner religious attitude of an individual, something that cannot be directly observed, while the latter denotes all observable and historically describable manifestations of a "religion." The two belong together and interact with one another.

Smith's suggestion that we abandon the concept of religion as misleading and replace it with more appropriate concepts has found influential followers. In Europe in the late 1980s, Dario Sabbatucci called for the "dissolution of the concept of religion in the concept of culture." Agreeing with this, Burkhard Gladigow saw "the actual achievement of religious studies" in a "consistent transformation" of its objects "into terms of cultural studies."[28] Similar views have been expressed in the English-speaking world by, for

---

[25] The "end" in this title is intentionally ambiguous, indicating both purpose and abolition.
[26] Smith (1963) 1978, 144–45.
[27] Ibid., 233n120.
[28] Sabbatucci 1988, 57; Gladigow 1988, 33.

example, Russell T. McCutcheon, Timothy Fitzgerald, and the literary and religious studies scholar Tomoko Masuzawa.[29]

A central argument against the academic utility of the concept of religion is based on the observation that this concept has developed within Western culture, and on the idea that other cultures or "religions" had no real equivalents for it. Therefore, any application of the concept in non-Western cultural areas would inevitably lead to misunderstandings and distortions. While the Western genesis of the concept of religion is undisputed, there has been much counterevidence forwarded to disprove its exclusively Western nature. Extensive studies have shown that there are indeed no exact equivalents to the concept of religion in non-Western cultures. However, their existence would hardly be possible, given that the term "religion" is highly complex even in the West, i.e., in its different languages and different epochs. By no means was it or is it always used with one exact meaning. Nevertheless, significant parallels can be found with its different aspects and facets.[30] Jens Schlieter therefore argues that the position "that no equivalents can be found to the European term 'religion' in non-European cultures is hardly tenable."[31] Moreover, it would be no easier to find exact equivalents to the concept of "culture" in non-Western languages and cultures—after all, it also originated within the West, where it is anything but unambiguous even within Western languages.[32] But should we then conclude that no culture or cultures exist outside the West? Or that applying the concept of culture outside the West inevitably leads to misunderstanding and distortion of these "cultures"?

As already mentioned, religious studies today widely accepts the criticism of an essentialist understanding of religion as such, as well as of individual religions, i.e., the criticism of an understanding that assumes that religion or religions each have something like their own specific and unchanging essence. Regarding the concept of religion, an alternative would be to use it as a cluster category, i.e., "polythetically."[33] This would mean seeing "religion" as a set of individual components and elements, such as a specific ("religious") community, rituals, a particular ethos, links to the sociopolitical dimension, ("sacred") scriptures, myths, narratives, certain teachings or ideas, reference to a supernatural, transcendent realm, and aesthetic and spiritual aspects.[34] Such components—and this is important for this ap-

---

[29] McCutcheon 1997; Fitzgerald 2000; Masuzawa 2005. For an overview and discussion, see also Bergunder 2011.
[30] See, for example, Haußig 1999; Schalk et al. 2013.
[31] Schlieter 2010, 266. Similarly, Seiwert 2020, 214–16.
[32] Consider, for example, the overlapping of "civilization" and "culture," and their nuances.
[33] As, for example, J. Z. Smith (1982, 1–8) already does in an essay from 1978.
[34] See Whaling 1986, 37–48.

proach—do not always have to be present in the same form, weighting, or even number in order to describe something meaningfully as "religion" or "religious." Rather, religions resemble each other in each case only with regard to some aspects that vary among themselves. According to this approach, the term "religion" is used in the sense of Wittgenstein's concept of "family resemblance."[35] Just as the family of "games" includes such different things as board games, card games, ball games, games of chance, etc., so "religion" also designates a family of highly diverse phenomena. Just as in a family some family members have the same hair color, but others have a similar eye color or a similarly shaped nose, so some religions also have partially matching characteristics, but not every religion shares all characteristics and certainly not in exactly the same form.

Such an understanding of "religion" has been proposed within religious studies apart from Frank Whaling by Ninian Smart[36] and Benson Saler,[37] and within the philosophy of religion by John Hick.[38] A question that remains open, though, is whether a certain component—namely, reference to a supernatural, transcendent realm—is given some prominence. I agree with Frank Whaling that this is indeed necessary, since traditional religions can otherwise no longer be distinguished conceptually from something like secular "religions" or ideologies.[39] It is, however, problematic if, like Saler, we distinguish the monotheistic religions with their characteristic elements as the "most prototypical cases" of the category "religion,"[40] since this would be to ignore the enormous internal diversity and mutability of all religions, including the great monotheistic religions themselves, and thus to lapse covertly into an essentialization of religion and religions. In any case, applying the concept of religion to non-Western cultures does not necessarily lead to distortions, if we remain conscious of intrareligious diversity, and make the concept of religion sufficiently flexible, without emptying it of all content.

Intrareligious diversity and mutability of religious traditions include among other things the diversity of their respective self-understandings and living forms; the diversity of different groups and currents, which is often tangible from the very beginning; the persistent tendency to split into different schools or denominations and their further ramifications; and the manifold changes of religions during different epochs and within different regions and cultural areas. But intrareligious diversity is not only a matter

---

[35]See Wittgenstein's *Philosophical Investigations* §§ 65–71. Wittgenstein 1986, 31–34.
[36]Smart 1996.
[37]Saler (1993) 2000.
[38]Hick 1989, 3–9.
[39]See Schmidt-Leukel 2017a, 175–79.
[40]Saler (1993) 2000, 225.

of these quasi-"official" forms of religious diversity. What should also be taken into account is the barely controllable but easily ascertainable diversity of religious attitudes, ideas, behaviors, etc., at the level of individual persons within particular religious groups—for religious diversity at the individual level does not always and necessarily coincide with the official prescriptions of the group, denomination, or tradition to which the individual belongs or is attributed. As Peter Antes has repeatedly noted with regard to the denominational diversity of Christianity, there are still all the different forms of being Christian that have emerged in the course of its historical development in the form of different denominations. But, says Antes, these forms now exist primarily *in* each of the respective denominations, so that the people within them would actually have to be redistributed among the various churches.[41] As this observation shows, religious diversity not only tends to branch out further; it also seems to replicate itself anew according to certain patterns.

As cognitive scientists have shown, the various forms of individual religiosity, which often deviate from the official prescriptions of the particular religious community to which the individual belongs, must be explained in a different way than by cultural influence alone. "Human behavior," says Jason Slone, "is not simply a product of culture."[42] Rather, according to cognitive science, the reason for both the phenomenon that individuals deviate in their behavior from cultural or religious prescriptions, and the occurrence of similar behavioral patterns in different cultures and religions must be seen in the uniformity of structures predetermined in the human mind/brain.[43] Thus, such biological constraints could be at least partly responsible both for the fact that individual behavior deviates from the respective religious community, and the similarity between certain behaviors in the context of different religions. According to Thomas Tweed, a theory of religion that wants to do justice to the fluidity of religions as well as to certain characteristics that recur in different religions must include both biologically rooted cognitive constraints and culturally mediated patterns.[44]

Also important here in the border area between these two dimensions is the psychology of religion, which since William James' epochal study of 1902 has linked religious and especially intrareligious diversity with the different psychological needs of different personality types.[45] But religious

---

[41] As stated in various lectures and confirmed by Peter Antes in a personal e-mail to the author, July 14, 2018.
[42] Slone 2005, 50.
[43] Ibid., 29–67, 121–25.
[44] Tweed 2006, 62–69. For approaches that take account of the findings of cognitive science of religion in the comparison of religious experience in general, and of contemplative experiences in particular, see Taves 2009 and Rose 2016.
[45] James (1902) 1990.

diversity can also be reflected at the level of the individual person. The psychology of religion has long dealt with the question of the religious development of individuals as they pass through different forms and types of religiosity.[46] That these differences have often been defined as lower and higher levels or different degrees of personal maturity is certainly not unproblematic.[47] However, it does not change the fact that quite a few people do actually pass through several forms of religiosity in the course of their lives—even beyond the particularly serious biographical fissures that can be observed in the case of religious conversions. In addition, the phenomenon of hybrid religiosity is now receiving increased attention, though currently more in the field of theological and religious studies than in the psychology of religion.[48] Here, religious diversity in the individual is not only diachronic in life history but also synchronic, so that we can sometimes observe an oscillation between different religious worlds for one and the same person.[49]

Criticism and Renewal of Comparative Religion

To explore the interplay between cognitively predetermined, culturally mediated, and psychologically describable patterns of religious ideas, behavior, and experience requires comparative studies. However, as already mentioned, in recent decades there has been an increasing departure from interreligious comparisons within the study of religions. This is partly due to the criticism of the phenomenology of religion and the shift toward an understanding of religious studies as cultural studies. The phenomenology of religion, which for decades has shaped how religious studies understands itself, regards "religion" as a distinct phenomenon of humanity that cannot be reduced to culture or society. According to phenomenology, the actual goal of *religious* studies consists in understanding better the specificity and essence of this distinct phenomenon, which is why religious studies is neither *cultural* studies nor *social* studies. In order to achieve this goal, the phenomenology of religion mainly used comparison. Hence, with the criticism of the phenomenology of religion and the increased shift toward a cultural studies approach, comparison as the central method of the phenomenology of religion also fell into disrepute. As a consequence, it was primarily particular and local studies with a narrow thematic, cultural, temporal, and

---

[46]Büttner & Dietrich 2000.
[47]Billmann-Mahecha 2003, 128–29.
[48]See, for example, Cornille 2002; Bernhardt & Schmidt-Leukel 2008; Knitter 2009; Drew 2011; Goosen 2011; D'Costa & Thompson 2016; Bidwell 2018; Sigalow 2019.
[49]Drew 2011, 224–27; Niculescu 2012.

spatial focus that established themselves; the goal was now no longer to understand the essence of religion, but at best to examine individual phenomena in other cultures, which in some vague, but mostly sociologically conceived sense can be seen as functional equivalents to what is associated in Western cultures with the term "religion." Besides such primarily anthropological, sociological, and narrowly localized studies, religious studies has been increasingly concerned in recent decades with itself: with discussing its own methods and categories, its demarcations against other disciplines, its ideological and political entanglements, its own particular determinacy and contextual situatedness, etc.

Both the turning away of religious studies from the comparison of religions as a central method, and the increasing focus on itself can also be seen as a concomitant of the influence of authors who are seen as representing postmodern and postcolonial ideologies. What both ideologies have in common is a so-called hermeneutics of suspicion, which articulates not so much a suspicion as rather an open accusation that Western—or, indeed, any—science serves not to broaden and deepen knowledge, but to expand and solidify power. Given the great influence of these ideologies in the social sciences, it is not without a certain irony that one of the leading sociologists of the twentieth century, Peter Berger, should characterize and criticize their hermeneutics as follows: "The basic method here is to translate affirmations of truth or virtue into expressions of allegedly underlying interests that have nothing to do with truth or virtue—interests of power, or greed, or lust. . . . So-called postmodernism has been a recent theoretical flowering of this worldview."[50]

Postmodern authors reject universal theories and claims to validity (with the exception, of course, of the alleged universal validity of their own theoretical claims). This is linked to the imperative of emphasizing the distinctive particularity and peculiarity of each individual phenomenon and its specific context. The accentuated "difference" of each phenomenon and its context in relation to everything else is often claimed to be unbridgeable or incommensurable. This of course raises the question of how such an assertion can be justified at all, since this would require being able to understand two supposedly incommensurable phenomena or contexts so well as to discern their incommensurability. But if such a comparative understanding is possible, then the incommensurability claimed cannot be so great that it can be played off against the fundamental possibility of comparison.

Unlike postmodern authors, postcolonial theorists strive to provide concrete evidence that cultural and religious theories during and since the

---

[50] Berger 2014, 11.

colonial era explicitly or implicitly articulate claims of cultural or religious, i.e., Christian, dominance. Postcolonial approaches have the advantage over postmodernism in that they can be better examined and thus either be confirmed or falsified. Moreover, they do not fundamentally question all categories regarding their universalizability, but only those whose application serves implicit or explicit claims to superiority. Thus, as Michael Bergunder has shown, a valid point of criticism leveled by postcolonial authors is that intercultural or interreligious comparisons often take the actual point of comparison, the *tertium comparationis*, from the culture or religion of those making the comparison, since the latter choose the point of comparison according to their own interests. In this way, they make their own culture or religion the norm for characterizing and evaluating the other culture or religion when it comes to the actual comparison. Every difference that the foreign culture or religion shows from their own therefore risks being interpreted as a deficit. In other words, their own culture or religion corresponds much better from the outset to the comparative yardstick than the other culture or religion.[51]

However, there are now also within religious studies individual voices that, despite this criticism, want to rehabilitate and reconceptualize comparative religion as a method,[52] arguing that it is possible to take up several points of criticism of the practice of comparison without rejecting the method altogether. Religious comparisons do not necessarily have to work with an essentialist concept of religion. Religious phenomena need not and must not be torn from their context; rather, it is essential that the comparison takes into account the actual contexts. It is vital to reflect critically on the categories of comparison and the respective interests behind each comparison, and to check their appropriateness. The fact that scholars of religion are also children of their time and of their own context, and can therefore never be completely objective or neutral, does not automatically render comparisons of religions useless. Rather, this insight calls for a critical perspective that reveals and controls the impact of such personal factors on the comparison.

In principle, the latter is particularly possible within theology, since theology positions itself from the outset and gives an account of its own standpoint. However, it was comparisons of religions carried out from a Christian perspective that suffered particularly strongly in the past from a theological-apologetic bias, since they distorted the religion of the other in order to present the superiority of their own religion. Yet, discussion today shows that this need not be the case. And so, while losing its importance

---

[51]Bergunder 2016, 36–40.
[52]See, for example, the contributions to Patton & Ray 2000 and Schmidt-Leukel & Nehring 2016, as well as the summary of the discussion in Freiberger 2019, 45–79.

within religious studies, the comparison of religions has now very much gained in importance in theology.[53]

1.2 COMPARING RELIGIONS IN THEOLOGY

Religious Studies and Theology

Oliver Freiberger has contributed substantially among scholars of religious studies to renewing in recent years the method of comparing religions.[54] Unlike the mainstream in religious studies, Freiberger also takes note of the increasing significance of interreligious comparisons within theology.[55] At the same time, though, he distances himself from a theological interest in comparing religions. According to Freiberger, religious studies encompasses all disciplines whose primary research interest is religion.[56] However, this, he claims, does not apply to theology, since, even in the form of comparative theology, this discipline is ultimately concerned with achieving a better understanding not of religion but of the divine.[57]

The relationship between religious studies and theology has been subject to long and complex debates,[58] with different positions having been put forward on the question of how the two differ from each other. Freiberger's position that theology and religious studies have a different object—"God" and "religion," respectively—is only one among several attempts at demarcation that have been made so far.[59] A closer look, however, reveals that Freiberger's demarcation remains too facile and conceals a far more important difference.

Even if the Greek meaning of the term "theo-logy" suggests that it is concerned with the "speaking" (*legein*) of and about "God" (*theos*), contemporary theology is largely aware of the fact that it can only speak of God in the refraction of faith in God, this faith manifesting itself in the form of religion. In this respect, theology treats the idea of God as a hypothesis,[60] which means, in the words of Wolfhart Pannenberg, "that God can be the object of theology only as a problem, not as an assured given."[61] The in-

---

[53] See Schmidt-Leukel & Nehring 2016.
[54] See especially Freiberger 2019 and his previous works mentioned there.
[55] Freiberger 2019, 42, 115.
[56] Ibid., 37.
[57] Ibid., 41–42.
[58] For example, Mann 1973; McCutcheon 1999; Löhr, G. 2000; Religionswissenschaft—Theologie 2012.
[59] See on this Schmidt-Leukel 2012, 50–54.
[60] Pannenberg 1987, 299–303.
[61] Ibid., 303.

sight that faith manifests itself in the form of religion implies that theology "surveys religions as to the extent to which self-expression of divine reality is documented in their traditions."[62]

These two aspects reveal the actual problem that usually underlies the various demarcations between theology and religious studies: it is not really about different objects, but about different interpretations of religion. Do we have to regard religion—from a scientific point of view—as a purely naturalistic phenomenon and thus as a form of human self-deception? Or is it also scientifically permissible to reckon with the hypothesis of a possible truth of religion and religions, insofar as religions in their respective forms of faith relate to a "divine" or transnatural reality, a reality transcending the boundaries of space and time?

Like many other scholars in religious studies, Freiberger too retreats in this respect to a "methodological agnosticism," i.e., to the obligation of refraining from any judgment regarding normative questions about the truth value of religions. The problem of this kind of refraining from judgment is, of course, that it is not "agnostic" at all, but highly normative; it admits in principle that religious phenomena can be interpreted as both deceptive and truthful, while at the same time normatively excluding both interpretations from its own interpretation of religion. However, the question of whether religion is a large-scale illusion or the expression of an openness of the human mind to a transnatural reality makes a fundamental difference, especially with regard to our understanding of religion.

By excluding both possible interpretations, religious studies constrains—in an academically highly problematic way and in contrast to its own explicit aims—its possible contribution to our understanding of religion. For example, Freiberger states with regard to the study of experiences of the presence of spiritual beings: "A study whose sole purpose is to prove that the spiritual beings do not exist would contribute little to our understanding of religion."[63] Well, such a study would be an inquiry into truth. Whether religion is illusory or not, however, is central to understanding it. Given that every science is fundamentally interested in coming closer to the truth and eliminating errors, it is rather strange if this maxim should not apply to the scientific exploration of religious phenomena.[64]

In contrast, a genuine methodological agnosticism would consist not in normatively excluding possible interpretations, but in characterizing them as hypotheses. Strictly speaking, agnosticism implies that we do not have definite knowledge concerning the question of an ultimately naturalistic or transnaturalistic interpretation of religion, and that the study of religion is

---

[62]Ibid., 317.
[63]Freiberger 2019, 207n22.
[64]Schmidt-Leukel 2020b.

therefore in this respect subject to a hypothetical proviso. In other words, an agnostic point of view means precisely that we would have to admit both a "methodological atheism" or "methodological naturalism," and "a methodological transnaturalism" (which hypothetically assumes that human consciousness of transcendence as evinced in religions has some substance).[65] Seen in this way, genuine agnosticism includes rather than excludes a theological approach in the comparison of religions, as long as a theological approach is not dogmatic, but hypothetical and thus open-ended.[66]

The contrast between religious studies and theology, then, is not that the former is about religion and the latter about God. It is rather a question of opposing interpretations of religion. Despite supposedly excluding both naturalistic and transnaturalistic interpretations, religious studies actually explains and interprets religious phenomena exclusively by means of this-worldly factors and constellations. Thus, in its actual work, it does not differ from a naturalistic or atheistic interpretation, but largely refuses to admit this and acknowledge explicitly a "methodological atheism" or "naturalism." In contrast, a theological comparison of religions discloses its methodological premises and working hypotheses, and is therefore much more in line with what Freiberger calls a "scholar-centered approach," which he himself favors.[67]

Freiberger has convincingly shown the importance of the individual religious scholar when it comes to carrying out a comparative study in practice, that is, the influence that the scholar's cultural and academic background, but also quite personal factors, can have on the investigation. It is striking, though, that Freiberger names as personal factors "gender, race, class, life experience, moral and political convictions, intellectual interests, career hopes, etc.,"[68] but skips religious or ideological beliefs. We may assume, however, that just these beliefs exert an especially strong influence in comparisons of religions, and that they should be reflected on and made transparent along the lines set out by Freiberger himself.[69] Freiberger notes elsewhere that the objectives of theological comparisons of religions are often apologetic in nature, which necessarily leads to unbalanced, i.e., oblique, comparisons. However, he also admits that this does not apply to all comparisons in theology, and points to the more recent comparative theology.[70] Indeed, it is true of today's generation of comparative theologians that they "openly

---

[65] See on this Schmidt-Leukel 2012.
[66] For the opposite positions, see Junginger 2021 and Wiebe 2020, who consider a naturalistic interpretation of religion to be the only scientific interpretation.
[67] Freiberger 2019, 81–110.
[68] Ibid., 96.
[69] Ibid., 101–3.
[70] Ibid., 40–41.

acknowledge the perspectival character of their comparisons" on the one hand, and "are willing to revise their theological judgments in light of the teachings of other traditions" on the other.[71] Thus, according to Hugh Nicholson, they are in principle able to leave behind the tendentious bias of earlier theological comparisons of religions.[72]

Comparative Theology, Theology of Religions, and Interreligious Theology

The central concern of comparative theology is to compare religions on the basis of a theological interest.[73] What all comparative theologians have in common is that they expect their comparisons to yield advances in theological understanding. However, they differ considerably with regard to a number of crucial questions: How much should comparative theologians remain bound to their own tradition, or how far can and must they go beyond it as a result of theological learning? Does comparative theology necessarily presuppose participation in a concrete religious tradition?[74] What is the nature of the processes of theological learning that are hoped for? What is the relationship between comparative theology and the theology of religions? Does this relationship have to be defined in terms of radical, mutually exclusive alternatives, as some comparative theologians initially understood it, or in terms of mutual complementarity, as it is now more often seen? And how do we do comparative theology? Are large-scale comparisons of religions, such as those carried out by Keith Ward[75] and Robert Neville,[76] permissible, or must they be, as Klaus von Stosch keeps demanding, "micrological," i.e., narrow and limited in scope, thereby following the postmodern interest in the particular?[77] How can we decide which comparison is adequate and which is theologically significant? How are the objects and points of comparison chosen? While comparative theology lacks uniformity when it comes to these theoretical and methodological issues, there is an increasing awareness of the problems and a growing discussion.[78]

Both comparative theology and the theology of religions grew out of

---

[71] Nicholson 2009, 634.

[72] Ibid., 634–35.

[73] For an overview, see Cornille 2020; Bernhardt & von Stosch 2009, and the recent handbooks Valkenberg 2022; Takacs and Kimmel 2024.

[74] Among the "Theology Without Walls" group, initiated by Jerry Martin, are some voices that call for such a theology as an option for all those who regard themselves as "spiritual but not religious." See Mercadante 2020.

[75] Ward 1987; 1994; 1996; 1998; 2000.

[76] Neville 2001a; 2001b; 2001c.

[77] For example, von Stosch 2012, 194–98; 2018, 39.

[78] See Clooney & Berthrong 2014; Voss Roberts 2016; Clooney & von Stosch 2018; Cornille 2020.

the serious efforts of Christian churches to engage in dialogue with people from other religious traditions. While such dialogue had already been called for and practiced sporadically in the first half of the twentieth century, it only became an activity widely affirmed and supported by the churches (across the denominational spectrum) in the second half of the century.[79] A classification, originating in the Roman Catholic Church, of interreligious dialogue into four different forms has now become widespread: (1) dialogue between people of different religions as it arises in everyday life (often referred to as "grassroots dialogue"); (2) dialogue in the course of practical cooperation among people of different faiths in promoting the common good (local, national, or international); (3) dialogue between religious experts from different religions; (4) dialogue as an exchange of religious experiences, including mutual participation and sharing in certain forms of religious practice, such as ritual ceremonies, forms of contemplative practice, and interreligious cohabitation in a monastic context.[80] We might now join Marianne Moyaert in adding a fifth form of dialogue: namely, dialogue as interreligious diplomacy, i.e., the cultivation of relationships between religious communities to avoid major conflicts and to promote the other four forms of dialogue.[81]

Especially in the context of the third and fourth forms of dialogue, an awareness has developed on the side of Christian theology to understand interreligious dialogue as a source of increased theological insight. For example, Leonard Swidler, one of the important pioneers of dialogue, established the "first rule" in his influential "Dialogue Decalogue" as, "The primary purpose of dialogue is to learn, that is, to change and grow in the perception and understanding of reality and then to act accordingly."[82] The change in understanding of reality addressed here concerns both the faith of the dialogue partner and the person's own faith. The first concern is manifest in the debate about an appropriate theology of religions, and the second in comparative theology.

The theology of religions is concerned with assessing religious diversity theologically. *Exclusivist* approaches assume that all other religions are "false," they do not convey salvific knowledge of transcendent reality, while

---

[79]There is now a vast literature on interreligious dialogue. An initial impression can be gained from Fu & Spiegler 1989; Swidler 1990; Cornille 2013; Dehn, Caspar-Seeger, & Bernstorff 2017; Dehn 2019. See also the series *Religions in Dialogue* (edited by Wolfram Weisse and published by Waxmann) and the journal *Studies in Interreligious Dialogue*. Useful information on various dialogue activities of the churches is found in the WCC's magazine *Current Dialogue*.

[80]On this, see the document *The Attitude of the Church towards the Followers of Other Religions: Reflections and Orientations on Dialogue and Mission* (nos. 29–35), issued in 1984 by the Vatican's Secretariat for Non-Christians prefigured in Sharpe 1974.

[81]Moyaert 2013, 203–4.

[82]Swidler 1990, 43.

inclusivist approaches assume that salvific knowledge can also be found in other religions, but in a deficient form, meaning that one's own religion or denomination is superior in this respect to all other forms of religion. These two positions are particularly prominent within Christianity and, analogously, within other religions, with a certain dominance of exclusivism within the Christian tradition. However, a third position has now developed, not least as a result of intensive dialogue.[83] *Pluralist* approaches give up the claim to the sole truth or unique superiority of one's own tradition, and reckon with the fact that other religious traditions contain different but equally valid forms of salvific knowledge of transcendent reality.[84] It is easy to see that, for logical reasons, there can be only one other position: namely, the *naturalist* claim that no religion has salvific knowledge of transcendent reality precisely because there is no transcendent reality. In other words, the claim that religions make to mediate salvific knowledge of transcendent reality is either always false (naturalism) or not always false. If the latter, then it is either true in only one case (exclusivism) or in more than one case. If it is true in more than one case, then there is either a singular maximum form of mediating salvific knowledge of transcendent reality represented in one religion (inclusivism) or not (pluralism). The strictly disjunctive character gives rise to the logically comprehensive nature of the classification. The first disjunction is already comprehensive, and only further differentiated in the subsequent steps.[85] Of course, the comprehensive nature of the classification applies only if we understand the theology of religions as the field where theology grapples with the claims made by religions to mediate salvific knowledge of transcendent reality. No one is obliged to do this. But constructing a theology of religions differently implies avoiding a theological response to the messages of salvation offered by other religions, with the result that any dialogue of a more specifically theological nature is abandoned.[86]

In German-speaking theology, it is especially Reinhold Bernhardt who has repeatedly suggested a model he calls "mutual" or "reciprocal inclusivism" ("Inklusivismus auf Gegenseitigkeit").[87] But it remains unclear what exactly this might mean. If the term "inclusivism" is used here in the

---

[83] On the different roots of the pluralist position within Christianity, see Schmidt-Leukel 2017a, 147–54 (= 2005, 166–71).

[84] For a discussion of all three positions within Christianity, see Schmidt-Leukel 2017a, 88–172 (= 2005, 96–192). An overview of pluralist positions within non-Christian religions can be found in Schmidt-Leukel 2017b, 32–106 (2019a, 62–169).

[85] See Schmidt-Leukel 2017a, 58–87 (= 2005, 62–95).

[86] An example of such an alternative conception of the theology of religions is the so-called hermeneutics of difference ("Differenzhermeneutik") proposed by Christian Danz (2020). For a critique, see Schmidt-Leukel 2020c.

[87] For example, Bernhardt 2005, 206–90; 2019a, 431–57.

sense of the position just defined, then claims of superiority raised against each other do not represent something like a new position in the theology of religions. Rather, "mutual inclusivism" is then a description of what we usually see in the reality of interreligious relations. The term would then describe the problem rather than a solution. If, however, "inclusivism" is meant differently—for example, in the hermeneutical sense that every theological interpretation of other religions is always co-determined by the religious beliefs and categories of one's own religion[88]—then this can certainly be agreed to. Indeed, exclusivist, inclusivist, and pluralist positions can each be formulated only from within a specific religious perspective.[89] This means, however, that a "mutual inclusivism" in such a hermeneutical sense is not another alternative to an exclusivist, inclusivist, or pluralist position. Rather, if we do not want to evade dealing theologically with the claims to salvation and truth made by other religious traditions, then we need to position ourselves within a religion-specific hermeneutical framework according to one of the three basic options.

In contrast to the theology of religions, comparative theology starts with a different question. It seeks to find out what new insights the dialogue with people and testimonies of other faiths can provide toward a better understanding of one's own faith-tradition. Some of the proponents of comparative theology had therefore initially claimed that comparative theology offered a fundamental alternative, not only to the questions, but also to the possible positions within the theology of religions.[90] However, many serious objections have been made since then to this initial stance, so that scholars now increasingly assume that these two currents complement each other.[91] Those comparing religions with a serious and express interest in truth or deeper theological knowledge will not be able to avoid adopting an evaluative position while carrying out the comparison. In other words, comparative theologians must face the question of whether they consider what they

---

[88]Thus explicitly in Nicholson 2009, 622–63. Reinhold Bernhardt (2019b, 204) too has now stated, "The concept of 'reciprocal inclusivism' ('Inklusivismus auf Gegenseitigkeit') does not mark a *material* ('inhaltliche') position in the theology of religions." In terms of material content, Bernhardt (2021, 61, 346–47, 375) has recently characterized his position as potential pluralism, with explicit proximity to Schubert Ogden. He holds that "in view of the available possibilities of knowledge and judgment more than such a modest answer in the mode of a potentialis would seem to me unjustifiable" (ibid., 375). Yet obviously he is unable to stick to this "modest answer" when he deals with Judaism (see ibid., 68–69). This raises the question of why a more affirmative position should be possible here but not in relation to other religions.

[89]See Schmidt-Leukel 2017b, 7–8 (= 2019a, 26–27).

[90]See, for example, Frederick 1995; 1999; von Stosch 2002; 2012, 216–30. Nicholson (2009, 620) has even called comparative theology "the antithesis of the theology of religions."

[91]See, for example, Kiblinger 2010; Hedges 2010, 52–55; Cornille 2020, 43–78; Moyaert 2020, 249. In the German-speaking world, it was especially Ulrich Winkler (2013, 361–481) who insisted on the complementarity of the two theological currents.

encounter in another religion to be aberrant and deceptive, or truthful and enriching—of course, with all due caution and always acknowledging their own susceptibility to error. According to Francis Clooney, a leading theorist of comparative theology, a theologian will at some point in the course of comparative work "begin to theologize as it were from both sides of the table, reflecting personally on old and new truths in an interior dialog."[92] This, however, implies that the comparative theologian inevitably enters the terrain of the theology of religions, for exclusivism excludes from the outset the possibility that other religions can have any "new truths" of a more specific theological relevance. And whether the new truths form only fragments of the old truth is still a matter of controversy between inclusivism and pluralism. Do the new truths merely place the superiority of the old truth in a new, even clearer light? Or is the realization of new truths able to allow both truths to appear in a different light, one that sees mutual claims to uniqueness or superiority evaporate like old shadows?

Klaus von Stosch, as one of the few scholars who still sees comparative theology as an alternative to a theology of religions, has argued that the latter presupposes judging religions as a whole, something that is not possible, at least not in a way that is scientifically responsible.[93] But von Stosch's premise is obviously wrong. Not only assessing entire complex traditions but already the consideration of some individual religious phenomena has the potential to radically undermine claims to exclusive uniqueness or inclusive superiority, and make pluralistic approaches more plausible. We should therefore understand as complementary the relationship between discussion within the theology of religions and the actual work of comparative theology.[94] In other words, comparative theology can contribute in no small measure to underpinning or undermining positions in the theology of religions, and can therefore also promote theological progress in relation to this discussion. Conversely, positions in the theology of religions need to be made plausible by drawing on observations from the comparison of religions. It is therefore not surprising (but often overlooked or ignored by representatives of comparative theology) that key figures of pluralist positions, such as Wilfred Cantwell Smith, Raimon Panikkar, or John Hick, produced extensive studies of a comparative nature long before the more recent comparative theology came into being.[95]

A pluralist and (albeit to a lesser extent) inclusivist theology of religions

---

[92]Clooney 2010a, 13.
[93]Von Stosch 2012, 217–25; 2019. Similarly, also Thatamanil 2017, 296–97.
[94]See already Schmidt-Leukel 2005, 87–95 (= 2017a, 80–87). Francis Clooney (2010a, 14–16, 114–17; 2010b, 195–96) has now clearly reinterpreted his initial plea for a "moratorium" in the theology of religions in this new direction.
[95]See Smith, W. C. 1979; 1993; Panikkar 1981; Hick 1989, 16–69; (1976) 1990.

makes possible a new form of theological work that can be characterized as "interreligious theology." This no longer draws only on the sources of its own tradition to deal with central theological questions, but also includes other religious traditions in order to arrive at new insights.[96] If the dialogical and constructive character of interreligious theology is highlighted, then we can follow John May in his seminal study *Buddhology and Christology*, and characterize it fittingly as "collaborative theology."[97] In this sense, comparative theology can also be understood as a form of interreligious theology, although there may be other forms besides this one in which the dialogical aspect of reciprocal and shared theological learning may be more pronounced than in most studies of comparative theology hitherto. The joint work of Mouhanad Khorchide and Klaus von Stosch in particular clearly demonstrates that comparative theology can also (and very successfully) be conducted in a collaborative-dialogical manner. Their comparative analysis of Islamic and Christian interpretations of Jesus opens up new perspectives on both sides, so that comparative theology emerges very clearly and fruitfully here as a form of interreligious theology.[98]

The by now quite broad field of comparative studies of religions motivated by theology and (though to a much lesser extent) religious studies could perhaps give rise to a new discipline spanning theology and religious studies, and including practical aspects of interreligious relations, that is called "Interreligious Studies."[99] Within the broad field of religious studies, dialogue, and comparative theology many important contributions to the comparative study of Christianity and Buddhism have been made in the last few decades,[100] including several recent studies that have undertaken such a comparison directly, with respect either to individual sub-aspects or to larger bodies of tradition. While some of these studies are clearly concerned with proving that, although the central contrasts between Christianity and Buddhism that I have sketched earlier may need modifying, they are basically still valid, other studies are marked by the endeavor to relativize such contrasts significantly.

I refer to several of these studies in the following chapters. My intention, though, is not to offer a summary of Christian-Buddhist comparisons, but rather to use the example of the comparison of Buddhism and Christianity to draw attention to the fact that structural patterns can be discerned in religious diversity that have the form of fractals. In other words, certain

---

[96] Bernhardt & Schmidt-Leukel 2013; Schmidt-Leukel 2017b, 107–245.
[97] May 2014. See also May 2019, 151–70.
[98] Khorchide & von Stosch 2016; 2018.
[99] See Leirvik 2015; Patel, Peace, & Silverman 2018; Gustafson 2020.
[100] On Christian-Buddhist dialogue, see the overviews in Spae 1980; Schmidt-Leukel 1992; Ingram 1988; 2009; von Brück & Lai 1997; Anderson & Cattoi 2023.

differences that are constitutive for our understanding of religious diversity are replicated through all three levels of religious diversity: the macro level of interreligious diversity, the meso level of intrareligious diversity, and the micro level of intrasubjective diversity. This calls for more explanation.

2

The Discovery of Fractal Structures

NEW PERSPECTIVES
FOR THE COMPARISON
OF RELIGIONS

2.1 PERSPECTIVES FROM CULTURAL AND RELIGIOUS STUDIES

From Structuralism to Poststructuralism—And Back Again

People represent and construct their image of reality in the form of cultural sign systems, the most fundamental being language. Yet language is linked to other systems such as culture-specific symbols, myths, narratives, rituals, conventions, institutions, aesthetics, and ethics. Structuralist approaches deal with such cultural reproductions and constructions of reality by viewing and analyzing them as systems of signs or meaning with clear structural regularities. From structural patterns, so the idea goes, specific conceptual connections can be deduced—i.e., *re*constructed—just as the structure of a triangle allows the significance and position of all its points to be deduced. By comparing different systems of meaning and their underlying patterns, we can make visible those overarching structures and patterns from which different cultural sign systems can be deduced and thereby understood even better. This is structuralism's key epistemological ideal.

The concern of structuralist thinkers thus corresponds to efforts within the phenomenology of religion: "comparison is generally used in phenomenology of religions as a hermeneutical instrument. It serves to capture the essence [of religion] and thus to understand not only individual religious phenomena but also their totality, and thus ultimately religion as a concept to which we subsume very different historical manifestations."[1] Specifically, this subsumption occurs by identifying elements that are essential to religion and interconnected in a particular basic structure. "Religions," writes C. J. Bleeker, "always have an inner logic…that dominates the structure."[2] The structures of individual religions vary a general basic structure in the form of different types of religion, which "are supposed to form the principle of a division and grouping of all religions."[3]

As mentioned in the previous chapter, criticism of the phenomenology of religion was an important reason for the widespread abandonment of interreligious comparisons within religious studies in the last fifty years. The comparative classification of different phenomena into common categories and systematic contexts, into a structure and its inner logic, was seen as surrendering the unmistakable uniqueness of the individual in the name of abstracting the general. This reproach reflects the central criticism that poststructuralists level at structuralism. They argue that structuralism's attempt to make reality transparent and comprehensible through the structural analysis of sign systems is doomed to fail, since those who deduce the particularity of the individual from the generality of structures construct the individual from the structural pattern given. The individual thus reconstructed is nothing but an abstract construct, an element of the system that the system itself creates. According to this critique, it is not possible to grasp in this way the particularity—the difference and uniqueness—of the actual individual. Instead, the individual phenomenon becomes a mere instance, "an illustration of the general pattern."[4]

At the beginning of his well-known 1970 essay *S/Z*, Roland Barthes used a "Buddhist" narrative to illustrate this criticism: "There are said to be certain Buddhists whose ascetic practices enable them to see a whole landscape in a bean."[5] This, according to Barthes, corresponds to the attempts of structuralists to see all the many stories of the world within a single structure. But this is precisely how each story loses its uniqueness, its difference from other stories.[6] To illustrate their idea that the multiplicity of individual phenomena cannot be expressed by the concept of a patterned structure, two other poststructuralists, Gilles Deleuze and Félix Guattari,

---

[1] Lanczkowski 1978, 13.
[2] Bleeker 1972, 45. Similarly ibid., 42.
[3] Lanczkowski 1978, 122.
[4] Belsey 2002, 43.
[5] Barthes 1974, 3. I have not yet been able to identify anywhere a Buddhist meditation technique of this kind. Did Barthes perhaps construct it by deriving it from his own system? The image, however, is reminiscent of the parable of Indra's net and of the *Avataṃsaka/Huayan* philosophy that it expresses. Barthes knew of this philosophy. He mentions it in his notes on Japan, which were originally published in 1970, the same year as *S/Z* (see Barthes 1992, 78).
[6] Barthes 1974, 3.

borrowed from biology the image of a rhizome, this being a network of roots that "assumes very diverse forms, from ramified surface extension in all directions to concretization into bulbs and tubers."[7] In geometric figures, and even in the geometric structure of a tree, they argue, each point is defined by the figure of the whole. But "there are no points or positions in a rhizome, such as those found in a structure, tree, or root. There are only lines."[8] Moreover, a rhizome has the capacity to proliferate. If it is broken at one point, "it will start up again on one of its old lines, or on new lines,"[9] thereby escaping any structural determination. Multiplicity, then, cannot be captured by a structural concept, and the individual can therefore only be adequately appreciated as such precisely if that individual is not seen as part of a given structure of multiplicity: "the only way the one belongs to the multiple: always subtracted."[10]

Despite the justified concern to point out the limitations of conceptual structures in comprehending concrete reality,[11] there is no way around the fact that we approach the world inevitably also through the prism of conceptual categories. Such categories allow us to establish relations between the individual and the general. The activity of unconscious and conscious comparison plays a logically indispensable and neurologically anchored role in this process.[12] Moreover, poststructuralists such as Barthes, Deleuze, Guattari, and others have greatly underestimated the power of structuralist approaches. Let us look again at the two images mentioned.

Only a year after the publication of the first French edition of *Rhizome* (1976), the mathematician Benoît Mandelbrot published his epochal work, *The Fractal Geometry of Nature* (1977). Mandelbrot's analysis of fractal structures can be applied to the image rejected by Barthes and to the image favored by Deleuze and Guattari. While it may be too farfetched to see the shape of a landscape in a bean, the shape of a mountain range may well already be seen in a single boulder. The basic concept of the fractal is self-replication, which means that a larger, complex structure is composed of smaller elements that repeat the structural pattern of the whole. This principle is particularly suitable for analyzing flexible, dynamic, even chaotic constellations that do not seem to fit into any geometric pattern—such as those of cloud formations or even those of rhizomes.[13] They all possess fractal structures. The rejection of structuralism was obviously just as premature

---

[7] Deleuze & Guattari 2006, 7.
[8] Ibid., 8.
[9] Ibid., 9.
[10] Ibid., 6.
[11] Barthes shows some sympathy for the radical Mahayana-Buddhist critique of concepts, which ultimately defeats all linguistic representation (Barthes 1992, 73–74).
[12] On this, see Paden 2000 and Sullivan 2000.
[13] For an application of fractal geometry and mathematics to rhizomes, see Majrashi et al. 2013.

as the view that living, complex, and changing phenomena elude structural analysis. This is also true with regard to a nonessentialist, nonreifying understanding of religion. As I show soon, it is precisely the flexibility of fractal structural patterns that makes them particularly suitable for the comparative analysis of religions. William Paden wrote with regard to the function of categories in comparative religion: "Though we cannot dispense with categories, we can fix them, change them, or make them better."[14] One such improvement can be achieved by applying fractal analysis.

The Fractal Face of Nature

Benoît Mandelbrot (1924–2010) introduced fractal geometry to make certain natural phenomena that defy Euclidean geometry more mathematically and geometrically comprehensible: "Clouds are not spheres, mountains are not cones, coastlines are not circles."[15] By means of fractal geometry, Mandelbrot argues, it will now be possible for natural scientists to approach in "vigorous and rigorous quantitative fashion" such shapes that they had previously had to call "grainy, hydralike, in between, pimply, pocky, ramified, seaweedy, strange, tangled, tortuous, wiggly, wispy, wrinkled, and the like."[16] Such shapes characterize the face of nature in both its inorganic and organic forms, which is why Mandelbrot proposed the thesis: "There is a fractal face to the geometry of nature."[17]

By "fractals," Mandelbrot means figures, patterns, structures, or forms that are characterized by strict or less strict self-replication across different scales. In other words, central elements of the entire structure replicate themselves either exactly or almost exactly with their regular and irregular aspects in their components.[18] The two central features of fractals are thus self-replication and relative scale invariance. A well-known example of a fractal geometric shape with strictly regular self-replication is the so-called Sierpinski triangle, which is composed of three smaller triangles, each of which is in turn composed of the same three triangles, and so on.[19] There is in principle an infinite iteration in such a case, i.e., the self-replication can theoretically be repeated infinitely into smaller and larger scales. In contrast, we are dealing in all phenomena of inorganic and organic nature known to us so far with less strict, similar forms of self-replication over a limited number of levels. The mountain range replicates its structural

---

[14]Paden 2000, 182.
[15]Mandelbrot 1983, 1.
[16]Ibid., 5.
[17]Ibid., 3.
[18]Ibid., 1.
[19]See ibid., 142.

features in individual mountains and smaller rock sections. An ice crystal replicates individual structural features in its smaller branches. The coastline, fringed by bays, peninsulas, fjords, and spits of land, repeats similar forms in a smaller format in the coastlines of each of these four forms. The structure of the cauliflower is found in each of its individual florets, the structure of many tree species in their respective branches, that of a fern leaf in its smaller leaves.

Fractal analysis is not limited to the spatial dimension, however. The self-replication that characterizes fractal patterns results from the repeated application (iteration) of the basic form-giving operation regarding each outcome. In the Sierpinski triangle, the first triangle is divided into three equal triangles, and each of these triangles is divided again in the same way. In nature, this repetition takes place in temporal processes. For example, the fractal bifurcation in the crown and root system of a tree occurs through growth, i.e., through the iteration of branching in time. Thus, uniform repetition at different scales enables the growth of "a structure or system that is complex, uniform, expansive, and detailed."[20]

However, in organic and inorganic nature, iteration leads not to exact but to similar self-replications. Moreover, it often contains unequal parts and replication errors (mutations), and is limited to a few levels. Nevertheless, the similarity remains clearly recognizable and approximately measurable by scaling and segmentation of the basic forms. Even if fractal geometry, like Euclidean geometry, is not realized anywhere in nature in a strict, abstract form, fractal geometry comes much closer to nature than Euclidean geometry, not least because it takes into account the dynamics of development and captures them as iteration.[21]

The Fractal Face of Culture

It is not only nature, but also culture, that exhibits a fractal face. According to William Jackson, "Cultures manifest cascades of recursive and mutually reflective eddies in song lyrics, music, verse, stories, voices, ideas, and visions. . . . Fractals seem a promising metaphor for explorations of the humanities, because they give us more models to help visualize some kinds of elusive complexities."[22] In my view, this is particularly true of the phenomenon of cultural diversity, where fractal features can be clearly discerned.

In contemporary intercultural philosophy, debates oscillate between

---

[20] Jackson, W. 2004, 245.
[21] Kenkel & Walker 1996, 78.
[22] Jackson, W. 2004, 25.

two opposing positions: the postmodern assertion that cultures are radically incommensurable on the one hand, and the assertion that they are completely commensurable or even fundamentally identical on the other. A number of authors strive to find a convincing middle ground between these two extremes. For example, the Indian philosopher Ram Adhar Mall, cofounder of intercultural philosophy in Germany, speaks of intercultural "overlappings," without which understanding and communication between cultures would be impossible.[23] A similar position is taken by the German intercultural philosopher Bernhard Waldenfels, who goes one step further than Mall with his concept of intercultural "intersection" ("Verschränkung"), meaning that what is culturally similar and what is culturally different, what is one's own and what is foreign, "are more or less entangled with each other." Waldenfels calls the boundaries between cultures "fuzzy," and argues that cultural differences are more about "accentuation, emphasis, and statistic frequency than clear-cut differentiation."[24] Intercultural intersection therefore means that something of one's own culture can always be found in the foreign culture, and vice versa.[25] In short, this amounts to a fractal interpretation of cultural diversity. Waldenfels sees confirmation for his position in the work, for example, of the Swiss intercultural philosopher Elmar Holenstein.[26]

Holenstein, who taught at the Universities of Bochum, Zurich, Tokyo, and Hong Kong, based his reflections primarily on his comparative studies of Western and Far Eastern cultures. According to Holenstein, "Structures that are very pronounced in one culture can . . . (at least to some extent) also be found in (almost all) other cultures."[27] One of his examples is the great variety of politeness-forms within the Japanese language. Such forms exist in all languages, but they are seemingly nowhere as pronounced as in Japanese.[28] Yet it would be misleading to assume that a particular characteristic—or cluster of particular characteristics—is exclusive to a specific language or culture. Rather, according to Holenstein, cultural differences are based on the fact that different characteristics are found in various cultures but with different orders of precedence and in different forms of elaboration.[29] That is, the range of variation *between* cultures is also reflected *within* cultures, and even *within a single individual*:[30]

---

[23] Mall 2000, 13–24.
[24] Both quotations from Waldenfels 1995, 54.
[25] Ibid., 56.
[26] Ibid., 55.
[27] Holenstein 1985, 133.
[28] Ibid.
[29] Ibid., 137–47.
[30] Ibid., 149–52.

In reality, the same oppositions that are thought to be ascertainable between two cultures (*interculturally*) can often be detected in the same kind and degree within one and the same culture (*intraculturally*), even within one and the same person (*intrasubjectively*) depending on age, surroundings, task or just on mood and humour.[31]

Holenstein thus distinguishes three levels of cultural diversity:

1. The *macro level* (or global level) *of intercultural* diversity
2. The *meso level of intracultural* diversity, i.e., diversity within each culture
3. The *micro level of intrasubjective* diversity, i.e., diversity within the mental cosmos of individual persons

His thesis implies that the various patterns of cultural multiplicity, to use a typical Mandelbrot term, are in a relationship of "scaling." In other words, the same patterns of cultural diversity are replicated along these three levels within a descending scale. The differences between cultures are reflected in the differences within each culture, and both in turn are reflected, to some degree, at the even smaller level of individuals. Thus, Holenstein rejects the notion of radical cultural difference in favor of the model of numerous variations of similar characteristics accompanied by wide-ranging structural analogies. Even if Holenstein himself does not use this term, this is in substance a fractal interpretation of cultural diversity.

The Fractal Face of Religion

Given the interconnectedness of culture and religion, it is not surprising that Holenstein's thesis also touches on the field of religions. According to Holenstein, common typologies of religion often suffer from the fact that they ignore intrareligious diversity. As an example, Holenstein cites Albert Schweitzer's and Friedrich Nietzsche's completely opposite characterizations of Christianity and Indian religions. While Nietzsche classifies Indian religiosity as life-affirming and Christianity as life-negating, Schweitzer does the complete opposite.[32] For Holenstein, though, it is not the case that one of the two comparisons is right and the other wrong. Rather, neither is nuanced enough: "Neither the Christian denominations nor Indian religions can be accommodated whole with all their developmental phases

---

[31]Holenstein 2003, 46.
[32]Holenstein 2003, 52–54.

and formations in the Procrustes-bed of a dualistic typology."[33] Within each major religious tradition, Holenstein argues, there exist quite different, even opposing, motifs, so that, depending on different historical and social constellations, sometimes one direction is more likely to come into play, and sometimes the other.[34]

As mentioned, the American religious studies scholar William Jackson already presented an extensive study in 2004 in which he showed the existence of fractal patterns in numerous works of literature, poetry, fine arts, architecture, music, and dance, and in mythologies, narratives, ideas, rituals, etc., from different cultural and religious traditions. Mandelbrot himself expressed enthusiasm.[35] But Jackson did not apply the concept of fractal patterns to the phenomenon of cultural and religious diversity itself. However, religious and cultural diversity do both also show a fractal face. Holenstein's distinction of three levels of cultural diversity can therefore easily be applied to the field of religious diversity.

Thus, the core idea of a fractal interpretation of religious diversity can now be formulated: The diversity of religions on the macro level (*interreligious diversity*) replicates itself on the meso level as internal diversity within the individual religions (*intrareligious diversity*), and finally on the micro level of common but intrinsically diverse dispositions of mind and psyche of individual people (*intrasubjective diversity*). Different types of religion or religiosity, different patterns of religious experience, different religious practices, beliefs, values, etc., replicate on all three levels. The fractal structure of religious diversity resembles the fractal patterns of rugged coastlines. Their typical elements, such as bays and peninsulas, fjords and spits, are replicated within each element as the viewer zooms in closer. For example, the coastline of a bay is itself interspersed with smaller bays, peninsulas, fjords, spits, and so on.

There have already been individual researchers within the phenomenology of religion who were well on their way to discovering fractal structures in religious diversity, one particularly clear example being Hilko Wiardo Schomerus (1879–1945). Schomerus distinguished the following four main types of religion: (1) "religions of the law" (e.g., "Mosaism"), (2) "magical-sacramental religions" (e.g., "the mysticism of India"), (3) "gnostic religions" (e.g., "ancient gnosis," "Buddhism"), and (4) "devotional religions" (e.g., "Indian bhakti religions" and some forms of "Mahāyāna Buddhism").[36] Schomerus developed this typology by drawing on the Hindu distinction

---
[33]Ibid., 53.
[34]Ibid., 51.
[35]See Mandelbrot's endorsement on the back cover of Jackson, W. 2004.
[36]Schomerus 1932, 22. The examples in parentheses and the terminology come from Schomerus himself.

of four different paths of salvation: the path of action (*karma mārga*), the path of meditation (*yoga mārga*), the path of knowledge (*jñāna mārga*), and the path of love of God (*bhakti mārga*).

According to Schomerus, however, actual religions cannot be strictly and unambiguously assigned to these four different types: "There are religious formations which comprise not only one of the said four major types but several or even all four of them, and this in a variegated mixture."[37] The fact that Hinduism includes all four types is thus only one example of a more general situation. According to Schomerus, the distinction between the four basic types should therefore be applied horizontally rather than vertically, even though one of the four types may well exert a dominant influence in some religions. How close Schomerus thus came to a fractal interpretation is obvious in this statement: "Religion as such hypostasizes itself in a few major types, which persistently recur and unfold everywhere in similar ways, everywhere giving rise to kindred forms and formations."[38]

Schomerus could of course not yet refer to the concept of fractals when he made this discovery. This is different with the Romanian historian of religion Ioan P. Couliano (also "Culianu") (1950–1991), who taught in Chicago for the last three years of his life. Couliano explicitly referred to Mandelbrot's concept of fractals, and recognized in it the opportunity to build on and improve structuralist approaches.[39] Couliano brings the dimension of time into play, arguing that fractal structures can be recognized in the historical differentiation of religious doctrines. He illustrates this by pointing to, among other things, the development of different Christological positions in the first centuries of Christianity. According to Couliano, we can analyze the complexity of this development by means of a fractal pattern. That is, we can see how this development replicates the underlying binary decision between interpreting Jesus as a human or as a divine being. Docetism views Jesus as purely divine, while early Adoptionism and Ebionism view him as purely human. Middle positions, which see Jesus as both divine and human, nevertheless tend more in one direction or the other. If Jesus is considered to be more divine, then the question arises as to whether he possessed a human soul alongside his divine soul. Again, the positions differ. If he is understood as more human, then the problem arises as to the nature of his connection with the divine, which also creates new differences. Seeing Jesus as equally divine and human raises the question as to whether the connection of the two natures is itself to be regarded as "natural" or as contingent, and so on. Depending on the direction in which the decision tends in each case, new problems constantly develop where

---
[37] Ibid., 22.
[38] Ibid., 26.
[39] Couliano 1992, 4–8, 267. I am grateful to Giovanni Casadio, who alerted me to Couliano's work.

it becomes possible and necessary to make a new decision in one or the other direction of the underlying basic decision. This results in a kind of tree structure of logically possible positions.[40]

The division of early Christianity according to different Christological positions thus does not follow social and (power-)political influences alone. Rather, these influences interact with the immanent logic of what the system of the core Christological question itself allows in terms of logical possibilities,[41] the latter being mathematizable rules of "mind games."[42] Whether, when, and under which circumstances the various possibilities of the mind game are actually realized remains open. This, in turn, depends on the other influences and remains historically contingent. In this respect, Couliano comes close to the positions in cognitive science mentioned in the previous chapter.[43]

Couliano then connects the intrareligious diversity that he analyzes with interreligious diversity, which fully reveals the fractal nature of the structure:

> Mind games have necessarily similar mechanisms (because the way the mind works and its capacity have remained unchanged for at least sixty thousand years), and therefore systems that have been sufficiently run in time would tend to overlap not only in shape but in substance. With complex data at hand, we should be able to demonstrate that portions of the map of the Buddhist system would overlap with portions of the Christian system . . . because all systems are infinite and tend to explore all possibilities given to them. Accordingly, when sufficiently extended, their maps of reality would certainly coincide.[44]

While Couliano's early death in a still unsolved murder prevented him from taking this idea further, James Ford has come to a similar conclusion in his comparative study of conceptions of ultimate reality. Ford outlines a "morphology" of ultimate reality by means of three typological oppositions: "one *versus* many," "personal *versus* impersonal," "transcendent *versus* immanent." But then he concludes as follows:

> I . . . do not assume that a particular tradition can be characterized by one of the particular poles of these dichotomies. But these dualities do reflect interesting tensions *between and within traditions* that are worth noting. The heterogeneous nature of these traditions suggests

---

[40] See the diagram in ibid., 15.
[41] Ibid., 16, 18–19.
[42] Ibid., 267–69.
[43] See above, p. 9.
[44] Couliano 1992, 268.

a fluidity that should problematize any essentialized or reified characterizations.[45]

Like Couliano, Ford thus also believes that there are logical possibilities of differentiation virtually embedded within the system itself. Logically, there could be one or more ultimate realities; ultimate reality can be thought of as a personal reality, i.e., as a personal God, or as an impersonal Absolute; it can be conceived as completely otherworldly (transcendent) or as present in everything (immanent). Other logically possible distinctions, combinations, or variants arise from this, and all or most of these possibilities have actually developed in some form or other within every major religious tradition. However, certain options can assume a particularly prominent and dominant position during this process.[46] It is precisely this fact, even though Ford himself does not use this terminology, that leads to a fractal effect: the distinctive differences *between* traditions (macro level) are found in analogous form *within* each tradition (meso level).[47] Going beyond Ford, we can add that, since these differences are ultimately possibilities of thought (or, in Couliano's terms, "mind games"), such different conceptions can also occur in the single individual (micro level). But how should we interpret the differences that replicate in the fractal patterns? This question takes us onto terrain that is relevant to theology.

2.2 PERSPECTIVES FROM INTERRELIGIOUS THEOLOGY

As mentioned, the widespread departure of religious studies from structuralism and phenomenology of religion has led to a real decline in comparative studies of religions. Thus, as far as I can see, no one has yet taken up the early exploration of fractal patterns and structures.[48] However, current interreligious theological work comprises an increasing number of examples where interreligious diversity is perceived along the lines of fractal patterns, even if these have not yet been named and studied as "fractals."[49]

Like Nathan Söderblom (1866–1931) before him, Friedrich Heiler (1892–1967) divided the so-called world religions into two main types: prophetic and mystical. In his dialogue with Julia Ching in *Chinese Religion*,

---
[45]Ford 2016, 308. My emphasis.
[46]Ibid., 308–19.
[47]Ibid., 325.
[48]See, however, the studies of fractal patterns in religious rituals carried out by Jens Kreinath (2012 and 2020).
[49]But initial discussions can now be found in Race & Knitter 2019; Faber 2019, 125–35; and May 2020.

first published in 1988, Küng then added a third type: namely, sapiential or wisdom religions.[50] The prophetic religions—Judaism, Christianity, Islam—are Semitic in origin; the mystical religions of Hinduism and Buddhism come from India; and the sapiential religions are Chinese Daoism and Confucianism. According to Küng, each of these three types has specific characteristics and in particular a different religious role model: the prophet, the mystic, and the sage. Yet Küng makes an important modification to his typology, arguing that prophetic religions also contain certain elements and characteristics of mystical and sapiential religions; mystical religions contain elements and characteristics of prophetic and sapiential religions; and sapiential religions contain prophetic and mystical elements or traits.[51] This observation corresponds to a fractal pattern: the diversity of prophetic, mystical, and sapiential types of religion is replicated in the form of intrareligious diversity, where typical elements of the prophetic, mystical, and sapiential recur.

However, in their discussions, neither Küng nor Ching pay much attention to this observation, although they do to its implications. According to Küng, the observation of "significant parallels and convergences" shows that, "in spite of all divergences and differences . . . enrichment through cross-fertilization is possible."[52] Indeed, the question of how to interpret and evaluate the content of fractal structures is of considerable importance for an interreligious theology: Do the different features from which individual fractal patterns emerge (such as, in this example, the features of the prophetic, mystical, and sapiential) form irreconcilable opposites? Are they mutually exclusive logical alternatives, or can they also be interpreted in terms of coherent, or even complementary, differences? The answer to this question ultimately decides how religious diversity will be evaluated theologically. The following examples all assume complementarity, but justify it in different ways.

Complementarity with Regard to Ultimate Reality

Three theologians highly influential within interreligious theology tend to discern fractal patterns within interreligious diversity, which each relates to the nature of ultimate reality. The American process theologian John Cobb distinguishes three different types of religion: *cosmic*, *acosmic*, and *theistic*.[53] According to Cobb, each corresponds to a specific notion of

---

[50]Küng & Ching 1989, xi–xix.
[51]Ibid., xv–xvi.
[52]Ibid., 279.
[53]For a summary of Cobb's theology of religions, see Griffin 2005.

ultimate reality and to a corresponding set of religious experiences. That is, cosmic religions (Cobb cites Daoism and Native American religions as examples) understand ultimate reality as the sacred nature of the cosmos itself. This corresponds to experiences that testify to "a kind of belonging to the cosmos, or kinship with other creatures, about which ordinary experience does not inform us."[54] As examples of acosmic notions of ultimate reality, Cobb cites the Mahayana-Buddhist concept of "emptiness" (*śūnyatā*) and the concept of "Brahman without form or qualities" (*nirguṇa brahman*) from the Hindu tradition of Advaita Vedanta.[55] Such concepts correspond to experiences like that of an "inward" nature, the "discovery of a 'depth' that is free from all the particularities of ordinary experience," or "a removal of all culturally and existentially determined barriers to openness to what is as it is."[56] Finally, the theistic concepts of ultimate reality—i.e., its conception as a personal God—correspond to experiences such as the presence of an invisible person with whom we are in communion, who guides and directs us, spurs us to a life of righteousness and love, and releases us from guilt.[57]

Cobb developed his classification of cosmic, acosmic, and theistic religions under the influence of the American religious scholar John A. Hutchison.[58] Like Hutchison, Cobb notes that "more than one of these types can be discerned in most of the great traditions."[59] That is, Cobb uses his typology to identify both differences *among* religions and different manifestations *within* each of these religions. In other words, Cobb states in essence a fractal pattern. Moreover, he sees the three basic elements of this fractal pattern as forming a complementary unit. For this purpose, he provides them with a metaphysical interpretation that he derives from his process theology. According to this, the three different concepts of ultimate reality relate to three different ultimates. To be more precise, they relate to three ontologically distinct, but interrelated and irreducible features of one complex ultimate reality: the *cosmos* forms in a sense the body of God, the *acosmic being itself* denotes that creative force and reality linking God and cosmos, and the *theistically* conceived God relates to the creative designer and true soul of the cosmos. I return to Cobb's process-theological metaphysics later.[60]

Something quite similar can be seen in Mark Heim's comparative reflec-

---

[54]Cobb 1999, 117.
[55]See Griffin 2005, 47.
[56]Cobb 1999, 118.
[57]Ibid.
[58]Ibid., 120. Cobb refers to the second edition of Hutchison's *Paths of Faiths* from 1975. Hutchison himself uses the terms "cosmic," "acosmic," and "historical religion." His terminology is obviously influenced by Mircea Eliade. However, in his description of these three types of religion, Cobb deviates from Hutchison, which is due to the fact that Cobb interprets the three types in line with his process theology.
[59]Cobb 1999, 121; Hutchison 1991, 17.
[60]See below, pp. 106–07 and 236.

tions regarding religious differences. Although Heim is not a representative of process theology, his interpretation of religious diversity has a certain similarity to Cobb's. More clearly than Cobb, Heim assumes only one ultimate reality, which, however, he also regards as internally complex. For Heim, this is the Christian Trinity. According to Heim, conceptions of ultimate reality in other religions can be related to different aspects or dimensions of the Trinity, which these conceptions more or less correctly capture.

According to Heim, the Trinity contains an *impersonal*, a *personal* (or *iconic*), and a *communial* (or interpersonal) dimension. These three dimensions are reflected in the different types of religion and their specific notions of ultimate reality. According to Heim, the *impersonal* dimension of ultimate reality consists on the one hand in the mutual indwelling of the three divine persons. That is, each person is completely one with the other two persons, and is therefore at the same time completely empty of itself and insofar "not-self" or "impersonal." On the other hand, the impersonal dimension of the Trinity consists in the fact that God holds back, so to speak, in order to give space to creation, but at the same time dwells in it as the power granting its existence. Some Buddhist doctrines, such as the doctrine of the "not-self," of nirvana, or of "emptiness" (*śūnyatā*), but also the nondualism of the Hindu Advaita Vedanta teaching can, according to Heim, be interpreted as partial realizations of this dimension of ultimate reality. Heim sees the *personal* or *iconic* dimension of the Trinity in the fact that "the three constitute one will, one purpose, one love toward creation."[61] This dimension of oneness or uniqueness is at the center of monotheistic conceptions of ultimate reality. But it is also found in the conception of one divine law, such as in Daoism or in ancient Stoa: "What is apprehended in these cases is the external unity of the Trinity,"[62] which appears here as *one* divine will without a person, i.e., as a heavenly law, as it were. According to Heim, the third (i.e., *communial*) dimension underlies the other two. It combines unity and difference in that the three persons participate and share in each other,[63] which is comparable to human relationships of "deep love or intimate friendship."[64] This dimension is at the heart of Christian notions of ultimate reality.

However, like Cobb, Heim also notes that "each great religious tradition in some measure recognizes the variety of dimensions we have described," and that each grasps "the set of dimensions *through* one of them."[65] These statements quite obviously imply a fractal pattern, too, since they suggest

---

[61] Heim 2003, 394.
[62] Ibid., 396.
[63] Ibid., 397.
[64] Ibid., 391.
[65] Both quotations ibid., 399.

that the differences between the various types of religion with their respective ideas of ultimate reality are also found within each one of them. He even admits that "formally" Christianity is not different from other religions in this respect.[66] Christianity, too, apprehends all three dimensions primarily through the lens of one dimension regarded as dominant, in this case the communial dimension. Thus, like Cobb, Heim also understands the typological differences between various notions of ultimate reality as complementary, even if he differs from Cobb in how he defines these differences in detail. And, like Cobb, Heim attributes this complementarity to the fact that the different concepts of ultimate reality actually reflect different dimensions of the complex nature of the ultimate.

A structurally similar approach has been proposed by John Thatamanil, who also argues that "religious differences are rooted in genuine distinctions within the divine life."[67] According to Thatamanil, "divine life" encompasses three dimensions: it is the *ground* of being of all things and makes everything, from the atom to the galaxy, exist in unmistakable *singularity* on the one hand, and, on the other hand, in inevitable interconnectedness and *relation*. The divine is thus the ground of being in its two essential characteristics of singularity and relation. For Thatamanil, this reflects the Christian Trinity of the Father as the ground of being, the Son as the source of singularity, and the Spirit as the bond of life-giving relation.[68] Yet he goes on to argue that the three dimensions are also reflected in the concepts of ultimate reality in other religions, with one dimension usually taking a dominant position: in Hindu Advaita Vedanta, the dimension of the ground; in Christianity, that of singularity; and, in Mahayana Buddhism, that of relation or inter-relation of all things.[69] However, says Thatamanil, this does not mean that the two corresponding dimensions are completely absent in each case. Nevertheless, according to Thatamanil, they are often insufficiently considered within the respective traditions or even rejected as heretical. Thus, there is the chance in interreligious theology to help each of the three dimensions to its rightful place, and thereby to arrive at a more appropriate perception of the divine life.[70]

Hence, Cobb, Heim, and Thatamanil not only describe fractal patterns of religious diversity but also interpret the differences constituting those patterns as complementary. This is because they all focus primarily on concepts of ultimate reality, and suggest that these differences reflect actual differences in ultimate reality itself. The complex but unitary nature of the

---

[66]Ibid.
[67]Thatamanil 2020, 246.
[68]Ibid., 219–20.
[69]Ibid., 218–42.
[70]Ibid., 242–48.

ultimate itself conditions the complementarity of the different conceptions of ultimate reality. This would also explain why each of these concepts is always accompanied by aspects of the alternative concepts. The occurrence of fractal patterns thus has its reason in the structure of ultimate reality itself, or more precisely in the correct recognition of this structure—or better, of its individual aspects and dimensions—within the different religions. But what if theologians are much more reserved than these three theologians regarding the human capacity to grasp and describe ultimate reality? That is, if they adhere more strongly than Cobb, Heim, and Thatamanil to the traditional position that ultimate reality is incomprehensible and ineffable? Even then it is possible to interpret fractal structures as complementary, but in a way that starts with the religious subject, i.e., the human being.

Complementarity with Regard to Human Predispositions

We can see in retrospect that initial reflections on the connection between religious diversity and human dispositions were already entertained by Rudolf Otto (1869–1937). He suggested that the large number of inter-religious parallels can be traced back to "the underlying congruent and common predisposition of humanity in general."[71] Influenced by Kant's transcendental philosophy, Otto interpreted this "common predisposition" as inherent structures of the human mind.[72] Such a "religious a priori," according to Otto, can explain not only the inherent possibility of religious experience but also the diversity of its forms and their replication within different religions.[73]

Bernhard Nitsche's work also moves along such transcendental-philosophical or transcendental-theological paths. In his recent publications, he distinguishes between monistic, theistic, and panentheistic types of religion.[74] Here, Nitsche postulates a connection between the respective concepts of ultimate reality and three basic forms of human relatedness: (1) relatedness to the world, as mediated by a person's own corporeality; (2) relatedness to other people, mediated by social contact; and (3) relatedness to oneself, mediated by the self-reflexive structure of the human mind. According to Nitsche, these three basic forms of human relatedness correspond to three different ways of thinking, which are in turn related to

---

[71] Otto 1923, 217; see also ibid., 222.

[72] In the cognitive science of religion, István Czachesz (2012) has suggested tracing religious conceptions of infinity to the mind's capacity to imagine infinite iteration. This, however, would apply only to the idea of an infinity within the limits of space and time, and not to the idea of a reality that transcends the finite limitations of space and time themselves.

[73] On this, see the classic account in Rudolf Otto's treatise *The Idea of the Holy (Das Heilige)* (1936), first published in 1917.

[74] Nitsche 2017; 2018a; 2018b—and most recently 2023a; 2023b.

different ideas of ultimate reality. Specifically, a dominance of the first corresponds, according to Nitsche, to a *cosmomorphic* way of thinking, which tends to *monistic* concepts of ultimate reality. The dominance of the second corresponds to a *sociomorphic* form of thinking, which favors *theistic* concepts of ultimate reality. Finally, the *noomorphic* form of thinking, which corresponds to the third form of human relatedness, tends to *panentheistic* conceptions. According to Nitsche, these connections are not compelling, but nevertheless reflect clear tendencies.

As for the distribution of these different ways of thinking and their corresponding conceptions of ultimate reality within the actual religions, Nitsche, too, suggests a fractal pattern: "Presumably, these basic forms of the reference to transcendence are thematized in all large and complex religious systems with different accentuations and combinations of dominant and subdominant as well as with different priorities and interferences."[75] The "leading melody of a religion," says Nitsche, "resounds . . . with different accompanying melodies" in quite varying "strength of presence."[76] However, since it is always the three basic forms anchored in the human mind that set the tone here, it is worthwhile in interreligious dialogue to "look comparatively for possible correspondences," without thereby leveling out the differences between the actual religious contexts and settings that diverge in each case.[77]

According to Nitsche, the three forms of thinking express *human relations* to divine reality. Before divine reality itself, however, each of these forms of thinking reaches its limits. They all stand under the proviso of a "mystical apophasis," since divine perfection exceeds every possibility of thinking.[78] In this respect, Nitsche also refers to the three forms of thinking as "resonances of human existence and its structural conditions."[79] He is explicitly concerned with finding an anthropological foundation for human relations to transcendence.[80] The unity and complementarity of the three forms of thinking are therefore based primarily on the unity of relations to the world, the social sphere, and the self as three cohesive dimensions of being human, none of which can ever be completely absent. However, Nitsche also suggests that divine reality as the ground of all reality is also constitutive of these three dimensions of human reality, and that it "operates in a manner appropriate to them."[81]

Nitsche's approach points to an important alternative to the three ap-

---

[75]Nitsche 2017, 60–61.
[76]Ibid., 51.
[77]Ibid.
[78]Ibid., 60; 2018b, 381–82, 385. See also Nitsche 2023a, 8.
[79]Nitsche 2017, 57.
[80]Ibid., 56.
[81]Nitsche 2018b, 383.

proaches just mentioned, since, unlike them, Nitsche takes into account the conviction—widespread among the great religious traditions—that a truly transcendent reality must also be transcendent in the conceptual sense. To paraphrase Augustine, a God who could be comprehended would not be God.[82] In contrast, Cobb, Heim, and Thatamanil give at best (if at all) a subordinate role to this apophatic proviso. Thus, Nitsche's attempt to root the complementarity of different ideas of transcendence in basic complementary features of the human mind—rather than in allegedly correctly apprehended different characteristics, properties, or dimensions of the divine itself—is and remains promising—even if, as Nitsche admits, this is *"work in progress"* requiring further reflection and modification.[83] In my view, a transcendental philosophy or theology, as shaped by Kant, would have to consider not only the theoretical forms of thinking but also the practical patterns of thought. That is, what are the anthropological predispositions forming the roots of human behavior, responsibility, pursuit of happiness,[84] and coping with suffering, as well as aesthetic and ethical sensibility? These aspects bring into play the different existentially relevant ideas of misery and salvation, such as guilt and forgiveness, egoism and altruism, delusion and insight, obduracy and openness, bondage and liberation, failure and fulfillment, ugliness and beauty, etc. This becomes especially clear when the focus is not solely on ideas of ultimate reality but also on different paths of salvation.

Complementarity with Regard to Different Paths of Salvation

Fractal patterns regarding different religious paths of salvation, combined with the thesis of their inner complementarity, can already be found in nuce in two important reform figures of modern Hinduism and Theravada Buddhism. As Ayon Maharaj (monastic name: Swami Medhananda) has shown, Swami Vivekananda (1863–1902) already provided something like a fractal interpretation of religious diversity.[85] Like Schomerus,[86] Vivekananda interprets religious diversity in terms of the distinction made in parts of the Hindu tradition between four different paths of salvation: the path of work (*karma yoga*), the path of love of God (*bhakti yoga*), the path of meditation (or, as Vivekananda can also say, of "psychology" [*rāja yoga*]), and the path of knowledge (*jñāna yoga*). On the one hand, Vivekananda claims, in accordance with the Hindu tradition, that the different paths of salvation

---

[82] Augustin, *Sermo* 117 (see below p. 103). See also the examples in Schmidt-Leukel 2017a, 179–87.
[83] Nitsche 2018b, 369.
[84] Schmidt-Leukel 2018, 198.
[85] Maharaj 2019, 105–8.
[86] I cannot say whether Schomerus might have been inspired by Vivekananda, but I would not exclude the possibility.

serve different temperaments and thus the different needs of individuals.[87] On the other, he identifies in a short remark the diversity of religions with the diversity of the paths of salvation: "each religion represents one."[88] This is obviously meant in the sense of a certain dominance of the respective path of salvation, since Vivekananda is fully aware of the internal multiformity of each individual religion: in all of them there are numerous divisions and further subdivisions.[89] For Vivekananda, the differences between the religions (macro level) recur in each of them (meso level), and in fact he sees them even on the micro level of diverse subjective inclinations.

Vivekananda understands the differences between the four principal paths of salvation as being complementary. In turn, this complementarity is related to the nature of the paths themselves:

> We may reach the same goal by different paths; and these paths I have generalised into four, viz those of work, love, psychology, and knowledge. But you must, at the same time, remember that these divisions are not very marked and quite exclusive of each other. Each blends into the other. But according to the type which prevails, we name the divisions. It is not that you can find men who have no other faculty than that of work, nor that you can find men who are no more than devoted worshippers only, nor that there are men who have no more than mere knowledge. These divisions are made in accordance with the type or the tendency that may be seen to prevail in a man. We have found that, in the end, all these four paths converge and become one.[90]

We find a comparable idea in the work of the Thai Buddhist reformer Bhikkhu Buddhadasa (1906–1993), who also takes up the notion of different paths of salvation. For him, what is necessary for the attainment of final liberation is found not only in Buddhism, but also in Christianity, Islam, and Hinduism, albeit with different emphases and in different forms.[91] Buddhism accentuates primarily "wisdom"; Christianity, "faith" or "trust"; and Islam, "willpower." According to Buddhadasa, these three central spiritual qualities form an inner unity, which means that, despite different emphases, all three qualities or paths can eventually be found in every religion: "each religion comprises all the three ways; the only difference is that a certain religion may give preference to one way or the other."[92] For Buddhadasa,

---

[87] Vivekananda 1994, vol. 4, 51–60.
[88] Ibid., vol. 8, 152.
[89] Ibid., vol. 4, 52.
[90] Ibid., vol. 1, 108.
[91] Buddhadāsa 1967, 12–14, 24–25, 38–39.
[92] Ibid., 13.

differences in the teachings of each religion result primarily from different cultural influences.[93] Interestingly, Buddhadasa refers not to a Buddhist authority for this view, but rather to the Qur'anic statement that there is a specific messenger for each nation (Surah 10:47).[94]

To assert that different paths of salvation have an inner cohesion, both Vivekananda and Buddhadasa draw on ideas from their respective traditions. The former draws on the one hand on the *adhikāra-bheda* principle, which says that people at different levels of spiritual development need different religious practices or "paths," and on the other hand on the teaching of the *Bhagavad Gītā*, which says that different paths can lead to salvation, inasmuch as they promote the inner attitude of nonattachment. Behind Buddhadasa's suggestion lies the traditional scheme of the three types of perfect future Buddhas (*samma-sambodhisatta*). According to the *Buddhavaṃsa*, Buddhahood can be attained in three ways, each of which differs according to which of the three qualities mentioned (wisdom, faith, willpower) dominates.[95] For Buddhadasa, what counts is that nonattachment and selflessness are practiced on each of the three paths.[96] Vivekananda and Buddhadasa therefore both argue that the complementarity of different paths of salvation is based on the fact that, despite their differences, they have equally salvific or liberating effects, an argument that could be much strengthened if it were further supported by transcendental anthropology. Vivekananda at least indicates this when he refers to a nature common to all human beings that nonetheless comprises different types and inclinations.

A connection of different paths of salvation, including their inherent ideas of salvation and transcendence, to different aspects of human existence was already the basis of the hermeneutic scheme that I proposed in my own early work on the relationship between Christianity and Buddhism.[97] According to this scheme, human existence includes different basic experiences, such as the experience of transience, of interpersonal relatedness, of freedom, creativity, responsibility, etc. Basic experiences are shared by people of all cultures and religions, but each is present in differently interpreted forms, which also has its impact on the actual nature of the experience. It is possible to discern some clear links between basic human experiences and the specific ways that different religions interpret human predicament and salvation/liberation. On the one hand, these links make their message of salvation universalizable, i.e., religions can count on the fact that their

---

[93]Ibid., 24–25.
[94]Ibid., 8.
[95]"Informed by wisdom" (*paññādhika*), "informed by faith/trust" (*saddhādhika*), "informed by willpower" (*viryādhika*).
[96]Buddhadāsa 1967, 13; Swearer 1989, 152, 168–69.
[97]Schmidt-Leukel 1984; 1992, 434–56, 655–83; 1993a.

message is relevant and in principle intelligible to all people. On the other, it also explains why the ideas held by the great religions with regard to salvation/liberation and human predicament differ. My suggestion is that it is largely to do with the fact that their analysis and evaluation each look at human existence from the perspective of different basic experiences.

For example, to understand the need for human salvation/liberation, Buddhism foregrounds the experience of transience, while Christianity foregrounds the experience of interpersonal relatedness and its challenges. Buddhism therefore understands deliverance primarily as deliverance from suffering under transience (a transience that the cycle of rebirth may perpetuate endlessly), while Christianity sees it as deliverance from guilt and as healing of broken relations. However, both religions also take into account the other basic experiences, albeit from somewhat different perspectives. What Buddhism is primarily interested in when it comes to the experience of interpersonal relatedness is how this experience can help deliverance from entanglement in transience, or whether it will even foster this entanglement. In contrast, Christianity sees death as the wages of sin, from whose bonds God's forgiving and healing love delivers the human being.

The fact that basic human experiences are cohesive implies that, despite the differing perspectives, there may be significant correspondences, convergences, and complementarities when looked at in more detail. Moreover, as both religions develop further, the emphasis that each places in its understanding of human existence can shift and vary, even if its original analysis of human existence may remain at work in the background. Hence, this hermeneutic approach already corresponded to a fractal pattern, even if I was unaware of this at the time.

A Fractal Interpretation of Religious Diversity and the Theology of Religions

The examples presented in the previous section show that the discovery of fractal structures in religious diversity is not dependent on any particular form of typological differentiation. Fractal patterns can apparently be encountered largely independently of the typological scheme that is chosen to define, classify, and analyze religious diversity. I therefore propose a fractal approach to religious diversity in a heuristic sense. According to William Paden, the purpose of categories in interreligious comparisons should generally be understood as heuristic—namely as "instruments of further discovery," including "the possibility of their own further differentiation, subtypologization, and problematization."[98] The heuristic use of fractal

---
[98] Paden 2000, 186.

44 The Celestial Web

analysis is appropriate in this sense, since it helps make actual comparative categories more flexible and nuanced. This corresponds when it comes to comparing religions to the insight that religions are not static and homogeneous entities. Rather, a fractal approach leads to a focus on the internal diversity and hybridity of the religions that are being compared, and helps take into account those aspects that the comparative description of religions tends to overlook or leave aside because they do not fit the prevailing picture.[99] If the personal background and starting point of the comparativist is also taken into account, and if this starting point is of a theological nature, then the fractal perspective leads us in the comparison of religions to look for analogous forms of diversity and hybridity within our own tradition, too. It is precisely this approach to viewing religious diversity that proves extremely fruitful when it comes to doing theology interreligiously.

In principle, the great religious traditions provide favorable conditions for a fractal approach: namely, in the form of the micro-macro-cosmos scheme that is common throughout the religions.[100] Since this scheme suggests a correspondence between micro- and macrocosmic structures, it discloses a fractal way of looking at the universe. This is often the case.[101] For example, it is said in Sufism, "The universe is a big man and man a little universe."[102] In Christianity, we find the widespread idea, probably going back to Augustine, of the image of the Trinity in the human soul. In the late Middle Ages, Heymericus de Campo (1395–1460) gave with his "Seal of Eternity" (*sigillum aeternitatis*) a splendidly fractal expression to the view that the entire world is structured triadically.[103] The image is also very reminiscent of similar attempts from Hinduism, such as in particular the well-known Śrī Yantra (also: Śrī Cakra). Its nine intersecting triangles have a multilayered symbolic meaning, which nonetheless revolves around the basic micro-/macrocosmic scheme. For example, they represent earth, air, and sun, which are reflected in body, breath, and consciousness, and are paralleled to other groups of three.[104] The irregular but clearly fractal structure is obvious. Finally, for Buddhism, we can point to the philosophy of the *Avataṃsaka Sūtra*, the central image of "Indra's net" that gives this book its title.[105]

---

[99] Jackson, W. 2004, 65.
[100] Lanczkowski 1978, 70–72.
[101] For numerous individual examples, see Jackson, W. 2004.
[102] Burckhardt 2008, 65.
[103] Meier-Staubach 2003; Geis 2007.
[104] Kak 2008–2009.
[105] See above, pp. xiii–xiv.

Fig. left: Sigillum Aeternitatis, © KIK-IRPA, Brussels, www.kikirpa.be
Fig. right: Sri Yantra, template: © yulianas—iStock.com

Thus, although religions have long been aware of the fractal replication of larger structures in their smaller components, they have, as far as I can see, barely applied this approach to religious diversity—at least not in a positive sense. A relatively widespread phenomenon, though, saw religious scholars sometimes parallel other religions, and especially new and hitherto unknown religions, with what their own tradition regarded as heterodox religious groupings. For example, representatives of older Buddhist schools accused the newly emerging Mahayana Buddhism of being merely a variant of Hindu Vedanta, and demonized both equally.[106] Or, when they first studied Indian religions, medieval Muslim theologians identified some of the Indian teachings with the "heretical" positions that they knew within Islam.[107] And when the first Jesuit missionaries in sixteenth-century Japan became acquainted with Pure Land Buddhism, they thought to recognize in it the same "heresy" that the devil had used to inspire Luther.[108] Such parallelizations of interreligious with intrareligious differences implicitly express a perception of fractal patterns. However, the cases mentioned did not perceive these differences as complementary, and therefore did not see them as enriching theology.

In 1870, Friedrich Max Müller coined his well-known dictum to explain the need for a method of comparing religions: "He who knows one [religion] knows none."[109] This was echoed by Adolf von Harnack about

---

[106] Schmidt-Leukel 2022a.
[107] Waardenburg 2003, 172, 174.
[108] Schmidt-Leukel 2020d, 238–40.
[109] Müller 1874, 13. From a lecture given by Müller in 1870.

three decades later in his equally well-known counterstatement: "He who does not know this religion [Christianity] knows none, and he who knows it together with its history knows all."[110] From the standpoint of a fractal interpretation of religious diversity, both were right in a sense. Harnack saw that essential elements of other religions can be found in Christianity, while Müller was right insofar as only comparison can reveal the fractal patterns in the relationships between Christianity and other religions. Only by comparison can we gain an adequate understanding of an individual religion in its particularity.

Müller's provocative thesis expressed the idea that "theoretical theology" could only make scientifically respectable progress when "comparative theology has completely collected, critically investigated, and sorted out all the facts that one can get hold of in the history of religions."[111] Harnack, on the other hand, was convinced that Christian theology could not really further its knowledge by studying other religions. His thesis that knowledge of Christianity means knowledge of all religions implied that in Christianity "the whole history of religion in the succession of its manifestations is repeated and unified"—and this especially "on the soil of Catholicism."[112] Thus, the Protestant Harnack also identifies other religions with those religious forms of his own tradition that are deemed deviant (in his case, Catholicism). But, according to Harnack, this all-encompassing nature applies to Christianity alone, and this for a dogmatic reason. Christianity, as Harnack understood it—i.e., "in its pure form"—is "not a religion among others, but the religion. But it is the religion because Jesus Christ is not a master among others, but the master."[113] His disciples, according to Harnack, recognized in him more than "just a teacher," but rather "the Lord and Savior." Therefore, Christianity, and only Christianity, is that "religion which offers what the others aspire to."[114] This is the real reason why, according to Harnack, genuine theological gains cannot be expected from studying other religions.

This poses the question: what does the observation of fractal patterns in religious diversity contribute to the debate about an appropriate theology of religions? Some authors see in my thesis—that religious diversity displays fractal patterns—a confirmation of a pluralist theology of religions.[115] For Kenneth Rose, the identification of fractal patterns supports the claim that the same salvific potential can be found in many variants in every major religious

---

[110] Von Harnack 1904, 168.
[111] Müller 1874, 19–20.
[112] Ibid., 170.
[113] Ibid., 172.
[114] Ibid., 173.
[115] On the pluralist theology of religions, see above, p. 18 and Schmidt-Leukel 2017a; 2017b, 15–106.

tradition, and can be further promoted through interreligious encounter.[116] According to Rose, a fractal interpretation holds the key to understanding similarity in diversity, and thus equivalence despite difference.[117] Similarly, Alan Race emphasizes that a fractal interpretation of religious diversity undermines the argument that different religions are incommensurable, and thereby all forms of exclusivism that are based on it. Since fractal structures can even be discerned in central religious concepts, for inclusivists it will also be more difficult to justify their claims to superiority.[118] "In this way, the fractal proposal provides some grounding in phenomenology for the pluralist hypothesis."[119] However, as Race also makes clear, this is only true if the fractal constellations can be shown to be complementary.

I share the assessments of Rose and Race insofar as the phenomenological identification of fractal patterns links very well with and strengthens a pluralist theology of religion. However, it does not entirely exclude alternative interpretations, and therefore does not constitute full evidence of religious pluralism. An *atheist* or *naturalist* can interpret the fractal patterns as structures of a great illusion of humanity—and as long as it cannot be proven that a reality transcending the limits of space and time really exists, the naturalist position remains a legitimate rational option. However, the atheist-naturalist interpretation loses an important argument if the demonstration of fractal patterns is combined with proof of substantive compatibilities, since atheism has often questioned the credibility of religious experience by arguing that all religions contradict each other. For David Hume, "In matters of religion, whatever is different is contrary."[120] This prop for an atheist position is removed if it is shown that especially in religion difference can also mean compatibility and even complementarity.[121] However, this does not defeat a naturalist position, since it still remains possible to interpret religious diversity as a diversity of structurally similar errors.

An *exclusivist* is in a more difficult position. Like the atheist, the exclusivist also interprets the majority of religious experience as illusory, but considers their own tradition as valid. Therefore, pointing out significant parallels between their own and other religious traditions poses a serious problem for any exclusivist approach.[122] Exclusivists can solve this problem by declaring the parallels to be either spurious or irrelevant. The Christian tradition has often done the former by interpreting non-Christian parallels

---

[116]Rose 2019, 32–34.
[117]Ibid., 37.
[118]Race 2019, 149–61.
[119]Ibid., 157. Similarly, May 2020, 379.
[120]Hume 1748 (1777), E 10.24.
[121]On this, see also Schmidt-Leukel 2016b.
[122]See the extensive discussion in Schmidt-Leukel 1997, 122–65; 2017a, 111–15 (= 2005, 122–27).

to Christian beliefs and rites as "diabolical imitation" (*imitatio diabolica*). Postmodern theories of incommensurability have also been drawn on more recently, the effect being to deny the validity of cross-religious parallels from the outset. A fractal interpretation undermines such attempts. However, exclusivists can also denote interreligious parallels as valid but irrelevant. For example, a Christian exclusivist may argue that such parallels do not touch on the core of the gospel; or the central person of Christianity, Jesus of Nazareth; or, according to Karl Barth, the true revelation, which is for him the "name Jesus Christ." But as soon as the question is about the religious interpretation of the gospel or of the person of Jesus or of his name, fractal patterns emerge once again, so that a fractal approach will also weaken exclusivist arguments. Yet above all, exclusivist positions come under pressure when certain forms of inter- and intrareligious diversity can be shown to be complementary, since any exclusivism sees diversity and difference as fundamentally pointing to falsity.

Regarding the demonstration of interreligious parallels, representatives of *inclusivist* positions are in a stronger position than exclusivists; inclusivists can accept interreligious parallels as valid and relevant, but not as signs of a real equivalence of different forms of knowledge of the transcendent and different paths of salvation/liberation. In order to defend the claim to the singular superiority of their own religion, they can interpret fractal patterns in two ways. On the one hand, they can argue that both the good and true sides of a religion, and its bad and false sides, are reflected in fractal patterns, but that as a whole the good and true aspects clearly predominate within their own religion. On the other hand, if certain fractal patterns are composed of good and true elements alone, they can claim that such patterns are found in the highest perfection only in their own religion, in whatever way they justify this in detail. This was already the position taken by Rudolf Otto, who argued that the superiority of a religion can be measured by whether it combines the different elements of religious experience "in healthy and lovely harmony."[123] In this, according to Otto, Christianity is superior to all other religions,[124] "not like the truth to the lie," but "like the firstborn to his brothers."[125] But why should it not be just as conceivable that other religions also combine various religious elements into different, but equally good harmonies? Otto, too, did not want to exclude this possibility completely.[126]

The phenomenological findings of fractal patterns are thoroughly compatible with a *pluralist* theology of religion. Inasmuch as a pluralist theology

---

[123] Otto 1936, 146; similarly, 173.
[124] Ibid., 146.
[125] Otto 1923, 223.
[126] Ibid., 222.

of religion leads to doing theology interreligiously, then tracing fractal patterns is a significant help. Such patterns show that interreligious points of reference are already laid out in the religions themselves and provide a basis for flourishing processes of interreligious learning, especially when the points of reference are complementary. However, this by no means implies that fractal patterns can be limited to what would be true, good, and holy in the religions. No one will seriously deny that there is also the false, the evil, and the demonic in all religions, and these phenomena are probably also part of fractal structures. But identifying fractal structures can foster learning processes even in this respect. Jesus' parable of the speck in one's neighbor's eye and the log in one's own eye (Matthew 7:3–5) can certainly be read in a fractal sense: the evil that we perceive particularly clearly in the religious other could and should sensitize us to the repressed dark sides in our own tradition.

Reinhold Bernhardt has derived from the fact that the observation of fractal patterns combines particularly well with a pluralist theology of religion the suspicion that the pluralist theology of religion is its secret prerequisite. According to Bernhardt, one would have to understand religious diversity from the outset as a unity, in order to be able to identify fractal patterns within this unity. The basis of this unity, though, consists in the "religion-transcendent ground of unity of the religions" that the pluralist theology of religion presupposes. But if one recognizes in the concept of religion "a construct of Occidental intellectual history that brings different—and ultimately not the same—currents of cultural history to the same denominator 'religion,' then this approach loses its basis."[127] But Bernhardt's objection does not hold, since, as the previous chapter showed, the fact that the concept of religion is a construct of Occidental intellectual history by no means automatically implies its uselessness. Speaking instead of "different currents of cultural history" follows no less an Occidental concept, namely that of "culture." Moreover, Bernhardt also uses the term "religion" without too many scruples. And what does he mean when he says that these currents are "ultimately not the same"? Does he mean, to echo poststructuralist positions, that they are incommensurable, because it is denied from the outset that comparative categories and overarching structures can have any universal validity? Quite apart from that, a fractal interpretation by no means claims that religious traditions are all the same: they are neither completely the same, nor incommensurably different, but resemble each other in their intrareligious diversity. This statement by no means presupposes a transcendent ground of unity; it can also be made on an atheistic

---

[127] Bernhardt 2019a, 369.

basis. Thus, the phenomenological observation of fractal structures does not depend on a hidden theological presupposition. However, the fact that it is particularly compatible with religious pluralism does not speak against, but for, such pluralism.

3

In the World

3.1 RENOUNCING THE WORLD OR AFFIRMING THE WORLD?

Apologetic Contrasts from a Christian Perspective

As already mentioned, comparisons between Buddhism and Christianity were particularly popular in the early phase of religious studies,[1] with most Western scholars tending to characterize Buddhism as world-renouncing, pessimistic, and passive, and Christianity as world-affirming, optimistic, and active.[2] For example, Hilko Wiardo Schomerus wrote,

> With Buddha, the world lies as in a dark shadow, and man creeps through it like a weary wanderer who has a heavy burden to carry, but does not know what he is carrying it for and where he should go. With Christ, the world lies as in a bright sunshine, and man rules and operates in it with a cheerful face, knowing what he has to do and what he is worth.[3]

Almost all Western scholars considered the reason for the world-renouncing nature of Buddhism to lie in the Buddhist understanding of suffering, and they mainly pointed here to the so-called Four Noble Truths, an ancient doctrinal formula widespread in Buddhism's different strands.[4] According to the traditional Buddhist narrative, Siddhartha Gautama, the "Buddha" (the "Enlightened One," the "Awakened One"), recognized these truths in his enlightenment or "awakening" (which is the literal translation of *bodhi*) and proclaimed them in his first sermon. "All life is suffering": this is how

---
[1] See pp. 2–3.
[2] See Schmidt-Leukel 1992, 36–141.
[3] Schomerus 1931, 41.
[4] See Schmidt-Leukel 2006a, 30–40.

Western scholars often summarized the content of the First Noble Truth, although this sentence does not appear there in that form.[5] Buddhism, it was said, downplays the joyful aspects of life and denies that human existence has any positive aspects, except that human life offers the chance of escaping suffering—namely, by renouncing life itself. For Schomerus, the underlying conviction of Buddhism is, "Suffering cannot be conquered; it can only be fled from."[6] And Alfred Bertholet formulated it thus: "Without world renunciation, there is no salvation."[7] Hence, such scholars argued that it made no sense from a Buddhist point of view to improve the world. Buddhism, it was held, is world-renouncing and deeply pessimistic. Belief in reincarnation simply reinforces this negative worldview—for given the prospect of constant rebirth, death offers no liberation from suffering in the world, but merely marks the transition from one life of suffering to the next. The endlessness of the cycle of rebirths implies that suffering may also be perpetuated endlessly. Liberation from suffering can therefore only be achieved through liberation from every kind of rebirth. There is no salvation apart from complete extinction of one's existence, meaning that a world-renouncing pessimism is combined here with existential nihilism.

A typical example of how Western scholars contrasted Buddhism with Christianity is Thomas Sterling Berry's influential comparative study from 1890. According to Berry, the "starting point of Buddhism is suffering," or, more precisely, "the necessary and inseparable connection between sorrow and existence." Every healthy person, says Berry, would "recognize that if human life has its dark side, it has also its joy and brightness. . . . But Buddhism refuses any brightness to life."[8] "Gautama taught that existence was an evil."[9] And as a result, says Berry, Gautama believed that "in the extinction of existence alone can rest be found."[10] Nirvana therefore originally meant "absolute extinction"[11] or "absolute annihilation."[12] Only later Mahayana Buddhism deviated from this.[13]

In order to achieve the longed-for state of complete "annihilation," Buddhism, according to Berry, found it necessary to give up all ties to the world, including all positive sentiments:

---

[5] According to the version in the *Saṃyutta Nikāya* (56:11), the First Noble Truth reads, "Now this, bhikkhus, is the noble truth of suffering: birth is suffering, aging is suffering, illness is suffering, death is suffering; union with what is displeasing is suffering; separation from what is pleasing is suffering; not to get what one wants is suffering; in brief, the five aggregates subject to clinging are suffering." Bodhi 2000, 1844; Schmidt-Leukel 2006a, 31.
[6] Schomerus 1931, 58.
[7] Bertholet 1909, 34.
[8] Berry 1890, 107.
[9] Ibid., 91.
[10] Ibid.
[11] Ibid.
[12] Ibid., 89.
[13] Ibid., 91–92.

The affections and emotions are but delusive ties and sorrow-causing fetters, . . . from first to last the supreme effort of the intelligent should be to crush and repress their nature until they have purified themselves from all taint of desire and made themselves the cold, passionless, emotionless beings, in which its ideal is realized and due preparation made for the consummation of extinction.[14]

In contrast, Berry presents Christianity as a religion that has never known such a negative attitude toward life as he imputes to Buddhism. According to the Christian view, it is not suffering but sin that is the real problem of human existence. For Berry, liberation from sin is not liberation from life, but on the contrary the promise of eternal life in communion with God and all the redeemed. At the same time, according to Berry, this promise is tied to the idea that people should already improve life on earth—whenever and wherever this seems possible.

As in several other comparisons of Buddhism and Christianity, Berry illustrates his arguments by juxtaposing the widespread Buddhist tale of Kisagotami with Jesus' raisings of the dead. In grief over the sudden death of her very young child, Kisagotami carried the tiny body to Gautama Buddha and asked him to heal her child. The Buddha replied that to do so he would need three mustard seeds from a house where no human or animal had ever died. When after a desperate search Kisagotami was unable to find such a house, she became aware of the omnipresence of death. She was able to let go of her child and accept her loss, and she then entered the Buddhist order of nuns.[15] "The story is touching and beautiful in its way," Berry acknowledges.[16] But ultimately the lesson is simply that no one can escape death, that "therefore you have no right to complain if you have to participate in that which is the common lot of all"—a lesson that offers "but cold comfort to the troubled heart."[17] In contrast, when Jesus met a widow in the city of Nain who had just lost her only son, he showed compassion for the mother and raised her son to life (Luke 7:11–17). According to Berry, this narrative not only expresses the Christian attitude of alleviating suffering in the here and now, but also stands for the hope of eternal life that Jesus brought. Unlike Buddhism, says Berry, Christianity is not about eradicating loving affection, but about cultivating it: "We believe that our affections and emotions are to be consecrated rather than repressed; for to us the first of all truths is contained in the declaration that 'God is Love.'"[18]

---

[14]Ibid., 111.
[15]The story is found in the commentarial literature on the *Therīgāthā* 212–223. See Schmidt-Leukel 2006a, 30.
[16]Berry 1890, 68.
[17]Ibid.
[18]Ibid., 112.

Such contrasts were shaped by a strong apologetic interest in defending Christianity and, accordingly, were highly biased. Although other comparisons, including those by Christian authors, were more nuanced in their judgments, they nevertheless show similar tendencies. For example, Edmund Hardy conceded that the Christian picture of the world was also not entirely unclouded, since the Christian redemption from sin also includes redemption from suffering as a consequence of sin.[19] For Hardy, Christianity promises a new heaven and earth to those who despair of this world, while in Buddhism every future world is the same as the last, and merely continues the conditions of suffering.[20] Some Buddhist ideals such as peacefulness and benevolence mean for Hardy that Buddhism has also had some positive effects on Indian society and culture since the reign of the Buddhist emperor Ashoka (third century BCE).[21] But, in contrast to the proactive attitude of Christianity, Buddhism is marked by "passivity and quietism."[22]

In contrast, the renowned English Indologist Monier-Williams acknowledged in much stronger terms the culturally creative power of Buddhism.[23] Moreover, like Hardy, he argued that Buddhism and Christianity both see the whole world groaning under pain and suffering. But then Monier-Williams characterized the key difference between the two religions in a similar way: while Christianity promises a final glorification, Buddhism promises redemption only through annihilation.[24] The maxim of Christianity is: "Fight and overcome the world"; that of Buddhism: "Shun the world, and withdraw from it."[25] "Work the works of God," teaches Christianity; "aim at inaction, indifference, and apathy," teaches Buddhism.[26]

Nor did authors such as Bryan de Kretser, Karl Kenntner, and Gustav Mensching deny the positive cultural effects of Buddhism. They explained the discrepancy between the world-shaping power of Buddhism on the one hand, and its supposedly world-renouncing and anti-life attitude on the other, by pointing to the difference between monastic Buddhism and the Buddhism of the laity. While monks and nuns at least ideally withdrew from life in the world, the Buddhist laity was allowed a certain form of involvement in the world.[27] This view has been taken up more recently by Melford Spiro[28] and Winston King,[29] who both argue that, at least for

---

[19]Hardy, E. 1919, 196.
[20]Ibid., 198.
[21]Ibid., 206–7.
[22]Ibid., 198.
[23]Monier-Williams 1889, 551.
[24]Ibid., 545.
[25]Ibid., 559.
[26]Ibid., 560.
[27]See Kenntner 1939, 88–94; Kretser 1954, 99, 105–13; Mensching 1978, 150.
[28]Spiro 1982.
[29]King, W. 1963.

Theravada Buddhism, there is a radical difference between the monastic path and the path taken by the laity. The layperson is active in the world, improves their karma through morally good actions, and strives for a better rebirth. Monks and nuns, on the other hand, withdraw from the world, leaving behind all personal relationships and worldly goals. Their goal is not a better rebirth, but nirvana. According to Spiro and King, they are not interested in morally good action in the usual sense, or in the betterment of society.[30] In contrast to such positions, Joseph Estlin Carpenter emphasized early on the continuity between monastic ethics and lay ethics, and pointed to the rather moderate ascetic character of Buddhist monastic rules.[31]

Despite all these different nuances, what has continued into the present is the trend of contrasting a world-renouncing Buddhism with a world-affirming Christianity. The most prominent example is perhaps Pope John Paul II's remarks about Buddhism in his book *Crossing the Threshold of Hope*. Here, he imputed to Buddhism an "almost exclusively negative soteriology." For Buddhism, "the world is bad" and is deemed the "source of evil and of suffering." Liberation, therefore, implies cutting off all ties to the world. "The more we are liberated from these ties, the more we become indifferent to what is in the world."[32] The pope explains nirvana as a "perfect indifference with regard to the world."[33] In contrast, Christianity inspires "a positive attitude toward creation" and helps build a civilization "which is marked by a positive approach to the world."[34] As is well known, these statements aroused strong protests on the Buddhist side. The Theravada scholar Bhikkhu Bodhi and the Mahayana scholar José Cabezón both argued against the pope, pointing out concurrently that liberation presupposes knowledge of rather than escape from the world, and that it is not the world that is evil, but suffering and its cause, delusion.[35]

Some Buddhist Perspectives

A similar apologetic motivation has also led some Buddhist authors to present at times sharp contrasts between Buddhist and Christian relations to the world. Whereas Western or Christian authors interpreted Buddhist spirituality as escapist and passive, Buddhist authors turned the tables and accused Christianity of cultivating various forms of attachment to the world, such as materialism, aspiration for power, and the unrestrained subjuga-

---
[30]Spiro 1982, 427–28; King, W. 1963, 59–60.
[31]Carpenter 1923, 98–104.
[32]Quoted from Sherwin & Kasimow 1999, 52.
[33]Ibid., 53.
[34]Ibid., 54.
[35]Bodhi 1995, 22–23; Cabezón 1999, 118.

tion of nature. For example, the influential Sri Lankan Buddhist reformer Anagarika Dharmapala (1864–1933) described Christianity as a religion rooted in the "materialistic monotheism" of Judaism. In essence, according to Dharmapala, Christianity

> is a political camouflage. Its three aspects are politics, trade and imperial expansion. It's [sic] weapons are the Bible, barrels of whisky and bullets.... The old war god of the Jews is yoked with the camouflaged god of love.[36]

Such statements unmistakably articulate the experience of colonial Christian domination. However, according to Dharmapala, the desire to dominate the world is already grounded in the beginnings of Christianity: in Jesus and his disciples. "The few illiterate fishermen of Galilee followed him as he had promised to make them judges to rule over Israel."[37] In particular, Dharmapala accused the Western colonial powers and their Christian missionaries of seeking to destroy Buddhism.

> Christianity as it is preached to Buddhists in Buddhist lands by materialistic missionaries is full of destructiveness. The purity of life which is enjoined in the noble eightfold path is beyond the grasp of the Christian who does not follow the ethics of the Sermon on the Mount.[38]

The last remark shows that Dharmapala appreciated the Sermon on the Mount. In fact, he saw in it a spirit akin to Buddhism and even expressed the suspicion that this might have been not the words of Jesus, but a borrowing from Buddhism.[39]

The Buddhist critique of the supposed Christian attachment to the world has played a special role in recent decades, especially against the background of increasing ecological crises. In 1967, Lynn White published his influential article "The Historical Roots of Our Ecological Crisis,"[40] where he attributed the ecological crisis to two ideological factors: first, to the fact that human beings, regarding themselves as masters rather than parts of nature, act ruthlessly toward it; and second, to the Judeo-Christian heritage, which continues to have an effect in post-Christian times, since the biblical myth of the human as the lord over creation has produced precisely this ecologically

---

[36] Guruge 1965, 439.
[37] Ibid., 475.
[38] Ibid., 29.
[39] "'The Sermon on the Mount' alleged to be the teachings of Jesus contain the re-echoings of Buddhist suttas in the Sutta Pitaka" (i.e., the Buddhist canon). Ibid., 26.
[40] White 1967.

In the World   57

disastrous attitude toward nature. For White, the idea of a divine order to control nature could manifest itself particularly well in the Western, Latin form of Christianity with its voluntaristic and activistic hue. White himself was a Christian and recommended as a cure a renewal of Franciscan spirituality where human and nature would be seen more strongly as one. But he also pointed as a possible alternative to Zen Buddhism, which was becoming popular in the West at the time. In fact, Daisetz Teitaro Suzuki, the most important protagonist of Zen in the West, had already in 1936 criticized the "Western" idea of subjugating nature for the benefit of humankind, contrasting it with the "Eastern" attitude, which sees nature as a friend and companion.[41] The ideas of White and Suzuki developed into a popular view within so-called eco-Buddhism, whose representatives proclaimed Buddhism to be much more eco-friendly than Christianity.[42] According to Joanna Macy, one of the movement's most prominent figures, Buddhist ecological engagement presupposes a spirituality whose "goal is not escape from the world, but transformation of the world."[43]

Ironically, though, eco-Buddhism is suspected of owing its ecological commitment to modern Western and Christian influences.[44] It can be seen as part of the larger movement of "socially engaged Buddhism," whose "genuine" Buddhist character is disputed even among Buddhists.[45] Christopher Queen, himself a follower of the movement, concedes that, in the genesis of "socially engaged Buddhism," "Buddhist and Christian—Asian, European and American—traditions have become inextricably intertwined."[46] For Queen, the really controversial issue is whether a social and ecological commitment is compatible with the basic Buddhist attitude toward the world. Is socially engaged Buddhism a Buddhist heresy?[47]

According to Richard Gombrich, the Buddha's "concern was to reform individuals and help them to leave society forever, not to reform the world. Life in the world he regarded as suffering, and the problem to which he offered a solution was the otherwise inevitable rebirth into the world."[48] Similarly, James Deitrick too holds that practical commitment to a good society has from a Buddhist perspective "no intrinsic value." Such a goal could at best be provisional, being "penultimately related to, and infinitely relativized by, Buddhism's ultimate goal—the liberation of every

---

[41]Suzuki 1973b, 334. This text from 1936 was later included in Suzuki's book *Zen and Japanese Culture*, which was first published in 1959, i.e., before White's essay.
[42]On the debate, see Harris, I. 2000 and Swearer 2006.
[43]Nisker, Gates, & Macy 2000, 160.
[44]Harris, I. 1995, 203–6.
[45]On the movement itself, see King, S. 2009; on the discussion, see Queen, Prebish, & Keown 2003.
[46]Queen 1996, 21.
[47]Ibid., 28–33.
[48]Gombrich 2006, 30.

individual from society and the world."[49] On the other hand, the stance of socially engaged Buddhism has found support among a number of highly influential figures in the Asian Buddhist world, such as B. R. Ambedkar, Thich Nhat Hanh, A. T. Ariaratne, Bhikkhu Buddhadasa, Sulak Sivaraksa, Daisaku Ikeda, and the fourteenth Dalai Lama. In addition, Asian religious scholars such as Hajime Nakamura,[50] Fumio Masutani,[51] and Chai-Shin Yu[52] have pointed out that older Buddhism also contains clear evidence of a socially and politically responsible ethics. In addition, Yu emphasizes that the basic objective of behavioral norms was of a nonworldly nature in early Christianity, as it was in early Buddhism.[53] In a 2016 interview, Queen responded to the specific question of whether socially engaged Buddhism dilutes the essence of Buddhist doctrine by pointing tellingly to the fluidity and multifaceted nature of the Buddhist tradition: "There is no Buddhism . . . , only buddhisms."[54]

Something like a fractal pattern is already apparent in these contrasting apologetic depictions of how Buddhism and Christianity relate to the world. On the one hand, world-renouncement and commitment to the world appear as characteristics to distinguish Christianity and Buddhism; on the other hand, they are also present as options within both traditions. I now want to consider this more closely.

3.2 RENOUNCING THE WORLD AND AFFIRMING THE WORLD IN BUDDHISM

The World-Renouncing Origins of Buddhism

Buddhism originated in India about five hundred years before Christ as part of the various ascetic movements, the so-called shramanas (*śramaṇa* = someone who strives and exerts himself). A shramana strives for liberation (*mokṣa*) and thus for the realization of a novel ideal or goal in life. According to the Brahminic tradition as found in the older parts of the Vedas, there were three life goals. First, gaining knowledge of, and living in accordance with, the *dharma*, the eternal order governing all areas of the cosmos and existence. Second, acquiring *artha*, i.e., wealth or power—the word encompasses both meanings (the rich have power, and the powerful are rich). Third, enjoying *kāma*, i.e., the pleasures of life, above all its

---

[49]Deitrick 2003, 263.
[50]Nakamura 1986.
[51]Masutani 1967.
[52]Yu, C.-S. 1981.
[53]Ibid., 218.
[54]Shuyin & Queen 2016.

sensual and erotic pleasures, which presupposed a certain wealth (*artha*). In contrast, the ascetic movements rejected *artha* and *kāma* as desirable goals in life, arguing that wealth/power and sensual pleasures cannot offer lasting satisfaction, but prove to be ultimately unsatisfying, so that people constantly desire more and something new.

Widespread among the ascetic movements was the belief in rebirth—or, as it was originally called, "re-death"—a belief not yet found in the older parts of the Vedas. It was suitable to support the conviction that the traditional Vedic goals of life were insufficient, since in the view of the ascetics the potentially endless repetition of life and death revealed all the more the fundamentally unsatisfactory character of earthly and even heavenly goods. For, even the life of the gods was considered finite and transient, at least by the Buddhists, so that heavenly joys are also not permanent. An ancient Buddhist text says that the stream of tears that a person has shed in countless lifetimes is more than the water in all the oceans of the world together. The person has experienced suffering and death again and again long enough to be disillusioned with everything that transient existence has to offer, long enough no longer to be attached to it, but instead to free themselves from it.[55] Liberation (*mokṣa*) from samsara (*saṃsāra*), the constant cycle of rebirth and re-death, thus became the new and highest goal of life for the shramanas. For them, living in accordance with the *dharma*, the eternal cosmic law, meant no longer pursuing wealth and pleasure, but following the path that leads to final liberation. The ascetic movements differed, however, in their more precise ideas of liberation. Some shramanas who were more committed to the Vedic tradition interpreted liberation as the final return to the divine source of all things. Others, such as the Jains, who would give rise to the later religion of Jainism, considered liberation to be the attainment of an omniscient, blissful, and eternal state, which they, like the Buddhists, called the "extinction (*nirvāṇa*)" of all suffering. Buddhists spoke of nirvana as a kind of "place" (*thāna, pada*) or "sphere" (*āyatana*) "where there is no earth, no water, no fire, no air, . . . neither this world nor another world, . . . no coming, no going, no staying, no deceasing, no uprising. Not fixed, not moveable, it has no support. Just this is the end of suffering."[56] Although this "description" mainly says what nirvana is not, the same canonical text emphasizes that nirvana really exists, and that without its existence liberation is impossible:

> There is, bhikkhus, a not-born, a not-brought-to-being, a not-made, a not-conditioned [*asaṅkhataṃ*]. If, bhikkhus, there were no not-born, not-brought-to-being, not-made, not-conditioned, no escape would

---
[55] *Saṃyutta Nikāya* 15:3.
[56] *Udāna* 8:1. Ireland 1977, 102.

be discerned from what is born, brought-to-being, made, conditioned. But since there is a not-born, a not-brought-to-being, a not-made, a not-conditioned, therefore an escape is discerned from what is born, brought-to-being, made, conditioned.[57]

Whatever ideas the various ascetic movements had regarding the specifics of final liberation, they all agreed that liberation would put an end to the unsatisfactory character of worldly life and its otherwise incessant repetition in the cycle of rebirths. Likewise, they agreed that final liberation involves overcoming all attachment to the world. This requires a special form of insight or realization, which by itself triggers the abandonment of attachment. Together with the rejection of *artha* and *kāma*, of wealth, power, and sensual pleasures as desirable goals in life, these beliefs led the shramanas to turn their backs on ordinary worldly life. They stopped working for a living and instead subsisted on alms; they left house and home, living either as hermits or, more often, in smaller, itinerant groups; they renounced marriage or left their families behind and led a celibate life. And they deemed all this necessary to reach the final liberating insight: "Household life is crowded and dusty; life gone forth is wide open. It is not easy, while living in a home, to lead the holy life," says an ancient scheme of the Buddhist path of salvation often repeated in its canonical scriptures.[58]

The Search for Syntheses

The ascetic movements posed an enormous challenge to traditional Indian society. For the Indian sociologist Daya Krishna, the teachings of the shramanas

> put the life of the ascetic renouncer at the heart of the Indian tradition and left it with the central problematic of how to reconcile the life of the householder with all its duties and obligations, with the ideal of the ascetic renouncer with no social or political obligations, who alone had access to the ultimate truth. . . . The status of the householder's

---

[57] *Udāna* 8:3. Translation following Ireland 1977, 103 (also *Itivuttaka* 43). It is not without a certain irony that a contemporary Buddhist such as Joanna Macy advocates precisely the opposite view. The Buddha, says Macy, rejected the existence of an unconditioned and unchanging reality, because otherwise "liberation" would mean renouncing the phenomenal world and turning toward this unconditioned reality (see Nisker, Gates, & Macy 2000, 151–55). Macy's position is untenable from a historical point of view (on this, see also the critique by Schmithausen 2010, 180, 211n74). On the other hand, the fact that Macy's position was included in a collection of key texts for eco-Buddhists (Kaza & Kraft 2000) demonstrates the broad range of the Buddhist spectrum.

[58] For example, *Dīgha Nikāya* 2 & 3, *Majjhima Nikāya* 27 & 28. Here quoted from Ñāṇamoli & Bodhi 2001, 272.

life in the context of the spiritual seeking of man was thus the great unsolved problem left by the diverse Śramaṇa traditions of India.[59]

From the perspective of this problem, it is possible to understand significant aspects of the dynamics of the wider history of Indian religion. The message of the shramanas was too persuasive for many simply to ignore, and the ties to worldly life were too strong for many simply to leave it behind. The internal developments of religion in India can be interpreted as various attempts to solve this problem, as the ongoing search for creative syntheses of renouncing the world and affirming the world, of other-worldly detachment and this-worldly involvement.

The texts of the Buddhist Pali canon (*tipiṭaka*) already contain not only testimonies of the tension between renunciation and affirmation of the world but also initial signs of the search for a synthesis. Characterizing the Buddhist path of salvation as the "Middle Way" can be interpreted in this light, since this path, it is said, avoids the extremes of striving for sensual pleasures on the one hand, and ascetic self-mortification on the other.[60] This interpretation is further illustrated by the legendary narrative of the life of the Buddha, Siddhartha Gautama. As a young prince, he enjoyed abundant wealth and sensual pleasures, and had the path to kingship open to him. However, by going forth into homelessness he rejected the Vedic goals of *artha* and *kāma*. The following years of harsh ascetic self-denial did not bring him to liberation, though, which led him to reject this life, too. Thus, the path that he finally found lay between these two extremes.

The beginnings of a synthesis can also be seen in how his life after the "awakening," i.e., after attaining Buddhahood, is characterized. He followed neither the inclination to keep his knowledge to himself, nor the temptation offered by the evil deity Mara (*māra*) to leave the world immediately.[61] Rather, out of compassion for other beings, he chose to remain in the world, to establish the Buddhist monastic community, and to preach his teachings "for the welfare of gods and men." This aspect of the Buddha legend illustrates a basic spiritual trait that was to prove extremely effective in the further development of Buddhism: namely, the inner unity of liberating wisdom (the Buddha's awakening) and active compassion (the Buddha's work in and for the world), the combination of detachment due to insight with involvement due to compassion. The narrative of the life of the Buddha that underpins all forms of Buddhism thus became a paradigmatic example. It is possible to live in the world without being attached to it. And

---

[59] Krishna 1996, 51–52.
[60] *Saṃyutta Nikāya* 56:11.
[61] *Majjhima Nikāya* 26; *Dīgha Nikāya* 16. See Schmidt-Leukel 2006a, 19–29.

true compassion, as practiced by the Buddha himself after his awakening, is not the same as attachment to the world, but instead is compatible with genuine inner detachment.

The tendency to synthesize inner detachment and compassionate involvement is evident not only in the traditional Buddha legend, though, but also in the fact that the Pali canon repeatedly recommends the development of kindness and compassion as a salvific practice. The love of a mother who protects her child at the risk of her own life is praised as a model of the mental attitude that a person should ideally adopt toward all sentient beings.[62] It is said explicitly that the development of loving-kindness has a "mind-releasing" (*ceto-vimutti*) quality.[63] This teaching is based on the belief already widespread in early Buddhism that a person's spiritual development depends above all on their inner attitude, since their mind gives rise to their words and deeds.[64]

Building on this belief, the Pali canon already shows a cautious relativization of the otherwise strict distinction between the "homeless," monastic followers of the Buddha on the one hand, and the "householder," his lay followers, who still actively participate in the life of the world, on the other. Thus, the *Aṅguttara Nikāya* (4:138) makes the astonishing statement that there are some people who have renounced the world physically but not spiritually, and others who have renounced the world spiritually but not physically. In the first case, "Some person resorts to remote lodgings in forests and jungle groves, but there he thinks sensual thoughts, thoughts of ill will, and thoughts of harming." In the second, "Some person does not resort to remote lodgings in forests and jungle groves, but he thinks thoughts of renunciation, thoughts of good will, and thoughts of harmlessness."[65] There are, it is said elsewhere, among those "who enjoy sensual pleasures" and "seek wealth" some who are not "tied to it, infatuated with it, and blindly absorbed in it," because they are "seeing the danger in it and understanding the escape."[66] The idea that someone still lives in the world while no longer being inwardly attached to it anticipates to a certain extent that resolution of the tension between world-renouncing asceticism and active participation in society for which the Hindu *Bhagavad Gītā* would later become well known: it is possible for a person to live a life in the world and fulfill their social duties, while at the same time cultivating an inner attitude of nonattachment. Living life this way constitutes a valid path to liberation

---

[62] As for example in the *Metta Sutta*, the *Sutta Nipāta* 149.
[63] *Ittivutaka* 27.
[64] *Dhammapada* 1–2. See also Harris, E. J. 1997.
[65] Bodhi 2012, 517.
[66] Ibid., 1458, 1461. *Aṅguttara Nikāya* 10:91.

(*mokṣa*).⁶⁷ This spiritualizes the ascetic renunciation of the world practiced by the shramanas, i.e., it turns renunciation into a primarily spiritual attitude of inner detachment that no longer requires actually withdrawing from worldly life.

Another form of synthesis operates less through spiritualization and more through hierarchization. That is, later forms of Hinduism no longer interpret the ascetic life goal of liberation as a counter-ideal to the two traditional goals of *artha* and *kāma*, but regard liberation (*moka*) as the superordinate and supreme goal. While subordinate to the goal of liberation, *artha* and *kāma* were thus nevertheless integrated into the pursuit of *mokṣa*.⁶⁸ This is particularly evident in the system of the four stages of life (*āśrama*), which has sometimes been correlated with the four goals of life (*puruṣārtha*). According to this system, man learns the *dharma* in his youth, acquires *artha* and enjoys *kāma* as a married householder, before then gradually withdrawing from the world in old age in order finally to renounce the world and prepare entirely for liberation (*mokṣa*).⁶⁹ Even various rebirths could now be interpreted as different phases of a gradual approach to the highest goal of liberation, which was also an attractive solution for Buddhism. By living according to the basic tenets of Buddhist ethics, the Buddhist layperson not only benefits religiously by acquiring good karma but is also able to undergo a spiritual development involving numerous rebirths in order to gradually approximate the ultimate goal of awakening.⁷⁰

The Buddha legend, together with a growing spiritualization of the notion of detachment from the world, had a formative influence on the development of the bodhisattva ideal in Mahayana Buddhism.⁷¹ Even before the beginnings of Mahayana Buddhism (which probably emerged in the first or second century BCE), the word *bodhisattva* ("enlightenment being") denoted a sentient being who would one day become a Buddha and not just an enlightened disciple of a Buddha. The bodhisattva path, that is, the aspiration to Buddhahood, became the general ideal in Mahayana Buddhism, since it was believed that, as a Buddha, a person could best help all other beings in their own quest for liberation. Those who follow the bodhisattva path, the path to Buddhahood, thus dedicate their religious lives to an altruistic purpose: their compassion for all sentient beings makes them vow to remain actively present in samsara, the world of rebirth, until all beings have attained release from suffering. However, if, as some Mahayana texts

---

⁶⁷See Malinar 2007, 5–6.
⁶⁸Tellingly, the *Bhagavad Gītā* (16:12) does not censure *artha* and *kāma* as such, but just the greedy attachment to them.
⁶⁹See Krishna 1996, 52–69; Kaelber 2007.
⁷⁰See Schmidt-Leukel 1996.
⁷¹On this, see also Schmidt-Leukel 2006a, 94–104.

claim, the number of sentient beings is infinite, then this remains a never-ending task. Having attained Buddhahood, the former bodhisattva remains in samsara. Through the power of his good karma the new Buddha creates his own Buddha land, where ideal conditions prevail for attaining awakening, so that all who are reborn there can attain liberation effortlessly.

Thus, from the very first stages of the bodhisattva path to its completion in Buddhahood, a bodhisattva remains within samsara, without being attached to it. The bodhisattva ideal therefore combines the aim of inner detachment with that of compassionate involvement in the world. Many Mahayana texts testify that the work of a bodhisattva for the liberation of all other beings also implies helping them in their very concrete needs, e.g., caring for the sick, feeding the poor, assisting the helpless, promoting peace.[72] The bodhisattva ideal therefore represents a strong synthesis, even convergence, of spiritualized renunciation of the world on the one hand, and an active commitment to the world on the other. According to the *Bodhicaryāvatāra* (6:126), a classical guide for those who follow the bodhisattva path, the Buddhas (i.e., those bodhisattvas who have achieved Buddhahood) have out of compassion made the whole world their self.[73] Here merge perfect detachment from the world and compassionate identification with the world.[74]

Mahayana Buddhism underwent fundamental changes in terms of how it not only related to the world but also understood it.[75] Since striving for Buddhahood became its general ideal, Mahayana Buddhism presupposed that all sentient beings in the cycle of rebirth—celestials, humans, animals, spirits, denizens of hell—have the potential to attain Buddhahood one day. In other words, they already carry within them the "germ/embryo of Buddhahood" or form the "womb of Buddhahood" (*tathāgatagarbha*, which can mean both); they have a hidden "Buddha nature" (*buddhadhātu*).[76] This notion expanded further in India, but especially in the Chinese cultural realm, so that finally not only all sentient beings in the cycle of rebirth were seen as participating in Buddha nature, but all reality per se. The world as a whole—or, more precisely, the infinite multiplicity of worlds that traditional Buddhist cosmology reckoned to exist—is a manifestation of the ultimate reality underlying and pervading them. At the same time,

---

[72]See, for example, *Bodhisattvabhūmi* 1.10 or *Vimalakīrti-Nirdeśa* 8.
[73]The *Bodhicaryāvatāra* ("Entering the Course toward Awakening") was composed in India in the seventh or eighth century and gained great popularity in large parts of the Buddhist world, especially in Tibet. See Schmidt-Leukel 2019b, 3–96.
[74]See Schmidt-Leukel 2019b, 298–303; 377–84.
[75]See Schmidt-Leukel 2006a, 115–26.
[76]While *tathāgatagarbha* and *buddhadhātu* came to be used more or less interchangeably during the later development of Mahayana Buddhism, some early texts reveal several conceptual differences. See Jones 2021, 13–14, 229–37.

In the World 65

ultimate reality is the supreme or true reality of every Buddha, his "dharma body" (*dharmakāya*). For human beings, the attainment of Buddhahood therefore means realizing their actual, true nature; they become aware of their deep unity with everything else and practice this unity in their lives. This notion gave rise to a Buddhist variant of theodicy, the problem of evil, since how could the existence of suffering and evil be reconciled with the Buddha nature of all reality? At the same time, these developments were also accompanied by changes in how nirvana was understood. These two points are taken up later.[77]

Institutional Aspects

The combination of world-renouncing and world-affirming tendencies is evident not only at the spiritual and doctrinal level, but also institutionally. The itinerant Buddhist world-renouncers settled down in their own monasteries and temples quite early on. There is clear evidence that this process entailed internal tensions between those groups who demanded a stricter ascetic way of life, and those who called for more moderate forms.[78] The tradition of following a harder asceticism is still preserved by some Buddhist movements today.[79] Even within the context of the bodhisattva ideal, a solitary ascetic lifestyle could be understood as an intensive preparation for the bodhisattva virtues that would be developed in later lives. However, what became the dominant form of life was the monastic community structured by comparatively mild rules and engaged in a more or less close exchange with the lay followers. Monasteries gradually came together to form various order-like groups, which soon also reflected different schools with slightly varying rules. Donations and state support enabled individual monasteries to gain considerable wealth and political influence over the centuries.

Besides the larger monasteries and nunneries, however, there were and still are smaller temple complexes, these being looked after by only a few or sometimes only one single monk. Some strands of Buddhism have even seen the former monasticism change completely (such as in the Japanese Jodo Shinshu, a school of Pure Land Buddhism) or almost completely (as in many Japanese and partly Korean forms of Buddhism) into a temple priesthood with married clergy, the "monasteries" then often functioning more as a kind of "seminary" that serves to train temple priests and that offers them only a temporary monastic life. Some forms of Tibetan Bud-

---

[77]See below, pp. 101–01, 186–88, 202–03, 228.
[78]For example, the Buddhist tradition connects to this controversy the conflict between Gautama Buddha and his relative Devadatta, which led to a split in the community.
[79]On this, see also Freiberger & Kleine 2011, 245–54.

dhism have also seen the development of a kind of lower clergy who are married, but are still distinguished from monasticism proper.

While Buddhist monasteries often became centers of learning and took on educational tasks, they also developed social and charitable functions in China under the influence of the bodhisattva ideal. According to Whalen Lai, the Christian monasteries in medieval Europe and the Buddhist monasteries in medieval China are very similar in this respect: they fed and clothed the needy, cared for the sick, and buried the dead.[80] There are many Buddhist charitable organizations today, these either being entirely run by laypeople or having close ties to monastic institutions.[81]

The bodhisattva ideal gave the laity a higher religious standing, since some influential Mahayana scriptures now proclaimed that bodhisattvas also carry out their work for the liberation of all beings through the actual work of laypeople. For example, the eighth chapter of the *Vimalakīrtinirdeśa-Sūtra* (a text dating perhaps from as early as the first or second century CE) states that bodhisattvas act among other things as political leaders, captains, advisers, and ministers to the king. It is therefore no coincidence that the text's eponymous figure, Vimalakirti, is himself a wealthy layman who uses his fortune to help the poor and defenseless (chapter 2). Although it is true that contemporary movements such as "socially engaged Buddhism" owe much to impulses from Western Christianity, these impulses have actually revitalized ancient Buddhist traditions.

The tension between world-renouncing and world-affirming tendencies, as well as attempts to synthesize the two, are reflected not least in Buddhist notions of state and politics. In some texts of the Pali canon, there is still a standard list of five great "dangers," these including not only fire, floods, bandits, and unloved heirs, but also kings.[82] Yet the belief quickly formed that a king should ideally be a Buddhist lay follower who governs the country according to the basic moral principles of Buddhism (*dharmarāja* = dharma king). Buddhist kings were and are often regarded, including in Theravada-Buddhist countries, as bodhisattvas and thus as future Buddhas.[83] Ancient canonical texts already sketched a parallelism between the Buddha, as the highest spiritual authority, and the world ruler (*cakravartin* = he who turns the wheel), as the highest political authority. While the *cakravartin* turns the wheel of worldly rule, the Buddha turns the wheel of dharma. Ideally, the two are not in competition with each other, but rather the ruler turns the wheel of politics in accordance with the dharma, i.e., the teachings of

---

[80] Lai, W. 1992.
[81] The Guide Star directory listed 1,756 Buddhist charities in 2021. See www.guidestar.org.
[82] For example, the *Aṅguttara Nikāya* 5:41.
[83] Tambiah 2007, 96–97.

the Buddha.[84] This means among other things that his government shall be peaceful and just, supporting the poor, providing protection and security for the inhabitants of his country, as well as for the animals of the earth and the air[85]—the latter being something to which ecologically committed Buddhists can rightly refer to today.[86]

Theravada-Buddhist countries eventually saw Buddhist monarchs attain superintendence over Buddhist religious communities (*saṅgha*), although ideally the religious authority of the sangha is above that of the king, who is after all merely a Buddhist layman. Thus, the sangha developed a kind of symbol of excommunication, the "turning over of the begging bowl" (*pattaṃ nikkujjana*),[87] which the sangha could use to signify that it no longer regarded the king as promoting and protecting Buddhism. In China, the question of whether Buddhist monks should be allowed to prostrate themselves before the emperor (as was expected as a symbolic gesture of submission) was long a source of fierce debates among Buddhists, before this kowtow then finally gained wide acceptance.[88] In the case of Tibet, the development even went so far that, from the seventeenth century onward, a monk, namely the head of the powerful Gelugpa order known as the "Dalai Lama," was also elevated to the position of political leader—which actually contradicts the early monastic understanding that monks and nuns should stay out of current day-to-day political business.[89] The idea was widespread in Asia that, if the ruler promoted Buddhism, financed the monasteries, or had scriptures copied and temples or stupas built, then he would obtain a very good karma, i.e., special religious merit, which in turn would benefit his rule and thus the entire country.[90] Wherever Buddhism attained social dominance, the sangha and the monarchy entered into a close reciprocal relationship, and Buddhism became the de facto and often also the de iure state religion.[91]

As this shows, Buddhism comprised and still comprises world-renouncing and world-affirming tendencies. Detachment from the world is based on the belief that the transient things of this world, and especially so when transient existence continues endlessly, do not provide any lasting fulfill-

---

[84]Ibid., 39–53; Lai, W. 2010.
[85]The *Dīgha Nikāya* 26:5.
[86]On the foundations of ecological activities in Buddhism, see Schmidt-Leukel 2020e (English version 2022b).
[87]By turning over the begging bowl, the monk symbolically indicates his refusal of food donations by a certain layperson. On the canonical foundation of this ritual, see the *Cullavagga* 5:20.3; the *Aṅguttara Nikāya* 8:87. See also Conze 1984, 98. In 2007, many Buddhist monks protesting against Myanmar's military regime used this gesture.
[88]Zürcher 2007, 106–8, 160–63, 231–38, 254–85.
[89]Snellgrove & Richardson 1986, 195–201; von Brück 1999, 64–71.
[90]Orzech 1998.
[91]See Spiro 1982, 379–82; Tambiah 2007, 76–101, 520–21.

ment. Rather, this can only be expected from an ineffable reality beyond. The world-affirming tendencies result from a spiritualization of world renunciation in the form of an inner nonattachment, which is combined with a benevolent and compassionate attitude, striving to alleviate the suffering of all sentient beings. Finally, even the understanding of the world underwent a change in being seen as the manifestation of ultimate reality. Let us now compare the world-renouncing and world-affirming motifs in Christianity.

3.3 AFFIRMING THE WORLD AND RENOUNCING THE WORLD IN CHRISTIANITY

Christianity began as an inner Jewish grouping: Jesus and the circle of his immediate followers. However, the early Christian communities transcended the boundaries of purely Jewish ethnicity soon after Jesus' death, even if the ties between Jewish communities and parts of Christendom continued to exist for a relatively long time in some regions.[92] The roots of early Christianity were thus fed on the one hand by the older traditions of Israel, and on the other by two important newer influences on Judaism at that time: Hellenistic or Greco-Roman culture and Jewish apocalyptic movements. The renunciant tendencies, as found in some parts of Jewish apocalypticism,[93] were quite strong in the beginnings of Christianity, but the this-worldly character of the older Jewish tradition also lived on in it.[94] As Christianity developed, it was these world-affirming tendencies that finally gained the upper hand, combining however with an ambiguous Greco-Roman notion of "world." The "new Israel," as the church soon understood itself, was no longer bound to the ethnic borders of the Jewish people (the "old" Israel), but saw itself increasingly as an entity that spanned the world.[95] The world-renouncing tendencies also entered into a connection with Hellenistic culture, merging with Gnostic, Platonic, and above all Neoplatonic ideas. At the institutional level, the emergence of Christian monasticism revitalized them and gave them a lasting manifestation.

New Testament Perspectives

Jesus and his followers were guided by the basic features of the Jewish faith traditions: the belief in the one and only God (Mark 10:18), the creator of the world and the ruler of its history. Above all, Jesus placed the fatherly

---

[92] Boyarin 2004.
[93] For textual evidence of such tendencies in Jewish apocalypticism, see Schrage 1964.
[94] For an overview on world-negation and world-affirmation in Christian origins, see Vollenweider 2014.
[95] See Küng 1994, 246–53.

goodness and mercy of this God at the center of his proclamation, a goodness that is shown not least in the work of his creation. God demonstrates his goodness by giving to all, bad and good, righteous and unrighteous alike, what they need for life: the light of the sun and the water of the rain (Matthew 5:45). He endows the lilies of the field with splendid beauty and feeds the birds of the air. All the greater is his care and concern for humankind (Matthew 6:25–33). The commandments that God gave to his people Israel were for the welfare of the human being. They were made for the human, and the human was not made for the commandments (Mark 2:27). The mercy that God shows to people is also to be practiced among them (Matthew 5:44–45; 12:7; Luke 6:36). For Jesus, love of God therefore coincides with love of one's neighbor. They are two sides of the same coin, and as such form the supreme commandment that encompasses all other commandments (Matthew 22:34–40). These underlying beliefs have always made it possible within Christianity to combine an existential orientation toward God with a commitment to the world marked by love and compassion. Nevertheless, early Christianity in particular was also shaped by a renunciant form of spirituality.

Jewish apocalypticism was based on the idea that God remains in control of the course of history, especially when history sees the emergence of forces of evil, resistance against God's good commandments, and the oppression of the "righteous" who follow these commandments. God's reign will eventually prevail against all the forces of evil. Its final and lasting establishment will be like the beginning of a new eon, a caesura that will be accompanied by cosmic catastrophes.[96] This is how Jesus prophesied according to the Gospel of Matthew (24:29):

> The sun will be darkened,
> and the moon will not give its light,
> the stars will fall from the sky
> and the powers of the heavens will be shaken.

After the collapse of the present world, it is expected that God will establish a new world, one that, according to early Christian belief, would be equivalent to a new creation. God creates "a new heaven and a new earth, for the first heaven and the first earth had passed away" (Revelation 21:1). God and people will finally be reconciled in the new world, and God will dwell in the midst of his people (Revelation 21:3–4):

---

[96] See the contributions by Paul Volz and Philipp Vielhauer in Koch & Schmidt 1982. On the presence of the idea of cosmic transformation in Jewish apocalyptic literature, see the overview in Collins, J. 2016, 8. According to Collins, "It is precisely this cosmic perspective that distinguishes the eschatology of these apocalypses from the older prophetic eschatology." Ibid., 327.

> God Himself will be among them,
> and He will wipe away every tear from their eyes;
> and there will no longer be any death;
> there will no longer be any mourning, or crying, or pain;
> the first things have passed away.

However, this hope for the divine creation of a new world free of suffering also expresses quite clearly the belief that the world of the old creation is by no means simply good and let alone perfect. Rather, it is an ambivalent world, full of suffering and death, shaped by sin and resistance to God's merciful rule.

Like many Jewish apocalyptics of his time, Jesus and his disciples believed that the end of the old world and the beginning of the new world was near.[97] The fact that people are already submitting themselves completely to God's rule means that the coming of God's kingdom, i.e., the new world determined by God's rule, is already dawning.[98] Even if the exact point in time could not be determined for certain (Matthew 24:36), Jesus was nevertheless sure that the apocalyptic events would still occur in his generation: "Truly, I say to you, this generation will not pass away until all these things take place" (Matthew 24:34; similarly, Mark 9:1; Matthew 10:23). About two decades later, Paul still held on to this imminent expectation. After some members of the church that he had founded in Thessalonica had already died, he assured them that everything would happen in their generation, and that the resurrected Jesus would return (1 Thessalonians 4:13–18). Paul linked this with a warning against slackening in the expectation of the near end and the exhortation to live accordingly. The events could come at any time, "like a thief in the night" (1 Thessalonians 5:1–11).

In fact, the imminent expectation of the apocalyptic events shaped the lives of the first Christian communities as much as it had already shaped the lives of Jesus and his disciples. Although for them it was a natural concern to follow God's commandments, their aim was not to bring about a lasting improvement in the state of the world, but rather to prepare themselves and others for the dramatic upheavals expected. In this spirit, Jesus was able to call his followers to give up family, job, and possessions, and to join him and his itinerant life.[99] Although many of his followers did return to their former lives after Jesus' crucifixion, their lives remained marked by the

---

[97]For a critical discussion of the objections to the association of Jesus with the apocalyptic movement, see Collins, J. 2016, 321–51, especially 322–27.

[98]See Vermes 1993, 245.

[99]According to B. J. Pitre (2001, 78), "Jesus was an eschatological prophet with a message of, among other things, apocalyptic asceticism."

real expectation that Jesus would return in the course of the supposedly imminent end. This attitude caused a form of inner detachment from the things of the world that could tie in with the respective motifs from Jewish apocalypticism.[100] Thus, Paul wrote in the First Letter to the Corinthians (7:29–31),

> But this I say, brothers, the time has been shortened, so that from now on those who have wives should be as though they had none; and those who weep, as though they did not weep; and those who rejoice, as though they did not rejoice; and those who buy, as though they did not possess; and those who use the world, as though they did not make full use of it; for the present form of this world is passing away.

Here, too, we can see a renunciation of the world being spiritualized. It is not a case of actually giving up family and possessions and no longer using the world (1 Corinthians 7:20, 27), but of living in family, job, and world in such a way that there is no longer an inner attachment to them. A similar spiritualization of renunciation can also be found in the writings of John, where Jesus is quoted as saying that his disciples should live *in* the world without being *of* the world (John 17:6–19). In Johannine usage, the term "world" often assumes a negative meaning. As here, it frequently stands not for God's good creation, but for the antidivine realm: the "world" is the domain of God's diabolical adversary (John 12:31; 14:30; 16:11; 1 John 5:19). Accordingly, the First Letter of John commands (2:15–18a),

> Do not love the world nor the things in the world. If anyone loves the world, the love of the Father is not in him. For all that is in the world, the lust of the flesh and the lust of the eyes and the boastful pride of life, is not from the Father, but is from the world. The world is passing away and also its lusts; but the one who does the will of God continues to live forever. Children, it is the last hour.

Again, it is clear that the inner detachment from the world is determined by the expectation of the imminent end. At the same time, however, we can discern another motif. The "world" becomes a symbol for the "lust of the flesh." A closer examination of the use of the word "flesh" (*sarx*) in John and especially in Paul shows that there are very strong parallels here with what Buddhism denotes as "defilements" (*kleśa*): greed, hate, and delusion.[101]

---

[100] See Schrage 1964.
[101] See Schmidt-Leukel 2019b, 113–14, 200.

Platonic and Gnostic Forms of Christian Spirituality

The concept of Christian spirituality as a way to overcome the "flesh"—the attachment to the world driven by desire—by the power of the divine Spirit became extraordinarily influential. A well-known example of this spirituality is Augustine (354–430), who became *the* teacher of nonattachment to the world in Western Christendom. For Augustine, people should not desire the things of this world, but rather use them without clinging to them. This is the central point of his well-known distinction between *uti* and *frui*, between the "use" (*uti*) of the world and the covetous "enjoyment" (*frui*) of it.[102] Augustine no longer foregrounds the motif of imminent expectation, or, to be more precise, he claims that the end of the world for each individual comes with death. The imminent end is as certain as death, and the exact time as uncertain as that of one's own death.[103] So, while originally based on the expectation that the apocalypse was imminent, detachment from the world is now based on the transience of one's own life. At the very beginning of his *Confessions*, Augustine turns as a human being who lives under the pressure of his mortality to God, while at the same time knowing that he is created for God, who alone can provide lasting peace. Augustine's theology is characterized by the feeling of a deep contrast between the unsatisfying and sorrowful attachment to the world on the one hand, and the liberating and fulfilling centering of life on God on the other. His theology comprises a close symbiosis of Christian faith and Neoplatonism, a philosophy in which the inner detachment from the world plays a central role as an integrative part of turning to the divine.

So, even if the imminent end of the world did not come about, Christians of the first three centuries often continued to cultivate an inner attitude of nonattachment to the world. This was undoubtedly also encouraged by the fact that various parts of the Roman Empire repeatedly saw reprisals and persecutions. The renunciant tendencies of early Christianity were particularly radical in those movements that can be assigned to Christian Gnosticism and Manichaeism (to which Augustine originally belonged). Here, the devil, as the master of the evil world, became an anti-deity (albeit one that was subordinate), and in some cases even the creative designer, the demiurge of the material world. It was necessary to escape from his sphere of power and to free the divine spark in the human soul from bondage to the material world. This required overcoming the desire chaining people to the world by means of knowledge or insight (*gnosis*). Only then could the divine spark of the soul, which does not belong to the material world,

---

[102] See Schmidt-Leukel 2020f.
[103] Augustine, *Epistula 199* (ad Hesychius), par. 3–4, accessed April 2023, https://www.augustinus.it/latino/lettere/lettera_204_testo.htm.

return with the death of the body to its true divine origin. If this liberation fails, then, according to many Gnostics and Platonists, the soul remains bound to further reincarnations.[104]

As recent research has shown, Gnosticism cannot simply be understood as a system alien to Christianity, one whose ideas infected the Christian faith like a virus and produced the Gnostic heresies in its fold. Rather, there is a fluid continuum of Gnostic ideas that reaches into the midst of some New Testament traditions. In other words, central motifs of Johannine and Pauline theology could easily be read in a Gnostic way. Couliano thus describes Gnosis and Christianity as two "perspectives on (and within) the same system."[105] Moreover, Gnostic and non-Gnostic forms of Christian spirituality were both located within the framework of Platonic modes of thought, which juxtaposed the imperfect (because material) beings of the world and the perfect spiritual reality of God. It is often difficult to draw clear boundaries.

One boundary marker consisted in the monotheistic heritage, or, more precisely, in the belief in the one divine origin of the world,[106] even if there was already something like a pre-Christian Jewish proto-Gnosis, which also assumed a subdivine creator figure.[107] The Gnostic idea of an evil or defective counter-deity who is responsible for the creation or shaping of the material world crossed this boundary, as was evident in the controversy surrounding Marcion (second century) and the Christian communities invoking him. Even if Marcion himself is not strictly related to Gnosticism, he also argued that the God described in the Hebrew Bible is an imperfect, even evil creator, who is not identical with the redeeming God of Jesus. According to the teachings of Mani (third century) and Manichaeism, the world, while not the creation of an evil counter-deity, nevertheless contains portions of both the good god of light and the evil lord of darkness. Hence, despite monotheistic demarcations, one must not forget that Marcion and his followers, as well as the vast majority of Gnostics, did see themselves as Christians. Mani referred to himself, for example, as an "apostle of Christ." From the perspective of religious history, Gnosis and Marcion should be regarded as parts both of internal Christian developments and ramifications, and also of course of syncretistic developments, as is especially clear with Manichaeism with its Zoroastrian and partly Buddhist[108] echoes. But syncretism is a feature of all great religious traditions.[109] Nor should it be

---

[104]Couliano 1992, 56–59, 103–9; Hoheisel 1984/85; Brox 1989.
[105]Couliano 1992, 18.
[106]Ibid., 24.
[107]Ibid., 54.
[108]According to Franz Winter (2008, 208–9), the Buddhist features are strong only in Eastern Manichaeism, but rather weak in its Western forms.
[109]See Schmidt-Leukel 2013.

forgotten that for large parts of Christianity, right up to the present day, the devil has retained his character as an evil, albeit subordinate, counter-deity, a supernatural figure that is associated above all with worldly attachment. Not only in this respect did the monotheistic boundary prove to be porous. The Christian explication of the *one* God as a God in three persons still continues to raise legitimate questions about the monotheistic character of Christianity, not to mention the proliferation of subordinate supernatural beings in Christian theology and popular piety in the form of the Mother of God, the saints, angels, and demons.

Political Profanization and Monastic Countermovement

After its official recognition and even promotion by the Roman Empire, Christianity was able to establish itself in the world. Now it could develop the Jewish heritage of a this-worldly spirituality much more strongly, and in doing so shape the state polity along theocratic lines. However, this meant being able not only to improve greatly its opportunities to act charitably in the world, but also to use state power in the fight against theological opponents (that is, Christians accusing each other of being "heretics") and against other religions (that is, Roman-Hellenistic cults and increasingly also Judaism). Besides its Jewish roots, the image of Christianity as a primarily world-affirming religion owes much to the close ties between Christendom and state power since the time of Emperor Constantine and his successors. These ties alone enabled the churches to implement their ideas of shaping the world politically.

A countermovement against this advancing profanization of Christianity that had begun in the fourth century came when Christian monasticism emerged at the same time. The early Christian ascetics and hermits often saw themselves as the spiritual heirs of the Christian martyrs. In a social situation that no longer required the readiness to suffer martyrdom, they kept alive the spirit of radical detachment from the world by realizing this detachment through the actual departure from worldly life. In contrast to the "red martyrdom" of Christian blood witnesses, they carried out what they themselves understood as a "white martyrdom" by living a life of renunciation beyond the world. *Fuga mundi* (flight from the world) and *contemptus muni* (contempt for the world) became key terms of monastic spirituality, and they continue to have an effect today. Marcionite and Gnostic communities already placed great value on—or even, as in Marcion's case, prescribed—various forms of asceticism and especially sexual abstinence. Mani divided his followers into two groups, the "hearers" and the "elect," the latter having to abstain from certain foods and drinks, manual labor, and sexual intercourse. Similar rules were also imposed by the first Christian hermits and monastic communities, who were often theologically close to or overlapped with Gnostic forms of Christianity and Neoplatonic philosophy. The resulting spiritual theology became especially influential in the Eastern Church. However, as monasticism and its ideas gained in influence, it too became more worldly. The number of monks increased enormously, and monks were often present as advisers in secular and spiritual matters in the Byzantine Empire. The monasteries became wealthy; "abuses and nuisances set in."[110] In the Latin church of the West, the Benedictine order, dating back to Benedict of Nursia (d. 547), became dominant. The Benedictine principle of *ora et labora* (pray and work) combined from its inception otherworldly tendencies (pray) with a this-worldly emphasis on formative and educational activity (work).

Despite growing in property, power, and influence, monastic orders continued to act as the strongest reminder within Christianity that the churches' engagement in and for the world should be accompanied by an inner detachment. In addition, the emergence of the mendicant orders in the thirteenth century proved that monasticism itself needed to be reminded of this, but was also capable of such detachment. Only with the crisis of monastic ways of life in the modern period and their decline after the Enlightenment was the renunciant dimension of Christian spirituality increasingly sidelined. It is therefore no surprise that many Christians today hope that the current dialogue between Buddhists and Christians will also revitalize the monastic form of Christian life. One example of this is the Trappist monk Thomas Merton (1915–1968). He was not only one of the pioneers of Christian-Buddhist dialogue, but also committed himself to renewing monastic life from within.[111] Dialogue between Buddhist and Christian monks has been one of the most intensive fields of interreligious encounter since the mid-1970s at the latest.[112] Part of this dialogue is the rediscovery of writings by learned monks among the early ascetics, such as those of Evagrius Ponticus (d. 399) and John Cassian (d. 435).[113] Like Edward Conze before,[114] Elaine Pagels, an expert on Christian Gnosis, has highlighted the remarkable similarities between Gnosis and Buddhism.[115] For Franz Winter, the sources do not allow us to clarify whether this is at least partly due to direct or indirect borrowings. There is no clear evidence

---

[110]Küng 1994, 280.

[111]See Cunningham 1999; Thurston & Bowman 2007; Sawicki 2020.

[112]For an overview, see Blée 2011 and the official website of DIMMID (Dialogue Interreligieux Monastique / Monastic Interreligious Dialogue): https://dimmid.org/.

[113]On the numerous parallels between the Buddhist *Dhammapada* and early monastic Christian theology, see Lefebure & Feldmeier 2011.

[114]Conze 1966.

[115]Pagels 1996.

either for this,[116] nor for possible Buddhist influences on the emergence of Christian monasticism.[117] It could simply be a matter of parallel developments due to similar existential attitudes.[118]

3.4 NONATTACHMENT AND LOVING INVOLVEMENT

This conjecture raises a number of broader questions: How can we interpret the fact that there are both world-renouncing and world-affirming attitudes in Buddhism and Christianity? Is this development of parallel intrareligious differences simply a phenomenon of logical options immanent to the respective systems? Do such more or less equivalent logical alternatives develop within different systems without requiring a special connection to existential experiences, as Couliano has suggested?[119] And are the world-renouncing and world-affirming tendencies mutually exclusive, having developed in both traditions simply because the respective system and its system-immanent presuppositions make them logically possible? Or can at least some aspects of this development be understood as reflecting certain existential experiences in which the two alternatives turn out to be complementary? Are there substantive reasons for assuming that world-renouncing and world-affirming motifs not only condition each other as mutually exclusive alternatives, but that, alternatively, they in some sense depend upon one another? That they complement each other and act in dynamic tension to protect one another from one-sided extremes?

Compatibility and Complementarity of Nonattachment and Love

In my view, it is likely that the attempts we can repeatedly observe in Buddhism and Christianity to synthesize the two tendencies suggest that such reasons do indeed exist, and that they lie primarily in the realm of existential experience. The Buddhist value of nonattachment is based on the experience of transience, while the Christian value of loving involvement is based on the experience of interpersonal relatedness. However, transience and interpersonal relatedness are experiences shared by all human beings. Christians as well as Buddhists live with both dimensions of human existence. The compatibility and even complementarity of nonattachment to the world on the one hand, and loving commitment to the world on the other—these hinge on the existential connectedness of mortality and interpersonal relatedness.

---

[116] Winter 2008, 206–7.
[117] Ibid., 275–76.
[118] See also Klimkeit 1986, 23–27.
[119] See Couliano 1992, 74. See also above, pp. 31–33.

The experience of transience plays an important role in both Buddhism and Christianity. In the context of the Four Noble Truths, it is the starting point for the analysis of suffering and the unsatisfactory character of human existence. According to the First Noble Truth, "Birth is suffering, aging is suffering, illness is suffering, death is suffering," with birth marking the beginning of transient existence.[120] Transience always involves painful loss: the separation from what the person is attached to, be it possessions, people, one's own life. Given that loss means suffering, it undoubtedly makes sense psychologically not to cling too tightly to what in any case cannot be kept forever. But Buddhism is about more than that. It is precisely the thought of a potentially endless repetition of transient existence that, for Buddhism, exposes the unsatisfactory nature of everything transient. Real detachment from the world therefore occurs only through the realization that anything transient cannot offer people genuine fulfillment because their deepest striving is directed toward an intransient reality.[121] "Nothing is worth holding to"[122]—this insight must be accompanied by the experience of peace and happiness, which spring not from power, wealth, and sensual pleasures (*artha* and *kāma*), but from the foretaste experienced in meditation of ultimate reality. Once he knew this bliss, said the Buddha, he no longer craved the pleasures of the senses.[123]

In Christianity, the expectation of the imminent end initially caused the attitude of nonattachment to the transient world. But Paul already introduces a new aspect. From his point of view, the biblical account of creation states that death is the wages of sin and as such belongs to the human predicament (Romans 6:23).[124] When the apocalyptic events did not occur, the transience of existence shifted to the center of reflections on how to relate to the world in Christianity, too. In conjunction with, but also beyond the expectation of, the world's imminent end, there developed in Christianity also a trust in God's mercy and love as a power that overcomes death. If God's mercy, as Jesus had taught and exemplified it, is greater and stronger than sin and guilt, then it also overcomes death as the wages of sin. According to Paul, God loves human beings even when—indeed, precisely when—they still live in enmity against God (Romans 5:10). Therefore, even death cannot separate them from God's love (Romans 8:38–39). Thus, trusting in God's mercy, a person can free themselves from any attachment to the transient world.

God's mercy urges and inspires imitation (Luke 6:36; 1 John 4:16, 19).

---

[120] See above, p. 52n5.

[121] See *Majjhima Nikāya* 26; see also Schmidt-Leukel 2006a, 33–36.

[122] *Aṅguttara Nikāya* 7:61. Bodhi 2012, 1061.

[123] See *Majjhima Nikāya* 75; Ñāṇamoli & Bodhi 2001, 611.

[124] As has been shown by James Barr (1992, 1–20), the biblical creation narrative can also be read as presenting death as a natural phenomenon. Paul's interpretation follows the tradition of Wisdom 2:23 (see ibid., 16–17).

Love of one's neighbor thereby enters into a synthesis with detachment from the world, insofar as it does not pursue its own, self-centered interests: "Love does not seek its own benefit" (1 Corinthians 13:5). This is shown on the one hand by the fact that love applies equally to friend and foe (Matthew 5:43–48), and on the other that the person is prepared in extreme cases to sacrifice their own life for the sake of others (John 15:13). Both criteria are also found in Buddhism, where lovingkindness and compassion also prove to be compatible with nonattachment in that on the one hand they must apply indiscriminately to all beings, whether friend or foe, and on the other that they must include the readiness to lay down one's own life for the sake of others.[125] The Buddha had repeatedly practiced the latter in his previous lives as a bodhisattva.[126] According to a Buddhist belief, nonattachment manifests itself especially in selflessness.

But why, according to the Buddhist view, is loving commitment to the world necessary at all? Is all that motivates this the example of the Buddha? *One* answer to this question can be found in the *Bodhicaryāvatāra*, a Mahayana text already mentioned, where it says, "Release (*nirvāṇa*) is the leaving behind of everything: and my mind strives for release. If I have to give up everything, it is better to give it to all beings" (3:11).[127] But why should it be "better" to give "everything," and, as the text clarifies in the next verses, especially oneself "to all beings"? The answer can be found in the text's eighth chapter: suffering is to be combated solely because it is suffering, without restriction to one's own suffering or that of others (8:102). Striving only to overcome one's own suffering would still be self-centered, but it is precisely this self-centeredness that is the nucleus of an attachment that causes suffering. The overcoming of self-centeredness consists in viewing all beings like or *as* one's own self. Striving for their liberation therefore coincides with striving for one's own liberation (8:111–139).

A similar aim is expressed by the *Visuddhimagga*, which is undoubtedly the most important classical spiritual manual in Theravada Buddhism. Dating from the fifth century CE, it says that nonattachment and loving commitment are mutually qualifying. Detached equanimity preserves lovingkindness from its "near enemy," greed. In other words, what looks like lovingkindness may all too easily hide self-centered motives. Conversely, lovingkindness preserves detached equanimity from its "near enemy," that is, "worldly, ignorant indifference." Lovingkindness counteracts the two "far enemies" of equanimity, greed and hate, and thereby unites with

---

[125] The popular *Metta Sutta* thus emphasizes both the readiness of a mother to protect her child with her own life, and the instruction to direct this kind of love indiscriminately toward all beings.
[126] On the motif of sacrificing one's life in Buddhism, see Ohnuma 2007.
[127] Schmidt-Leukel 2019b, 163.

equanimity.[128] The "Great Beings," i.e., the bodhisattvas, "are unshakably resolute upon beings' welfare and happiness. Through unshakable lovingkindness (*mettā*) they place them first [before themselves]. Through equanimity (*upekkhā*), they expect no reward."[129] Not only Mahayana but also Theravada Buddhism censures an attitude that strives exclusively for one's own salvation, as would be the case with detachment unaccompanied by loving commitment.[130]

One of the most influential classics of Christian spirituality, the *Imitatio Christi* by Thomas à Kempis (d. 1471), places a similar emphasis on true love being free from attachment and self-centeredness.[131] "Now, that which seems to be charity is oftentimes really sensuality, for man's own inclination . . . and his self-interest, are motives seldom absent. . . . He who has true and perfect charity seeks self in nothing" (I 15:2–3). "Love is never self-seeking, for in whatever a person seeks himself there he falls from love" (III 5:7). "Nature works for its own interest . . . , is covetous" and "loves to have its own." Grace, however, is "kind and openhearted" and "does not cling to those which are temporal" (III 54:2–4). He who has "great charity" considers the transient glory of the world to be "folly" (I 3:6, alluding to Philippians 3:8). "It is more blessed to give than to receive" (Acts 20:35)—according to Thomas, this attitude shows the bond between true love and nonattachment (III 54:4), a view that, without his knowing it, agrees with the *Bodhicaryāvatāra*.[132]

Some Personal Testimonies

It is especially in the reflections of people whose spirituality draws from both Buddhism and Christianity that we find personal testimonies suggesting that nonattachment and love are complementary.

Thich Nhat Hanh (1926–2022) gained international renown first through his pacifist activities during the Vietnam War, later primarily through the Tiep Hien Order ("Order of Interbeing"),[133] which he founded in 1964 and is now primarily active in the West, and then through the influential center Plum Village in France.[134] At the age of sixteen, he was ordained in a

---

[128] *Visuddhimagga* 9:98–101. See Schmidt-Leukel 2006a, 71–72.
[129] *Visuddhimagga* 9:124. Translation following Ñāṇamoli 1999, 318.
[130] See *Aṅguttara Nikāya* 7:68: "The person who is practicing for his own welfare but not for the welfare of others is in that respect blameworthy; the person who is practicing for his own welfare and for the welfare of others is in that respect praiseworthy." Bodhi 2012, 1083.
[131] All subsequent quotations from the translation by A. Croft and H. Bolton: Thomas à Kempis 2012.
[132] See the *Bodhicaryāvatāra* 8:125: "'If I give, what will I eat?' Such concern for the sake of oneself is the character of a meat-eating demon. 'If I eat, what will I give?' Such concern for the sake of others is the character of a king of gods." Schmidt-Leukel 2019b, 389.
[133] See https://orderofinterbeing.org/.
[134] See https://plumvillage.org/de/.

Vietnamese order belonging to the Zen (*thiền*) tradition. Through meeting Christians such as Martin Luther King, Thomas Merton, and Daniel Berrigan, however, he increasingly also embraced Christianity.[135] As he himself once put it: as a Buddhist, the Buddha naturally was his spiritual ancestor; but now he had adopted Jesus Christ as a further spiritual ancestor.[136] Buddhist compassion commands that a "monk should engage himself in the work of helping and caring" where suffering occurs. "In the situation of war, a monk cannot just sit in the meditation hall while bombs are being dropped all around."[137] For him, the real meaning of love is to alleviate suffering,[138] which means that "the question is not whether to be engaged or not," but "how to engage without losing the contemplative life."[139]

According to Thich Nhat Hanh, the answer lies in the practice of mindfulness, which leads to the experience of the transience of all things. Things have no immutable or essential core, but rather exist only as a component in the interconnectedness of everything with everything. The perception of transience therefore becomes a realization of "the nature of interbeing."[140] Compassion grows out of this experience. "When you are mindful, you realize that the other person suffers. . . . When you begin to see the suffering in the other person, compassion is born."[141] In other words, there arises an empathic and sympathetic identification with the other, even with the enemy.[142] This kind of understanding, according to Thich Nhat Hanh, "is the very foundation of love."[143] But for him, there are Buddhists who become caught up in the doctrine of the nonsubstantiality of things without penetrating to the insight of interbeing.[144] Instead of remaining attached to the doctrine of not-self, the person should become free from self through sensitivity to the suffering of all.[145] Such an unattached love transcends the self[146] and is not possessive: "True love is a love without possessiveness. You love and still you are free, and the other person is also free."[147] In the most extreme case, a person will be prepared to sacrifice themselves for the other out of compassion—as was the case with the Vietnamese monks

---

[135] Hanh 1996, 4–6. On Thich Nhat Hanh's biography, see von Brück & Lai 1997, 560–68, and DeVido 2019.
[136] Hanh 2005, 41. Also Hanh 1999, 190–91, 194–95.
[137] Hanh 1996, 174–75.
[138] Hanh 1999, 32.
[139] Hanh 1996, 175.
[140] Ibid., 182–86.
[141] Hanh 1999, 34.
[142] Ibid.; Hanh 1996, 78–79, 84–86.
[143] Hanh 1999, 36.
[144] See ibid., 21–23, 25–27.
[145] Ibid., 36–38.
[146] Hanh 1996, 184–86.
[147] Hanh 1999, 69.

and nuns who immolated themselves during the Vietnam War, or indeed, as Hanh says, with Jesus.[148]

Sallie B. King is an American scholar of religious studies and at the same time a practicing Buddhist (Zen) and Christian (Quaker).[149] In an autobiographical essay, King describes her experiences as a mother torn between loving commitment to her own children and the Buddhist teaching of nonattachment. King identifies different tendencies within Buddhism. On the one hand, there are forms of spirituality that are articulated in such a way that they appear to be completely incompatible with the loving devotion of a mother for her child. On the other, there are texts such as the *Metta Sutta* that elevate motherly love to the archetype of the Buddhist understanding of benevolence and compassion.[150] But King also perceives ambivalences in Christianity: images of a frightening God on the one hand, and the idea of love as the noblest fruit of the Holy Spirit on the other.[151]

King describes how she experienced love for her children as a form of attachment and stands by this. For her, it is an attachment that goes hand in hand with suffering, and yet that is exactly what love urges her to do. But she also experiences a radical form of selflessness in this love, the putting aside and giving up of all self-centered interests in favor of caring for the child. And when children grow up and go their own ways, the important thing is to let go, since doing so, King says, is part of love, even of clinging love.[152] Although Buddhist nonattachment and Christian love are not so easily reconciled, her experience as a mother in particular has taught her that she needs both.[153] There are situations that call for more of one attitude, and those that call for more of the other. According to King, this in a sense also reflects something of the different contexts of a monastic life on the one hand, and the life of the laity on the other.[154]

It is indeed possible to describe the tense complementarity of nonattachment and loving commitment as a reciprocal integration of monastic and nonmonastic spirituality. According to Raimon Panikkar (1918–2010), who saw himself as a Catholic, a Hindu, and a Buddhist, "Traditional monks may have reenacted in their own way 'something' that we [i.e., nonmonks] too may be called upon to realize, but in a different manner."[155] According to Panikkar, monasticism is in a sense the institutionalized form of awareness

---

[148]Hanh 1996, 81–82; 2010, 87.
[149]She retired in 2015. For further biographical details, see Drew 2011, 31–35.
[150]See King, S. 2003, 164–65, 167–68.
[151]See ibid., 160, 163–64.
[152]Ibid., 169.
[153]Ibid., 170.
[154]For example, in an interview with Rose Drew; see Drew 2011, 142–43.
[155]Panikkar 1989, 14. Quotations are taken from the e-book edition of Panikkar's *Opera Omnia*, I.2 (Orbis Books).

both of the transience of this world and of the presence of an absolute reality.[156] But there is a danger, he says, of failing to recognize that the absolute is also present in the transient itself. "Always we have known that to love God is to love one's neighbor, that to seek *nirvāṇa* is really to aid *saṃsāra*. . . . The old masters knew well that one has to integrate death into life."[157]

Panikkar's allusion here to the bodhisattva ideal is also found in Sallie King: the love of the mother for her child corresponds to the willingness of the bodhisattva not to leave the world, but to remain in samsara for the benefit of all beings.[158] This recourse to the bodhisattva ideal is not surprising; within Mahayana Buddhism it has actually helped relativize a strict distinction between monastic and lay status.[159] Existentially, says Panikkar, the tension between renouncing and affirming the world is ultimately about the question of the relationship between nonattachment and commitment, this being particularly evident in the question of a celibate or a noncelibate life.[160] But the monk's renunciation of the world retains its own special significance for the world, since it makes the monk "the nonconformist." A monk swims against the current of the world by not adhering to its rules.[161] His way of life alone questions "how problems are seen." For Panikkar, this also implies an important critical potential toward the rules made by the powerful.[162]

Political Implications

Having looked at the micro level of religious diversity, we are brought back by Panikkar's last statement to the social implications of the relationship between world-renunciation and world-affirmation. Buddhism and Christianity both display the whole range of the spectrum: from complete renunciation of society to the almost complete identification between state and religion, yet it is precisely the complementary tension between the two opposing tendencies that has often produced attitudes that fruitfully counteracted any one-sidedness.

As examples of an understanding of political rule shaped by both tendencies, James Fredericks has compared Augustine's *On the State of God / De Civitate Dei* (fifth century CE) with *The Story (of the Great Deeds) of Ashoka /Aśokāvadāna* (second century CE). Fredericks recognizes in both works a deep questioning of the idea that the state manifests a cosmologi-

---

[156] Panikkar 1989, 134.
[157] Ibid., 137.
[158] King, S. 2003, 167.
[159] See above, p. 66.
[160] Panikkar 1989, 141–42.
[161] Ibid., 50, 139–40.
[162] Ibid., 139–41.

cal truth.[163] With Augustine, it is the insight into the finitude of this world and the expectation of the divine future that forbids any absolutization of the state. Christians, according to Augustine, have no "lasting city" in this world (Hebrews 13:14). Nor can the Christian state ever replicate, or let alone usurp, the human being's eschatological goal. For Augustine, the earthly peace that in the best case the state provides is not identical to eternal peace.[164] The *Aśokāvadāna* portrays the life and personality of Emperor Ashoka, the first great protectionist of Buddhism in India, in a way that in some respects deviates considerably from the common Buddhist cliché of glorifying Ashoka as the ideal ruler. According to the *Aśokāvadāna*, Ashoka corresponded only partially to the ideal of the Buddhist world ruler (*cacravartin*), since, even as a promoter of Buddhism, he still retains extraordinarily violent traits in this text. Of particular interest, according to Fredericks, is that the *Aśokāvadāna* ends with the narration of Pushyamitra (*Puṣyamitra*), who is presented here as the last descendant of Ashoka's Maurya dynasty.[165] Unlike his predecessors, Pushyamitra becomes an enemy and persecutor of Buddhism, and destroys Ashoka's work, which Fredericks sees as a stylistic device to express the Buddhist doctrine of the transience of all things.

From the perspective of the *Aśokāvadāna*, the sangha is forbidden to cling to a Buddhist state, which, too, will pass away.[166] And according to Fredericks, a central message in Augustine is that imperial "Rome," even in its Christian guise, is by no means "eternal."[167] "Both Buddhism and Christianity share . . . an existential sense of the fragility of existence and the illusory trust we place in transitory things."[168] But Fredericks also makes clear that actually quite different concepts of the relation between religion and politics have also proven to be effective in both religions, concepts that were clearly less aimed at a permanent distance from state rule, but instead saw in the latter an earthly image of God's rule, or an integrative part of the cosmic dharma. Hence, the warning against the illusory trust in the state shaped by religion is still relevant today.[169]

According to Fredericks, however, a fundamental spiritual distance from what the state is and is not capable of doing does not obstruct social engage-

---

[163]Fredericks 2015, 76.

[164]According to Fredericks' reading of *De Civitate Dei* 19. See ibid., 77–78, 86.

[165]According to Brahminical sources, though, Pushyamitra did not belong to the Maurya dynasty, but usurped the throne after murdering Brihadratha (*Bṛhadratha*), the last Mauriya ruler. See Strong 2016a, 292; Hazra 1995, 46–47.

[166]Fredericks 2015, 82–83, 86–87.

[167]Ibid., 83–84.

[168]Ibid., 84.

[169]Ibid., 87–89.

ment in either tradition, but rather gives it its leeway.[170] This is consistent with the findings of a comparison that Robin W. Lovin undertook between social-ethical aspects of monasticism in Western Christianity and in Theravada Buddhism: "In both traditions this insistence on a human destiny that transcends any possible social achievement provides the basis for a flexible social ethics that takes social relationships seriously but does not make the creation of any particular social order to be the goal of religious life."[171] Thus, it also becomes apparent with regard to social reality that the world-renouncing and world-affirming tendencies in Buddhism and Christianity have the potential to complement each other and to guard against one-sided conceptions of either a radical turning away of religion from politics or its complete assimilation—even though these extremes have undoubtedly always existed and still exist in both traditions.

Both Fredericks and Lovin see a clear difference between Christianity and Buddhism in the apocalyptic or eschatological orientation of Christianity, arguing that the transience of the world that Christianity speaks of is the transience of a history that nevertheless has a *telos*, a final goal, which God will bring about.[172] In contrast, the Buddhist doctrine of samsara lacks such a fulfillment of history, and there remains instead a constant cyclical up and down, especially regarding the respective state of societal conditions.[173] But how sharp is this difference? Lovin admits that millenarian hopes for the future, i.e., the hope for groundbreaking changes through the appearance of the future Buddha, Maitreya, are not alien to Buddhism either.[174] On the other hand, however, Maitreya's new age will also pass away. Only nirvana remains imperishable. Conversely, on the Christian side, God is conceived not only as the future consummator of history but also as its author and director. Such questions about the relationship between the transient world and the imperishable absolute point to the differences in the understanding of ultimate reality, as there are between, but also within, Buddhism and Christianity.

---

[170] Ibid., 89.
[171] Lovin 1992, 204.
[172] Ibid., 191, 201, 204; Fredericks 2015, 84–85.
[173] Lovin 1992, 205; Fredericks 2015, 85. On the expectation of Maitreya and its significance, see below, pp. 204–206.
[174] Lovin 1992, 272n3.

4

Ultimate Reality

4.1 IMPERSONAL ABSOLUTE OR PERSONAL GOD?

Numerous comparisons of Buddhism and Christianity have presented the central difference between the two as lying in the contrast between a theistic and an atheistic religion—Christianity and Buddhism, respectively. In the West, however, "atheism" is understood not as a religion, but as a non- or even anti-religious worldview. Thus, the unusual word combination of an "atheistic religion" already points to a certain ambiguity in this use of the predicate "atheistic" (or, alternatively, in the description of Buddhism as a "religion"). The problem is illustrated by the book *Buddhism: An Atheistic Religion* by the Indologist and religious scholar Helmuth von Glasenapp (1891–1963). This was the title of the book's second edition, published in 1966 by Szczesny Verlag, a publisher that pursued an "atheist" (in the Western sense) program between 1961 and 1968.[1] The title of the first edition of 1954 was much more apt and circumspect: namely, *Buddhism and the Idea of God: Buddhist Teachings of Supra-worldly Beings and Powers, and Their Parallels in the History of Religion.*[2]

In the book itself, von Glasenapp deals with both "the Buddhist arguments against theism" and "the Buddhist teachings about the absolute." Using a great deal of textual evidence, von Glasenapp makes it abundantly clear that both the older Buddhism and Mahayana Buddhism are guided by the idea of an absolute reality that transcends the world, an idea that each expresses in different forms.[3] This, however, is incompatible with the Western concept of an atheistic worldview. Accordingly, the title was changed again in 1970 in the English translation of the book, with Buddhism no longer being called

---

[1] See the Spiegel article "So Sad," July 1, 1968, https://www.spiegel.de/spiegel/print/d-45997607.html (March 2021).

[2] "Buddhismus und Gottesidee. Die buddhistischen Lehren von den überweltlichen Wesen und Mächten und ihre religionsgeschichtlichen Parallelen."

[3] Von Glasenapp 1966, 141–63. For the English edition see Von Glasenapp 1970.

an "atheistic" but instead a "non-theistic religion." The Buddhist denial of a personal creator God is after all not the same as denying any form of supramundane or transcendent reality. This difference is extremely important when it comes to comparing Buddhism and Christianity since it shows ultimately that it is about different notions of transcendence.

Atheism or Nontheism?

Christian missionaries who first came into direct contact with Buddhism in the modern period often considered it atheistic. For example, the Jesuit missionary Matteo Ricci (1552–1610), who became acquainted with Buddhism in China, described the "big difference" between Buddhism and Christianity: the former denies and revolts against the Lord of Heaven while the latter obeys and serves him.[4] Ricci grounds this judgment primarily by interpreting the Mahayana-Buddhist concept of emptiness (*śūnyatā*) as a mere nothingness. Although briefly raising the possibility that this interpretation might be wrong, he nonetheless dismisses that possibility.[5] If the Buddha, he concludes, did not recognize the existence of the creator, then he was ignorant. But if he recognized but did not explicitly acknowledge him, then this amounted to a rebellion against God. This verdict corresponds to a central idea in modern Christian apologetics that claims that the rational arguments for the existence of God are so strong and evident that anyone who denies God must be either stupid or evil. "Buddha," says Ricci, "worships his own spirit nature (心 性) and wishes to obscure the omnipotence of the Lord."[6] In other words, for Ricci, Buddha placed himself in the role of God.

More cautious was the Jesuit missionary Ippolito Desideri (1684–1733), who encountered Tibetan Buddhism between 1715 and 1721. Desideri too emphasized that, since Buddhists deny the existence of the "true God" or any other god on the basis of their doctrine of emptiness, they could be called atheists. However, they are not atheists, he argued, if by that is meant people who deny any divinity, any life after death, and any morality. According to Desideri, the Buddhists of Tibet profess and worship in the form of their "saints" (i.e., the supernatural Buddhas and bodhisattvas) a reality that is free from all evils, omniscient, ready to help anyone, and perfect in compassion. Moreover, they believed in a supreme, blissful, eternal, and unchanging goal for all sentient beings. Thus, for Desideri, they accept God in substance, albeit in a way that is deluded and unconscious.[7]

Two Methodist missionaries and scholars, Daniel Gogerly (1792–1862)

---

[4]Kern, I. 1984/5, 79–80.
[5]Ibid., 81.
[6]Ibid., 96.
[7]Desideri 2010, 374–77.

and Robert Spence Hardy (1803–1868), studied the Theravada Buddhism of Sri Lanka in the nineteenth century, both holding that Buddhists do not believe in God and that the goal of the Buddhist path is the complete annihilation of one's own existence.[8] Spence Hardy did know that Mahayana Buddhism contained the belief in supernatural Buddhas and bodhisattvas, and even notions of creation, but he deemed these to be regional phenomena that went against the actual teachings of Buddhism.[9] Similar attitudes strongly influenced early research on Buddhism in the West, one of its main pioneers, Jules Barthélemy Saint-Hilaire (1805–1895), drawing among others on Spence Hardy to depict Buddhism as atheistic and nihilistic.[10] The great Sanskrit scholar Monier Monier-Williams (1819–1899) adopted this view, but modified it with regard to the Mahayana branch of Buddhism, arguing in a comparative study of 1889 that Buddhism, at least in its original form, "refused to admit the existence of a personal Creator, or of man's dependence on a higher Power."[11] However, he also argued that in later forms of Buddhism, i.e., in Mahayana, one could see "the gradual sliding of its atheism and agnosticism into theism and polytheism."[12]

The juxtaposition of Buddhist atheism and Christian theism became a widespread motif in comparative studies at the turn of the twentieth century, with several authors seeing the denial of a personal creator and of an immortal soul as evidence of the atheistic and nihilistic character of Buddhism, at least in its original form.[13] A remark by Hilko Wiardo Schomerus shows how strongly entrenched was the belief that the older Buddhism was atheistic. While aware that the older Buddhist texts do not explicitly deny the existence of God, Schomerus argues that this reveals all the more its atheistic character, since, for Buddha, "God . . . is so much a nothing that he does not even bother to deal with him in any way, to deny his existence or to prove his non-existence. A more consistent atheist cannot really be imagined."[14]

Many authors understood Buddhist atheism in a radical, i.e., materialistic and nihilistic, sense. In their view, Buddhism denies any form of ultimate reality, insofar as this means a reality that transcends the limits of space and time, and thus the limits of contingent and transient existence.[15] For them,

---

[8]Harris, E. J. 2006, 69.
[9]Spence Hardy, R. 1874, 17–18.
[10]Welbon 1968, 67–79, 90.
[11]Monier-Williams 1889, 539.
[12]Ibid., 541.
[13]E.g., Bertholet 1909, 18–22; Wecker & Koch 1910, 29; Hardy 1919, 195–99.
[14]See Schomerus 1931, 25. However, Schomerus did not want to interpret nirvana in a completely nihilistic way, even though he came close to this position. See below p. 190–91.
[15]The term "ultimate reality" remains inevitably vague, but is sufficiently distinct. According to Wesley Wildman (2017, 6–8), ultimate reality is not conditioned by anything else; everything else is dependent on it; it forms the context of everything, but is not itself part of a still larger context. More

Buddhism is therefore actually not a religion, but a pessimistic philosophy. Some Western scholars of Buddhism, as well as Buddhists who are mainly influenced by the West, still defend such a strong atheist interpretation.[16] In contrast, other authors have interpreted Buddhism as a nontheistic religion, seeing Buddhism as atheistic only in the sense that it rejects the belief in a personal creator God. For these authors, Buddhism does not deny the existence of an ultimate, transcendent reality per se, and is in this respect best seen as similar to mysticism. And this, they hold, is by no means only true for later developments within Mahayana Buddhism.

The French Indologist Jules Mohl contradicted Barthélemy Saint-Hilaire's atheistic or nihilistic interpretation of Buddhism as early as 1855, arguing that nirvana certainly does not mean complete annihilation, but rather represents "the goal common to all mysticism: reunion of the soul with God." This goal, Mohl continues, is always spoken of by the mystics of all religions only in images and comparisons.[17] Other authors, such as the philosophers Adolphe Franck and Adolphe Garnier, pointed out that mystical traditions within religions often use negative language to refer to the ineffability of ultimate reality, and that such negative formulations should not be mistaken for atheism or nihilism.[18] Interpreting Buddhism as a form of mysticism also continued into the twentieth century, strongly supported by the German religious studies scholars Rudolf Otto, Friedrich Heiler, and Gustav Mensching. Buddhism, according to Mensching, is "a genuine mysticism . . . and thus also religion, which is always connected with something numinous, and not atheism. This is the case in both basic forms of Buddhism, Theravada, and Mahayana Buddhism."[19]

According to Bhikkhu Bodhi, Theravada monk and internationally recognized translator of numerous canonical works, many Buddhists prefer the term "nontheistic," since "atheistic" suggests a purely materialist worldview.[20] However, there is some evidence that even those Buddhists who emphasize the atheistic character of Buddhism interpret it, on closer

---

simply, and perhaps more aptly, John Hick (1993, 164) says that it is a reality "which transcends everything other than itself but is not transcended by anything other than itself."

[16]For example, Asanga Tilakaratne (2016) in Theravada Buddhism, and Stephen Batchelor (1998; 2011) in Mahayana Buddhism. Mark Siderits and Jay Garfield can also be mentioned from Western Buddhist scholarship, both arguing that, at least according to Nagarjuna's philosophy, "the ultimate truth is that there is no ultimate truth" (Garfield 2002, 99; Siderits 2007, 182; for a philological critique, see, for example, Ferraro 2013). Tilakaratne (2016, 92–94), however, acknowledges that other opinions are possible, and actually have been and still are held in the tradition. Batchelor is also aware that he is turning away from traditional Buddhist positions, but claims to be at least partially closer to the original position of the Buddha (Batchelor 1998, 4–5, 34–38, 114–15; 2011, 38–39, 130–31, 174–83).

[17]Quoted from Welbon 1968, 70.

[18]Ibid., 77–79.

[19]Mensching 1978, 244.

[20]Bodhi 1995, 24.

inspection, in a nontheistic rather than nihilistic sense. The Theravada-Buddhist reformer Anagarika Dharmapala (1864–1933) consistently affirmed the Buddhist rejection of a creator god, but said that Buddhism was neither monotheistic, atheistic, materialist, nor nihilistic;[21] rather, it contains a psychology of "transcendental mysticism,"[22] which is based on a "transcendental metaphysics."[23] For him, nirvana exists outside "the law of the cosmic processes,"[24] and is "beyond speech," "inexpressible," "eternal," and "unconditioned." Only those who experience it know what it is.[25] Dharmapala explicitly rejected the nihilistic interpretation of nirvana as annihilation.[26]

More recently, the Sri Lankan scholar Gunapala Dharmasiri (d. 2015) has highlighted the atheistic nature of Buddhism, and linked it to a detailed critique of the Christian concept of God.[27] Initially, Dharmasiri also did not shy away from speaking of nirvana as "absolute extinction" and from rejecting the interpretation of nirvana in terms of a mystical reality.[28] However, he then acknowledged in a later "postscript"[29] a certain similarity between Buddhism and the Hindu tradition of Advaita Vedanta, arguing that the Buddha's "attempt was to rescue the ultimate principle from degradation to the conceptual level." This is the reason, according to Dharmasiri, that the Buddha spoke via negation about nirvana, even though he occasionally intimated, as in *Udāna* 8:3,[30] that he accepted the positive existence of such an ultimate principle.[31] In this respect, he, Dharmasiri, had criticized the Christian concept of God as "a primitive and undeveloped conception of the perfect and ultimate Reality."[32]

In China, the Buddhist reformer Taixu (1890–1974) highlighted the atheistic character of Buddhism, and rejected theistic ideas of God as inherently contradictory and incompatible with modern science.[33] However, as shown not least by Taixu's discussion with his Buddhist contemporary Ouyang Jingwu, he was primarily concerned with rejecting dualistic notions of transcendence. The "suchness" (*zhenru*, *tathatā*) of ultimate reality affirmed

---

[21]Guruge 1965, 33.
[22]Ibid., 80.
[23]Ibid., 8.
[24]Ibid., 288.
[25]Ibid., 80–81; see also 190.
[26]Ibid., 354–55.
[27]Dharmasiri 1988.
[28]Ibid., 152–83.
[29]This postscript is not contained in the first edition of *A Buddhist Critique of the Christian Concept of God* (Dharmasiri 1974). Remarks in Dharmasiri 1976 already point in a similar direction, however.
[30]See above, p. 60.
[31]Dharmasiri 1988, 269.
[32]Ibid., 259.
[33]See Pittman 2001, 243–49.

in Mahayana Buddhism must, according to Taixu, be thought of as both transcendent and immanent,[34] with all people participating in the absolute reality that constitutes their Buddha nature and not, as in Christianity, Jesus alone.[35] Taixu even occasionally described the concept of God as a false or insufficient way of conceptualizing this absolute reality.[36]

A similar position was taken in Japan by Taixu's contemporary, Daisetz Teitaro Suzuki (1870–1966), who also explicitly rejected the belief in a creator god. However, unlike Taixu, Suzuki believed that defining Buddhism as "atheistic" was misleading, since it gave the impression that Buddhism had an agnostic and materialist view of the world.[37] In his influential 1907 work *Outlines of Mahāyāna Buddhism*, Suzuki wrote, "Buddhism outspokenly acknowledges the presence in the world of a reality which transcends the limitations of phenomenality, but which is nevertheless immanent everywhere and manifests itself in its full glory, and in which we live and move and have our being."[38] This allusion to Acts 17:28 already indicates his point of view, which is that the Mahayana concept of the dharma body (*dharmakāya*) is the Buddhist equivalent of the concept of God. At the same time, Suzuki equates the dharma body with the Buddha nature immanent in all phenomenal reality.[39] Fifty years later, in 1957, Suzuki explicitly presented Zen Buddhism as a form of mysticism, and highlighted significant parallels between Zen and the Christian mysticism of Meister Eckhart.[40] A further eight years later, he then revoked his definition of Zen as "mystical" on the grounds that this term had connotations such as "obscure," "hidden," and "secret" that in no way applied to the spirituality of Zen.[41] This shows that, like the term "atheistic," those such as "mysticism" and "mystical" have many and various connotations, meaning that it is only possible or sensible to use them in a very nuanced way.

My final example is the Zen-Buddhist philosopher Keiji Nishitani (1900–1990). He was also not averse to drawing strong parallels between Zen and the mysticism of Meister Eckhart, and he explicitly rejected equating Mahayana Buddhism with a nihilistic or materialist atheism.[42] For him, the Buddhist viewpoint is beyond atheism and theism. "To be sure," Nishitani argues, "even in Buddhism . . . a transcendence to the far side, or the 'yonder shore,' is spoken of. But this yonder shore may be called an

---

[34]Ibid., 247. See also Yu, X. 2003, 174.
[35]Pittman 2001, 119, 248.
[36]Yu, X. 2003, 183.
[37]Suzuki 1977, 219.
[38]Ibid.
[39]Ibid., 217–41.
[40]In his book *Mysticism: Christian and Buddhist* (Suzuki [1957] 2007). See also on this, Reichl 2021.
[41]Suzuki 1965.
[42]Nishitani 1983, 98–99.

absolute near side in the sense that it has gone beyond the usual opposition of the near and the far."[43] For Nishitani, Eckhart's conception of "nothing" or the "Godhead" as the basis of the relationship between the soul and God comes very close to such an understanding of transcendence.[44]

In dialogues between Christians and Zen Buddhists, characterizing Buddhism as a form of mysticism, or at least as being close to Christian mysticism is still widespread. However, this is now done with a greater sensitivity to the hermeneutical problems entailed in applying the category "mysticism" to Buddhism. But even experts as hermeneutically sensitive and cautious as Jan van Bragt and Paul Mommaers see good reasons for arguing that many questions and experiences that are assigned to "mystical theology" within Christianity have a central place in Buddhism. This applies in particular to the apophatic tradition of Christian theology, which asserts that one can only say of God what God is *not*. This tradition, say van Bragt and Mommaers, "has much in common with the 'tenacious process of negation' that pervades the whole of Buddhism, but especially Mahāyāna Buddhism."[45] Christian Steineck speaks of a "plurality of mystical approaches," but does not shy away from understanding Zen Buddhism as a form of mysticism.[46] Janett Williams avoids classifying Buddhism or Zen Buddhism as mysticism, but nonetheless arrives at a finding very similar to van Bragt and Mommaers in her comparative study of Dogen (1200–1253) on the one hand, and Pseudo-Dionysus the Areopagite and Maximus Confessor on the other: namely that of an astonishing consonance in the apophatic attitude toward ultimate reality.[47]

Impersonal versus Personal Understanding of Transcendence

Whether the category of "mysticism" is appropriate or not to Buddhism or particular forms of Buddhism, many Christians engaged in dialogue with Buddhists now agree that Buddhism cannot be characterized as "atheism" if this means the denial of any form of transcendent or ultimate reality.[48] Modern Western atheism has usually denied the existence not only of a personal creator God but also of any unconditioned reality transcending space and time.[49] However, it is also uncontested that there are Buddhists

---

[43]Ibid., 99. The "other" or "yonder shore" is one of the classic Buddhist metaphors for nirvana. See Collins, S. 1998, 222–24.

[44]Nishitani 1983, 90, 99, 115–16.

[45]Mommaers & Van Bragt 1995, 33.

[46]See Steineck 2000, 10–12, 259–67.

[47]Williams, J. P. 2000, 185. Katharina Ceming (2004) assigns many strands of Buddhism to mysticism, and, like Janett Williams, sees the main reason for this as lying in the various forms of apophaticism.

[48]See on this also the overview in von Brück & Lai 1997, 349–478.

[49]See also the distinction proposed by Jeanine Diller between "global atheism," the denial of any

today who understand their worldview as atheistic in precisely this Western sense—just as there are Christians today who abandon any notion of a metaphysical reality and, echoing Ludwig Feuerbach, regard the term "God" as merely a symbolic cipher for particular human values.[50]

However, such a radical denial of transcendence can hardly be applied to Buddhism, even in its early forms.[51] Early Buddhism in particular emphasized the supramundane or transcendent character of nirvana as an unconditioned and imperishable reality.[52] Nor did Mahayana Buddhism, especially those varieties that developed in the Chinese cultural sphere, deny transcendence. The denial often relates to dualistic conceptions. Transcendence is intrinsically united with radical immanence. In China, the influence of Daoism played a not insignificant role in this respect. The Indian foundations are provided with Nagarjuna's (second century CE) criticism of any form of a conceptual worldview. According to Nagarjuna, true reality (literally "that-ness/such-ness": *tattva*) cannot be expressed in concepts, which means that even the distinction between samsara and nirvana, between this-worldly and other-worldly reality is at best only temporary, but not absolute.[53]

But if Buddhist "atheism" does not mean the denial of a transcendent reality per se, then the difference between Buddhist nontheism and Christian theism should be seen as a difference between different understandings and conceptions of transcendent reality. Quite a few Christians and Buddhists, however, still regard this difference as an insurmountable opposition. For example, Keith Yandell and Harold Netland explicitly note in their comparison of Buddhism and Christianity that, according to traditional Buddhist understanding, nirvana denotes an unconditioned reality free from all transience.[54] However, since nirvana is "not conceived as personal or capable of action," it has nothing in common with the Christian understanding of God.[55] Similarly, Paul Williams, who first converted to Buddhism and later to Catholicism, says that the concept of nirvana as a supreme reality does not allow us to see in it another version of what Christians understand as "God." This is because no personal relation to nirvana is possible, nor is nirvana in any way creative.[56] Drawing on rich evidence, Steven Collins shows in the

---

form of divine or transcendent reality, and "local atheism," the denial of a particular idea of transcendent reality (Diller 2016).

[50] See, for example, the positions of Hasenhüttl 1979, 115–35, and Cupitt 2003, 276–77.

[51] This seems questionable even for the position of the Sautrantikas, to whom the idea of final annihilation is often imputed. Cf. Pandit 1993, 312–39; Pande 1999, 443–51.

[52] Schmidt-Leukel 2016c.

[53] *Mūlamadhyamakakārikā* 18.7–11. Schmidt-Leukel 2006a, 118–24.

[54] Yandell & Netland 2009, 22–26.

[55] Ibid., 183.

[56] Williams, P. 2011, 161.

most detailed study so far that the canonical texts of Theravada Buddhism understand nirvana as an unconditioned, timeless, and ineffable reality that also forms the real and ultimate goal of human striving. Nevertheless, Collins argues, a comparison with the idea of God is not possible, since nirvana (Pali: *nibbāna*) "is never said to be the origin or ground of the universe."[57] A similar view is taken by Peter Harvey[58] and Christopher Gowans, the latter concluding in his study on the philosophy of Theravada Buddhism,

> insofar as *Nibbāna* is portrayed as ultimate reality that is beyond change and conditioning, and that, when attained, enables us to overcome suffering, it might invite comparison with the God of the theistic traditions of Judaism, Christianity, and Islam. There are points of similarity. . . . *Nibbāna* is transcendent reality in a broad sense of the term. . . . But the differences are quite significant. The most important are that, unlike God, *Nibbāna* is not the ultimate cause of the universe, and it is not a personal being who is omnipotent, omniscient, and all-loving.[59]

Yet are these differences in the Buddhist and Christian understanding of transcendence really so irreconcilable? Here, too, it may be helpful to note that the difference between an impersonal and a personal understanding of transcendence can be found not only *between* Buddhism and Christianity but also *within* both traditions. If, however, paths have developed within both traditions that assume a complementarity between personal and impersonal conceptions of transcendence, then can such a complementarity not also be assumed for the relationship between the two religions? The situation also turns out to be more complex than has often been assumed so far regarding the question of the creative nature of ultimate reality. For neither in Buddhism nor in Christianity is the understanding of what is meant by "creation" completely unambiguous or homogeneous. As will be seen in the last section of this chapter, a more careful consideration of the details in the respective conceptions of creation leads to new perspectives here, too.

When speaking of "impersonal" conceptions of transcendence, we can use the word "impersonal" in two different senses: cataphatically—i.e., positively—and apophatically—i.e., purely negatively. In the *first*, cataphatic sense, "impersonal" can mean that transcendent or ultimate reality is spoken of in terms, images, or metaphors that are not borrowed from the personal reality of human beings, i.e., are not anthropomorphic. To speak of ultimate reality as "Father" or "Mother" would be a personal, anthropomorphic way

---

[57]Collins, S. 1998, 176–77; similarly, Collins, S. 2010, 53–54.
[58]Harvey 2019, 1–2, 35–37.
[59]Gowans 2003, 150–51.

of speaking. In contrast, designating this reality as the "yonder shore" or "safe island" is an impersonal (or, if you like, "physicomorphic") way of speaking. To speak of the effect and meaning of ultimate reality as "divine will" is a personal way of speaking, whereas designating it as "cosmic law" is an impersonal (in this case, a "nomomorphic") way.

Besides such a cataphatic use of concrete and descriptive, yet not personal, expressions, "impersonal conception of transcendence" can also mean, *second*, something quite different: namely, a purely negative or apophatic way of speaking. This expresses the conviction that ultimate reality cannot be adequately spelled out in human terms and images at all—neither in those terms and images borrowed from the personal nor those from the nonpersonal world of experience. In this case, then, it is not emphasized how or what ultimate reality is like; rather, here it is articulated that all terms and images—personal and impersonal—do not apply to ultimate reality in any literal sense.

We can find impersonal language in the second, apophatic sense in both Buddhism and Christianity, along with the affirmation that this is, on balance, the more appropriate way of talking about transcendent reality—if this reality allows for any way of speaking at all.[60] But both traditions also contain personal and impersonal language in the first sense, too, i.e., in the use of descriptive notions from the personal and the nonpersonal world. As far as this cataphatic way of speaking is concerned, we can probably say that a personal way of speaking prevails in Christianity, while an impersonal way of speaking prevails in Buddhism. Although the use of personal and impersonal language at the cataphatic level is more balanced in many forms of Mahayana Buddhism, and in some cases even a personal imagery seems to dominate, it is also true that personal images (mediated by the ideas of Buddhas and bodhisattvas) still in general relate back to the more fundamental impersonal metaphors and conceptions.

4.2 IMPERSONAL AND PERSONAL NOTIONS OF TRANSCENDENCE IN BUDDHISM

Early Buddhism and Theravada

Early Buddhism often referred to nirvana as "the deathless" (*amṛta, amata*), which depicts the nature of nirvana as liberation from otherwise endless "re-death" (*punarmṛtyu*—the original term for what is later called "rebirth")

---

[60]See also the comparative overview of the apophatic traditions in Buddhism and Christianity in C. D. Sebastian (2016, 19–50). However, Sebastian, unfortunately, presents Buddhism one-sidedly from the rather reductive perspective of authors such as Mark Siderits, Jay Garfield, and others.

in the cycle of samsara. On the one hand, it could be said that the term "the deathless" is a purely negative, apophatic way of speaking, one that simply denies that any form of death and mortality applies to nirvana. On the other, the term is also associated with the metaphor of a *deathless place* or *realm*,[61] or else a sea or ocean of the deathless into which one can "plunge."[62] Furthermore, as we have already seen, nirvana is also called the "yonder" or "further shore" that we reach safely after crossing the stream of samsara, or the "safe island," a "firm ground" that provides protection from the "great flood" of samsara. Nirvana is also likened to a "safe" or "happy city" that offers freedom from fear, or to a delightful "cool place" where respite can be found from unbearable heat. In fact, canonical and postcanonical texts use many different impersonal images for nirvana, all of which emphasize the motif of liberation from the transient and unsatisfying world of samsara.[63]

This motif is also the key reason why influential traditional Buddhist treatises such as the *Milindapañha* (fourth–fifth centuries CE, with significantly older layers) and the *Visuddhimagga* (fifth century CE) insist explicitly that nirvana must be a "non-conditioned" or "unconditioned" (*asaṃskṛta, asaṅkhata*) reality. According to traditional Buddhist teaching, everything that is subject to the principle of dependent origination (*pratītyasamutpāda*), i.e., arising from causes and conditions, is also subject to decay. Thus, both texts argue that, in order actually to be a deathless reality, nirvana must be an unconditioned reality.[64] This implies, according to the two texts, that nirvana cannot be defined as the spiritual state of an awakened (enlightened) person, since, arising as it does from the completion of the Noble Eightfold Path, such a state would be a conditionally arisen reality. However, insofar as nirvana is an "unconditioned" reality, it exists regardless of whether someone attains it. This line of reasoning in traditional Theravada-Buddhist dogmatics also remains at the level of purely negative statements, though, since it only says what nirvana cannot be, i.e., neither conditioned nor caused. The other canonical attributes— the "not-born," "not-brought-to-being," "not-made"—are all also purely negative in nature, as is the "non-conditioned."[65] Indeed, it is affirmed quite early on that nirvana can only be expressed metaphorically, hence being inexpressible in a strict sense, and cannot be described adequately in concepts.[66] Ultimately, according to the early canonical *Sutta Nipāta* (1149), nirvana even remains incomparable.

---

[61] See Collins, S. 1998, 146–47.
[62] Ibid., 221–22.
[63] Overviews of all the designations of nirvana in the canonical scriptures of Theravada Buddhism can be found in Chandrkaew 1982, 20–44, and Collins, S. 1998, 135–233.
[64] *Milindapañha* 4.7.13–17; *Visuddhimagga* 16.67–74.
[65] See above, p. 60.
[66] See Collins, S. 1998, 97, 162–63.

Nirvāṇa (nibbana) is not the only concept that early Buddhism uses to point to an ultimate reality, another being *dharma (dhamma)*, the eternal cosmic law or the teaching in which the Buddha reveals this law. A *Buddha*, i.e., a fully awakened person, is according to traditional Buddhism not someone who makes up or invents his teaching. Rather, the idea is that a Buddha, in his awakening, not only experiences nirvana, but also recognizes the dharma. More precisely, a "Buddha" is someone who rediscovers the dharma at a time when it has long been forgotten, and who at the same time is able to proclaim the dharma in his teaching in such a way that it helps other people also find the path to awakening. According to Buddhism, the dharma thus contains those laws or truths that people need to know and implement in their lives in order to follow the path to nirvana. This path, like its goal, are themselves part of the dharma. "Law" (*dharma*) is also an impersonal concept. But as in the case of nirvana, dharma too is said to be "subtle" and "transcending mere thought" (*Majjhima Nikaya* 26:19). *Dharma* is thus almost, though not completely, inexpressible, since a Buddha can articulate it in such a way that he can show people the path to the strictly inexpressible nirvana.

From this close relationship between nirvana and dharma as two aspects of ultimate reality, traditional Buddhism derives a third concept, which it uses to refer to the immanence of transcendent reality: namely, the concept or figure of a *Buddha*. This has far-reaching implications, particularly in Mahayana Buddhism. The canonical writings of Theravada Buddhism had already depicted the Buddha as embodying dharma and nirvana. "One who sees the Dharma sees me; one who sees me sees the Dharma," says the Buddha. The context makes it perfectly clear that this is not about the physical appearance of the Buddha, but about what he embodies through the spiritual qualities of a Buddha.[67] This is further underlined by the Buddha legend that says that the life of every Buddha always follows the same underlying pattern, and thus illustrates nothing other than the fundamentals of Buddhist teachings, i.e., the dharma. Similarly, it also says that every enlightened person embodies dharma and nirvana.[68] When asked in what way nirvana is "directly visible, immediate," the Buddha replies,

> When lust is abandoned, ... when hate is abandoned, ... when delusion is abandoned he does not intend for his own affliction, for the affliction of others, or for the affliction of both, and he does not experience mental suffering and dejection. It is in this way ... that nibbāna is directly visible.[69]

---

[67] *Saṃyutta Nikāya* 22.87.
[68] *Aṅguttara Nikāya* 3.54–55.
[69] *Aṅguttara Nikāya* 3.55. Translation following Bodhi 2012, 253.

The same is said beforehand about the visibility of dharma. Ultimate reality thus acquires a personal face in the figure of the Buddha, and indeed in every enlightened person. Experiencing ultimate reality transforms human life into a life filled with wisdom and compassion, a life liberated from greed, hate, and delusion. It is precisely this transformation that makes ultimate reality "visible." Ultimate reality manifests itself in the form of perfected human beings. The Buddha and any awakened one thus become personal representations of ultimate reality, albeit in dependence on primarily impersonal concepts such as nirvana and dharma.

Mahayana Buddhism

Such ideas had a considerable impact within Mahayana Buddhism.[70] The influential *Lotus-Sūtra* projects the timelessness of nirvana and the eternity of dharma onto the figure of the Buddha, arguing that his appearance as a mortal being was only a magic trick, a clever pedagogical means to disseminate his teachings. It was also intended to establish a loving and devoted relationship to the Buddha, since his followers missed him greatly after mistakenly believing that he had entered extinction and would no longer be accessible to them:

> Yet I have not actually entered nirvana,
> But continually abide here expounding the Dharma.
> Although I am always among these erring beings,
> With my transcendent powers,
> I prevent them from seeing me.
> The sentient beings,
> Seeing me enter perfect extinction
> Earnestly revere my relics
> And, filled with longing,
> Yearn for me.
> When the sentient beings become
> Sincere, mild, and receptive,
> And, wanting wholeheartedly to meet the Buddha,
> Are willing to give unsparingly
> Of their bodies and lives,
> Then I, together with the sangha,
> Will appear on Mount Gṛdhrakūṭa.
> I will declare this to sentient beings:
> Although I am always here without extinction,

---
[70] See Schmidt-Leukel 2006a, 105–14.

Through the power of skillful means
I manifest extinction and nonextinction.[71]

The message of the *Lotus-Sūtra* is that the Buddha is essentially a supernatural reality beyond all time. Even though it still speaks of his awakening as taking place in an unimaginable past, it in fact presents the Buddha as a reality removed from time; at least this is the dominant line in the Chinese Buddhist reading of the text.[72] Thus, ultimate reality has personal traits not only in the earthly Buddha but already in the supramundane Buddha. The *Lotus-Sūtra* refers to him as "the father of the world."[73] Whenever necessary, he takes a human form to guide people onto the right path. With these ideas, the *Lotus-Sūtra* takes a similar position to the more or less contemporaneous Hindu *Bhagavad Gītā*. This also sees the divine as a reality removed from time that nevertheless becomes incarnate whenever the dharma falls into disrepair, and also names this reality "father of the world."[74]

A further development is represented by the Mahayanist doctrine of the "Three Buddha Bodies" (*trikāya*), according to which it is possible to distinguish between three "bodies" or three forms of reality of the Buddha. First, there are the numerous Buddhas who appear in a mutable "transformation body" (*nirmāṇakāya*), i.e., in human form. Second, there are supramundane Buddhas that manifest or incarnate in the human Buddhas. The supramundane Buddhas represent the actual Buddhas, i.e., the highest form of perfection that a sentient being on the path to Buddhahood (in other words, a bodhisattva) can attain. Their form of reality is therefore called the "enjoyment body" (*saṃbhogakāya*): the bodhisattva "enjoys," so to speak, what he has striven for. But there is a third form of reality: "dharma body" (*dharmakāya*), which originally referred above all to the qualities that make up a Buddha, his spiritual "embodiment" of the dharma. Gradually, however, the term *dharmakāya* came to refer to the supreme, ineffable reality embodied in the Buddhas, whether earthly or supramundane. Mahayana Buddhism expressed this by referring to the transformation body and the enjoyment body both as "form bodies," while the dharma body was deemed "formless," meaning here that this reality transcends any conceptual or comprehensible form. Hence, it is the negative or apophatic reference to ultimate reality, which is accessible to us only in the form of

---

[71] Kubo & Yuyama 2007, 228. (For the German version, see von Borsig 1992, 287–88). Kubo & Yuyama's translation (as well as von Borsig's) follows Kumārajīva's classical Chinese translation of the *Lotus-Sūtra* here. For an English translation of the Sanskrit text of the equivalent passage, see Kern 1884, 307–8. The corresponding fifteenth chapter of the Sanskrit text appears in the Chinese translations as chapter sixteen.

[72] Williams, P. 2009, 157–58.

[73] *Saddharmapuṇḍarīka-Sūtra* 15.21 (Kern 1884, 309); see also Kubo & Yuyama 2007, 230.

[74] *Bhagavad Gītā* 9.17; 11.43. For other obvious parallels between the *Lotus-Sūtra* and the *Gītā*, see Kern, H. 1884, xxv–xxxi.

the supramundane Buddhas and their earthly manifestations.

The doctrine of the "Three Buddha Bodies" thus contains another strongly personal representation of ultimate reality, one that is nonetheless closely linked to an impersonal, apophatic element: the dharma body. In religious practice, the earthly and supramundane Buddhas are the object of intense devotion, ritual veneration, and pictorial meditation, along with some highly developed bodhisattvas, who are also considered supramundane beings and are often in no way less important than the Buddhas. What is especially revered and praised in all these figures is the wisdom and compassion that they embody. In other words, ultimate reality, which in itself is ineffable and inconceivable, reveals itself to us in the form of earthly and divine figures who are full of wisdom and compassion, such as the bodhisattva Avalokiteshvara and the supramundane Buddha Amitabha (= infinite light; also known as Amitayus = infinite life). Avalokiteshvara is thought to embody universal compassion in a very special way. The *Lotus-Sūtra* already presents him as a helper and refuge for all emergencies and needs. An Indian Buddhist text from the fourth or fifth century CE even depicts him as the very origin of the cosmos.[75] In China, this bodhisattva attained great popularity in his female form as Guanyin (Japanese: Kannon or Kwanon). This is no less true for Buddha Amitabha (Chinese: Amituo, Japanese: Amida), who prepared out of his all-encompassing compassion a path for all people without exception to achieve liberation simply by entrusting themselves to him. According to the Chinese scholar Tan-luan (fifth–sixth century), we can see in Buddha Amituo that from the ineffable ultimate reality of the dharma body a power emerges that strives for our salvation. By means of figures such as Guanyin and Amida and the respective narratives, Buddhism brought a particularly strong personal trait to the religious world of China—quite contrary to the popular Western assumption that Buddhism is primarily or even exclusively linked to impersonal concepts of transcendence. Writing in medieval Japan, Shinran, who regarded Shakyamuni (i.e., Gautama Buddha) as an incarnation of Amida,[76] could speak of both as "our father and our mother, full of love and compassion for us."[77] In one of his letters, Shinran writes that Shakyamuni "rejoices in people of *shinjin* [trust in Amida]" and considers them his "true companions."[78] But despite such an intensely personal way of speaking, the awareness persists that ultimate reality is actually beyond anything imaginable or conceivable.

---

[75] *Kāraṇḍavyūha Sūtra*, ch. 4. See Studholme 2002, 37–59, 123–24. According to Studholme, the older version of the text presents Avalokiteshvara (in imitation of the Vedic *puruṣa* myth) merely as the creator of the gods and not of the material order (see ibid., 44). But neither in the *Ṛg-Veda* nor in the *Kāraṇḍavyūha-Sūtra* are the gods mentioned distinct from the "material" realities associated with them (e.g., sun, moon, wind, earth, sky), as if they merely bore their names.
[76] Hirota 1997, 349.
[77] Ibid., 380.
[78] Ibid., 526.

As for our question concerning personal and impersonal notions of transcendence in Buddhism, there are two further developments in Mahayana Buddhism that are particularly important: the idea of the universal Buddha nature and the idea of the indistinguishability of nirvana and samsara. Connected to the bodhisattva ideal[79] in Mahayana Buddhism is the notion that every being in the cycle of rebirth carries within them the potential, called the "Buddha germ" or "Buddha embryo" (*tathāgatagarbha*), to become a Buddha one day. This potential is the hidden Buddha nature that every sentient being carries within. The idea is presumably rooted among other things in the canonical doctrine that the human mind is actually luminous and pure by nature.[80] The evils of greed, hate, and delusion are therefore only "defilements" of the mind, and do not correspond to its true nature. In a later stage of its development, Mahayana Buddhism identified this true nature of the mind with the Buddha nature on the one hand, and with the dharma body, i.e., a Buddha's highest form of reality, on the other. But this means nothing else than that every being in samsara participates in ultimate reality through the actual essence of their mind—a doctrine that is strongly reminiscent of the Brahman-Atman doctrine of the Hindu Upanishads, which stresses the inseparable unity between the essence of the self (*ātman*) and the essence of the world (*brahman*).

The idea that the dharma body is also the hidden nature of all reality gave rise to the belief that not only the mind possesses Buddha nature, but all reality. Although originating in India, this idea became particularly influential in Chinese Buddhism, which was also undoubtedly fostered by Daoist influence, since the Dao is also considered a transcendent reality that is simultaneously deeply immanent in everything that exists. David Eckel has aptly summarized the result of this process: "'Nature' in the Indian tradition was a world to be transcended, while in East Asia it took on the capacity to symbolize transcendence itself."[81] But, as a symbol of transcendence, nature encompasses both impersonal and personal phenomena, both the beauty of untouched nature and the beauty of human beings living in harmony with nature—a motif that recurs both in Daoist art and the Buddhist art that it influences.

As already mentioned briefly, the influential Buddhist philosopher Nagarjuna taught that all conceptual distinctions miss the true essence of reality. A concept superimposes on a phenomenon an essence, an "intrinsic nature," as well as certain properties and relations. But, for Nagarjuna, a closer analysis shows that everything is "empty" (*śūnya*), i.e., empty of a

---

[79] See above, pp. 63–64.
[80] Harvey 1995, 166–76, 213–14, 250–51.
[81] Eckel 1997, 339.

conceptually definable essence and further determinants belonging to it. Therefore, he argues, the distinction between nirvana and samsara is also only valid provisionally; it does not hold from the standpoint of supreme truth. Interpreting this indistinguishability of nirvana and samsara is still the subject of much debate both within and outside Buddhism. Historically, however, it supported the process of viewing the contingent and transient reality of samsara as a manifestation of the supreme reality of nirvana. The reality beyond our conceptually structured perception is what Nagarjuna calls "thatness" or "suchness" (*tattva*) or "supreme reality" (*paramārthasatya*) in contrast to its "worldly veiled" form (*lokasaṃvṛtisatya*). He equates insight into and realization of supreme reality with the attainment of nirvana.

As Mahayana Buddhism developed further, the emptiness (*śūnyatā*) of all things of a conceptually tangible independent nature, the suchness of reality, became identified with the dharma body and the Buddha nature, which in turn is manifested both in nature and in the Buddhas. A typical example is the Japanese Buddhist Shinran Shonin (1173–1263), who claimed that nirvana has "innumerable names": "extinction of passions, the uncreated, peaceful happiness, eternal bliss, true reality, dharma-body, dharma-nature, suchness, oneness, and Buddha-nature." But, for him, Buddha nature is nothing other than Amida Buddha, who "pervades the countless worlds; it fills the heart and mind of the ocean of all beings. Thus, plants, trees, and land all attain Buddhahood."[82] For Shinran, Amida is the visible form that the inherently formless and indescribable dharma body assumes in order to reveal itself as all-encompassing compassion.[83] Here, too, we can see a dense symbiosis of personal and impersonal notions of transcendence that take into account both the cataphatic and the apophatic.

4.3 PERSONAL AND IMPERSONAL NOTIONS OF TRANSCENDENCE IN CHRISTIANITY

As mentioned in the previous chapter, Christianity emerged as an apocalyptic Jewish sect, and its notions of transcendence are therefore shaped by its Jewish roots. Originally, Israel also assumed the existence of numerous deities, but several gods—in particular Baal, El, and YHWH ("Yahweh")—then merged in the course of time into a single figure: Yahweh, who absorbed features of other deities ("Isra-El" still preserves the name "El"). Faced with widespread and longstanding polytheism, some followers of Yahweh demanded that only he be worshipped. They argued that Yahweh had made a

---

[82]Hirota 1997, 461. Shinran talks here of the *tathāgata*, but refers by this title to Buddha Amida.
[83]Ibid.

covenant with his people, and that, as long as they kept the commandments associated with the covenant and did not worship any other gods besides him, Yahweh would remain faithful to his people, protect them, and guide them through the course of time. It was only since the period of the Babylonian exile (sixth century BCE) that the Jewish image of God gradually became monotheistic: the God of Israel is now increasingly seen as actually the one and only true God, the creator of the world who controls the fate of all peoples and whom all people will at some future time recognize and worship as the one and only true God.[84]

The Hellenization of the Jewish world made Platonic philosophy an influential source for the further development of the idea of God as the ultimate and sole source of reality.[85] This applies to both Judaism and Christianity, and later to Islam. As far as Christianity is concerned, it was above all Neoplatonism that helped shape from about the fourth century onward how its key doctrines developed. Christian practice and religious life certainly continued to be dominated by a personal image of God, which may have been due in particular to the fact that Jesus himself addressed God as "Father"—or, as it says in the Gospel of John, as "my father and your father" (John 20:17). A central feature of Jesus' message was that God's attitude toward human beings is like that of a merciful father in whom we can confide, and whose love and kindness we should reflect in how we behave toward our fellow human beings.

Influenced by Platonism, nascent Christian theology supplemented and modified this personal image of God. The idea of a trinitarian God, consisting of Father, Son/Logos, and Holy Spirit, developed from the end of the second century, but especially in the third and fourth centuries, Jesus now being seen increasingly as the incarnation of the eternal Word or *logos* of God, and in this sense as God's eternal "Son." At the same time, Jesus was understood as someone who was filled with the divine "Spirit," which had inspired the prophets and breathed life into the divine creation. Under Neoplatonic influence, the divine *logos* was interpreted in terms of the Platonic *nous* (Greek for "mind"/"intellect"), i.e., as the eternal truth of divine ideas, while the divine Spirit was equated with the Neoplatonic *psyche* (Greek for "soul"), i.e., with the life-giving power that emanates from *logos*/*nous* and permeates the whole creation.

Above all, however, Neoplatonism reinforced the apophatic tendencies of the developing Christian theology. In the Neoplatonic philosophy of Plotinus (205–270), *hen* (the "One") stood above *psyche* and *nous* as the

---

[84]On the development of the notions of gods and God in ancient Israel, see Römer 2018. For a concise summary, see Bauks 2011.
[85]See Kelly 1977, 3–28.

origin of both. Being beyond all diversity and forms of thought, the One is inconceivable and ineffable. Christian theology identified it with the divine origin ("Father"), whose essential nature was now equally designated as transcending all concepts and words. After that, an impersonal, i.e., apophatic, notion of transcendence became the norm in many strands of classical and medieval Christian theology—and by no means, as is sometimes claimed, only in its mystical peripheries: God's essence could only be accurately named through the negation of all conceptual (cataphatic) attributions, be they personal or impersonal. A God who can be conceived is not God, says Augustine (354–430).[86] According to Thomas Aquinas (1225–1274), the highest knowledge of God consists in recognizing that God necessarily transcends all knowledge.[87] And contemporary theologians, especially Karl Rahner (1904–1984), have spoken of God as the "absolute" or "holy mystery" ("das heilige Geheimnis"), a reality that essentially eludes any conceptual classification and to which the word "God" refers only in that it ultimately cancels itself out.[88]

However, such judgments do not owe themselves to Platonic influence alone. Platonic ideas could probably gain such a strong influence precisely because they fell on fertile ground. In the Hebrew Bible, the prohibition against making a cult image (a "carved image" that one "serves")—the second of the "Ten Commandments" (Exodus 20:4)—is closely related to the first commandment, which is not to worship any other gods besides Yahweh. Although the latter was perhaps initially about not worshipping the images of other gods besides the cult image of Yahweh, it finally became a general prohibition of cult images in the course of the developing monotheism[89]—in other words, the prohibition against worshipping any kind of human-made image and thus elevating it to a divine rank. The Septuagint, the Greek translation of the Hebrew Bible that emerged from the third century BCE, uses the term *eidolon* ("image") with the connotation of "mirage" or "phantom."[90] Everything that is depictable, everything that has form, cannot correspond to the One who is the origin of everything. In early rabbinic Judaism, the decisive criterion for the admission or prohibition of images of any kind was whether they were intended as objects of cultic worship that would thereby take the place of the undepictable God.[91] For the Platonically influenced Jewish scholar Philo of Alexandria (first century CE),

---

[86]"Si enim comprehendis, non est Deus." Augustinus, *Sermo* 117 (3.5). See above, p. 40.
[87]Thomas Aquinas, *De potentia*, q. 7, a. 5.
[88]E.g., Rahner 1977, 54–61, 67–75, 82, 125–26, 137, and elsewhere. For the English translation: Rahner 1978, 44–51, 57–66, 74, 119–20, 131, etc.
[89]See Römer 2018, 157–76, 260–61.
[90]See Doering 2020, 21–23.
[91]Ibid., 47.

God is "pure being" and without any determinable quality (*ápoios*).[92] The Greek tradition of thinking the origin of all reality as a One on the one hand, and as what exceeds all individual definitions of manifold reality on the other, could be combined well with the tendency within Judaism toward monotheism and the prohibition of worshipping created things as images of God or as God.

In the New Testament, the idea that God cannot be depicted is adopted in a paradoxical way. Jesus is described in 2 Corinthians 4:4 and Colossians 1:15 as the "image" (*eikōn*) of God, but in the letter to the Colossians as image of the "invisible"—and thus truly undepictable—God. This paradox is presumably mediated by the biblical idea that God created the human being in his "image" (*eikōn* in the Septuagint) (Genesis 1:26–27). Since the New Testament often understands Jesus as the "new Adam," i.e., as the human being who is as God originally intended him to be, Jesus conforms to this creaturely image far better than the first Adam.

However, this understanding of human beings and in particular Jesus as the image of God does not annul the indescribability of God. Hence, it is no surprise that, besides all the personal and even anthropomorphic ways of speaking of Jesus as the "Son" of God, and of God as the "Father of Jesus Christ" in Christianity, there is also an unbroken tradition that rejects such anthropomorphisms. Impersonal images, metaphors, and concepts can have a double function here. On the one hand, there are images that remain tied to the primary and personal way of speaking—for example, when, as is often the case in the Hebrew Bible, God is spoken of as a "rock" to indicate his constancy and reliability,[93] or as a "fortress" (Psalms 18:2; 31:3), which expresses the trustworthiness of God as a safe refuge and was popularized by Martin Luther's paraphrase of God as "a mighty fortress" ("ein feste Burg"). Even if such metaphors are reminiscent of the Buddhist image of nirvana as "firm ground" and "safe city," the personal connotation is unmistakable in biblical usage. On the other hand, however, there are also images in which the personal connection is weaker or that even lead away from this connection—for example, in the case of the luminosity of God (Psalms 104:2, Isaiah 60:19–20), before which darkness cannot endure (Psalms 139:12; Daniel 2:22). This luminosity can be an expression of hope in God (Isaiah 9:1),[94] but it can also refer to God's invisibility or unknowability, as in the First Letter to Timothy (6:16), where it is said of God that he "dwells in unapproachable light" and that "no one has ever seen or can see" him. When it is said in the New Testament that "God is love" (1 John 4:16), this statement also oscil-

---

[92]Kelly 1977, 9.
[93]See Steinberg 2010.
[94]See Wilke 2016.

lates between a personal reading, according to which God loves or "has" love, and an impersonal reading, according to which God is recognized or experienced in love itself (both in the same verse). Here, too, God's being love is connected with a reference to the invisibility of God (1 John 4:12). In addition, the statement "whoever abides in love abides in God, and God abides in him" (1 John 4:16) draws on a spatial metaphor. According to Psalm 139, God is a reality that surrounds and permeates us, and remains incomprehensible to us. And Acts 17:28 says of God that in "him we live and move and have our being." Such spatial metaphors continue to have an impact in contemporary theology especially in speaking of God as the ultimate horizon of all being and thinking that cannot be transcended any further—a parlance that Karl Rahner in particular liked to use.[95] Paul Tillich (1886–1965) speaks of God as the depth of all being, which is also a spatial metaphor.[96] Tillich thus continues the tradition of speaking of God as the ground of being or, as in the case of Meister Eckhart, of a "ground of God" ("Gottesgrund") that lies beyond the idea of a personal God. Tillich, too, is concerned with overcoming the "God of theism." For Tillich, this means not only the personal and anthropomorphic conceptions of God; rather, he is concerned with thinking of God not as part of a larger overall reality, i.e., not as a supreme being beside and among other beings. Instead, for Tillich, such a dualistic conception should be abandoned. The God beyond theism, the "God above God," transcends for him every form of descriptiveness, including that of mysticism.[97]

Tillich's concern is not as modern as it may seem. Both the theology of the first millennium and the theology of the Middle Ages were often concerned with thinking of God not as one being among others, but as "being itself" (*ipsum esse*) or "being as such" (*esse tantum*). As already stated, Thomas Aquinas held that the word "God" refers to a reality that strictly speaking transcends all concepts and all positive naming. Hence, according to Thomas, ultimately we can speak about God only by negations, but can also speak in analogies, provided that we remain aware of the insufficient character of such an analogical way of speaking. In philosophical terms, the best analogous way of speaking is for Thomas speaking of God as "being as such." Everything that *is* has its existence through this being. According to Thomas, this implies that the divine reality on the one hand transcends every concrete being (and thus is not *a* being), and on the other hand is deeply immanent in every being as the ultimate source of its reality.[98]

These few examples may suffice to show that the use of impersonal lan-

---

[95]E.g., Rahner 1977, 70–73 = 1978, 61–65.
[96]Tillich 1987, 55.
[97]Tillich 2015, 124–29.
[98]Thomas Aquinas, *Summa theologiae* I, q. 8, 1, ad 1.

guage with regard to ultimate reality is no less familiar to Christianity than to Buddhism. This is especially true of the impersonal way of speaking in an apophatic sense. But as has been shown, at the cataphatic level, we find in Christianity, despite the dominance of the personal mode of expression, also several significant images and concepts of an impersonal or abstract nature. This is confirmed not only by the history of theology. According to recent surveys, significantly more people in Germany believe in the existence of an impersonal divine reality or power than in a personal God.[99] At the same time, the "Religionsmonitor 2008," a global empirical survey, found that 37 percent of people in Buddhist Thailand testify to religious experiences with a personal "You," and 89 percent show a pattern of theistic spirituality overall.[100] Such findings also highlight the fact that the supposedly essential and characteristic differences *between* religious traditions are no less manifest *within* them.

Let us now turn to the question of how far the difference between personal and impersonal ideas of transcendence may be understood as being complementary.

4.4 SPEAKING OF THE INEFFABLE

Image and Experience

Personal and impersonal notions of ultimate reality can be regarded as incompatible, which would mean that either only one or none of them is true. The latter is the position of atheist or naturalist criticism of religion, which argues that, since there is no reality that transcends the contingencies of spatiotemporal reality, no conception of such reality can hold true. The position that only one notion is true radically limits the possible compatibility of personal and impersonal language. In this case, personal language, say, can be interpreted as provisional or poetic articulations of a strictly impersonal reality, or vice versa.[101] However, there are two other alternatives. The first consists in interpreting ultimate reality as an intrinsically complex reality whose essence includes both personal and impersonal aspects. Yet this solution would exclude or at least radically marginalize the apophatic option. It could for instance be argued that what eludes our comprehension and thus our means of expression is only the more precise understanding of how the different aspects of ultimate reality are arranged. Yet in its essential features, ultimate reality would nonetheless be discernible and intelligible. This

---

[99]Pollack & Rosta 2015, 133–37.
[100]Bertelsmann Stiftung 2007, 236.
[101]See on this also Wildman 2017, 17–18.

alternative is pursued above all in the process theology of John Cobb and David Griffin, but also by scholars such as Mark Heim and John Thatamanil (as has already been discussed in more detail in chapter 2).[102] In contrast, the second alternative begins with the apophatic option. Unlike atheism, it does not deny the existence of an ultimate reality, but it does refrain from relating personal and impersonal notions directly to ultimate reality itself, arguing instead that these notions reflect different human impressions and experiences of a reality that is by its nature incomprehensible and ineffable. This alternative is represented above all in more recent discussions by the approach of John Hick. In order to understand his often misunderstood and distorted approach better, it will help to first revisit the distinction between cataphaticism and apophaticism with regard to the implications of each for interreligious comparison and interreligious theology.

While the apophatic position does not posit its own specific notion of ultimate reality, it nevertheless underlines the special character of ultimate reality by negating its categorial determinability.[103] In this respect, it would be to misunderstand the apophatic concern if we regarded negation as a mere addition to a certain form of cataphatic language that would itself suffice to determine the nature of ultimate reality. It is correct that apophaticism needs, so to say, a cataphatic substructure, i.e., a linguistic and conceptual agreement regarding the kind of reality which is claimed to be transcategorial and about the reasons for such a claim. However, the apophatic proviso also relativizes its respective cataphatic starting point, which cannot be seen as being valid in an all-encompassing and exclusive way, since that would make the apophatic negation completely superfluous and indeed nonsensical.[104] The apophatic option therefore includes the possibility that different cataphatic starting points, despite their diversity, nevertheless point to the same ultimate reality. In other words, the apophatic option forbids concluding compellingly from the diversity of the cataphatic starting points alone that these do not refer indirectly to the same ultimate reality.

This argument pertains, for example, to the comparison made by C. D. Sebastian between the apophaticism of Nagarjuna and John of the Cross. Despite being very similar in their apophatic criticism, says Sebastian, "both thinkers speak of different things": while John of the Cross refers to the ineffability of God, Nagarjuna deals with the nonsubstantiality of all things and their merely conventional construction.[105] "Nāgārjuna is a Buddhist Mādhyamika and God *means nothing* for his philosophical-religious scheme. John of the Cross is a theistic Christian and God *means everything*

---
[102]See above, pp. 34–38.
[103]Thus rightly also Wildman 2017, 41, 79.
[104]See on this also Schmidt-Leukel 217a, 204–8 (= 2005, 228–33).
[105]Sebastian 2016, 110.

for him."[106] We could also of course state just as easily that nirvana means nothing for John of the Cross, while it means everything for Nagarjuna, who after all makes it explicitly clear that his apophatic criticism serves the attainment of nirvana.[107] While Nagarjuna does in fact conduct a comprehensive critique of language in order to prove the aporetic and provisional nature of all conceptual representations of reality, it is precisely within this that he also anchors the ineffability of nirvana. Is it not the case, then, that "nirvana" and "God" can be regarded as conceptually and terminologically different starting points that from within different religious contexts each point to the same ineffable reality? Contrary to Sebastian's opinion, the different starting points by no means necessitate that we answer this question in the negative—and this precisely due to the apophaticism of Nagarjuna and John of the Cross.

The apophatic option, however, makes an affirmative answer merely possible, but not obligatory. Answering affirmatively will depend on further criteria, these having to do above all with how far the cataphatic ideas are connected with an existential behavior that would in fact be classified in the two religions as salvific. But answering affirmatively remains hypothetical even then. Accepting this hypothesis would require defining more precisely the relationship between the different cataphatic starting points on the one hand, and the unimaginable ultimate reality on the other. In pursuing this task, we can then investigate whether the different cataphatic notions might complement each other. This is precisely what John Hick does.

Hick distinguishes between ultimate reality in itself ("the Real *an sich*")—i.e., ultimate reality in its suchness that transcends all human categories—and "the Real as humanly experienced and thought of." Being limited and multiply conditioned (biologically, historically, culturally, psychologically, etc.), our cognitive capacities cannot adequately grasp and articulate the unlimited nature of ultimate reality, meaning that it is in its essence ("*an sich*") "transcategorial" and "ineffable." The images, stories, and notions about ultimate reality that we find in the world of religions are thus to be interpreted not as descriptions of the essence of ultimate reality. Rather, they reflect different forms or modes in which people have experienced and thus thought of the presence of this reality. According to Hick's hypothesis, people authentically experience the one ultimate reality, but this experience always occurs in accordance with the human capacities and limitations of experience. It is, so to speak, a matter of limited experiential impressions of an unlimited reality.

---

[106]Ibid., 108, emphasis in the original. Similarly, ibid., 6–7.
[107]See *Mūlamadhyamakakārikā* 24:9. Although Sebastian (2016, 30) points through a quotation from Paul Numrich to nirvana as the starting point of Nagarjuna's language criticism, this remains inconsequential for his interpretation of Nagarjuna and even more so for the comparison with John of the Cross. This is probably also due to his closeness to the positions of Siderits and Garfield.

Ultimate Reality   109

The "*an sich*" in Hick's phrase "the Real *an sich*" refers to the transcategorial essence of ultimate reality as it exceeds human cognitive and experiential capacities. But it does not mean that ultimate reality cannot be experienced at all. To explain his distinction between "the Real *an sich*" and "the Real as humanly experienced and thought of," Hick draws, as an analogy, on Immanuel Kant's distinction between *noumenon* and *phenomenon*, i.e., between things as they are "*an sich*," beyond our cognitive capacities, and things as we actually perceive them. Hick uses this analogy to argue that "the noumenal world exists independently of our perception of it and the phenomenal world is that same world as it appears to our human consciousness."[108] At the same time, Hick emphasizes that he is using this distinction only analogically, since Kant himself does not apply it to the experience of God, which Kant denies is possible.[109] However, this is exactly the form that many misunderstandings of Hick's work take, as if Hick wanted to use Kantian epistemology to justify the claim that ultimate reality is unknowable and beyond experience. The opposite is in fact the case. Hick wants to show that, despite the conviction widespread in all great religious traditions that ultimate reality is incomprehensible and ineffable, genuine, though limited, experiences of ultimate reality are nonetheless still conceivable. At the same time, he wants to grant the positive statements about ultimate reality their proper status and thus their validity by relating them not directly to ultimate reality (to "the Real *an sich*"), but to the different human experiences of ultimate reality. He draws on Kant not to substantiate apophaticism, but rather, faced with the strong apophatic tradition in all great religions, to make sense of cataphaticism.[110]

According to Hick, this cataphatic realm, i.e., ultimate reality as we experience and think of it, is divided into two large worlds of forms: personal and impersonal. Hick denotes the various personal gods or personal notions of God and the various impersonal absolutes as "*personae*" and "*impersonae*" of ultimate reality. These *personae* and *impersonae* condense, make concrete, and hand down countless experiences and ideas concerning ultimate reality in the form of collective memory. They constitute a direct point of reference for all concrete and positive language about ultimate reality, while at the same time being subject to historical change. Were all

---

[108] Hick 1989, 241.

[109] See ibid., 242.

[110] See also Schmidt-Leukel 2022a. In the new and detailed introduction to the second edition of *An Interpretation of Religion* (Hick 2004, xvii–xlii), Hick distinguishes his understanding of transcategoriality from a "negative (apophatic) . . . doctrine" (ibid., xx). For him, "transcategoriality" excludes both the negative and positive attribution of properties, which, says Hick, is exactly what has been taught by almost all great thinkers in the various religions (ibid.). But precisely this doctrine that ultimate reality transcends all categories corresponds to the traditional understanding of radical apophaticism, which is not reduced solely to the negation of certain properties within a particular category. See also the positive reception of the apophatic tradition in Hick 1999, 79–90.

these statements about ultimate reality related directly to this reality itself, then they would inevitably contradict each other. However, since they relate to different manifestations of human experience of ultimate reality, they must not necessarily be seen as contradictory.[111]

Yet Hick goes even further, also claiming that personal and impersonal parlances are in principle complementary, this complementarity being mediated by different modes of experience:

> The relation between these two very different ways of conceiving and experiencing the Real, as personal and as non-personal, is perhaps a complementarity analogous . . . to that between the two ways of conceiving and registering light, namely as waves and particles. That is to say, the purely physical structure of light is not directly observable; but under different sets of experimental conditions it is found to have wave-like and particle-like properties respectively. If we act upon it in one way it appears to behave like a shower of particles, and if in another way, like a succession of waves. The reality itself is such that it is able to be validly conceived and observed in both of these ways. Analogously the divine Reality is not directly known *an sich*. But when human beings relate themselves to it in the mode of I-Thou encounter they experience it as personal. Indeed in the context of that relationship it is personal, not It but He or She. When human beings relate themselves to the Real in the mode of non-personal awareness they experience it as non-personal, and in the context of this relationship it is non-personal.[112]

As Hick makes clear elsewhere, he is speaking here of prayer and meditation as two fundamental ways of relating to ultimate reality.[113] Each corresponds to a personal or impersonal notion of ultimate reality, while in turn also evoking such notions. Prayer and meditation are of course embedded in broader religious structures that ground such forms of spiritual practice and lend them concrete meaning. As I have already argued, I believe that they are concerned not with the experience and corresponding understanding of ultimate reality in isolation, but with the experience of human existence in the light of transcendence.[114] Human existence has different facets, including fundamentally the experience of its transience as well as the experience of interpersonal relatedness. Some impersonal notions of transcendence, such as of nirvana as the "deathless," point to the fact that the experience

---

[111] See Hick 1995, 43.
[112] Hick 1989, 245.
[113] Hick 1999, 41.
[114] See above, pp. 42–43, 76–78.

of transience is dominant in the understanding of the human predicament and the specific promise of salvation. On the other hand, personal notions of transcendence, such as that of a merciful Father, point to the fact that the experience of interpersonal relatedness is dominant. Since life can never be viewed from only one dimension of experience, it is not surprising that Buddhism and Christianity contain both types of notions of transcendence. Thus, many Buddhists refer to ultimate reality in a personal mode, and seek refuge with the compassion of supramundane bodhisattvas and Buddhas in prayer and worship, while quite a few Christians relate to ultimate reality in a contemplative mode by immersing themselves in being itself or in the ground of being as that which is beyond all transience.

Wesley Wildman has suggested seeing the apophatic proviso primarily as an antipole to personal, i.e., anthropomorphic, ideas of transcendence, arguing that the further we move away from anthropomorphic notions of God, the more we follow the apophatic impulse. For Wildman, impersonal notions of transcendence are therefore altogether more accurate than personal ones.[115] Since at the cataphatic level he thus favors impersonal notions, the apophatic impulse becomes imbalanced. For Hick, on the other hand, personal and impersonal manifestations of experiencing transcendence are in principle equally valid and both fall equally under the apophatic proviso. Neither form is inherently superior to the other, since the transcategoriality of ultimate reality transcends personal and impersonal categories in the same way. For Hick, assessing their cataphatic or relative validity must be derived from their effects in existential practice.[116] However, Hick is well aware that some impersonal concepts serve both a cataphatic and an apophatic function. As examples, he cites the notion of divine Brahman in Advaita Vedanta and the notion of emptiness in Mahayana Buddhism. The "Brahman with qualities" (*saguṇa brahman*), for example, as "existence-consciousness-bliss" (*satcitānanda*), corresponds to an impersonal representation and therefore falls under the *impersonae* of ultimate reality. As "Brahman without qualities" (*nirguṇa brahman*), however, Brahman refers to the ineffability of ultimate reality and therefore corresponds to what Hick himself calls "the Real *an sich*."[117] Something similar applies, according to Hick, to the notion of emptiness. "Emptiness" is also partly used as an impersonal cataphatic representation of ultimate reality, for instance when it refers to a new form of experiencing the world freed from all egocentrism. But, according to Hick, "emptiness" can and does also refer to the fact that reality cannot be comprehended and expressed in any form.[118]

---

[115] See Wildman 2017, 75–81.
[116] See Hick 189, 299–342.
[117] Ibid., 282–83.
[118] Ibid., 287–92.

But will this not imply that ultimately the impersonal way of speaking about transcendence is at an advantage over the personal, since the former, unlike the latter, also points beyond the cataphatic level to the ineffability of ultimate reality? According to Lynn de Silva (1919–1982), a Sri Lankan Methodist who was an important pioneer of Buddhist-Christian dialogue,[119] the two ways of speaking are complementary in this respect, too. In an essay published posthumously, de Silva assigns personal and impersonal ways of speaking to different aspects[120] of the experience of transcendence: "The personal . . . *evokes* a sense of intimacy and the impersonal evokes a sense of ultimacy."[121] For de Silva, the latter indeed reinforces the sense of the intrinsic ineffability of ultimate reality. Using the Buddhist notion of "the Unborn" for ultimate reality, de Silva writes, "The impersonal points to the ultimacy of the Unborn which cannot be defined."[122] The personal way of speaking, on the other hand, refers to the intimacy or closeness that is experienced with regard to ultimate reality, and it is here that the specificity and strength of the personal way of speaking lie. According to de Silva, the two aspects of ultimacy and intimacy coincide and intertwine: in the experience of ultimate reality, loving intimacy draws us ever deeper into the divine mystery, while conversely, the experience of ultimate mysteriousness drives personal representation: "The personification of the ultimate is unavoidable; man is driven to it by a psychological necessity."[123] The image of the Buddha "evokes in the worshipper a deep sense of intimacy with the Transcendent."[124] Thus, according to de Silva, both aspects are necessary and balance each other: "Ultimacy gives depth to intimacy and intimacy gives vitality to ultimacy."[125]

While for de Silva it is the case that impersonal ways of speaking about ultimate reality dominate in Buddhism, and personal ways in Christianity, both forms are present in both traditions, which he explains by pointing to the necessary coincidence and complementarity of the different aspects of experience that correspond to these ways of speaking. And because, according to de Silva, this intrareligious diversity of notions of transcendence is rooted in religious experience itself, it is also evident at the micro level of the individual religious person: "Ultimacy and intimacy are coincidental aspects in the religious life of everyone."[126] A good example of this from the perspective of a lived Christian and Buddhist spirituality is provided by the

---

[119] See Harris & Schmidt-Leukel 2021.
[120] De Silva 1982, 49.
[121] Ibid., 50.
[122] Ibid., 49.
[123] Ibid.
[124] Ibid., 53.
[125] Ibid., 51.
[126] Ibid., 53.

autobiographical comments of Paul Knitter,[127] who says that the personal way of speaking about God is justified since it mediates ultimate reality to us as something "trustworthy,"[128] while Buddhism strengthens him in the conviction that " 'mystery' always holds priority over words."[129]

De Silva saw support for his reflections not least in the works of the two Western Buddhists Marco Pallis (1895–1989) and Maurice O'Connell Walshe (1911–1998). For example, he takes over from Walshe in particular the underlying scheme, reminiscent of Hick, that distinguishes between the one transcendent reality ("the Unborn") and its two complementary representations in impersonal and personal language.[130] Walshe himself invokes here among other things the mystical traditions of Christianity with which he was extremely familiar, since he was a professor of Middle High German and a recognized specialist in the work of Meister Eckhart. He was also vice president of the Buddhist Society of the United Kingdom and known in particular for his English translation of the *Dīgha Nikāya*.[131]

As we have seen, Hick's and de Silva's attempts to think of personal and impersonal notions of ultimate reality as complementary are based on the distinction between the transcategoriality and ineffability of ultimate reality on the one hand, and the different forms and aspects of the human experience of transcendence on the other. Their approaches differ fundamentally from the attempts already mentioned to relate impersonal and personal notions to objective impersonal and personal properties of an intrinsically complex ultimate reality.[132] Whereas such approaches assume a strong correspondence between human notions and ultimate reality, Hick and de Silva emphasize an inevitable noncorrespondence. Any complementarity of personal and impersonal notions can only relate to the subjective side, the experiential dimension. How far the correlation between specific cataphatic notions of transcendence and respective forms and aspects of the human experience of transcendence, as proposed by Hick and de Silva, can be substantiated still requires more in-depth research. In this respect, not only psychological studies of religion, but also transcendental philosophical reflections such as those of Bernhard Nitsche[133] and Fabian Völker,[134] are likely to be relevant. In addition, studies in cognitive science and neurophysiology could provide further insights, the latter possibly demonstrating a link between certain forms of contemplative practice and personal as well as impersonal

---

[127]Knitter 2009.
[128]Ibid., 43.
[129]Ibid., 59.
[130]See Walshe 1982, 5–6.
[131]https://obo.genaud.net/backmatter/gallery/walshe.htm (October 2023).
[132]See above, pp. 106–07.
[133]See above, pp. 38–40.
[134]See Völker 2016; 2018a; 2018b; 2019; 2020.

notions at the cataphatic level. Meditative experiences of an objectless, pure awareness could be intrinsically related to the apophatic option.[135] All this could explain the spread of both personal and impersonal ideas within the different major religious traditions.

There are also undoubtedly philosophical or, in a broader sense, "theological" reasons that in each individual case tip the scales in favor of one particular notion. Nishitani, for example, has put forward the notable argument that it is precisely the idea of the perfection of God's love that necessarily gives the notion of his personhood an impersonal aspect, since perfect love is indifferent—not in the sense of a cold indifference, but in that it faces everyone in the same way and does not arbitrarily select according to its own interests. The law-like regularity of this divine "indifference of love" gives it an impersonal trait.[136] Not infrequently, however, the problem of theodicy that emerges precisely because of such love is put forward as an argument for an impersonal rather than a personal notion of transcendence.[137] As is well known, the Jewish theologian Richard Rubenstein, faced with the Holocaust, rejected the belief in a personal God who guides the fate of his people and of all peoples, and instead approached the notion borrowed from Jewish mysticism of God as *En Sof*, the indeterminable and impersonal source of being—a "holy nothingness" that Rubenstein parallels with Buddhist emptiness.[138] The connection between a personal notion of ultimate reality and the problem of evil and suffering in the world takes us now back to the question of the creative dimension of ultimate reality.

Ultimate Reality as Ground and Goal of the World

As mentioned above, Buddhism experts such as Steven Collins, Peter Harvey, and Christopher Gowans have pointed out that, while nirvana does indeed signify a transcendent reality, it bears the features neither of a divine person nor of a creator. So far, I have shown that ultimate reality has been and still is imagined in personal and impersonal ways in both Buddhism and Christianity. This does not at all mean that nirvana or the dharma body is regarded as a personal God. But both are so closely related to the reality of a Buddha that they also gain a personal representation through and in the figure of the Buddha. I would now like to add some further comments on how far both traditions understand ultimate reality as creative.[139]

---

[135] As has been suggested by Kenneth Rose (2016, 23). For empirical studies of these states of consciousness and the practices leading to them, see Nash, Newberg & Awasthi 2013, 8.
[136] See Nishitani 1983, 57–61, 69–76.
[137] E.g., Wildman 2017, 204, 220–27.
[138] See Rubenstein 1995.
[139] See also my extensive discussion of the subject in Schmidt-Leukel 2006b and in 2017b, 204–21.

According to Steven Collins, the canonical texts of Theravada Buddhism define nirvana exclusively as liberation from samsara, and thus as release from suffering and transience, but not as the origin, ground, or source of the universe, since "there is no ultimate beginning of things in Buddhism."[140] This remark is interesting in three respects. First, it arises from the frequently encountered but by no means self-evident understanding of creation in terms of a temporal beginning of the universe. Second, Collins presupposes here the (presumably) later Buddhist doctrine of a beginningless chain of successive worlds. Third, he seems to assume that the reality that guarantees release from the world has no creative implications. Let us look at these three assumptions a little more closely.

The idea that God created the world at a certain point *within time* is likely to be held by many believers, even though we have no precise data on how widespread this idea actually is. In any case, it does raise some insoluble theological problems: What was God doing before God created the world? Or why did God create the world so late? These questions can always be asked, if one presupposes that creation took place at some point in time, so that always a beginningless, infinitely long time preceded creation. What should God have waited for? In contrast to the idea of a creation *in time*, a standard position widespread in theology at least since Clement of Alexandria (second–third centuries) is that time itself belongs to the world and is therefore also created.[141] Creation thus encompasses the entire world with all its time. It is, strictly speaking, misleading from this perspective to say that God *has* created the world, as if it were an event in the past. Rather, it is true that the world *is* persistently a creation of God.

The doctrine that God created the world *out of nothing* (*creatio ex nihilo*) must therefore, according to Thomas Aquinas, not be understood as if God created the world *after nothing* (*post nihilum*).[142] The idea that time itself is created implies for Thomas that the question whether the world has a divine creator does not depend on whether it has a temporal beginning or not. Even a world without a temporal beginning could still be a divine creation.[143] Moreover, according to Thomas, God is not the efficient cause of the world (*causa efficiens*) in the sense of efficiency as it applies within the world and its chronological sequence, according to which the cause temporally precedes the effect. Rather, according to Thomas, God is "cause" of the world in a metaphysical sense independent of the question of its temporal

---

[140]Collins, S. 1998, 177.

[141]See on this also the information in Pannenberg 1991, 52–56.

[142]See *quaestiones* 44–46 in *Summa theologiae* I.

[143]Drawing on the biblical account of creation, Thomas does indeed assume a temporal beginning of the world, but this has no influence on his basic understanding of creation as a nontemporal relationship of dependence.

116   The Celestial Web

beginning, Thomas obviously understanding metaphysical causation in a primarily teleological sense.[144] That is, the world as a whole exists *because of* God, this "because of" being conceived in the sense of a "wherefore." God is the ultimate and proper goal of the world. As this wherefore of the world, God is the cause of its existence. Thomas is following the philosophy of Aristotle here, which had a decisive influence on his thinking, since God for Aristotle is the "cause" of the world in the sense of the "unmoved mover." As the beloved attracts the lover sometimes without any activity on the part of the beloved, so the eternal God causes by God's sheer existence, without further activity ("unmoved"), the existence ("motion") of the world. The world exists—even if it has no temporal beginning, as Aristotle actually presupposes—because it strives toward God as its true fulfillment. Eternity is the goal of the temporal, which exists only through the attractive force of this goal. According to Thomas, the teleological causation, the end-cause (*causa finalis*), has priority among all causes. Without this end-cause, no further cause would exist, because all causes are toward some end.[145] If we consider such notions of creation, which are very influential within Christianity, then it is somewhat premature to deduce *only* from the Buddhist doctrine that the universe or the chains of successive worlds have no beginning, an incompatibility with the idea of their being created.

Several passages in the canonical writings of Theravada Buddhism count the question of the (temporal) finiteness or infiniteness (*sassata, asassata*), as well as the (spatial?) finiteness or infiniteness (*antavā, anantavā*), as being among the "unanswered questions" (*avyākatā*).[146] This obviously also implies the question of an initial finiteness (a temporal beginning) or infiniteness (beginninglessness) of the world. Other passages explicitly state that samsara is without a "discernible beginning" (*anamataggo*),[147] which also seems to leave the question of a temporal beginning deliberately unanswered. Later, though, the standard Buddhist position became more or less that the chains of successive worlds are without a temporal beginning, this being motivated by the emerging concept of karmic creation, which says that each new world system arises from the karma of the beings of a previous world—and there are countless parallel chains of such successive worlds.[148]

But what is the real impetus behind this karmic dynamic that keeps creating new worlds? The Buddhist tradition names "thirst" and "delusion" here,

---

[144]See *Summa contra gentiles* I 13 and I 37. See also Schmidt-Leukel 2006b, 166–68.

[145]*Summa theologiae* I-II, 1, a. 2.

[146]See, for example, *Majjhima Nikāya* 63 & 72. "They relate to the problem of whether the universe is finite or infinite in terms of time (*sassato, asassato*) and space (*antavā, anantavā*)." Karunadasa 2007, 9.

[147]*Samyutta Nikāya* 2.15, 1–20. See also Bodhi 2000, 795n254.

[148]See, for example, *Abhidharmakośa* 4.1; *Yogācārabhūmi* 30.21; 36.19.

the two being closely interwoven, insofar as thirst is the deluded attitude toward the things of this world. The inherent striving of every being for the intransient, for nirvana, where alone all striving comes to rest, is falsely directed—precisely through delusion—toward the transient, which, however, is never able to quench this thirst permanently.[149] Thus, in its delusion and by means of the rebirth triggered by it, the thirst itself ultimately brings forward the objects that incite it again and again, but leave it unsatisfied. A remarkable passage of the Pali Canon says that all things are rooted in "thirst" (*chanda*), but that liberation is their very core, the deathless their true "goal" (*gadhā*), and nirvana their "fulfillment" or "end" (*pariosānā*).[150] This notion almost appears as a variation on the idea that the world exists only for the sake of its transcendent goal, which it strives toward and in which it eventually merges or dissolves. The world perpetuates itself, as it were, because of the nonattainment of its goal. But it exists out of the inner dynamic toward this goal. Insofar as the dharma describes the inner laws that determine the path to this goal, it is as such not only the law of salvation, but also the law of the world.

In Mahayana Buddhism, this underlying motif developed in different ways, containing two further variations of the idea of creation. Already quite early in Buddhism the idea emerged that Buddhas through their actions "purify" their environment or "field." In the religions of ancient India, as well as in numerous other religions, "purity" is a fertile metaphor for something to be aspired to, often signifying the opening of the human being to the transcendent. It frequently denotes the goal of salvation within Buddhism, as is the case with Buddhaghosa's classic treatise from the fifth century CE, *The Way to Purity* (*Visuddhimagga*), which is concerned with purifying the inherently pure spirit of its "defilements"—greed, hate, and delusion—and thus leading the person to the experience of nirvana. The idea soon arises in Mahayana Buddhism that the Buddhas, due to their perfect compassion and the power of the good karma that they have accumulated in countless existences, each create their own "pure" Buddha land, these Buddha lands then providing the optimal conditions for attaining nirvana. This idea is thus also based on the notion of karmic creation. But here this notion expresses even more strongly the direct finalization of the Buddha lands toward the goal of salvation, and declares this to be the very reason for their creation by the Buddhas. Several relatively ancient and enormously influential Mahayana texts, such as the *Lotus-Sūtra* and the *Vimalakīrtinirdeśa-Sūtra*, teach that the present world, with all its evil and suffering, is in truth also

---

[149] See Schmidt-Leukel 2006a, 33–36.
[150] *Aṅguttara Nikāya* 10.58.

a pure Buddha land,[151] but that our delusion prevents us from seeing this. According to the *Vimalakīrtinirdeśa-Sūtra* (chapters X and XI), this means that we do not realize that only in a world like ours can the spiritual and moral virtues of a bodhisattva be developed. In other words, only in a world where suffering is possible can human beings develop those attitudes and qualities that will overcome suffering. In truth, then, our world is a world with optimal conditions for the path of salvation and, as such, is the creation of a Buddha. Thus, for José Cabezón, a Buddhist scholar-practitioner, it is "not implausible for Mahāyānists to argue that all universes everywhere are the pure fields of enlightened beings." Here, Cabezón argues, "Buddhists may have a point for dialogue with Christians and Jews, for whom the creation of the world has always been conceived of as an act of love."[152]

A further, but quite convergent, line developed from the incarnational motif that a Buddha, and ultimately every Awakened One, embodies dharma and nirvana. As has been shown, this led in Mahayana Buddhism first to the notion that all samsaric beings possess Buddha nature, and then eventually to the belief that Buddha nature is manifested in all reality. It was then possible within this line of thought sometimes to draw on the motif of a quasidivine creation. As already mentioned, the *Kāraṇḍavyūha-Sūtra* takes up the Vedic myth about the creation of the world from the divine organism of Purusha, and identifies Purusha with Avalokiteshvara, the latter being referred to throughout the text as *īśvara* ("Lord" in the sense of a creator God). Thus, if the entire world is a creation—or, perhaps better, manifestation—of the bodhisattva Avalokiteshvara, then this expresses figuratively that the entire world serves the purpose of bringing its beings to awakening or salvation, since this is precisely what a bodhisattva vows to do.

In a later revision of the *Kāraṇḍavyūha-Sūtra*, Avalokiteshvara himself is portrayed as an emanation of the *ādibuddha*, i.e., that primordial ground (*ādi* = first or primordial) from which all Buddhas originate.[153] This primordial ground stands in later Mahayanist terminology for the supreme wisdom associated with ultimate reality. The same line of thought is seen when, for example, the *Hevajra Tantra* (1.5.16), an Indian text from the eighth century, says that the highest wisdom (*prajñā*) is called "the Mother, because she gives birth to the world."[154] Such statements are not isolated. As Eva Neumaier argues, "Certain strands of Mahayana Buddhism affirmed a 'creation' as manifestation of the ultimate Reality whereby the two, mani-

---

[151]See *Saddharmapuṇḍarīka-Sūtra* 15.11–14 (Kern 1884, 308); *Vimalakīrtinirdeśa-Sūtra* 1 (Thurman 1976, 18–19).
[152]Cabezón 2016, 40.
[153]See Studholme 2002, 45.
[154]Snellgrove 1971, 62.

festation and 'ground,' are syn-existential."[155] Although several classical and philosophical texts of Mahayana Buddhism use numerous arguments against the belief in a personal creator God,[156] it has also developed ideas that are themselves quite close to this belief.[157]

Jeanine Diller draws two conclusions from what is probably to date the most comprehensive compilation and analysis of different notions of ultimate reality.[158] First, none of the major religious traditions is uniform, with each having many different forms and models of ultimate reality. Second, certain types of notions of transcendence can be found simultaneously in several religious traditions. Hence there is not only an astonishing diversity within religions, but also an even more astonishing congruence between religions with regard to certain ways of thinking about ultimate reality.[159]

The evidence provided in this chapter substantiates this finding with regard to personal and impersonal notions of ultimate reality. If we take into account that there is a certain dominance of impersonal notions in Buddhism, and of personal notions in Christianity, then we can see clearly a fractal pattern that extends over the macro and meso level down to the micro level of the religious person. As Diller also points out, however, the interreligious parallels relate to certain ideal-typical models and not to how these models are actually instantiated. Given the enormous variety of religious particularities, they also always retain their unmistakable specificity.[160]

---

[155]Neumaier 2016, 57. See also Neumaier-Dargyay 1992.
[156]On the Buddhist antitheistic arguments, see Schmidt-Leukel 2006, 123–41; 2017b, 207–11.
[157]See for a similar assessment Jackson, R. 1999, 473–74.
[158]Diller & Kasher 2013.
[159]Diller 2013.
[160]See ibid., 1027.

5

What Is Wrong with Us?

5.1 DELUSION OR SIN?

Many older comparative studies saw a structural similarity between Christianity and Buddhism in the fact that both promise redemption or liberation, and are thus "religions of redemption."[1] But redemption from what? In this respect, religious scholars have suggested strong contrasts.

Often key here was how comparative scholars interpreted the Christian and Buddhist relationship to the world.[2] According to Karl Kenntner, for example, Buddhism proclaims a "redemption *from* empirical life," while Christianity proclaims a "redemption *of* empirical life."[3] Such sharp and one-sided contrasts ignored the fact of course that in Christianity too the ultimate goal of salvation was often understood as a new reality that was not simply an improvement or redeemed extension of the present world. However, comparisons often appeared sweeping and confrontational even when they paid more attention to the specific phenomena of "empirical life" to which the idea of redemption relates in both religions, i.e., with its transience and suffering, with the suffering of life also including the morally reprehensible infliction of suffering.

Most of the early comparisons saw the key difference between the two religions in how each analyzed the cause of the human predicament, the unanimous verdict in Christianity being that the real cause of all evil was sin, whereas in Buddhism it was "thirst" (*taṇhā, tṛṣṇā*) and ignorance (*avijjā, avidyā*) or delusion (*moha*).[4] This vacillation in Buddhism between thirst and delusion derives from the differences between two old Buddhist

---

[1] For a problematization of the category "religions of redemption," see Colpe 1990.
[2] See above, pp. 51–58.
[3] Kenntner 1939, 68.
[4] Ignorance/not-knowing and delusion are usually used synonymously in Buddhism, since the ignorant are unaware of their not-knowing, but erroneously consider it to be knowledge and are thus blind or deluded. Iconographically, too, ignorance is symbolized in the classical depiction of *pratītyasamutpāda* by a blind woman. See Zin & Schlingloff 2007, 127–28; Schmidt-Leukel 1992, 52–56, 73–84.

doctrinal schemes. While the "Four Noble Truths" name thirst as the cause of suffering, the doctrine of "dependent origination" (*paticcasumuppāda, pratītyasamutpāda*) traces thirst via various intermediate links to delusion.[5] However, there is a genuine link between thirst and delusion, since thirst denotes a deluded orientation of human life to the transient things of this world instead of salvation/liberation as the only satisfying goal.[6]

According to Gustav Mensching, Buddhism does not understand "not-knowing" as "theoretical ignorance," but uses it to denote the "missing contact with the reality of the numinous."[7] This missing contact with the numinous, he says, articulates itself in the desire for—and the false identification with—individualized existence.[8] Thus, the suffering or human predicament that Buddhism speaks of consists in "the found separation of man from the salvific reality of nirvana."[9] Mensching sees a structural similarity to Christianity here, since, according to Christian belief, the human predicament also arises from the "separation or isolation of man from a transcendent reality," i.e., through "sin."[10]

For Mensching, though, this structural similarity between delusion and sin takes very opposite forms. In Christianity, the human predicament is manifested primarily in the "frightened conscience" and bears the character of a "debt." For Mensching, this is not primarily a matter of individual sins, but, echoing Martin Luther, of an essential sin, "an overall existential attitude of a guilty nature, which can be described as a self-assured isolation from God." This is "self-assertion before God, ego-addicted existence as distinguished from ego-ish existence, which is regarded as predicament in Buddhism."[11] Thus, Christianity sees "ego-addiction" as the root of evil, whereas Buddhism sees it as being "ego-illusion." For Mensching, this difference becomes key insofar as in Buddhism any willing presupposes and perpetuates the ego-illusion, whereas in Christianity only the direction of the will ("away from God toward the world, and that is toward the ego and its cravings") is regarded as malign.[12]

Although Mensching discerns and names some important structural parallels here, it is this last point that we need to question, since Buddhism also recognizes a right, i.e., rightly directed, will. Thus, for example, the scheme of the Four Noble Truths designates as the sixth limb of the Noble Eightfold Path to liberation the "right effort," that is, the effort directed

---
[5]See Schmidt-Leukel 2006a, 30–33, 46–48.
[6]Ibid., 33–34.
[7]Mensching 1978, 126.
[8]Ibid., 128–31.
[9]Ibid., 138.
[10]Ibid.
[11]Ibid.
[12]Ibid., 140–43.

toward nirvana. The striving for nirvana, which essentially includes will, is designated as "noble search," in contrast to "ignoble search," which is directed toward the transient things of the world.[13] Buddhism is therefore also concerned with the direction of the will or of existential striving.

The opposition of delusion/ignorance and sin as two fundamentally different interpretations of the human predicament can be found not only in older, but also in relatively recent comparisons of the two religions.[14] According to the orthodox theologian Ernest Valea, ignorance is the strongest equivalent in Buddhism of the Christian concept of sin, but this structural similarity cannot hide the irreconcilable differences between the two concepts. For Valea, Christianity understands sin as the absence of the right relationship to God and other human beings, whereas, lacking any concept of God, Buddhism deems the Christian concept of sin to be unacceptable. Conversely, Christianity cannot accept the Buddhist understanding of delusion, since, at least in Mahayana Buddhism, this understanding presupposes that the human being has a hidden cognitive faculty covered by delusion that as such forms the basis of redemption or enlightenment. In contrast, he argues, Christianity does not assume such a positive basis within human nature, but sees the human heart as being deeply determined by sin.[15]

Keith Yandell and Harold Netland identify the central differences between Buddhist and Christian understandings of the human predicament in a similar way. While according to them Buddhism and Christianity agree "that things are not right," they disagree over the question of how things are wrong and how the situation can possibly be rectified. For them, Christianity sees sin as "a type of rebellion against our own nature and against God. Sins are self-destructive, preventing our flourishing, and set a barrier between us and God."[16] Healing lies in repentance and divine forgiveness. In contrast, Buddhism sees delusion as the false belief in an ego and the repression of universal transience, the remedy therefore being knowledge accompanied by the overcoming of all attachment.[17] That the two conceptions are incompatible is shown by the fact that Christianity sees evil as lying ultimately in the corruption of the human being's heart or inner person, and that the Christian notion of sin is based on the notion of God, a notion that is completely lacking in Buddhism.[18]

Yandell and Netland justify their argument among others by quoting

---

[13] Schmidt-Leukel 2006a, 33–34.
[14] See, for example, the sweeping judgment made by Harold Coward (2003, 128): "There is no sin in the sense of disobedience to God or to some blindly believed scripture. Rather, for Buddhism there is the karmic ignorance caused by the many false views that assail us on all sides."
[15] Valea 2008, 131–35.
[16] Yandell & Netland 2009, 180–81.
[17] Ibid., 177–81.
[18] Ibid., 201–3. See also above p. 92.

the statement of the Buddhist scholar Walpola Rahula: "There is no 'sin' in Buddhism, as sin is understood in some religions. The root of all evil is ignorance (*avijja*) and wrong views (*micchaditthi*)."[19] Other Buddhist scholars, however, such as the Japanese religious studies scholar Hajime Nakamura, have resisted such simplistic dichotomies, citing the internal diversity of Christianity *and* Buddhism. To reduce a religious tradition to a narrow and static type is for Nakamura to overlook those "movements of life and thought which are not confined to any one tradition."[20] While also seeing a difference between the two religions as lying in the fact that Christianity understands sin as alienation from the divine creator, Nakamura says that this difference becomes relativized if we consider that parts of Mahayana Buddhism also present the Buddha as an Eternal Being, and as the "Father of the worlds."[21] But, for Nakamura, Buddhism does not have the idea of a divine punishment for sin,[22] with Buddhism seeing the consequences of good or evil deeds as resulting instead from the law of karma, from an independent moral causality.[23] However, Nakamura emphasizes that Christianity also sees sin not only in terms of punishment, but also sometimes as a kind of illness requiring not the judge, but the physician, which again somewhat resembles the Buddhist diagnosis of the human predicament.[24] According to Nakamura, ignorance and thirst constitute an inner unity, and, since Buddhism considers knowledge and will to be closely connected, it presupposes that true knowledge is always accompanied by a virtuous development. This connection, says Nakamura, has also been perceived in Christianity: Ephesians 4:18 mentions "ignorance" as the reason for alienation from God and thus for sin, while John 8:32 says that it is "the truth" that sets the human being free.[25]

Nakamura's comparative observations already suggest something like a fractal approach: the different conceptions of the human predicament in Buddhism and Christianity reappear at least to some extent also within each of the two religions. At the end of his monumental comparative history of ideas, Nakamura concludes that the different religious and philosophical traditions address "more or less the same problems," which shows that, despite all the differences within humanity, "human nature and human concerns are also vastly similar."[26] In the following section, I sketch and illustrate Nakamura's observation that in both traditions we find different

---
[19]Ibid., 203. Quoted from Rahula 1974, 3.
[20]Nakamura 1986, 152.
[21]Ibid., 151. Nakamura is alluding here primarily to the influential *Lotus-Sūtra*.
[22]Nakamura 1986, 38.
[23]Ibid., 43–46.
[24]Ibid., 38–39.
[25]Ibid., 64–65.
[26]Nakamura 1992, 565.

124   The Celestial Web

conceptions of the cause of the human predicament that in their polarity, however, are structurally similar to each other, before returning to his claim that this structural similarity is due to anthropological factors.

5.2 DELUSION AND SINFUL SELF-ATTACHMENT IN BUDDHISM

Sin and Punishments for Sin

Contrary to the widespread tendency to deny that Buddhism has a concept of sin, several experts have recently pointed out that especially in Buddhism notions of sin and sins, as well as the corresponding infernal punishments, are actually rife. They criticize the fact that some scholars in Buddhist studies pay too little attention to or even ignore the presence of notions of sin in Buddhism—probably also because this would relativize the cliché that Buddhism and Christianity are radically different. For example, Alan Cole writes, "Though Western discussions of Buddhism tend to ignore the role of sin in Buddhist culture, it seems that certain notions of sin are central to Buddhism in most of its manifestations."[27] And according to James Robson, "In much contemporary writing on Buddhism . . . it has generally been regarded as a sin itself to discuss the concept of sin in relation to Buddhism."[28] For him, however, there is no question that "notions of sin—or transgressions—and repentance can be found both in mainstream Buddhist teachings as well as in later Mahāyāna developments."[29] And, according to Phyllis Granoff, it is true of all traditional Indian religions that the nature of sin and the consequences of sin were themes of central importance, and remained so until the beginning of the modern period.[30]

The discrepancy between such statements and the denial that there is a concept of sin in Buddhism is based at least partly on questions of translation. How far is it legitimate to translate Sanskrit terms such as *pāpa* (Chinese *zui* 罪 : violation, crime, guilt, sin; also as an adverb), *mithyā* (wrong, unseemly, bad, sinful), *akuśala* (evil, bad, corrupt, unwholesome), or *apunya* (wrong, karmically bad, culpable) as "sin" or "sinful"? The answer partly depends on how narrowly or broadly we understand the concept of "sin." If it refers in a religious context to the violation of moral or ritual commandments, prohibitions, rules, principles, obligations, etc., then the translation seems quite appropriate—precisely because it expresses the religious dimension

---

[27] Cole 1998, 8.
[28] Robson 2012, 74.
[29] Ibid., 77.
[30] Granoff 2012, 175.

of the transgression. It is more difficult, however, if "sin" is understood in a narrower theological sense or in the sense of specific Christian conceptions such as that of "original sin," where the translation may sometimes be misleading. It is therefore important to clarify which aspects of "sin" are covered by the relevant Buddhist terms, and which are not.[31]

Buddhism does not consider moral and ritual rules to be commandments of a creator God. But they are nonetheless a subaspect of the dharma and thus part of an eternal cosmic law that the Buddhas recognize and proclaim. In this sense, they are not rules that the Buddhas[32] command, but rules that they reveal and whose validity does not depend on the consent of the individual. In their supposedly timeless validity and obligatoriness, Buddhist laws and rules thus share an important feature with the theistic "commandments." Moreover, there are parallels to the concept of "original sin" insofar as this refers to a fundamental existential condition of the human being; for Buddhism also believes that ordinary beings in the cycle of rebirth are already born in a state of delusion and thirst, i.e., with a quasi-"sinful" inclination. Sinful behavior—in thoughts, words, and deeds (the three areas of karma)—is not understood in Buddhism as rebellion against a creator God, but the idea that sinful behavior is also an offense against the Buddhas is by no means foreign to Buddhism. I will return to both aspects: the "originally sinful" unwholesome inclination, and "sin" against the Buddha. But I would first like to address a further aspect briefly.

As already shown with the example of Hajime Nakamura, scholars, sometimes critically, hold as a peculiarity of Buddhism that it lacks the idea of "punishment for sins," seeing the negative consequences that sins entail for the sinner as being not a divine punishment, but the result of the law of karma. Although it is correct to point to the causal connection, almost as in laws of nature, between deed and retribution (in the positive as well as negative sense of "having deserved"), the negative "deserving" is often also understood as "punishment," and especially so when it is the infernal punishments often painted in grisly detail in classical Buddhist texts.[33] According to a belief widespread in Buddhism, it is the deity Yama who rules over the infernal realms. According to some texts,[34] the deceased must first appear before Yama, who asks them about their misdeeds and why they had not taken seriously the warnings about the negative consequences of their misdeeds and the death that was sure to come. The guards of hell then take

---

[31] See Robson 2012, 74–76.
[32] In this case, this also includes the so-called solitary Buddhas (*pratyekabuddha*), since, in contrast to the widespread misconception that solitary Buddhas do not teach at all, they do in fact—according to numerous classical Buddhist texts—teach, but mainly the moral laws. They differ from the Buddhas in the full sense in that they do not establish a sangha and do not show the full path to salvation.
[33] On Buddhist hells, see Matsunaga & Matsunaga 1972, Van Put 2015, and Tiefenauer 2017.
[34] E.g., *Majjhima Nikāya* 130.

them to that particular hell that corresponds to their deeds. In other texts, however, Yama also assumes the role of a judge "who decides on wrongdoings and acts of merits," and who "punishes the guilty according to his law."[35] This idea has expanded in Chinese Buddhism into the concept of a court, presided over by the "ten kings" who judge the deceased according to merit and misdeed, and assign them the next form of existence according to the law of karma. Here, too, Yama retains the role of lord over the hells, i.e., it is Yama who condemns the deceased to hell.[36] Yama thus functions as the personification of the law of karma, so to speak. Seen in this way, the karmic consequences appear on the one hand as inflicted by one's own behavior, and on the other as punishments imposed by Yama. Taking account of this personalized way of looking at the law of karma clearly relativizes the sharp distinction between punishment for sins and karmic consequences.

Repentance, Forgiveness, and Liberation

Even if Buddhism in principle does not hold the idea of an eternal, irreversible punishment in hell,[37] the period of time for people's stay in the various hells is calculated in inconceivably long periods, and the tortures and torments are of unsurpassable cruelty. Thus, the prospect of infernal punishment was no less frightening, and this fear no less widespread, in Buddhism than in Christianity.[38] According to Alan Cole, "A closer look at the historical record shows that Buddhism without anxiety would not be Buddhism."[39] The question of whether the punishments of sin or the negative karmic consequences are avoidable is therefore also of tremendous existential importance in Buddhism.

One means of avoidance here is to compensate for negative karma by accumulating good karma. But what if one's own good karma appears to be too little? Another path opens up here, since the idea developed especially (but by no means only) in Mahayana Buddhism that people could out of compassion transfer their own karmic merits to other beings who lack such merits.[40] Thus, a person without special karmic merits can turn to the great bodhisattvas, who are full of compassion, and trust them to share their almost

---

[35] Thus in the influential *Saddharmasmṛtypasthāna-Sūtra*. Quoted in Van Put 2015, 36. See also ibid., 152.

[36] Van Put 2015, 37. See also Teiser 1994.

[37] Shantideva possibly hints in the *Bodhicaryāvatāra* (4:21–22) at the idea that negative karma can continue to be produced in hell, too—for example, through thoughts of hatred. This would then imply a potentially endless perpetuation of the stay in hell. See on this problem Schmidt-Leukel 2019b, 187–88nn14, 15.

[38] For a brief comparison of Buddhist and Christian hells, see Schmidt-Leukel 2019b, 331–45.

[39] Cole 1998, 9.

[40] See on this also below pp. 175–77.

immeasurable merits with oneself.[41] Under their "protection," the person then escapes the threatening consequences of their own misdeeds[42]—an idea that became extremely important especially in Pure Land Buddhism, where the karmic merits of the Buddha Amitabha or Amitayus (Japanese: Amida) open a path of salvation for all beings.

On the other hand, there are also references in the Buddhist tradition to practices that can purify people directly of negative karma, such as recitation, listening to certain sutras, and invoking the names of Buddhas.[43] Repenting one's own sinful misdeeds is also often said to have such a purifying effect, with some texts claiming that doing so can even lead directly to enlightenment.[44] The influential *Abhidharmakośabhāṣya* (2:28) notes that it must be proper repentance, however, i.e., repentance (*kaukṛtya*) is good only if it actually relates to misdeeds, and not, for example, to a good action.[45] This remark is instructive, since it implies that purifying repentance must also involve some insight or understanding.

Buddhist texts often mention "repentance" in relation to confessions of sin.[46] Ritualized confessions were and still are widespread in the Buddhist world, both for laypeople and, especially, for monks and nuns.[47] They form an integral part of many Buddhist rituals,[48] and often include a resolution to improve—as is the case, for example, with the detailed confessional formula in the Mahayana-Buddhist *Golden-Light-Sūtra*.[49] They may also, as this sutra does, contain an explicit request to the Buddhas and bodhisattvas for forgiveness:

> May the Buddhas watch over me with minds attentive. May they forgive my sins with minds given over to compassion. . . . All the Buddhas are compassionate. They remove the fear of all beings. May they forgive my sin and may they deliver me from fear. May the Tathāgatas take away for me the defilement of impurities (and) acts. And may the Buddhas bathe me with the surging waters of compassion.[50]

---

[41] See Dayal 1932, 192–93; Basham 1997, 32–38; Williams 2009, 203; Schlieter 2013, 464.
[42] See Schmidt-Leukel 2019b, 150–52.
[43] Granoff 2012, 183; Robson 2012, 82.
[44] Granoff 2012, 186.
[45] See ibid., 189. See Pruden 1991, vol. 1, 196–97.
[46] See Granoff 2012, 211; Robson 2012, 80–81; Groner 2012, 216.
[47] As an example of the regular use of a confession formula for laypeople in the context of the bodhisattva ideal, see the references in Nattier 2003, 117–21. For the use of confession among laypeople on Buddhist holidays, see Groner 2012, 217.
[48] See Robson 2012, 80–82.
[49] *Suvarṇaprabhāsottama-Sūtra* 20–44. Emmerick 1970, 8–17. The formula is also cited in *Śikṣāsamuccaya* 8. See Bendall & Rouse 1922, 159–60.
[50] *Suvarṇaprabhāsottama-Sūtra* 30–31. Emmerick 1970, 12.

Such requests for forgiveness can also be found in the context of Theravada Buddhism. Peter Harvey reports that in Sri Lanka and Thailand there are recitations that ask Buddha, dharma, and sangha for forgiveness for all wrongs done to them.[51] In both Mahayana and Theravada Buddhism the willingness to forgive is part of the spiritual virtue known as *kṣānti*. Often translated as "patience," *kṣānti* also strongly connotes "toleration," and by extension "forbearance." A person should show such forbearance to the very person who has inflicted harm on them. In this respect *kṣānti* approximates to the idea of forgiveness.

But in what sense is sinful behavior considered an offense against the Buddhas, so that a person can ask for their forgiveness? One answer is provided by the *Bodhicaryāvatāra*,[52] which develops the idea that the Buddhas have overcome any egocentric notion of an "I," instead making in their encompassing compassion the whole world of beings their "self." Thus, since the Buddhas identify with all beings as their own self, whatever suffering one person inflicts on other beings is suffering also done to the Buddhas:

> This is why today I wish to confess as sin to have caused all Those of great compassion to suffer by bringing suffering to people. May the Sages bear with what caused them distress.[53]

But Shantideva (as tradition calls the author of this text) also deduces from this that the true worship of the Buddhas lies in serving all beings and striving to eliminate their suffering,[54] an idea that incidentally also found its way into Theravada Buddhism. Here, the learned Sri Ramacandra Bharati composed probably in the thirteenth century the Buddha hymn *Bhaktiśataka*, where he writes in verse 33 about the worship of the Buddha,

> To do good to the world is to serve you alone;
> To do evil to the world is to torment you.[55]

The request for forgiveness is tied in the *Bodhicaryāvatāra* to the underlying idea that *bodhicitta*, the "spirit of awakening," i.e., the compassionate desire to strive for the liberation of all beings, purifies from all negative

---

[51] Harvey 2000, 28. It is noteworthy that this request is also addressed to the impersonal dharma.
[52] On the *Bodhicaryāvatāra*, see above, pp. 64, 78.
[53] *Bodhicaryāvatāra* 6.124. Translation by Ernst Steinkellner in Schmidt-Leukel 2019b, 296. For the whole argument, see ibid., 295–303.
[54] *Bodhicaryāvatāra* 6.125–27.
[55] Quoted from the German translation in Otto 1917, 141–60, here 148. Ramacandra could indeed be influenced by the *Bodhicaryāvatāra* because at his time this text was well-known and popular in Sri Lanka, too. See Schmidt-Leukel 2019b, 506n30.

Sigillum Aeternitatis, © KIK-IRPA, Brussels, www.kikirpa.be

Sri Yantra, template: © yulianas—iStock.com

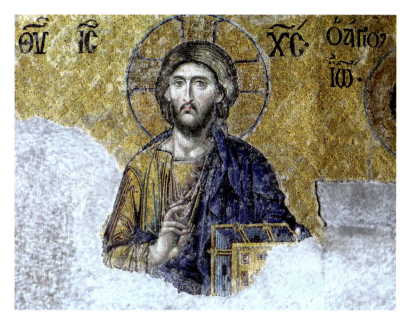

Pantocrator Christ icon, template: © gunthersimmermacher / 38—pixabay

Enso Zen circle, template: © Elina Li—shutterstock.com

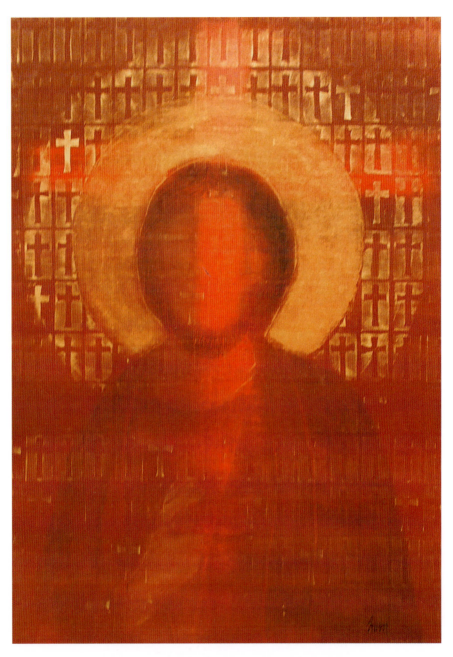

Christ, © Satish Gupta, http://www.satishgupta.com/

karma.[56] Forgiveness thus takes effect by promoting *bodhicitta*. The notion of *bodhicitta* as the actual antidote to sin is in turn related to an idea central to the Buddhist understanding of sin, which says that all sinful behavior in thoughts, words, and deeds originates from a deeply rooted egocentricity or self-attachment in the person. The three central "defilements" or "impurities" (*kleśa*) of the human spirit are greed, hate, and delusion, these being inseparable, since greed is understood as the deluded attitude toward what is pleasant, and hate as the deluded attitude toward what is unpleasant.[57] The standard Buddhist depiction of the cycle of rebirth expresses this interconnectedness by symbolizing the three defilements as three animals—dove (greed), snake (hate), and pig (delusion)—biting each other's tails and thus forming a circle. This circle forms the hub around which the wheel of rebirth turns.[58] Greed and hate originate from self-attachment, since at its center is concern for one's own self. Self-attachment is therefore the ground from which greed and hate arise, and is considered to be the real form of delusion. In this respect, *bodhicitta*, the spirit of awakening, is the opposite attitude: striving for the good of others without distinguishing between friend and foe.

Insofar as delusion is understood as the root and structural principle of sinful transgressions, awakening is considered to be the perfection of knowledge/insight, which is accompanied by a complete liberation from greed, hate, and delusion. This liberation is also considered permanent, since the root of sin has been eliminated. The vast majority of Buddhist texts assume that it is necessary to combat evil with its opposite, which is the reason that the development of knowledge is the most important factor in the fight against the defilements. The Theravada canon calls knowledge the morning-red of all wholesome things.[59] When the sixth-century Mahayana philosopher Bhaviveka (also called Bhavaviveka or Bhavya) says that "the wise burn sin through insight," he places himself within the mainstream of fundamental Buddhist convictions.[60] And yet the matter is more complicated in Buddhism, too.

If delusion denotes the absence of insight, then how can liberating insight arise at all? And what if the means that are supposed to lead to insight, such as knowledge of the Buddha's teachings, do not yield the success hoped for,

---

[56]*Bodhicaryāvatāra* 1.11 and 27. Similarly in *Śikṣāsamuccaya* 177 (see Bendall & Rouse 1922, 173)—an anthology ascribed to Shantideva.

[57]*Aṅguttara Nikāya* 3.68.

[58]Zin & Schlingloff 2007, 22–23, 115–16. In later developments, the bird representing greed was no longer seen as a female dove (whose pleasant cooing awakens the greed of the male doves) as in the original versions, but became interpreted as a (greedy) cockerel. See Schmidt-Leukel 2020a, 95.

[59]*Aṅguttara Nikāya* 10.121.

[60]*Madhyamakahṛdayakārikā* 9.60.

with the sinful inclinations remaining unabated? Shantideva, for example, writes in his guide for bodhisattvas,

> Yet I ignore the word of the omniscient physician who eliminates all pain. Disgrace to me in my abysmal blindness!
>
> Countless Buddhas have passed by, searching for any kind of being; through my own fault, their art of healing was not directed at me.
>
> If I do not do what is wholesome although capable of doing the wholesome, how will I do the same when I am distraught by the sufferings in bad destinies?
>
> And if I do not do what is wholesome but rather accumulate evil, then even the word "good destiny" is wiped out [for me] for hundreds of millions of eons.
>
> I do not know how, but I have gained a site of [possible] advantage extremely difficult to reach, and although I am now aware of it, I am still being led . . . to the same hells.
>
> I do not know what to make of it. As if deluded by spells, I do not know by whom I am bewildered, who is here in me. Enemies such as greed and hate have neither hands nor feet, are neither brave nor wise. How have they been able to enslave me?
>
> They have already penetrated my mind and fight me from a safe position, yet I am not even angry with them. Shame on this misplaced tolerance!
>
> Where can that which sits in my mind go if it has been driven out? Where can it reside and work on my destruction? Yet weak of mind, I do not exert myself. The miserable defilements can only be defeated by the direct awareness that is insight [*prajñā*].[61]

There is a strong awareness in texts such as this of the profound power and deep-seatedness of delusion. It is, as John Makransky writes, an awareness "that persons find themselves in a state of bondage to self-clinging and vice which severely limits their capacity to choose and do the good."[62] In the same vein, Shantideva laments that he deems himself unable to follow the Buddha's teaching and do what is wholesome, even though he is aware of its healing character and believes in his ability to do the good. He experiences delusion and sin as a personified power that enslaves him and permeates his mind. He holds to the view that only perfect, transcendent wisdom (*prajñā*) can liberate him. But it remains open how this wisdom

---

[61] *Bodhicaryāvatāra* 2.57; 4.13, 18–19, 26–29, 46. Translation by Steinkellner in Schmidt-Leukel 2029b, 146, 185–86, 190–92.

[62] Makransky 2005, 6.

succeeds in breaking the spell of delusion that bewitches and blinds him. How can the love of the good, i.e., compassion for others, become so strong that it defeats the love of self? According to Shantideva, the solution lies in viewing others as one's own self, so that altruism becomes the true form of self-love.[63] But, again, this can only happen through insight. Thus, until this insight liberates him, he has no choice but to entrust himself to those who have already fully embodied this insight and the corresponding compassion: namely, to the Buddhas and great bodhisattvas. The hope is articulated here that relying on their selfless compassion will also in him evoke, sustain, and ultimately perfect the "spirit of awakening":[64] "I seek my refuge in these treasure troves of happiness."[65]

The tendency to rely on trust in the face of delusion and its sinful manifestations is particularly strong in the teachings of Shinran Shonin (1173–1263), and in the Japanese "True School of Pure Land" (Jōdō Shinshū) that he inspired. Here, trust no longer appears merely as the path to insight, but as the form of insight appropriate to the depth of human delusion. According to Shinran, "The self . . . is unable to distinguish right from wrong, good from evil," and "has no claim even for little deeds of love and compassion."[66] The deluded attitude of self-attachment is so pervasive for Shinran that it ultimately infuses all supposedly good deeds, i.e., these deeds essentially serve an egocentric agenda. At the same time, this is accompanied by a lack of knowledge of the truth. Thus, Shinran says of himself, "I know nothing at all of good and evil. . . . with a foolish being full of blind passions . . . all matters without exception are empty and false, totally without truth and sincerity."[67] Since he is not capable of any good work, he cannot escape hell anyway, and thus has no other choice but to entrust himself completely to the all-embracing mercy of Buddha Amida and his vow to redeem everyone and exclude no one.[68] But, according to Shinran, not even this entrusting (*shinjin*) arises from the self; rather, it is actually the trust or confidence that Amida had when he was the bodhisattva Dharmakara in attaining Buddhahood and thus in realizing his all-encompassing compassion. It is precisely this spirit of trust that Amida gives to the deluded person. In other words, it is only in the form of entrusting that the transcendent reality of salvation can break through in the person who is deeply entangled in their self-attachment and inclination toward greed and hate:

---

[63] See Schmidt-Leukel 2019b, 391–402.
[64] See ibid., 130–52.
[65] *Bodhicaryāvatāra* 1.36. Schmidt-Leukel 2029b, 128.
[66] *Shūjishō* 2. Suzuki 1973a, 122–23.
[67] *Tannishō* Postscript. Hirota 1997, 679.
[68] *Tannishō* 2 and 3. Shinran reinterprets the exclusion of the great malefactors, found in the canonical text of this vow, in such a way that ultimately all beings fall under this category, and that consequently no one is actually excluded.

When foolish beings of delusion and defilements awaken shinjin [entrusting], they realize that birth-and-death is itself nirvana.[69]

According to Shinran, the insight regarded as the highest knowledge in Mahayana Buddhism into the nonduality of nirvana and samsara is realized paradoxically precisely when the hopelessness of a person's own delusion and sinful inclinations is seen in the light of entrusting oneself to Amida. Thus, for Shinran, entrusting (*shinjin*) is the form of liberating insight that is appropriate to the human being's delusion.

5.3 SINFUL SELF-ATTACHMENT AND DELUSION IN CHRISTIANITY

Biblical Perspectives

"I once was lost, but now I'm found, was blind, but now I see."[70] These are the words from "Amazing Grace," one of the world's best-known Christian hymns. This is how the former slave trader John Henry Newton (1725–1807) described his salvation from a life of sin, presupposing as a matter of course a close link between sin and spiritual blindness (ignorance) or delusion. But this link is overshadowed by another, more prevalent understanding of sin: namely, as debt.[71] The Lord's Prayer says, "Forgive us our trespasses" (literally: "forgive us our debts"). This petition associates sin less with a lack of insight than with a defect of the will, the lack of will to do what is good. However, the aspect of delusion may not be completely absent from the Lord's Prayer. In the Aramaic reconstruction, the last petition ("deliver us from evil") is about deliverance from *bīšā*, a word that can mean both "fault" and "error."[72]

The economic metaphor of debt (or debts) understands sin as the nonfulfillment of what we owe to someone else. It thus refers to a third aspect that precedes the other two aspects in terms of the history of thought, and probably needs to be seen as the more comprehensive aspect in a religious sense: namely, the understanding of sin as the rupture of a relationship, both with other people, and in particular with God. Human beings remain short on something decisive that they owe to fellow human beings and to God. This relationship aspect can be shown in the Hebrew Bible, and thus

---

[69]*Shōshinge* 81–82. Hirota 1997, 72.
[70]Turner 2009.
[71]See on this the overview in Anderson 2009.
[72]See Bubolz 2019, 68, 651–59.

What Is Wrong with Us? 133

in one of the roots of Christianity, to be the primary characteristic of sin.[73] Sin thus represents the malign counterpart to what Jesus names as the core of a salvific life: namely, the link between love of God and love of one's neighbor. This was again expressed in an economic metaphor: a person acquires merit, a "treasure in heaven," that outweighs their debts. Like Buddhism, Christianity also sees generosity—the giving of gifts—as one of the central means of earning merit.[74] Above all, though, in the context of this economic metaphor the idea could develop that redemption from sin occurs because Jesus Christ paid for the debt(s) of sinners with his life.[75]

In Paul's writings, the concept of sin is extremely complex. What is significant is that Paul presupposes sin as being a universal phenomenon,[76] which means that sin must not only be understood as a violation of the Jewish law. Instead, for Paul, all people, Jews and non-Jews alike, are under the rule of sin (Romans 3:9, 23). The "power of sin" (Romans 6:18) consists in an inner desire that Paul characterizes as being "hostile to God" (Romans 8:7). The "wages of sin," again an economic metaphor, is death (Romans 6:23). Thus, for Paul, the very mortality of all people proves that all are under sin (Romans 5:12). Sin, then, is more than just debt in the sense of a violation of the law given to the Jewish people. Rather, it is the violation of the law written on the heart of every human being (Romans 2:15). Ultimately, it is the refusal to acknowledge God: something nondivine is substituted for God, and the human being lacks insight, love, and mercy (Romans 1:25–31).

The aspect of delusion is thus not absent, but involved as a lack of insight. In Paul, sin is virtually a personified power. First it "deceives" us (Romans 7:11), before then enslaving us so that we can no longer help but sin (Romans 6 and 7:14–25). The difference between the two stages is of course significant, since those who are deceived or blinded by sin act sinfully because they do not know any better and act according to their deceived will. But those enslaved by sin act sinfully even against their better knowledge and perhaps against their own will.[77]

Paul stresses the aspect of deception or not-knowing both for non-Jews ("Gentiles") and for those Jews who did not join Jesus. Given over to their lusts, the Gentiles "do not know God" (1 Thessalonians 4:4–5). "The world through its wisdom did not know God" (1 Corinthians 1:21), and so its wisdom is in truth "folly with God" (1 Corinthians 3:19). Paul attributes the rejection of Jesus by a large proportion of Jews to "blindness" or being

---

[73] See Kiefer 2017, 21–22.
[74] See Anderson 2009, 9–14, 135–51.
[75] Ibid., 111–32.
[76] See also Sanders 2015, 643–44.
[77] See ibid., 646–57, and Dunn 2006, 111–14.

spiritually "hardened" (Romans 11:7); their "zeal for God is not based on knowledge" (Romans 10:2). According to Paul, though, it is ultimately God who numbs the minds and blinds the eyes of Jews (Romans 11:8), so that the message of salvation could also reach non-Jews (Romans 11:11–12). Eventually, however, all of Israel will be saved (Romans 11:25–26). For Paul, the thinking of unbelievers is fundamentally blinded (2 Corinthians 4:4), and he also apparently relates sinning among Christians to a failure to recognize (*agnosian*) God (1 Corinthians 15:34). Conversely, he describes growth in faith, or spiritual maturing, as a process where "love may abound more and more in knowledge and depth of insight" (Philippians 1:9).

According to the pseudo-Pauline Second Letter to the Thessalonians, all who reject Jesus are considered not to love the truth and thus to have fallen into the power of error (2 Thessalonians 2:10–11). Other texts among the later New Testament writings, such as the Letter to the Ephesians and the First Letter of Peter, also link sin closely with ignorance (*agnosia*) (Ephesians 4:18; 1 Peter 1:14). This is true above all of the Gospel of John,[78] which also initially ties in with the motif that the hearts of the Jews have been "hardened" (John 12:37–41), but then turns this idea into a general position. According to Rainer Metzner, the Gospel of John defines "the essence of sin as *spiritual blindness and unbelief* towards the revealer."[79] Hence, it is knowledge of the truth that sets people free from sin (John 8:32). This knowledge also includes the knowledge of sin itself, which without this insight is not perceived as sin at all (John 16:8). The light of truth dispels the darkness of blinded self-appraisal. However, the aspect of a deliberate willful guilt is not completely absent in John, either. Metzler speaks here of a "guilty not-willing to see,"[80] this then leading to enslavement to sin (John 8:34).

The understanding of sin as blindness that characterizes the Gospel of John makes the healing of the blind man (John 9) a symbol for Jesus' act of salvation, this having a lasting impact on Christian symbolic language and iconography.[81] Likewise, the motif of the hardening of the hearts of the Jews found its pictorial expression in the depiction of a woman who cannot see because she is blindfolded—the blind synagogue as counterpart to the seeing church.[82] This conception of sin implies a different emphasis with regard to God's act of salvation—for while the idea of debt corresponds to

---

[78]There are similar, but less clearly developed, ideas in the Synoptic Gospels. See, for example, what (according to Luke) Jesus says on the cross, when he asks God to forgive his executors because they do not know what they do (Luke 23:34), or the motif of hardening in Matthew 13:13–15.
[79]Metzner 2000, 113.
[80]Ibid., 98, in view of John 9:40–41.
[81]See Hartmann 2011.
[82]See Raddatz 2006.

What Is Wrong with Us? 135

the idea of the remission of debt(s) or indeed forgiveness, delusion calls for healing through knowledge/insight.[83]

Later Developments

Both aspects of sin—its understanding as a lack of knowledge and its understanding as a lack of good will—remained influential in the history of Christian theology. However, the question of how to relate both dimensions more precisely remained unclear and contested. Is the lack of will to do good due primarily to a lack of knowledge, i.e., delusion? To the fact that we do not recognize what the true good is? Or has the power of sin so greatly damaged our will that not even appropriate insight can move us toward the good? The different answers to these questions correspond, also within Christianity, to different conceptions of salvation, and thus to differences in how the role of Jesus and of our role in the process of salvation are understood.

Paula Fredriksen has illustrated this paradigmatically by comparing the concept of sin in Origen (c. 185–254) and in Augustine (354–430). Origen, according to Fredriksen, presupposes, in line with the Platonic tradition, that knowledge of the truth implies love of the truth: "'sin'—a turning from God—accordingly implies *error*, since no one would ever knowingly turn from truth or willingly make a mistake. . . . One chooses according to what one knows. Once one knows the truth, one turns freely to the truth, because one loves it."[84] Salvation is interpreted as a lifelong learning process in which the person gradually recognizes their own errors, repents of them, and overcomes them through love of the truth.[85] The material world as a spiritual field of learning will remain until all beings have come to the full realization of the truth and thus of God.[86] Hell, too, is not eternal, but ultimately serves a pedagogical purpose as an agony of conscience for the soul.[87] Christ is savior insofar as he is the great teacher and the perfect example of a life led completely in harmony with the truth/God.[88]

What remains difficult to explain in this concept, however, is why an original apostasy of beings from God occurred at all. Origen can only attribute this to the imperfection, mutability, and freedom of will of the created

---

[83] See also Stimpfle (1996, 122), who writes with regard to the Gospel of John: "Sin does not mean misconduct in the areas of common decency, morality and (divine) law, but rather the state of unbelief, i.e., ignorance . . . As such a state, sin cannot simply be forgiven, but it can be uncovered and removed."
[84] Fredriksen 2012, 104.
[85] Ibid., 106.
[86] Ibid., 106–9.
[87] Ibid., 111–12.
[88] Ibid., 111.

beings, who in this respect lag inevitably behind the perfection of God.[89] But the question remains as to why, if everybody supposedly loves the known truth and nobody acts against their knowledge, people would turn sinfully and willfully away from the truth in the first place.

According to Augustine, too, there is a human orientation toward God that is based in creation: an existential longing that reaches its lasting fulfillment only in finding God. Echoing the Gospel of John, Augustine says that "blindness is unbelief and enlightenment is faith."[90] But in his spiritual development Augustine became increasingly convinced that the will does not follow knowledge alone, and that wickedness is therefore more than mere folly or delusion.[91] The fall of Adam affected human nature as a whole, both its ability to know and its will. Thus, Augustine can on the one hand ask for knowledge: "Make me seek You, Father, free me from error."[92] But on the other also for God to heal his mistaken will: "Give what Thou commandest, and command what Thou wilt."[93] Christian faith and the grace that works through it involve both knowledge and will. Faith can help the mind to achieve that wisdom that is hidden to mind alone. And grace is able at least gradually to direct the will back to the good. "The mind is receptive to enlightenment, and the will is receptive to grace."[94]

As Fredriksen points out, Augustine understands Adam's sin as a fall of human nature. In other words, the fall means that human will is no longer free:[95] "the will is defective: a person now functions with a sort of diminished capacity, unable if unassisted by grace to achieve the good."[96] The will follows desire, and humans on their own have no control over desire. The person is no longer moved by what they know, but by the force of desire.[97] Thus, will is divided between the desire determined by sin and the striving for God rooted in creation. According to Augustine, the brokenness of will, its enslavement by desire, is paradigmatically exemplified by sexuality. After the fall, man (and Augustine thinks here primarily of males) can no longer perform the sexual act necessary for procreation by will alone. Instead, this requires lust, a form of desire to which will is subject. Ultimately, however, it is primarily self-love that constitutes the basic structure of desire and forms the real antithesis to the love of God.[98] Only in the state of final redemption

---

[89] Ibid., 104–5.
[90] "Caecitas est infidelitas et illuminatio fides." Augustine, *In Ionnis Evangelium Tractatus* 44.1.
[91] See Flasch 194, 104.
[92] "Fac me, pater, quaerere te, vindica me ab errore." Augustine, *Soliloquia* 1.6.
[93] "Da, quod iubes, et iube, quod vis." Augustine, *Confessiones* 10.29.31.37.
[94] Flasch 1994, 409.
[95] Fredriksen 2012, 115–16.
[96] Ibid., 116.
[97] Ibid., 117.
[98] Jenson 2006, 6–28.

will human will no longer take pleasure in sin, but be completely devoted to the divine and find its true fulfillment in it.[99]

Martin Luther radicalized the Augustinian notion of sin as human desire fixated on itself. Taking up Augustinian motifs, he coined the formula of "the person being curved in on oneself" (*homo incurvatus in se*).[100] Luther sees this as a comprehensive definition of the human condition from which no aspect of human existence is excluded.[101] The liberation from egocentric self-love to love of God and neighbor, but also to true self-acceptance, cannot come from human beings themselves. Rather, it results entirely "from outside," i.e., from the promise of divine care, forgiveness, and acceptance. It is not knowledge that brings liberation, but trust in grace.[102] Knowledge is reduced at best to knowing, in the light of grace, one's own incapacity of salvation.[103]

When it comes to its understanding of sin, Christianity has always contained different views regarding the respective extent as well as interaction between defective knowledge and defective will. There is no such thing as *one* normative Christian conception. Particularly contested within theology have been and still are the question of free will on the one hand, and the dependence of will on knowledge on the other. But parts of Christian theology have also been concerned with the question of how far a lack of knowledge may be due to a lack of will. According to Thomas Aquinas, ignorance (*ignorantia*) can be a sin if it refers to something that a person can and should know, but willfully fails to make an effort to know.[104] Yet this position, which is also echoed in Kant's well-known definition of "enlightenment" as "man's emergence from his self-imposed immaturity," only shifts the underlying problem to a higher level: Why do people willingly—or in a "self-imposed" manner—not seek the knowledge that is important for them? Is this again due to an ignorance of a higher order or in the end still to a misdirection of the will? Even in modernity, ideas that echo Augustine in regarding human delusion as chronic, due to self-love and to affects that the mind does not or cannot control, remain prominent. The fact that today such contexts and connections of delusion are often construed as collectively and socially grounded does not really change the underlying problem.[105]

---

[99] Fredriksen 2012, 117–34.
[100] For precursors of this formula, see Bosch 2015, 50–52.
[101] Jenson 2006, 68–70.
[102] Ibid., 71–72.
[103] Ibid., 82.
[104] Thomas Aquinas, *Summa theologiae* I-II.76.2.
[105] See also the overview in Hühn 2001.

5.4 INSIGHT AND TRUST

"Human existence," writes the American theologian Roger Haight, "poses the basic question of itself to itself: our very being elicits wonder at who we are and what we are."[106] This wondering imposes itself especially with regard to the dark side of human existence. Who and what are we in view of the fact that, despite all the undisputed progress of civilization, we accept—can and even perhaps must accept—situations that love and compassion never accept? Such as the fact that a large proportion of humanity live in abject poverty, and even in acute hunger, while a tiny proportion have immense wealth? According to an Oxfam study of 2016, the eight richest people in the world own more than the poorer half of the world's population.[107] Globally, immense sums are spent on armaments (nearly $2 trillion in 2020)[108] in the persistent reestablishment of a balance of weaponry in order to prevent global or local wars, the latter with much less success. According to *Terre des Hommes*, there are 420 million children living in a war or conflict zone at the beginning of the twenty-first century.[109] Many other examples could be given, especially when it comes to the horrors that people inflict on each other day after day. We all know that there is something very fundamentally wrong with humanity—with us. But what exactly? Why do we seem to be so much "more proficient at producing suffering than happiness"?[110]

With their long traditions, religions—or, more precisely, the people in these religions—try to provide answers to such questions. As this chapter has suggested, Buddhism and Christianity provide two typologically different answers. The first sees the primary cause in a defect of insight, i.e., in not-knowing or delusion, while the second identifies the primary cause of evil in a defect of human nature, i.e., primarily in a defect of the human will. Both answers can be found in both traditions, albeit with varying emphases; both traditions also attest that an immoral will and insufficient insight are intertwined; and both identify the source of illusion and depravation in the baleful self-centeredness of the human being. To echo Nakamura, we can explain this structural similarity between both traditions with the assumption that all human beings share a common nature. It is this nature that raises more or less the same existential questions for all human beings, and that leads to similar or intertwined answers.[111]

---

[106] Haight in Haight & Knitter 2015, 117.
[107] https://www.oxfam.de/ueber-uns/aktuelles/2017-01-16-8-maenner-besitzen-so-viel-aermere-haelfte-weltbevoelkerung.
[108] https://www.faz.net/aktuell/politik/ausland/weltweite-militaerausgaben-steigen-auf-neuen-hoechststand-17312126.html.
[109] https://www.tdh.de/was-wir-tun/arbeitsfelder/kinder-im-krieg/.
[110] Knitter in Haight & Knitter 2015, 124.
[111] See above, p. 123.

Roger Haight and Paul Knitter's 2015 comparative discussion of how Buddhism and Christianity understand the human predicament follows largely the mainstream of previous comparisons. It argues that Buddhism points primarily to delusion, while Christianity points to a defect of human nature in terms of its egocentric inclinations.[112] In their normative perspectives, Haight and Knitter make the point that Christianity should learn from Buddhism by reinterpreting the doctrine of original sin as one of original delusion or "original ignorance."[113] While both theologians agree on this, Haight is somewhat more reserved than Knitter: the latter calls explicitly for sin to be reconstructed as ignorance or delusion,[114] and therefore prioritizes, from a soteriological perspective, the promotion of wisdom.[115] According to Haight, though, ignorance/delusion is only *one* factor that stimulates moral depravity.[116] Moreover, it is not within people's own power to become what they long to be,[117] since the causes of antisocial behavior could well also lie in the evolutionary history of human nature.[118]

When it comes to analyzing the human predicament, we can perhaps not say whether it is a lack of insight or a defect of the will that is key. Everyday life tells us both: that insight can indeed lead people to changing their negative behavior (and apparently, a change of behavior is lasting only if it results from a person's own insight). But we also know from experience that will can resist our own insight, and that we may act against our better knowledge. In addition, we know the even more confusing situation that at times our good will is not strong enough to determine our action, but that our deeds seem to follow a dynamic that neither our better knowledge nor our good will can break. Paul is aiming at precisely this in the seventh chapter of his Letter to the Romans, where he expounds that evil is rooted in a "dichotomy between willing and doing, and thus ultimately in the inability to truly live according to the law recognized as good and just."[119]

As already shown, a similar experience is reported in Shantideva's *Bodhicaryāvatāra*. It may well be true that Shantideva also counts primarily on insight to solve the problem of the human predicament, an insight being so strong that it frees a person's will and actions from defilements. But we have also seen that Shantideva, until he has finally achieved this goal of liberating insight, counts on help as it were "from outside": namely, on the compassion of the Buddhas and bodhisattvas to protect him from the negative consequences (the negative karma) of his sins, and to help

---

[112] Haight & Knitter 2015, 117–34.
[113] Ibid., 133–34.
[114] Knitter in ibid., 125. Similarly in Knitter 2009, 50.
[115] Knitter in Knitter & Schmidt-Leukel 2021, 340.
[116] Haight in Haight & Knitter 2015, 130.
[117] Haight in ibid., 122.
[118] See ibid., 130, 132n7.
[119] Röhser 2012, 89.

him on his path.[120] This motif of trusting in external help, in some "other power," seems to be all the stronger in both religions, the more our own actions are perceived as a form of self-imprisonment that neither an effort of will nor our own insight can free us from. This is especially evident in developments within Pure Land Buddhism.[121] "Our eyes of wisdom are lost and our feet of practice have withered," says Shinran's teacher Honen Shonin (1133–1212).[122] Fumio Masutani argues from a Buddhist perspective that Pure Land Buddhism and Christianity are structurally very similar when it comes to their understanding of sin.[123] In both traditions it is the experience of being unable to do good that moves a person to trust in the mercy of someone else.[124]

"If we understand sin as something that has gone wrong within our constitution, then the solution will have to come from outside. . . . But if our fundamental problem is ignorance of what we already are, then the solution will have to be discovered within us."[125] In my view, Knitter's analysis points in the right direction, but I suggest that the difference between these two conceptions of the human predicament can be construed as complementing rather than mutually excluding the other. That help that comes "from outside" can be understood as a healing intervention and not merely mechanically as a kind of "repair."[126] What is more, if we consider the interpersonal dimension of sin (and this is obligatory in both Buddhism and Christianity), then overcoming sin also involves forgiveness, which must come to the sinner primarily from the outside. It may be important that we forgive ourselves, too—but this can hardly replace forgiveness on the part of the other. Recognizing our own debt is only one side of the solution; healing in the sense of reconciliation also requires active and interpersonal forgiveness.

Thich Nhat Hanh is right in that it is easier to forgive other people if we recognize that they have acted badly due to their lack of insight.[127] But this is by no means the only possibility. We can also practice forgiveness because we have experienced forgiveness ourselves. In Christianity, this entails both forgiveness by those against whom one has become guilty, as well as the forgiveness by God that the believer trusts in. As has been shown, in Buddhism, too, trust in the help of the Buddhas and bodhisattvas, especially in the face of seeing one's own sinfulness, is by no means

---

[120]See above, pp. 130–31.
[121]See above, pp. 131–32.
[122]*Jōdoshū ryakushō*. Quoted from Masutani 1967, 85.
[123]Masutani 1967, 110–12.
[124]Ibid., 118–19, 114–15.
[125]Knitter in Haight & Knitter 2015, 124.
[126]See Knitter 2009, 99–100.
[127]Hanh 1996, 85–86.

absent. Knitter argues that, given the nondualist philosophy of Mahayana Buddhism, the "other power" of the Buddhas and bodhisattvas is ultimately not an "other power" at all, but in truth one's "own power." Yet, we should also point out, as Knitter himself also notes, that the distinction between "other" and "own" has no ultimate validity from a nondual perspective.[128] This, however, relativizes both sides: the idea of *other* help, as well as the idea of one's *own* insight. Nonduality does not mean revoking one-sidedly the former in favor of the latter. And at the same time both conceptions retain their justification in the world of conceptual distinctions in which we find ourselves.

---

[128]Knitter 2009, 35–37.

6

Bearers of Hope

As shown in the previous chapter, both Buddhism and Christianity see the cause of human misery as lying in a defect of both knowledge *and* will. Differences within both traditions can be seen among other things in the fact that determining the cause of the human predicament sometimes gives weight more to the one, and sometimes more to the other explanation. These differences also correspond to a certain extent to the different understandings of the role of the respective bearer of hope. If the root of evil is deemed to be delusion, then the bearer of hope brings salvation by bringing about insight. But, if it is deemed to be a defect of the will, then the bearer of hope brings about healing through reconciliation and trust.

However, it is by no means this correspondence alone that shapes how the mediation of salvation is understood in each case. Of even more fundamental importance might be the question of how Gautama, the "Awakened One" (= "Buddha"), and Jesus, the "Son of God," open up an encounter for the human being with ultimate reality.

6.1 AWAKENED TEACHER OR SON OF GOD INCARNATE?

Many religious comparisons have focused repeatedly on the lives of the two central figures or on how the authoritative texts in each tradition have described their lives.[1] However, their real goal was usually to compare typologically the concepts of salvific mediation as reflected in the respective accounts of their lives. I leave aside the hagiographic comparison of the two central figures here, and concentrate instead on the typological aspects. These served, and sometimes still serve, the argument that, when it comes

---

[1] See, for example, Spence Hardy 1874; Scott 1890, 126–91; Wecker 1908; Carpenter 1923, 167–231; Grimm 1928; Schomerus 1931; Streeter 1932, 39–72; Mensching 1978, 55–85; Siegmund 1980, 152–69 (= 1983, 253–80); Lefebure 1993, 3–56; Luz & Michaels 2006 (= 2002); Gwynne 2014.

to the mediation of salvation, there is a central difference between the role of the Buddha and that of the Son of God incarnate. Along this line, a sharp contrast has been established between Buddhism as a human philosophy or doctrine of wisdom, and Christianity as a religion in the proper sense. Although Buddhist interpretations of Jesus are diverse and complex,[2] some Buddhist apologists have interpreted the difference between Gautama, the Awakened One, and Jesus, the Son of God, as paradigmatic for the difference between a rational and scientifically compatible teaching without dogma and compulsion to believe on the one hand, and its opposite on the other.[3] Conversely, many Christian apologists have interpreted the differences between the two foundational figures as showing the contrast between a human seeker who is prone to error, and a divine revealer who brings salvation.[4]

Writing in his famous epic poem *Buddhacarita* ("The Life of the Buddha") in the second century CE, the Indian Buddhist poet Ashvaghosha described the birth of Prince Siddhartha Gautama thus:

Like the sun bursting from a cloud in the morning,—so he too, when he was born from his mother's womb, made the world bright like gold, bursting forth with his rays which dispelled the darkness.[5]

Ashvaghosha gives a very special meaning to the legend that Gautama was born by emerging from the right-hand, i.e., noble, side of his mother "without pain and without illness":

As was Aurva's birth from the thigh, and Pṛthu's from the hand, and Mandhatṛ's, who was like Indra himself, from the forehead, and Kakshīvat from the upper arm,—thus too was his birth.[6]

The supernatural birth of these mythical figures was considered a sign of their special role and of their divine nature. Aurva was considered a descendant and Prithu an incarnation (*avatāra*) of the god Vishnu, while Mandhatri and Kakhsivat were Vedic "seers" (*ṛṣi*) and thus "revealers" respectively. The very symbolism alludes to the ancient Vedic myth of the creation of the world from the various body parts of the purusha (*puruṣa*), i.e., the one divine primordial organism underlying all created reality. Ashvaghosha echoes this myth by referring to Indra, the king of gods, who, according to

---

[2] See now the comprehensive study by Mathias Schneider (Schneider 2023) of Buddhist images of Jesus.
[3] See Notz, 1984, 168–75; Usarski 2001, 122–24.
[4] See Schmidt-Leukel 1992, 36–68.
[5] Cowell 1894, 5.
[6] Ibid., 6.

the Vedas, was born from the head of the purusha. Ashvaghosha uses these comparisons and echoes to lend the birth of Gautama a cosmic significance and the traits of a divine incarnation, a visible manifestation of supreme reality and ultimate truth.

The first comparisons between Buddha and Christ written in the West about seventeen hundred years later present a very different picture. Many nineteenth-century authors were anxious to portray the Buddha as a mere man and philosophically minded teacher, and to contrast him with Christ as the incarnate Son of God and savior of the world. For example, according to Thomas Sterling Berry, "Gautama taught a system; but Christ preached a Gospel."[7] Gautama's disciples "thought of him mainly as the Teacher, whereas the primary conception of the early Christians was of our Lord as the Saviour, who had accomplished, not merely taught, the salvation of the world."[8] For Archibald Scott, Gautama "came in his own name; but Jesus, as one sent by Him into the world, went forth in the Name of His Father. . . . The authority of the Buddha sprang from his acknowledged intellectual superiority, but the authority of Jesus sprang from spiritual insight."[9] Writing along the same lines, Monier-Williams argued that probably the most important contrast between the two figures is that "Christ constantly insisted on the fact that He was God-sent, whereas the Buddha always described himself as self sent."[10] But the "so-called Light of Knowledge" that the Buddha brought was, according to Monier-Williams, rather dim, if it existed at all. In virtually all "momentous questions," the Buddha declared himself to be "a downright Agnostic."[11] Consistent with a contrast construed in this way, most religious comparisons in the West argued that Buddhism, as far as the original Buddha is concerned, is more a philosophy than a religion. According to Monier-Williams, "Christianity is a religion, while Buddhism, at least in its earliest and truest form, is no religion at all, but a mere system of morality and philosophy founded on a pessimistic theory of life."[12]

The contrast between the Buddha as a teacher of wisdom and Christ as the Son of God is also present in the work of Buddhist authors and Western sympathizers of Buddhism—but with a reversed evaluation. An interesting variant of this contrast is provided by Paul Carus (1852–1919), a Protestant admirer of Buddhism.[13] Carus deals directly and critically with the

---

[7] Berry 1890, 69.
[8] Ibid., 31.
[9] Scott 1890, 151.
[10] Monier-William 1889, 553.
[11] Ibid., 544.
[12] Ibid., 537.
[13] See Jackson, C. T. 1968; Verhoeven 2004.

theses put forward by Monier-Williams, arguing that Buddhism is indeed a religion, but a religion of the heart and of morality,[14] and that Buddha's enlightenment is primarily an "enlightenment of the heart."[15] For Carus, this contrasts above all with Christian dogmatism, which, though, is a product of the church, and not something that Christ himself demanded. Christ had demanded "faith," "a moral quality implying steadfast confidence," rather than dogmatic, unquestionable belief. People, according to Carus, cannot live without "faith," while "belief," on the other hand, is at best provisional and must be replaced by the pursuit of knowledge.[16] Moreover, Carus points out that the Buddha was also seen as an incarnation of a divine or supernatural reality. However, Buddhism sees reality as a whole as being permeated by the supernatural, and the Buddha, unlike Christianity, is by no means regarded as the sole incarnation.[17] As we will see, the latter objection is one that Buddhists have repeatedly raised against Christianity.

The contrast between teacher of wisdom and incarnate redeemer continues to resonate today. For example, no less a figure than the British religious studies scholar Ninian Smart has reaffirmed this very contrast by saying, "Jesus saved humanity through his deeds and death—he was a sacrifice which restored the breach between human beings and the Divine. . . . The Buddha saves through his teaching above all."[18] Anthony Clark agrees with Smart, adding, "Christ, who identified himself as both God and human, reconciled humanity . . . to a divine God; but the Buddha identified himself as the bearer of a special teaching, or Dharma, that helps humanity."[19] And Yandell and Netland note that "whereas Gautama presents teachings and practices leading to enlightenment, Jesus does not merely teach the way to reconciliation with God—he himself is the Way to salvation."[20]

A particularly noteworthy example of this kind of contrast can be found in Romano Guardini's (1885–1968) widely read work *The Lord*, which was first published in 1937. It is noteworthy insofar as Guardini, a prominent Roman Catholic theologian, assesses Gautama in an unusually positive way. On the one hand, Guardini argues that so far no one has really said what the Buddha might mean to Christians.[21] According to Guardini,

---

[14] Carus 1897, 290–93.
[15] Ibid., 296.
[16] Ibid., 292. The distinction between "faith" and "belief" became an important theoretical tool for Wilfred Cantwell Smith in the twentieth century, although, as far as I can tell, he nowhere refers to Carus. See Smith, W. C. 1979.
[17] Carus 1897, 196–97, 228–30.
[18] Smart 1993, 13.
[19] Clark 2018, 62.
[20] Yandell & Netland 2009, 209.
[21] Guardini 1997, 367.

> There is but one person whom we might be inclined to compare with Jesus: Buddha. This man is a great mystery. He lived in an awful, almost superhuman freedom, at the same time his kindness is as mighty as a cosmic force.[22]

But then Guardini performs a volte-face and reverts to the traditional contrast, arguing that, unlike the Buddha, Jesus not only brings "new insights" or teaches "people to face each other in a more pure way." Rather, in the case of Jesus, there is "a mind from beyond the world" that is expressing itself, and not only in a way that a person speaks who in terms of morality or religion has broken through the world from within.[23] Thus, for Guardini, there is "no earthly compare" for the work of Christ in the world.[24] The Buddha is at best another "precursor" of Christ, comparable to John the Baptist or Socrates. Like them, the Buddha did not come from beyond the world, but actually from within it. He is a teacher who recognized the "vanity of this fallen world" from which he sought liberation. Buddha's freedom results from his insight, "but his freedom is not that of Christ. . . . Christ's freedom comes from the fact that he stands completely in the love of God."[25]

While thus remaining faithful to the common pattern of seeing the Buddha as a human teacher of wisdom and Jesus as the Son of God incarnate, Guardini's appraisal of the Buddha was much more positive than that of many other Christian theologians of his time. One particularly extreme example was Winfried Philipp Englert, then professor of Roman Catholic theology at the University of Bonn, who argued in a comparison of Christ and Buddha in 1898 that such a comparison is "valuable," since it helps the reader to discern "the true dew of paradise from the poison spread by the snakes."[26] Englert's image of the snake in paradise portrayed the Buddha and Buddhism as a satanic temptation. The reason for this demonization lies in Englert's interpretation of the Buddha as an atheist philosopher who wanted to destroy belief in God. The practical conclusions that Englert drew from his comparison are alarming. In "our days," Englert concludes his book, "European civilization" is bringing the light of Christ to "those deprived peoples" who are "sitting in the darkness of Buddhism." This, though, requires the sword, i.e., military conquest, to precede the cross: "For it is a harsh law, but a law of history, that to such deep depravity the cross will appear only after the sword."[27]

---

[22]Ibid.
[23]Ibid., 369.
[24]Ibid.
[25]Ibid., 367.
[26]Englert 1898, Preface (no pages).
[27]Ibid., 123.

Such forthright justification of aggressive imperialism in the name of Christian mission can be found among several Christian authors since the beginning of modern colonialism. This makes only too understandable Carus' more or less contemporaneous comment that "Christianity (and this is both its strength and its weakness) has been especially successful in teaching surrender of self without at the same time disturbing the egotism so strongly developed in the Western nations."[28] However, Western colonialism also led Buddhists to create their own demonizations, one example being an eighteenth-century folktale prevalent in Sri Lanka that reflects the experience of Sri Lankan Buddhists under Portuguese colonial rule in the sixteenth and seventeenth centuries. This folktale refers to Jesus as the "carpenter-demon" or "carpenter-heretic." He was not the son or incarnation of God, but an incarnation and the son of Mara, a figure that in Buddhism represents the demonic adversary of the Buddha.[29] Demonizing those religious and political groups perceived as a threat to Buddhism by calling them "Maras" or "sons of Maras" has a long tradition in Buddhism.[30] In a 2014 article posted on LankaWeb, Buddhist activist Senaka Weeraratna pointed to Sri Lanka's history since the 1950s and argued that, behind "the unrelenting march of Abrahamic religions into the hinterland of Buddhist Asia," there is "a diabolical scheme underway to undermine Buddhism." Faced with this situation, Weeraratna calls "on China to assume leadership of the Buddhist world. We need a powerhouse to protect Buddhism. China meets that description. China too faces the same challenge from Abrahamic religions as the rest of Buddhist Asia and even Hindu India."[31] This example illustrates rather clearly how the reciprocal interreligious perceptions documented in comparisons of religions have their impact even in the field of current politics.

6.2 AWAKENING, PROCLAMATION, AND INCARNATION

An Imbalanced Picture and Its Correction

Usually, those who presented or still present the difference between Gautama and Jesus as a contrast between the awakened teacher and the Son

---

[28]Carus 1897, 234.
[29]See Young & Senanayaka 1998. See also above, p. 61.
[30]See Schmidt-Leukel 2022a.
[31]Senaka Weeraratna, "Mettananda's Grim Warning of 'A Conspiracy against Buddhism' (1956) Still Worthy of Serious Attention," Lankaweb, November 10, 2014, http://www.lankaweb.com/news/items/2014/11/10/mettanandas-grim-warning-of-a-conspiracy-against-buddhism-1956-still-worthy-of-serious-attention/.

of God incarnate were and are well aware that the matter is actually more complicated, since in Buddhism too—especially, but by no means only, in Mahayana Buddhism—the idea exists that a Buddha is the incarnation of a higher reality.[32] Those making these comparisons were normally aware of the early identification of the Buddha with the cosmic dharma; they were familiar with the doctrine of the *Lotus-Sūtra*, which says that the earthly Buddha is a manifestation of the supramundane and eternal Buddha; and they sometimes mentioned the Mahayana doctrine of the "Three Buddha Bodies," which claims that both the human and the supramundane Buddhas are manifestations of the ineffable ultimate reality.[33] However, they dismissed these traditional interpretations of the Buddha as later developments, as forms of a "deification" of Gautama that corresponded neither to how Gautama saw himself, nor to how early Buddhism saw him. The problem, however, is that they did not take such a historical-critical perspective when interpreting Jesus as Son of God and incarnate Savior, which inevitably made the comparative view skewed. It is essential that we correct this view by taking a historical perspective with regard to both figures.

Historical-critical exegesis of the New Testament and research on the history of Christian dogma have produced a great deal of evidence that Jesus in all historical probability did not see himself as God incarnate or as the incarnation of the second person of a triune deity.[34] Rather, he shared the monotheistic faith of the Jewish people and sharply distinguished himself as a human being from the one and only God. When addressed with the words "Good Teacher" (*didáskale agathe*), Jesus replies, "Why do you call me good? No one is good but God alone" (Mark 10:17–18).[35] And he does not criticize the address then changed to just "Teacher" (Mark 10:20).

A historical approach shows that both religions contain both the concept of the "awakened" or inspired teacher, and that of the incarnate savior, which relativizes the common juxtaposition of Buddha and Christ. However, only a handful of comparativists have taken this viewpoint, one such being the Oxford exegete, theologian, philosopher, and religious studies scholar Burnett Hillman Streeter (1874–1937).[36] In his comparison, *The Buddha and the Christ*, from 1932, Streeter pointed out clearly how the understand-

---

[32]On the ideas of the Buddha's supramundane nature in the pre-Mahayana schools, see Weber 1994 and 1998; on different developments within Mahayana, see the contributions by Tauscher, von Borsig, and Schmidt-Leukel in Schmidt-Leukel 1998.

[33]See above, pp. 98–100.

[34]See, for example, Young, F. 1983; Dunn 1989; Vermes 2001.

[35]Compare also the congruent judgments of Hans Küng and Wolfhart Pannenberg in Küng et al. 1986, 117 (= Küng et al. 1984, 184); Pannenberg 1994, 372 (= Pannenberg 1991, 415).

[36]On Streeter's significance for Christian-Buddhist dialogue, see also Lai, P.-C. 2009.

ing of Gautama and Jesus had developed and changed over time. Streeter compared the interpretation of Gautama as the incarnation of a supramundane reality in Mahayana Buddhism with the interpretation of Jesus as the incarnate Word of God in the Gospel of John,[37] arguing that interest in the teachings of both had shifted in both cases to the question of the meaning of their person.[38] Despite all sociocultural differences between the two initial situations, Streeter argued, both religions had become increasingly similar in the course of their inner development to the point of "convergence."[39] This thesis anticipates somewhat Couliano's view already discussed that systems that have already been running for a sufficiently long time "tend," because their fractal structure always continues to further branch out, "to overlap not only in shape but in substance."[40]

Within the context of Greek culture, the person of Jesus was construed, Streeter argues, either according to the model of apotheosis, i.e., as a "deification," or according to the model of theophany, i.e., as a "manifestation of the divine." While the first model would tend toward an adoptionist understanding of incarnation that sees Jesus' sonship with God as being more like an adoption, the second tended toward a docetic understanding of incarnation that sees Jesus as being only apparently a human being, but in reality God. For Streeter, the Christological formula articulated at the Council of Chalcedon ("truly God and truly man") had not been able to establish the sought-after median between the two conceptions. In actual practice, though, it was the docetic understanding that had prevailed again and again, largely pushing the idea of Jesus as a real human being to the margins.[41] In this respect, Streeter holds, the development of the concept of incarnation in Christianity is remarkably similar to its development in Buddhism, since the latter also conceived incarnation in a primarily docetic way.[42]

Another scholar who deviated relatively early from the common juxtaposition of Buddha and Christ was the Sanskritist, philosopher, and religious studies scholar Joseph Estlin Carpenter (1844–1927), who also taught at Oxford. In his 1923 book *Buddhism and Christianity: A Contrast and a Parallel*, Carpenter comes close to a fractal interpretation when he summarizes the relationship between the two religions: "There are as many diversities *between* them as there are *within* the internal development of each."[43] While not explicitly comparing the differences *between* the two

---

[37]Streeter 1932, 83.
[38]Ibid.
[39]Ibid., 76–77.
[40]Couliano 1992, 268. See above, pp. 31–33.
[41]Streeter 1932, 131–35.
[42]Ibid., 86, 134.
[43]Carpenter 1923, 306 (emphasis mine).

traditions with the differences *within* each of them, he does nonetheless at least suggest such a parallel when he writes about the understanding of Gautama and Jesus in Buddhism and Christianity:

> Both present a Person as an object of faith, who in a human life devotes himself to teaching. . . . Both ultimately interpret the person of their Founders by philosophical conceptions linking them with the Infinite and Eternal Source of all existence. . . . Each [of the two religions] rests on some form of Revelation.[44]

Such judgments can be well justified from a historical perspective that recognizes the internal diversity of both traditions. Even if some New Testament texts already show the early beginnings of the Christian belief in incarnation,[45] a historical perspective does not allow us to suggest that this is how Jesus understood himself. It may remain difficult to determine what exactly Jesus' self-understanding had been. Yet it is possible to discern what can be excluded and hence belongs to later developments. The Christian belief in incarnation emerged during a long and complicated process full of (sometimes violent) disputes, without, as Streeter already pointed out, ever reaching a consensus among all Christians. Thus, there is actually no such thing as *the* Christian belief in incarnation, at least not in a homogeneous form, but it still exists only in a rather great variety of different conceptions. And, even if there are some formulations in some New Testament passages that speak of Father, Son, and Holy Spirit, the doctrine of a trinitarian God did not develop until the end of the second century CE. Moreover, this doctrine too by no means led to a uniform idea, but instead to a multitude of variants.[46]

Even more complicated is the quest for the historical Buddha. According to Bernard Faure, we can say with more or less certainty "that he was born, he lived, and he died. The rest remains lost in the mists of myth and legend."[47] John Strong suggests that we can add some more details to this, such as his name, his tribal affiliation, where he lived, and, with much less certainty, roughly when he lived—but only because of "the lack of any contradictory evidence."[48] What we can glean from the Buddhist texts is not a sketch of a historical person, but rather "the impression that the Buddha made on his followers and subsequent generations."[49]

---

[44]Ibid., 305–7.
[45]See Vermes 2001; Schreiber 2015.
[46]See Hübner 1996; Ohlig 1999.
[47]Faure 2009, 12.
[48]Strong 2016b, 140.
[49]Freiberger & Kleine 2011, 36.

Given this state of affairs, it is methodologically unsound to compare Jesus with Gautama in such a way that Jesus is seen entirely through the lens of a developed doctrine of incarnation, while a similar perspective on Gautama is rejected as unhistorical and secondary. A more sound comparison must therefore start deliberately with the testimonies of the faith-traditions themselves. This is something that Robert Elinor does quite consistently in his book *Buddha and Christ*, since he does not rely solely on the textual testimonies, but also takes account above all of the rich iconographic material,[50] and thus judging,

> But Buddhists do not take refuge in Gautama the sage, nor do Christians worship Jesus the rabbi. Neither Buddha nor Christ has lived primarily as a historical figure. Pictures of transcendent Buddhas far outnumber those of Gautama, just as Christ the holy child, vicarious sacrifice, triumphant judge, and glorious redeemer is pictured far more frequently than the Galilean teacher. Narratives of their ministries portray them as transfigured Lords.[51]

This type of comparative approach certainly does not mean ignoring the historical perspective. Rather, it includes the question of why and how Buddhists and Christians, in the course of history, have each understood and glorified their teachers as manifestation or incarnation of ultimate reality.

Embodied Teaching

The canonical Buddhist texts often call Gautama "teacher" (*śāstṛ*), "great teacher" (*mahācārya*), or "king of the dharma" (*dharma-rāja*).[52] The Gospels call Jesus "teacher" (*didáskalos*) forty-one times—a Christological title used more often than any other one.[53] Mark 14:14 suggests that this is how Jesus referred to himself: "Say to the master of the house, 'The Teacher asks, "Where is my guest room, where I may eat the Passover with my disciples?"'" The second century still saw much of early Christianity regarding Jesus' redemptive function as lying primarily in his role as teacher of the truth. The light of the truth he spreads dispels the darkness of sin, with salvation often being understood as a process of growth in understanding ultimate truth.[54] The idea that Jesus' teaching brings about redemptive

---

[50] Elinor 2000.
[51] Ibid., 24, 40.
[52] See Weber 1994, 14; Griffiths 1994, 60–66.
[53] See Feulner 2016, 14.
[54] Ibid., 15, and Kelly 1977, 163–70.

knowledge never left Christianity completely,[55] and not even then when changes in the understanding of sin were accompanied by changes in the interpretation of Jesus' role.[56]

In Buddhism, as in Christianity, the designation of Gautama and Jesus as teachers was accompanied by the affirmation that their teaching is of a special nature. Gautama was not understood simply as one religious teacher among many, nor was Jesus seen as a more or less ordinary rabbi. The Buddhist texts present Gautama as the truly enlightened or awakened teacher. The light that he brings is compared at one point with the light of the sun, while the light of the other teachers is compared to that of glowworms.[57] According to early Buddhist scholasticism, a "Buddha" in the full sense (*samyaksambuddha*) differs from both an ordinary enlightened person, an *arhat*, and from a so-called solitary Buddha (a *pratyekabuddha*). An *arhat* attains enlightenment by following the teachings of a Buddha, whereas a Buddha comes to know the dharma by himself—even though he may have been given the impetus to do so by a previous Buddha in a distant life. This is also true for a solitary Buddha, from whom a Buddha in the full sense differs in that the latter is able to teach the dharma in such a way that other people also attain enlightenment. This allows a Buddha in the full sense to establish a long-term salvific community, the sangha.[58] It is therefore the case at least for the older Buddhism that there cannot be two Buddhas at the same time.[59] The implication is that a new Buddha can appear and establish a new sangha only when the sangha of the previous Buddha has degenerated completely and the dharma fallen into oblivion. Thus, according to the testimony of the canonical texts, Gautama proclaims after his enlightenment,

> I have no teacher, and one like me
> Exists nowhere in all the world
> With all its gods, because I have
> No person for my counterpart.[60]

---

[55]On this, see in particular Feulner 2016.

[56]An example of this is the development of Augustine. While in his early writings he saw redemption as purifying knowledge brought about by Christ as the teacher of the right life and the embodiment of the eternal truth, in his later works he understood Christ as the one who purchased redemption from Satan's rule through his death (Flasch 1994, 153–54, 326–27, 378), a view that was further reinforced by Anselm of Canterbury and Martin Luther.

[57]See *Udāna* 6.10.

[58]Introductions to Buddhism often claim that a *pratyekhabuddha* does not teach at all. This does not correspond to the statements of Buddhist scriptures, which often also portray *pratyekhabuddhas* as teaching. However, they mostly teach only Buddhist morality and not the whole path of salvation. Above all, they do not establish a sangha, which means that their work is less salvific than that of a Buddha in the full sense.

[59]*Aṅguttara Nikāya* 1.25; *Milindapañha* 4.6.4–10.

[60]*Majjhima Nikāya* 26. Ñāṇamoli & Bodhi 2001, 263.

According to Axel Michaels, we can by no means rule out that the Buddha saw "himself as a superhuman (*lokottara*), extraordinary being," and that this "was the reason why so many followed him, not just the content of his teaching."[61] Be that as it may, the canonical texts characterize the teaching of the Buddha by no means as a kind of philosophical search for truth, but rather as the authoritative proclamation of that cosmic truth that the Buddha had beheld in his awakening. Peter Masefield has therefore rightly depicted the Buddha's teachings as an act of revelation.[62] The fact that every Buddhist sutra begins with the words "Thus have I heard" may very well be interpreted as a kind of seal that the Buddhist community used to mark the Buddha's teachings as *śruti*, meaning "what has been heard."[63] For *śruti* is traditionally the technical term used by the Brahmins to affirm the revealed status of the Vedic scriptures. The Vedic "seers" (*ṛṣi*) had received revelation through spiritual vision—and therefore in a mode comparable to the Buddha's insight gained in his awakening. Revealed knowledge is "heard" through the recitation of the Vedic hymns or, in the case of Buddhism, through the recitation of the Buddhist sutras.

Similarly, the Gospels emphasize that Jesus taught not "as the scribes," but "as one having authority" (*exousia*) (Mark 1:22). His authority is based on the experience of the divine Spirit at his baptism, an event that all four Gospels place at the beginning of his public ministry. The belief that Jesus was guided by the Spirit places him alongside the Jewish prophets,[64] and may well reflect how he viewed himself. According to Ed Sanders, Jesus can be called a "charismatic and autonomous prophet," since "he thought that he had been especially commissioned to speak for God, and this conviction was based on a feeling of personal intimacy with the deity."[65]

Jesus taught not only the dawn of God's reign, but especially the character of this reign. As already stated in chapter 4, Jesus compared God's relationship with human beings to that of a merciful father. Living by the rules of God's reign therefore means not only entrusting oneself to God's goodness, but also imitating and reflecting God's mercy in one's own behavior. This is undoubtedly something that Jesus made use of for his own person.[66] If he understood himself as someone whose life reflected the mercy of God's

---

[61] Michaels in Luz & Michaels 2002, 151. The term "superman" in the English translation (Luz & Michaels 2006, 136) is misleading.
[62] See Masefield 1986.
[63] Arvind Sharma (2005, 69) has also proposed this interpretation. According to the traditional Buddhist interpretation, the words, "Thus have I heard," means that Ananda, Gautama's close companion, recited all the canonical sutras at the first council shortly after the master's death, thus vouching for their authenticity.
[64] See Lampe 1977.
[65] Sanders 1995, 239.
[66] Vermes 1981, 43–44.

reign, then it would also be conceivable that he regarded himself, as some exegetes suppose, as the "Son of Man" whom God will appoint as judge in the final judgment. But this is not certain.[67] In any case, though, Jesus was for his followers the primary model of a life under God's rule, the reflection of God's mercy. This helps us understand at least one root of the emerging Christian belief in Jesus as a divine incarnation: like other prophets before him, Jesus was regarded as someone who proclaimed the Word of God. Yet he not only taught the Word; he *embodied* it in his life and death. Thus, the prologue of the Gospel of John speaks of Jesus as someone in whom the divine Word has "become flesh" (John 1:14). And it is in this sense that here he is also called the "only begotten [Son] from the Father" (John 1:14).[68]

As repeatedly mentioned, the idea of the Buddha as the visible embodiment of the dharma can already be found in the pre-Mahayana scriptures, and one might well say that the dharma has become flesh in the Buddha.[69] This idea is closely linked to the Buddhological honorific title *tathāgata*, which literally means the "thus gone." That is, the Buddha lived as he taught. His life corresponded to the dharma, and especially to the life schema of every Buddha, since, according to the ancient Buddhist view, the life of every Buddha always follows the same pattern, albeit with some minor individual variations. This pattern *is* in essence how Buddhism understands the dharma: it comprises the carelessness of youth, the encounter with transience in the form of the four excursions, the search for the "deathless," its fulfillment in the experience of awakening, and the subsequent proclamation of the dharma with the founding of the sangha.[70] By experiencing nirvana in his awakening, the Buddha became in a sense "nirvanized." In other words, like any truly enlightened person, he becomes through his compassionate activity a visible representation of the invisible and ineffable ultimate reality of nirvana,[71] a notion that has clear structural parallels to the belief in Jesus as image of the invisible God (Colossians 1:15; 2 Corinthians 4:4). Just as the life and teaching of the Buddha show what the ineffable ultimate reality means for us, so the life and teaching of Jesus show how the ineffable God relates to us. In both cases, this incarnational language does not cite how Gautama or Jesus saw themselves, but reflects an experience and belief that they evoked in the lives of their followers. Thus, as Roger Haight writes, "Jesus and Buddha both open up the human imagination to the immanent experience of ultimate reality."[72]

---

[67]See on this Luz in Luz & Michaels 2002, 140–47 (= 2006, 127–31).
[68]See Schreiben 2015, 192–93.
[69]In Theravada Buddhism in particular, the Buddha is understood as a superhuman being, but not docetistically as an illusory being (see Weber 1994, 65–86).
[70]See Schmidt-Leukel 2006a, 19–29; Griffiths 1994, 87–90.
[71]*Aṅguttara Nikāya* 3.55–56. See above, pp. 96–97.
[72]Haight in Haight & Knitter 2015, 63.

Fractal Structure

We can thus observe an inner interconnectedness between awakening and incarnation, between the belief in Gautama as the "Awakened One" and in Jesus as the Son of God incarnate. This interconnectedness is mediated by the idea of authoritative proclamation, or, we might say, by the category of revelation or the prophetic. As categories underlying belief in central religious figures, awakening, incarnation, and prophetic proclamation stand in a fractal relationship with each other: each of the three categories contains aspects of the other two. This fractal structure is rooted in what Mircea Eliade, so often reviled in contemporary religious studies, has aptly called a "hierophany" or "epiphany of the holy," that is the "manifestation . . . of the sacred in a fragment of the universe."[73] This "fragment" can be a part of nature, a human artifact, a text, or even a human person. In each of these cases, something finite and limited becomes the medium of a transcendent reality, this medium articulating the experience of ultimate reality, the "awakening" to this reality. Thus, the medium reveals the transcendent on the one hand, while pointing beyond itself to the transcendent reality on the other:

- Siddhartha Gautama, under the tree of enlightenment, *awakens* to the ultimate refuge from suffering, nirvana, and, out of compassion, *proclaims* to others the path to liberation that he himself lives, thereby *embodying* nirvana and dharma.
- Jesus, in his baptism in the waters of the Jordan and his subsequent retreat to the desert, *awakens* to the ultimate source of life, which he calls "Father," and, by imitating and reflecting the Father's mercy, he *proclaims* and lives the good news of God's imminent reign, thereby himself *embodying* the eternal Word.

We can also include Islam in this structure:[74]

- Muhammad, in the solitude of the mountains, *awakens* to the ultimate unity of true reality and, out of divine commission, *proclaims* God's oneness, justice, and mercy of God to which he henceforth submits his life, thus *embodying* both the eternal Word of God in his message and the submission to God as the true essence of all reality.

Thus, Muslims may discover through comparative or interreligious theology that, and how, prophetic existence also contains certain features of incarna-

---
[73] Eliade 1996, 463.
[74] This idea is further developed in Schmidt-Leukel 2017b, 193–203, 235–37.

tion and awakening. The mainstream of Islam[75] does not regard Muhammad as an incarnation of the divine Word in the same way as Christianity does with regard to Jesus. But this certainly does not mean that the aspect of incarnation is completely absent. Prophets are human beings with whom the Word of God is incarnate in the form of their prophetic message—with all the sociocultural and historical (that is, human) conditionality and limitedness as they are given through the language, terminology, and context of the message. In this respect, the Qur'an mediated by Muhammad is also a kind of incarnation of the divine Word. The indissoluble interweaving between the Qur'anic suras and the life of Muhammad also shows that there is a continuity between the prophet and the incarnation of the Word in his message. In Sufism, Muhammad is venerated as the embodiment of the cosmic "Muhammad reality" that existed before Adam, the first human being. This reality constitutes the primary archetype of all creation, and finds its perfect incarnation or manifestation in the prophet Muhammad. The possibility to be a prophet of God and thus a bearer of the divine Word incarnate in human language, without ceasing to be a real human being, is thus already inherent in human nature. The prophet "awakens" to this, his true nature. The structural similarities between the Sufi idea of a "Muhammad reality" and the Buddhist idea of a general "Buddha nature" have been identified and stressed on both the Islamic and the Buddhist side.[76]

Understanding the fractal link between awakening, incarnation, and prophetic proclamation in comparing Buddhism and Christianity can make Buddhists more sensitive to the prophetic dimension in the proclamation of the dharma. After all, someone becomes a Buddha only by proclaiming the dharma in such a way that it opens the path to salvation, and leads to the establishment of the salvific community. There is already a prophetic element in this. At the same time, noticing that there is an inner link between all three categories could strengthen the awareness that the incarnational dimension of Buddhahood also entitles us to use personal ways of expression and imagination with regard to the experienceable dimension of ultimate reality, as is in fact the case in large parts of the Buddhist tradition. Conversely, Christians can learn to acknowledge the incarnational dimension of awakening, and thus take more account theologically of the fact that incarnational ideas have their roots and foundation in prophetic proclamation. For Jesus embodies—incarnates—the Word of God in his message and in his life. The fractal connection of the three central categories not only enables a process of mutual learning and reciprocal illumination; it directly

---

[75] In more minor currents of the Islamic tradition, the idea of God's or the divine spirit's incarnation in human beings is by no means absent. According to Kriztina Kehl-Bodrogi, "Belief in the divine incarnation in human form is clearly part of the Alevi religion" (Kehl-Bodrogi 1988, 140).

[76] See Izutsu 2008, 170–71; Shah-Kazemi 2010, 59–60, 72.

invites it.[77] It disentangles the concept of incarnation from its constraints; it entangles the spirit of Buddha and the spirit of Christ.

6.3 DISENTANGLEMENT AND ENTANGLEMENT

The Question of the Uniqueness of Incarnation

If the categories of Buddhahood and incarnation are fractally intertwined by the joint aspect of authoritative proclamation, then the inevitable question arises whether incarnation is unique, since Buddhahood and prophetic teaching are not limited to uniqueness. It is, however, important to resist seeing the difference between Buddhism and Christianity simply and too quickly as an opposition between belief in multiple incarnations on the one hand, and belief in the uniqueness of incarnation on the other. Although such a distinction tends to have a point, a closer look reveals a more complex—and, indeed, fractal—relationship here, too: just as there are approaches in Buddhism that emphasize the relative uniqueness of the Buddha, so there are approaches in Christianity that pluralize the idea of incarnation. As already said, the older Buddhist view is that there is only one Buddha at a time, i.e., for as long as the sangha founded by this Buddha continues to exist in a form where it is able to teach the dharma effectively. Thus, according to the early Buddhist treatise *Milindapañha* (4.6.9),

> Whatever is mighty in the world is singular. . . . A Tathāgata, an Arahat Buddha supreme, is great; and he is alone in the world. Wherever any one of these spring up, then there is no room for a second. And therefore . . . is it that only one Tathāgata, an Arahat Buddha supreme, can appear at one time in the world.[78]

The phrase "any one of these" reveals of course that this uniqueness is not absolute, but indeed relative. There are Buddhas in other worlds and in one world at different times. Such ideas meant that the widespread Buddhist ideal was initially to follow the path taught by the Buddha and to become an enlightened arhat. This changed with the emerging idea, which then became more or less the norm in Mahayana Buddhism, that it is better, because altogether more beneficial, to strive for Buddhahood, i.e., to become a Buddha oneself in another time and another world, and thereby show as many beings as possible the way to enlightenment. The belief,

---
[77] See Schmidt-Leukel 2024.
[78] Rhys Davids 1894, 50–51.

widespread in ancient India—that there are countless different worlds, both simultaneously and successively, since each vanishing world is succeeded by a new one—made it possible to make the striving for Buddhahood a general religious goal. This in turn presupposed that all beings in the cycle of rebirth have the potential for this, i.e., that they carry within themselves an embryonic Buddha nature (*tathāgatagarbha*). The further development of this doctrine in the Chinese cultural area, and especially the idea that everything that exists participates in Buddha nature, sometimes relativized the older idea that there cannot be two Buddhas at the same time. In addition, the doctrine of the "Three Buddha Bodies" established the belief in a plurality of simultaneously existing supramundane Buddhas, while both this-worldly and supramundane Buddhas were regarded as various manifestations of the one ultimate reality of the dharma body (*dharmakāya*).

Buddhists from this strand of the tradition have therefore criticized Christianity for its idea of the uniqueness of incarnation, without addressing the fact that this idea also existed and still exists in their own tradition, at least in the form of a relational uniqueness. From such a Buddhist perspective, José Cabezón, for example, holds that "the problem lies not in the claim that Jesus is the incarnation or manifestation of a deity." Rather, the problem is the Christian image of God on the one hand, and, on the other, "the claim that Jesus is unique in being such a manifestation."[79] According to Daisetz Suzuki, Mahayana Buddhists see "an incarnation of the Dharmakāya in every spiritual leader regardless of his nationality or professed creed," and therefore "recognize a Buddha in Socrates, Mohammed, Jesus, Francis of Assisi, Confucius, Laotze, and many others."[80] Thich Nhat Hanh goes even further: "As the child of Mary and Joseph, Jesus is the Son of Woman and Man. As someone animated by the energy of the Holy Spirit, He is the Son of God. The fact that Jesus is both the Son of Man and the Son of God is not difficult for a Buddhist to accept."[81] Rather, the problem lies in the claim to uniqueness: "We are all, at the same time, the sons and daughters of God and the children of our parents."[82] "Of course Christ is unique. But who is not unique? Socrates, Mohammed, the Buddha, you and I are all unique." Behind the Christian claim that Jesus' sonship of God is unique, Thich Nhat Hanh discerns the idea "that Christianity provides the only way of salvation and all other religious traditions are of no use."[83]

Thich Nhat Hanh may present his criticism here in an oversimplified

---

[79] Cabezón 2000, 24.
[80] Suzuki 1977, 63.
[81] Hanh 1996, 36. Similar objections are also documented for the encounter between Buddhists and Christians in the sixteenth–seventeenth centuries in Japan and China. See Elison 1991, 377; Kern, I. 2001, 38.
[82] Hanh 1996, 44.
[83] Ibid., 193.

and somewhat exaggerated form, but he does make two points that should be taken seriously: those interpretations of Jesus who see him as a real human being—and this applies at least formally to most of the Christologies common in theology today—will have to justify the claim that incarnation is unique in such a way that this claim does not collide with this real humanness. According, for example, to Karl Rahner, the openness to the divine mystery is not fundamentally different with regard to Jesus than it is to all other human beings. It is just the case that Jesus corresponded to this general disposition (Rahner calls it the "supernatural existential") far better than all other human beings. In this respect, the incarnation of God in Jesus is for Rahner "the unique and *highest* instance of the actualization of the essence of human reality, which consists in this: that man is insofar as he abandons himself away to the absolute mystery whom we call God."[84] But precisely if, like Rahner, we see incarnation as the "highest case" of what is inherent in the "essence" of every human being, then the claim to uniqueness seems arbitrary. Indeed, it raises the suspicion that it is ultimately a matter of asserting the superiority of Christianity. While Rahner did make an effort to appreciate other religions, even as paths of salvation, he also held to the view that Christianity is "the absolute religion, intended for all men, which cannot recognize any other religion beside itself as of equal right."[85] For him, any positive significance of other religions is provisional. Other religions are oriented toward their being surpassed and fulfilled by Christianity. Rahner tries to buttress this view by claiming that religious history contains no other human being whose life can be understood as an irreversible self-promise on the part of God to humankind.[86] But even this argument is barely able to escape the impression of arbitrariness, since Rahner is well aware that religious history has "saviour figures" who are also given a "final and definitive sense."[87]

Thus, some Christian theologians engaged in dialogue with Buddhists have accepted and shared the Buddhist criticism of the claim regarding the uniqueness of incarnation.[88] This is particularly clear in the case of Paul Knitter, who draws explicitly on the emphasis on the real humanness of

---

[84]Rahner 1978, 218. In the German original, this crucial statement reads, "Die Menschwerdung Gottes ist von daher gesehen der einmalig *höchste* Fall des Wesensvollzugs der menschlichen Wirklichkeit, der darin besteht, daß der Mensch ist, indem er sich weggibt in das absolute Geheimnis hinein, das wir Gott nennen." Rahner 1977, 216. Note that, when Rahner refers to the "absolute mystery" called "God," he uses the neuter relative pronoun "das" ("that"), whereas the English translation uses the personal pronoun "whom."

[85]Rahner 2001, 22. The German original reads, "Das Christentum versteht sich als die für alle Menschen bestimmte, absolute Religion, die keine andere als gleichberechtigt neben sich anerkennen kann." Rahner 1964, 139.

[86]See on this the overview and discussion in Schmidt-Leukel 1997, 532–42.

[87]Rahner 1978, 321.

[88]See also Pieris 1988, 124–35; Keel 1995, 180–81.

Jesus in Karl Rahner's Christological approach, but avoids Rahner's superiority claims.[89] According to Knitter, a pluralized notion of incarnation can be combined with the attribution of a particular form of uniqueness or singularity to each central incarnation or manifestation of the divine.[90] Like Aloysius Pieris, Knitter sees Jesus' uniqueness or singularity in the fact that he embodies "God's defense pact with the poor." "The God embodied in Jesus suffers not only for the victims of this world; this God suffers *like* them and *with* them."[91]

In pluralizing the idea of incarnation, Knitter also draws on those "New Testament perspectives that saw Jesus' divinity in terms of his total responsiveness and transparency to the Spirit of God."[92] Indeed, when it comes to the question of plurality and uniqueness, it is the case that both are present in both traditions. Just as Buddhism has, besides the idea of a plurality of Buddhas, also the idea of a relative uniqueness, so Christianity has, besides its emphasis on the uniqueness of Christ, also the idea of a pluralization of the sonship of God. This is especially true of Paul, who in Romans (8:14) writes, "For all who are led by the Spirit of God are sons of God." Those who love God, he continues, are "predestined to be conformed to the image of his Son, in order that he might be the firstborn among many brothers" (Romans 8:29; similarly, Galatians 3:26–27). Paul holds that for the person led by the Spirit, it is Christ who lives in them and no longer their old self (Galatians 2:20; similarly, 4:19; Romans 8:10). This motif has very much taken a back seat in the history of Christianity to the dogmatic emphasis on the uniqueness and singularity of Jesus. However, the motif has always played a special role in Christian mysticism.[93] Also, Buddhists such as Keiji Nishitani and Shizuteru Ueda have come upon the Pauline notion of the Spirit-Christ or inward Christ in their dialogue with Christians, leading them to question the Christian claim regarding the uniqueness of incarnation.[94]

Buddha Mind and Christ Mind

In 2008, Paul Knitter officially took refuge in Buddha, dharma, and sangha, and took the bodhisattva vows. In doing so, he formally became a Buddhist without ceasing to see himself as both a Christian and a Roman Catholic theologian.[95] Methodist Elizabeth Harris reveres the Buddha for the quali-

---

[89] See Knitter 2009, 116.
[90] See Knitter 1997; 2009, 92–130; Haight & Knitter 2015, 57–75.
[91] Knitter 2009, 126.
[92] Ibid., 122. See also ibid., 129–30, 196–201.
[93] See also the hints in Riches 2008, 137–43.
[94] See Ueda S. 2001, 53–55.
[95] Knitter 2009, 213–17.

ties that he embodies, which she believes resonate with those of Jesus.[96] Anglican Ross Thompson sees Christ and Buddha as distinct but "genuine incarnations of the divine or the Dharmakaya."[97] On the Buddhist side, the Thai Theravada Buddhist Bhikkhu Buddhadasa has called Jesus a Buddha—despite the Theravada dogma that there can at this time be no second Buddha.[98] For Tenzin Gyatso, the fourteenth Dalai Lama, Jesus was either a Buddha ("a fully enlightened being") "or a bodhisattva of a very high spiritual realization."[99] The Zen Buddhist Masao Abe, like D. T. Suzuki before him, spoke of Jesus as an incarnation of the dharma body.[100] And the Pure Land Buddhist John Yokota saw Jesus as a manifestation of the wisdom and compassion of the supranatural Amida Buddha.[101] Such voices are by no means representative of the respective Christian denominations or Buddhist traditions, but they do show how wide the spectrum is that we can identify today among confessional options. That there are people who now see themselves as Christians and Buddhists at the same time is a growing phenomenon and something that raises increasingly the attention of scholars.[102] For me, a key reason for the reciprocal appreciation that some Buddhists and Christians show today with regard to the central figures in each tradition religion is that they perceive an intense affinity between what can be called the Buddha mind and the Christ mind. This opens up another important field for those processes of interreligious learning that revolve around the understanding of Gautama and Jesus.

Gautama's compassion is considered a constitutive part of his Buddhahood, since he became a Buddha in the full sense not through his awakening alone, but through his compassionate resolve to preach the dharma and establish the sangha. Before attaining Buddhahood, he is designated as a "bodhisattva," which denoted long before the emergence of Mahayana Buddhism a being who is moving toward Buddhahood. This is the reason that the canonical texts use the term *the bodhisattva* (Pali: *bodhisatta*) not only for Siddhartha Gautama before his awakening, but also for all his previous existences, whether as deity, human, or animal. According to general Buddhist belief, it was in these previous lives that he cultivated those spiritual virtues and qualities that eventually enabled him to attain Buddhahood in his final life, with the development of selfless compassion playing a crucial role among these qualities. Numerous *Jātakas* and *Avadānas*, i.e., stories about the Buddha's previous lives, illustrate this point by describing how,

---

[96] Harris, E. 2000.
[97] Thompson 2010, 53.
[98] Buddhadasa 1967, 104–10. See on this also Schmidt-Leukel 2017b, 80–82.
[99] Dalai Lama 2002, 83.
[100] Suzuki 1977, 63; Abe 1985, 184–88.
[101] Yokota 2005, 100.
[102] See above, p. 10.

as a bodhisattva, he repeatedly sacrificed his life out of compassion for other beings.

A particularly well-known example is the popular *Sasa Jātaka* (*Jātaka 316*). It explains why it is possible to discern not only a face in the shadows of the full moon, but—as so often documented in Asian art and iconography—the image of a hare. Once, the story goes, the bodhisattva lived as a pious hare in a forest. Indra, the king of the gods, here called "Sakka" (Sanskrit: Śakra), decided to try the hare. On the next full-moon day (the "holy" day in Buddhism), he appeared to the hare as a renunciant beggar asking for some alms food. However, since the hare had nothing to give, he asked the beggar to gather firewood and light a fire. When the fire was burning, the hare jumped into the flames to sacrifice himself as a meal for the beggar. Before doing so, though, the hare shook his fur of the tiny insects living there three times, so that none would suffer any harm. Sakka then revealed his true identity and rescued the hare from the flames unharmed. He painted the hare's image on the disc of the full moon so that everyone would be reminded of the hare's selfless virtue: the virtue of "giving" or "generosity" (*dāna*), the first and primary of all the six or ten bodhisattva virtues.[103] As such, the virtue also represents the essence of a bodhisattva's existence, since a bodhisattva strives for Buddhahood in order to be, as a Buddha, of the greatest possible benefit for all other beings. His life is thus pro-existence, a life entirely devoted to striving for the salvation of other beings. There are strong analogies here between the Buddhist symbol of the hare in the moon and the Christian symbol of the crucified Christ who gives his life for others, as well as the ritual of the Lord's Supper that celebrates the gift of bread and wine as the body and blood of Christ in remembrance of his self-sacrifice and the spirit that it expresses.

With the Mahayana change of the goal of religious life to striving for full Buddhahood instead of the enlightened state of an arhat, the motif of perfecting the bodhisattva virtues became the focus of spirituality. The Mahayana Buddhist who follows the example of the Buddha or the path of the bodhisattva vows not to slacken his efforts while even a single being is still suffering. That is, the bodhisattva vows to remain in samsara, the cycle of rebirth, until all beings are saved—which, as already mentioned, could mean forever.[104] Several Mahayana texts assume that the number of beings in the cycle of rebirth is infinite. Thus, the path of the bodhisattva itself becomes the goal. It is about developing an unreservedly kind and compassionate attitude toward all beings, excluding no one. This mind is

---

[103] See Schmidt-Leukel 2006a, 99–101.
[104] See above, p. 64.

called *bodhicitta*, literally "mind (*citta*) of awakening (*bodhi*)." It reaches perfection with the attainment of Buddhahood, and is thus the Buddha mind.

The *Bodhicaryāvatāra*, the guide for bodhisattvas that I have mentioned several times, characterizes this Buddha mind as follows. First, it strives for the salvation of others more than for one's own salvation (1:23–26). Second, it involves a readiness to sacrifice one's life for others (5:87; 6:25; 8:105). Third, it implies an "exchange of others and oneself," by which is meant the acceptance of others as one's own self (8:111–173). The Buddhas brought this exchange to perfection: "In their compassionate nature they have made this whole world of sentient beings their own self" (6:126), and one therefore truly venerates the Buddhas by becoming "a servant for the world with all my heart" (6:125).[105]

There are strong affinities here with Jesus' compassion and selfless love, and his identification with those who suffer. According to Matthew (25:31–46), Jesus not only identified with the poor, with strangers, and with those in prison; he also declared that every service rendered to them is in truth rendered to him. According to Luke (23:34), Jesus asked God to forgive even those who had tortured and crucified him. In this attitude, Jesus demonstrated through sacrificing his own life the limitlessness of divine mercy, which even embraces the mortal enemy. The power of forgiveness and thus of God's love is stronger than all sin and all hate, and shows its strength precisely in an act of utter weakness and helplessness.

Given such striking resonances between the bodhisattva ideal and the New Testament image of Christ, it is not surprising that a question often raised is whether Jesus can be regarded as a bodhisattva, with some Buddhists and Christians answering in the affirmative.[106] On the Christian side, for example, the Korean theologian Hee-Sung Keel suggested in 1996 that understanding Jesus in terms of the bodhisattva ideal could not only make Jesus more meaningful within an Asian context, but also help Christians to see Jesus in a new light.[107] From a Christian perspective, says Keel, "bodhisattvas are certainly manifestations or 'incarnations' of the Logos."[108] For Paul Williams, however, calling Jesus a bodhisattva is "radically unsatisfactory."[109] Not only would it deny his divinity, Williams argues; it could also suggest that Jesus is subordinate to a Buddha, or that he is understood in a docetic manner as pseudo-human, which would im-

---

[105] Schmidt-Leukel 2019b, 296.
[106] See Schmidt-Leukel 2016a. On the position of Chunyi Zhang (1871–1955), who first became a Christian and later a Buddhist, see Lai & So 2003; 2007. See also below, pp. 185–86.
[107] See Keel 1996, 172–73.
[108] Ibid., 184.
[109] Williams, P. 2011, 166.

ply that he did not really suffer. In any case, Williams argues, suffering is incompatible with the status of Buddhahood—or even with the status of a very highly developed bodhisattva.[110]

However, Williams does not take into account that the Christian side has similar problems, since much of the Christian tradition also sees God as being, on account of his perfection, completely free of suffering. This led Friedrich Schleiermacher to make the critical remark that the divine nature of Christ could therefore not have suffered at all on the cross.[111] Moreover, Williams makes no effort to distinguish between suffering and compassion. While briefly addressing the problem elsewhere, he questions whether it is actually possible to speak of genuine "compassion" with regard to a Buddha.[112] However, Tenzin Gyatso, the fourteenth Dalai Lama, writing from within that Buddhist tradition to which Williams refers, has rejected the idea that Buddhahood is a state of unfeeling apathy lacking all empathy.[113]

In Buddhist-Christian dialogue it has repeatedly been pointed out that Buddha mind, *bodhicitta*, and Christ mind converge precisely in their shared motif of self-renunciation and self-emptying out of love and compassion for others.[114] The Sri Lankan theologian Lynn de Silva,[115] whom I mentioned in chapter 4, already pointed in 1982 to the Christological hymn in Philippians (2:6–11) that says of Christ, he "emptied himself, taking the form of a slave." According to de Silva, this "kenotic" (*ek-kénōsis* = self-emptying) attitude on the part of Christ shows some remarkable "affinities with the Buddhist doctrine of Sunyata" (*śūnyatā* = emptiness), and "is very close to the idea of the Bodhisattva."[116] De Silva is echoing here positions previously held by the Zen Buddhist philosophers Keiji Nishitani (1900–1990) and Masao Abe (1915–2006).[117] Nishitani saw the notion of the self-emptying character of Christ's love as agreeing fundamentally with the ideal of the bodhisattva, who through his "great compassion" (*mahākaruṇā*) achieves the wisdom of "emptiness."[118] And Masao Abe held "that Christ is a kind of bodhisattva," since he embodied the truth of self-emptying.[119]

The Indian artist Satish Gupta has given these considerations an awesome artistic expression in his portrait of Christ.[120] His painting clearly echoes the well-known depiction of Jesus Christ as Pantocrator, the omnipotent ruler

---

[110] Ibid., 166–69.
[111] See his *Glaubenslehre* § 104(4). Schleiermacher 1960, vol. 2, 129.
[112] Williams, P. 2006a, 63.
[113] Dalai Lama 2005, 26–27. See on this also Schmidt-Leukel 2019b, 438.
[114] See, for example, Lopez & Rockefeller 1987; May 2014, 54–70.
[115] See above, pp. 112–13.
[116] De Silva 1982, 57–58.
[117] See Schmidt-Leukel 2021, 108, 112–13.
[118] See Nishitani 1983, 57–61.
[119] As reported in Fredericks 2003, 227.
[120] See Amaladass & Löwner 2012, 188.

Bearers of Hope 165

of the world, as found in the Hagia Sophia in Istanbul and elsewhere. But, strongly influenced by Zen Buddhism,[121] Gupta gives this traditional image a completely different twist. His image of Christ is entirely dominated by the cross. The power of Christ is the power of his weakness, his complete self-emptying or self-surrender on the cross in the name of God's love. Christ's face thereby assumes the shape of the well-known Zen-Buddhist symbol of emptiness: the open empty circle. The Buddhist ideal of the bodhisattva who embodies the wisdom of emptiness and great compassion sheds light on the life, death, and nature of Christ, just as Christ sheds light on the bodhisattva ideal.

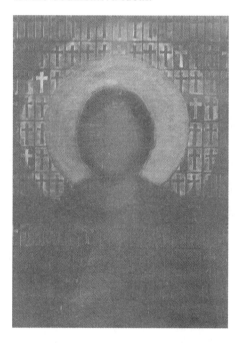

Fig. left: Christ, © Satish Gupta, http://www.satishgupta.com/
Fig. top right: Pantocrator Christ icon, template: © gunthersimmermacher / 38—pixabay
Fig. bottom right: Enso Zen circle, template: © Elina Li—shutterstock.com

Lynn de Silva has highlighted that in the Letter to the Philippians, Paul refers to the hymn of Christ as a means of spiritual encouragement, which is the reason that he prefaces the hymn with his own words: "Let the same mind

---

[121]"Though born a Hindu, I am drawn to Zen Buddhism. . . . I love the emptiness in the calligraphic works of Zen masters, their use of asymmetry, simplicity, and, above all, the silence. Zen philosophy provides inspiration—I feel an affinity to the form and the silence, which match my way of thinking." Gupta 2005, 14.

be in you that was in Christ" (Philippians 2:5).[122] According to Nishitani, the ideal of Christ's attitude is also about Christians imitating or practicing this self-emptying perfection.[123] Yet how can this ideal be realized? How can the mediation of ultimate reality that Buddhists and Christians recognize in the figure of Buddha and Christ transform life with all its deep-seated self-centeredness and entanglement in greed, hate, and delusion? This question takes us to the traditional contrast between salvation by self-effort and salvation by grace.

---

[122]See de Silva 1982, 57.
[123]See Nishitani 1983, 59.

7

The Path

Let us now turn to a further contrast that is often used to distinguish Buddhism from Christianity: the contrast in the understanding of the path of salvation between self-redemption on the one hand, and redemption through others (redemption by grace) on the other. First, I again briefly outline how this contrast has been drawn in older and more recent interreligious comparisons, before then showing in line with the theory of fractal structures that this contrast is found also within Christianity and Buddhism. Finally, I present some reflections on why this contrast—or, perhaps better, difference—might have developed in both religions, where I focus on two aspects: the nature of the self, and the understanding of virtue in the process of salvation/liberation, the second being closely tied to the problem of evil.

7.1 SALVATION: SELF-HELP OR OTHER-HELP?

Christian Perspectives

When older comparative studies contrasted Buddhism as a religion of self-redemption with Christianity as a religion of grace, this assessment was often based on an interpretation of Buddhism as a form of atheism. Given this premise, the logic seems to be conclusive. If there is no divine or transcendent reality whatsoever, then it is inevitable that, when seeking salvation or liberation from evil, people are left to fend for themselves. As already explained in chapter 3, "salvation," however, can then only mean complete extinction.[1] In the comparative studies of Western authors, Buddhism thus appeared as a system in which the person had to strive by their own efforts to be liberated from the cycle of rebirth—a liberation that was nothing but sheer and definitive annihilation. Ethically good or virtuous behavior was

---
[1] See above, pp. 52–53.

deemed to be part of this path to liberation, but only in a rather weak and provisional manner, since, so Western authors often argued, Buddhist ethics aims ultimately to abstain from good as well as evil deeds. At least in the higher forms of the path of salvation, it is a matter of generating neither good nor bad karma, since both lead to rebirth. For most Western authors, Buddhist morality is also fundamentally selfish, since it is concerned either with self-redemption, as in the actual path of salvation, or with improving one's own karma, as in the morality of Buddhist lay followers. In both cases, these Western authors argue, Buddhist morality is never really about the welfare of others, but always and only about one's own self, which in turn contradicts the Buddhist notion that the "self" is only an illusion, an expression of delusion. Buddhism, argued Monier-Williams, establishes the "paradox" of "the perfecting of one's self by accumulating merit with the ultimate view of annihilating all consciousness of self."[2]

Such an understanding of Buddhist self-redemption was usually the starting point for the contrast with Christianity. Thus, Archibald Scott wrote in 1890,

> In a universe where Moi-mệme is the only god, and a man's own Nirvana his only goal, the primary motive of action can rise no higher than fear or self-interest. . . . Others are regarded only as occasions of acquiring merit. Instead of serving them as Christ enjoins us to do, the Buddhist serves himself of them. It is a religion of every man for himself. . . . His very self-abnegation had egoism at its core. Between the Christian surrender of self to God for the sake of others, and the Buddhist surrender to others for the sake of self, there is a great gulf fixed. The first springs from a sense of indebtedness, a consciousness of mercy unmerited, but freely bestowed; but the other, having no sense of forgiveness received, has no real mercy to show. The mercy of God is the spring of all true human compassion, for he who truly receives it finds it impossible to withhold it.[3]

Monier-Williams drew a similar picture, arguing that all Buddhist morality is self-centered and incapable of establishing true altruism. The "righteousness of the Buddhist," he argued, consists in "the perfection of merit-making, with the view of earning happiness for himself in a higher state hereafter. For every Buddhist is like a trader who keeps a ledger, with a regular debtor and creditor account, and a daily entry of profit and loss."[4] In truth, there-

---
[2] Monier-Williams 1889, 143.
[3] Scott 1890, 233–36.
[4] Monier-Williams 1889, 143.

fore, Buddhist selflessness is quite self-centered and radically different from Christianity. For Monier-Williams, "Christianity demands the suppression of selfishness; Buddhism demands the suppression of self, with the one object of extinguishing all consciousness of self"; in Christianity, "the true self is elevated and intensified," while, in Buddhism, "the true self is annihilated by the practice of a false form of non-selfishness, which has for its real object, not the good of others, but the annihilation of the Ego, the utter extinction of the illusion of personal individuality."[5] Monier-Williams sums up the difference between the Buddhist and the Christian concept of redemption thus:

> Buddhism . . . says: Act righteously through your own efforts, and for the final getting rid of all suffering, of all individuality, of all life in yourselves. Christianity says: Be righteous through a power implanted in you from above, through the power of a life-giving principle, freely given to you, and always abiding in you. The Buddha said to his followers: "Take nothing from me, trust to yourselves alone." Christ said: "Take all from Me; trust not to yourselves. I give unto you eternal life, I give unto you the bread of heaven, I give unto you living water." Not that these priceless gifts involve any passive condition of inaction. On the contrary, they stir the soul of the recipient with a living energy. They stimulate him to noble deeds, and self-sacrificing efforts. They compel him to act as the worthy, grateful, and appreciative possessor of so inestimable a treasure.[6]

Similar judgments can be found in a number of other comparisons, such as in Friedrich Weinrich's *Love in Buddhism and Christianity*, which was particularly influential in Germany.[7] Indeed, Gustav Mensching still drew on Weinrich's book in his own comparison.[8] While accepting in essence the opposition between redemption by self-help and other-help, Mensching nevertheless rightly pointed out that in Buddhism, too, "the actual salvific enlightenment (bodhi) does not fall within the power of disposal of the one striving for salvation."[9]

Judgments such as those made by Scott, Monier-Williams, and Weinrich are usually based on a reading of Buddhist texts that is shaped by the doctrinal presuppositions of the interpreters. Monier-Williams, for example,

---
[5] Ibid., 558–59.
[6] Ibid., 551.
[7] *Die Liebe im Buddhismus und im Christentum*. Weinrich 1935, 15–17.
[8] Mensching 1978, 172–73.
[9] Ibid., 169.

claims that all non-Christian religions, such as Hinduism, Zoroastrianism, Confucianism, Islam, and Buddhism, are driven by the selfish motivation to acquire merit and avoid demerit.[10] These are "irrepressible and deep-seated tendencies in humanity which nothing but the divine force imparted by Christianity can ever eradicate."[11] Archibald Scott shows the same Protestant-biased view when he writes that the "blessedness" in the Buddha's teaching "was the blessedness of the Old Covenant, not of the New—the blessedness, not of them who love much because they have been forgiven much, but of them who keep the law."[12] In his 1954 comparison of the Buddhist and Christian concepts of the human being, Bryan de Kretser freely admitted that he had used for this the theological "tools" of the dialectical theology of Karl Barth, Hendrik Kraemer, and others.[13] But if dogma dictates from the outset that only Christianity—or a certain variety of it—can defeat human self-interest and put an end to the "works righteousness" associated with it, then the verdict that Buddhism is a religion of self-redemption has been decided before the comparative work is actually done.

Comparativists who start from such premises tend to ignore or downplay counterevidence, with regard to both Buddhism *and* Christianity. Sterling Berry, who also held the view that the Buddhist notion of self-redemption necessarily gives all morality a selfish character, briefly raised the question of whether something similar might not in fact apply to Christian spirituality, too. Does not, he asks, "the reward of heaven and the fear of hell occupy in our religion the same place that the striving for Nirvana has for the Buddhist"?[14] But Scott promptly dismisses this idea by claiming that in Christianity heaven and hell do not constitute the "motives" of a person's religious life, but the "results." If someone's behavior is motivated by the pursuit of heavenly reward, then they will certainly miss the mark. Rather, the right motivation comes from the desire to do God's will and from the "constraining power of the love of Christ."[15]

A number of recent comparisons also emphasize the contrast between Buddhism as a religion of redemption by self-help and Christianity as a religion of redemption by other-help, and tend to downplay findings to the contrary. For example, Keith Yandell and Harold Netland do concede that the Buddha's proclamation of the dharma is seen as a crucial aid on the path to salvation, and that the central role of bodhisattvas in Mahayana Buddhism is to work for the salvation of others. But, they argue, at least

---

[10]Monier-Williams 1889, 547–48.
[11]Ibid., 546.
[12]Scott 1890, 226.
[13]Kretser 1954, ii, 6.
[14]Berry 1890, 109.
[15]Ibid.

"the Buddha himself seems to have regarded each person as responsible for his or her own destiny."[16] In other words, "It is up to the individual himself to grasp the dharma, to appropriate it, and thereby to attain nirvana."[17] In contrast, "the Christian Scriptures" teach that "human beings cannot save themselves; we are utterly helpless and hopeless apart from the grace of God and the atoning work of Jesus Christ on the cross for us." "The New Testament," moreover, "consistently presents Jesus as the one Savior for all people in all cultures."[18]

One further example may be briefly mentioned here. According to a recent comparison by Robert Magliola,

> The irreducible difference between Buddhism and Catholic Christianity, as I see it, is that Buddhism is ultimately a "self-help" (or "self-power" or "self-effort") religion and Catholic Christianity is ultimately an "other-help" (or "other-power") religion. That is, Buddhism asserts that human beings can and must ultimately earn their supra-mundane beatitude, and Catholics assert that human beings can only receive supra-mundane beatitude as a gratuitous gift from Another-power with whom they freely cooperate.[19]

Magliola, too, admits that there are some features in Buddhism, and especially in Pure Land Buddhism, that question the accuracy of such a clear-cut contrast. But he insists that even here "practitioners must still ultimately liberate themselves. The Buddha's other-power is to facilitate self-power."[20] The only "conspicuous exception" that Magliola acknowledges is Shinran's version of Pure Land Buddhism, but he does not elaborate further on this supposed "exception," or on its reasons and implications.

Buddhist Perspectives

Buddhist authors have also emphasized the contrast between Buddhism and Christianity in terms of a religion of redemption by self-help versus a religion of redemption by other-help. For example, the Chinese Buddhist reformer Taixu (1890–1947) in his essay "On Atheism" (1913) rejected belief in salvation through a divine agent and the idea of divine forgiveness, arguing that such ideas contradicted Buddhist ethics and the law of karma.

---

[16] Yandell & Netland 2009, 210.
[17] Ibid., 209.
[18] This and the previous citation, ibid., 210.
[19] Magliola 2014, 36–37.
[20] Ibid., 54.

According to Taixu, the salvific role of Gautama Buddha is confined to being "the prime example of one who faithfully pursued the salvific path that leads to Buddhahood."[21] Taixu attacked the Christian belief in utter dependence on God as an obstacle to freedom and equality, arguing that the ideal of absolute surrender to God and the belief in a God who saves only those whom he favors function as the ideological superstructure of inequality and hierarchy in a feudal society, and as such could not underpin democracy.[22]

According to the Sri Lankan Buddhist modernist Anagarika Dharmapala (1864–1933), belief in redemption through God and the forgiveness of sins is not only "foolish," but also fosters moral laxity or negligence.[23] In contrast, moral seriousness results from the insight that "man is the inheritor of its own karma."[24] "No vicarious savior is needed" to enter heaven, which, Dharmapala argues, pointing to Matthew 7:21, is what Jesus himself has taught.[25] Yet, in Buddhism, all self-effort is directed toward "self-abnegation." "Selflessness," he says, "is the panacea to realize the happiness of Nirvana."[26]

Similar objections have been raised in more recent times by Gunapala Dharmasiri (d. 2015), most notably in his 1974 book *A Buddhist Critique of the Christian Concept of God*. According to Dharmasiri, belief in divine redemption and grace renders the free will of human beings pointless and undermines any serious spiritual struggle and pursuit of salvation. The idea of redemption by divine grace ultimately comes down to the idea of divine predestination, which, in turn, implies a kind of determinism that is "positively harmful to moral and religious ideals."[27] Responding to the Christian criticism that the idea of self-redemption inevitably leads to moral egoism and prevents true altruism, he counters that "any theory of salvation is necessarily egoistic ultimately."[28] If people do not worry about themselves, then nor will they worry about salvation, be it in a Christian or a Buddhist sense. According to Dharmasiri, Buddhist ethics transcends the distinction between egoism and altruism in that spiritual progress and the regard for others are inseparably entwined.[29]

However, there are also Buddhist scholars who question the distinction between Buddhism as a religion of redemption by self-help and Christianity

---

[21] As summarized in Pittman 1993, 78.
[22] Yu, X. 2003, 165. See also So 2017, 365–66.
[23] Guruge 1965, 33.
[24] Ibid., 27.
[25] Ibid.
[26] Ibid., 436.
[27] Dharmasiri 1988, 57. See also ibid., 104–6.
[28] Ibid., 87.
[29] Ibid., 66–67, 87.

as a religion of other-help. Fumio Masutani (former professor of history of religion at Taisho University, Tokyo) compares the difference between the Jewish spirituality of fulfilling the law and Paul's doctrine of justification by faith and grace on the one hand, with what he considers to be a parallel development from the beginnings of Buddhism to Mahayana Buddhism and especially to Pure Land Buddhism on the other.[30] He sees a synthesis of self-interest and altruism realized in both the Christian ideal of love as a response to God's love, and in the Buddhist ideal of compassion and mercy as resulting from insight into the suffering of all beings.[31] In view of the typological distinction between redemption by self-help and other-help, Hajime Nakamura (1912–1999) stated quite decidedly, "In each tradition, we find both types. It is misleading to identify any one religion with one type only."[32] And he further explained, "Even where the one emphasis predominates, echoes of the other remain, with tensions maintained between the two."[33] With that, Nakamura came remarkably close to identifying a fractal structure. Let me now look at this in more detail.

7.2 SALVATION BY SELF-HELP AND OTHER-HELP IN BUDDHISM

Aspects of Grace in Theravada Buddhism

The typological distinction between redemption by self-help and other-help raises the question of what each of the two religions regards as "self" and what as "other." In most cases, the category of redemption by other-help is linked unquestioningly to a personal concept of transcendence. Christianity usually presents divine reality as guarantor of redemption in the form of a merciful father. But the awareness remains in many forms of theology, and especially classical theology, that these are images for a reality that is actually imageless and undepictable. Although the idea of redemption by other-help is often linked to a personal conception of transcendence, this is by no means necessarily so. The fundamental idea that our redemption depends on the existence of a transcendent reality can also be expressed within the framework of impersonal concepts of transcendence. This is easily overlooked, if one identifies redemption by other-help from the outset with a personal idea of transcendence. Buddha's well-known words from *Udāna*

---

[30]Masutani 1967, 117–20.
[31]Ibid., 163–74.
[32]Nakamura 1986, 107.
[33]Ibid., 152.

8:3 and *Itivuttaka* 43 say explicitly that liberation from samsara would be impossible without nirvana, and that nirvana is a "not-made" (*akataṃ*) reality.[34] Along the same lines is the scholastic depiction of nirvana as the "efficient cause" (*kāraṇahetu*) or "cognitive support" (*ālambanapratyaya*) of that kind of insight that liberates the person from the "defilements" of greed, hate, and delusion.[35] Nirvana is very clearly understood here not as a state brought about or "made" by the human being through their own efforts, but as a transcendent, timeless reality that is both the goal and the precondition of liberation. This dependence of redemption on a transcendent reality is not expressed as divine "grace" or "mercy," however, since such personal notions are foreign to this particular impersonal idiom. Nevertheless, the dependence of liberation on the existence of an other reality is articulated very clearly.

However, even certain traits of the idea of grace become tangible when the canonical writings of Theravada Buddhism say that those who have attained nirvana have attained it "for free" or "free of charge" (*laddhā mudhā*).[36] The Theravada scholar Mahinda Palihawadana emphasizes very clearly in his remarkable essay "Is There a Theravada Buddhist Idea of Grace?"[37] the structural analogy to the concept of grace. According to him, for Theravada Buddhism, too, "The supreme truth to be realized is not a product of 'my' efforts."[38] For Palihawadana, the Buddhist and the theistic world share the common belief that "the redeeming change in a person takes place not ultimately by exercising the will, but at its cessation, which is an indispensable factor for contact with supreme reality; it is this contact that truly renews and transforms the person."[39]

Thus, within the context of impersonal conceptions of transcendence there are also structural similarities to what is referred to in personal terms as "grace." The clearest manifestations of the concept of redemption by other-help can also of course be found in Buddhism, where it uses personal notions to refer to the ultimate, i.e., in connection with the Buddhist discourse on Buddha and sangha. On the path of salvation, a Buddhist takes refuge in the Buddha, dharma, and sangha. This "refuge" clearly implies the expectation of essential support here. According to the Buddha legend, when the god Brahma persuaded the Buddha to proclaim the dharma to others, he did so with the argument that the "world will be lost, the world will

---

[34] See above, p. 60.
[35] On this, see the discussion in *Abhidharmakośabhāṣyam* on verses 50–62; Pruden 1991, 255–303.
[36] *Khuddaka-Pāṭha* 6.6.
[37] Palihawadana 1978.
[38] Ibid., 193.
[39] Ibid., 194.

perish" if the Buddha should remain silent about the truth.[40] This narrative clearly illustrates how much the Buddha and dharma were perceived as a crucial aid on the path of salvation. Something similar applies to the sangha, which the Buddha established not only to provide the best conditions for its members on their path of liberation, but also "out of compassion for the world, for the good, for the gain, and for the welfare of gods and men."[41] For, it is the sangha that shall guarantee after the Buddha's death the continuing transmission of the dharma in a salvifically effective way. Thus, Theravada Buddhism, too, teaches that it is better to strive for one's own liberation *and* the liberation of others than just for one's own liberation.[42] This canonical statement explicitly rejects the accusation that the teaching of the Buddha only serves one's own liberation.[43]

All this implies that a person can receive crucial help from others on the path of salvation. What undoubtedly matters is to tread the path to nirvana oneself. But, in a certain way, nirvana also approaches the person in the form of the Buddhas, who show others the path to nirvana and help and stand by them on this path. The works of Gautama (Pali: Gotama) can therefore already be characterized in the Pali canon as an active and saving intervention: "It is as if a man were to seize someone by the hair who had stumbled and was falling into a pit, and to set him on firm ground—just so, I, who was falling into the pit, have been saved by the Reverend Gotama" (*Dīgha Nikāya* 12:78).[44]

Merit Transfer and Altruism

The underlying motif of saving action has gained particular prominence in the form of the bodhisattva ideal. As we have seen, a bodhisattva strives for Buddhahood because, as a Buddha, he can work far better for the liberation of others than he could as an arhat. Thus, bodhisattvas not only devote their whole religious striving to the goal of reaching a status where they can most benefit others; they also help others on their very path to Buddhahood by among other things transferring the good karma acquired through their own merits to those whose karma is less good. The idea of transferring one's own karmic merits to others (*pariṇāmanā*) had obviously arisen even before Mahayana Buddhism came into being. Several canonical texts of Theravada Buddhism, such as the *Kathāvatthu*, dispute that such a transfer of merit is

---

[40] *Majjhima Nikāka* 26; Ñāṇamoli & Bodhi 2001, 261. See above, pp. 61, 161.
[41] *Vinayapiṭaka Mahāvagga* 1.11.1; Rhys Davids & Oldenberg 1881, 112–13.
[42] *Aṅguttara Nikāya* 4.95.
[43] *Aṅguttara Nikāya* 3.61.
[44] Walshe 1995, 185.

possible, while others, such as the *Buddhāpadāna*, presuppose it as valid.[45] An inscription from the second century CE testifies "that someone could be expected to obtain *nirvāṇa* as the result of an act of *pūjā* [= a meritorious and usually ritual act] undertaken on his behalf by another."[46] Overall, the practice of transferring merit became widespread not only in Mahayana but also in Theravada Buddhism. There is also sometimes the notion that the merit transferred is received through the joyful assent of the recipient.[47] This is reflected in Mahayana Buddhism in the practice of taking grateful refuge in the major supranatural bodhisattvas, whose merits and compassion are deemed immeasurable. If we keep in mind that a view widespread in Mahayana Buddhism is that the compassion of the Buddhas and bodhisattvas, which materializes in their work for the salvation of others, is an outflow of their Buddha nature and thus of the immanence of ultimate reality, then the structural analogy to the idea of grace in theistic religions becomes evident.

Discussions on the transfer of merit (both within Buddhism itself and among scholars of Buddhism) have repeatedly raised the question of whether this idea does not in fact contradict and indeed force open the notion of karma as a strict cause-and-effect relationship. The religious studies scholar and philosopher Steven G. Smith has pointed out here that "merit" (*puṇya*; Pali: *puñña*) does not have to be understood only as what someone is necessarily entitled to, but can also contain the aspect of a special distinction or honor.[48] "Merit transfer" may seem less contradictory when compared to the transfer of an honor, and indeed even when it is an unmerited transfer that is made in the hope that the recipient will at some time prove worthy of it. Thus, the bodhisattva may assume that transferring their merits to others will also prove to be such an incentive. This interpretation would explain why the recipient's joyful assent has such significance. But the loving devotion shown by the person transferring merit already bestows upon the recipient a different and somewhat elevated status, the very love of the lover already giving the beloved a special honor.[49] Finally, this interpretation is also supported by the fact that *kṣānti* (patience, forbearance, lenience) is one of the central bodhisattva virtues, since, as I have already suggested in chapter 5, this virtue also includes the aspect of forgiveness.[50] Several key Mahayana texts contain rituals that include confessing one's sins to the Buddhas and bodhisattvas, appealing to their compassion, asking for their help, and in some cases (as has been shown) asking for forgiveness.[51]

---

[45]See Bechert 1992.
[46]Schopen 1997, 36. Insertion mine.
[47]See Bechert 1992, 99–100.
[48]See Smith, S. G. 2021.
[49]See ibid., 204–5.
[50]See above, pp. 127–28.
[51]See Dayal 1932, 54–58 and p. 127, above. On the integration of this ritual into the *Gaṇḍavyūha-*

The tension between self-interest and altruism that so often accompanies discussion of redemption by self-help or other-help is a central theme in the *Bodhicaryāvatāra*, which attempts to resolve the tension through the message that altruism is ultimately in one's own interest—or, in religious terms, that one's own liberation lies in striving for the liberation of others.[52] Thus, it says,

> All those who are suffering in the world are so out of longing for their own happiness. All those who are happy in the world are so out of longing for the happiness of others (8:129).[53]

The pursuit of one's own liberation is replaced by the pursuit of the liberation of others—or, better, the two become one, since the bodhisattva not only loves others as himself or herself, but identifies with them as his or her own self:

> To calm my own suffering and to calm the suffering of others, I therefore offer myself to others and adopt others as myself (8:136).[54]

Aspects of Grace in Pure Land Buddhism

Several Mahayana texts say that, when a bodhisattva finally attains Buddhahood, he creates by means of his good karmic merits accumulated in innumerable rebirths his own Buddha land, i.e., a world where he functions as Buddha.[55] In this world, he establishes for all beings reborn there the optimal conditions for their liberation. Of the numerous Buddha lands mentioned, it is the "Pure Land" of the Buddha Amitabha that has become particularly prominent. Amitabha (Chinese: Amituo; Japanese: Amida = "infinite light"), or Amitayus ("infinite life"), is the name of a supramundane Buddha. When he was once the bodhisattva Dharmakara, he vowed to create the Buddha land Sukhavati (*Sukhāvatī* = "Blissful [Land]"). By hearing and confidently invoking his name, a person can be reborn in this land in order to attain enlightenment there without great effort.

The veneration of Amitabha appears to be very old, probably dating to the first century BCE.[56] After first spreading within India, the practice became especially in Chinese cultural circles one of the predominant forms of

---

Sūtra and thus also into the *Avataṃsaka Sutra*, see Cleary 1993, 1511–18.
[52] See Schmidt-Leukel 2019b, 391–400.
[53] Ibid., 389.
[54] Ibid., 390.
[55] On this, see p. 118 above.
[56] See Tanaka 1990, 3, 7.

Buddhism. The medieval Japanese Buddhist Shinran Shonin (1173–1263) developed a particularly radical interpretation of this practice, arguing that Amida's compassion encompasses all beings, including and especially those who have committed the most serious offenses. The only factor determining rebirth in Amida's Pure Land is entrusting oneself to his promise, and even this entrusting (*shinjin*) is not something that the person can produce themselves, but a gift bestowed by Amida. Liberation, according to Shinran, can in truth never be achieved by "self-power" (*jiriki*), since the ego-self is the core of the person's entanglement in greed, hate, and delusion. Liberation comes only from "other power" (*tariki*), i.e., from the boundless merits of Amida and his compassionate resolve to dedicate his merits to the salvation of all beings.

Shinran did not hesitate to accuse the other Buddhist schools of his time of relying too much on self-power and ignoring the crucial importance of "other power." And yet, Shinran's dualism of "self-power" and "other power" is also underpinned by his strong recourse to the nondualistic philosophical currents of Mahayana Buddhism. Thus, for Shinran, the Pure Land is a symbol of nirvana, and nirvana is not different from samsara, but rather, in a sense, its hidden side. A person born into the Pure Land also returns to this world as a bodhisattva. And both birth into the Pure Land and return into samsara already take place to some extent in the act of entrusting. According to Shinran, the trust in Amida that Amida himself gives to the human being is again nothing other than Amida's own spirit. Amida himself is the perfect expression of the unfathomable dharma body (*dharmakāya*) that pervades all reality and "fills the hearts and minds of the ocean of all beings."[57] Thus, Amida represents not only the all-encompassing compassion that flows from ultimate reality itself, but also the originally pure mind that will overcome the self-centered ego-mind. According to Shinran, the person who trusts in Amida participates in both realities.[58] "This self," he says, "is false and insincere," and yet at the same time, "Mind nature is from the beginning pure."[59] When European Jesuit missionaries arrived in Japan in the sixteenth century and learned about Shinran's version of Pure Land Buddhism, they reported back to Europe that this doctrine was identical in essence to the heresy that the devil had inspired in Luther.[60] As already mentioned, this remark nicely illustrates the fractal insight that the tension between redemption by self-help and other-help is present in both Buddhism and Christianity.[61] A brief look at Christianity may clarify this insight further.

---

[57] Hirota 1997, 461.
[58] On this, see also Schmidt-Leukel 2020g.
[59] *Shōzōmatsu wasan*, verses 94 and 107. Hirota 1997, 421, 423. See also *Jōdo monrui jushō*, ibid., 311.
[60] Valignano 1944, 160–61.
[61] See above, p. 45.

7.3 SALVATION BY OTHER-HELP AND SELF-HELP IN CHRISTIANITY

Faith and Deeds

The synoptic Gospels of the New Testament show Jesus as someone who taught faith in God's merciful and fatherly love on the one hand, and who also preached the fulfillment of the divine will by sharing God's love with one's neighbor on the other. Paul's theology deems faith to be key. Paul sees in Abraham the exemplar of a person who is "righteous" in the eyes of God because he had faith in God and relied on God's promise (Galatians 3:6–18; Romans 4:1–22). In the theology of James, which also belongs to the New Testament, the emphasis is placed on deeds, with genuine faith proving itself in the works that correspond to such faith—without such works, faith would be "dead" (James 2:14–26). But Paul also sees the deeds of the human being as anything but irrelevant. He argues that those who are justified in the eyes of God because of their faith in the promise given by God through Jesus are to live by the Spirit of Jesus and not according to what Paul calls the "flesh." Those who live by the Spirit will develop "love, joy, peace, patience, kindness, goodness, faithfulness, gentleness, self-control" (Galatians 5:22–23), which are opposed to "the works of the flesh": "sexual immorality, impurity, sensuality, idolatry, sorcery, enmity, strife, jealousy, fits of anger, rivalries, dissensions, divisions, envy, drunkenness, orgies, and things like these. . . . Those who do such things will not inherit the kingdom of God" (Galatians 5:19–21). Paul's theology combines redemption by self-help and redemption by other-help in a paradoxical way when he writes, "Work out your own salvation with fear and trembling, for it is God who works in you, both to will and to do for His good pleasure" (Philippians 2:12–13).

Grace and Personal Responsibility

The history of Christianity has seen the theological pendulum swing back and forth between the two poles of this paradox. One of the best-known examples within the ancient church of the West is perhaps the dispute between Pelagius (~350–420?) and Augustine (354–430), and between their respective followers. While Pelagius emphasized the significance of one's own efforts to salvation, Augustine developed an increasingly radical understanding of both human sin and divine grace, which culminated in his theory of "double predestination." According to this theory, it is ultimately divine grace alone that determines who will attain salvation and who will not.[62]

---

[62]See Flasch 1990.

For Pelagius, on the other hand, even after the fall of Adam, people are still granted the incentive and the real chance to resist sin, with grace consisting precisely in the fact that God gave this freedom and responsibility to us permanently. Following Winrich Löhr, we can discern a legitimate concern on both sides: "For Pelagius, Augustine's doctrine of grace was demoralizing and thus not suitable to guide to the true Christian life; conversely, Augustine criticized Pelagius that his concept of grace was underdetermined and thus did not grasp the essentially healing effect of grace."[63]

Augustine's strong influence led to the classification of Pelagius as a heretic in Western Christianity, while the latter "lives on in all harmlessness and uncriticized" in Eastern Orthodox Christianity.[64] But the frequency with which the accusation of "Pelagianism" has been flung since the Pelagian controversy shows that the positions and concerns of both sides, those of Augustine and those of Pelagius, remained significant for the West, too.

In a sense, the Pelagian controversy was continued—or even renewed—in the disputes of the sixteenth century, i.e., in the attacks on the scholastic and late scholastic theology of the Roman Church made by Reformers such as Martin Luther (1483–1546) and John Calvin (1509–1564). Put very simply, it was the Reformation side that emphasized here the all-determining role of grace and thus of salvation through other power, while Catholic theologians strove to give human responsibility a legitimate place in salvation. It is therefore no surprise that the Jesuit missionaries who supported the Catholic Counter-Reformation saw a certain similarity between the controversies within the Buddhist traditions in Japan regarding the question of salvation by self-help or other-help, and the controversies between Catholics and Protestant Reformers in Europe. But also within the European disputes new controversies developed on each of the two sides, Catholics and Protestants, about the exact allocation of human and divine responsibility—controversies that never reached a conclusion satisfying both sides. According to Alan Sell, divine sovereignty and human responsibility constitute a permanent antinomy in the Christian concept of redemption. As the driving force behind Christian faith and life, he argues, the two aspects are both difficult to reconcile but nonetheless indispensable.[65] Such judgments can also be read as an admission that there is no such thing as *the* Christian understanding of redemption, but rather a diversity of theological conceptions that always all revolve in numerous variations around the two poles mentioned. The actual persistence of these conceptions and their theological "indispensability" may point to an inner complementarity.

---

[63]See Löhr, W. 2007, 197. See also the very similar judgment of Sell 1977, 117–18.
[64]Heyer 1977, 163. See also Demacopoulos & Papanikolaou 2008, 31.
[65]See Sell 1977, 118, 140–43.

Given the frequency with which religious comparisons have contrasted Buddhism as a religion of self-help and Christianity as a religion of other-help, it is surprising that Christian-Buddhist dialogue has yet to pay much attention to this issue.[66] Leo Lefebure has pointed out that the tension within Christianity between Pelagian and Augustinian tendencies in the understanding of the path of salvation is very similar to the tension within Buddhism between the emphasis on one's own efforts and the emphasis on faith in the "other power."[67] Yet even a work as voluminous as Paul Chung's *Martin Luther and Buddhism* deals surprisingly little with this issue.[68] John May has therefore rightly called for the relationship between grace and self-effort to be put on the future agenda of a Buddhist-Christian "collaborative theology."[69] A fractal perspective may well prove particularly helpful here. Even my rather sketchy observations suffice perhaps to show that the tension between redemption by self-help and other-help is present within each of the two religious traditions. But why is that so? Is there perhaps an indispensable polarity? I would now like to present two arguments that suggest that that could well be the case.

7.4 SALVATION OF THE SELF FROM THE SELF

The Nature of the Self

Looking at the analysis of the self with regard to the respective doctrines of redemption reveals something like a dialectical structure of thesis, antithesis, and synthesis in both Buddhism and Christianity. First, the analysis of the self is related in each case to a concrete individual, i.e., to a specific "self." The *thesis* would thus be that "oneself" or "one's own self" is in need of salvation or liberation, which therefore needs to be appropriated by oneself in order to materialize. Second, however, the message is that it is precisely the self that is at the center of the problem requiring a solution, i.e., salvation/liberation. Thus, Buddhism considers suffering (*duḥkha*) to be the result of the deluded attachment to the transient things of this world, and this deluded attachment has at its core the attitude of clinging, the wish to own, and of ego-identification—in other words, the attitude of "This is mine, this am I," as the standard Buddhist not-self sermon puts it.[70] In Chris-

---

[66] See, however, the two unpublished dissertations: Suwanbubbha 1994 and O'Grady 2010. The comparison of Shinran and Luther in Oguro 1985 is careful and illuminating, but does not enter the level of constructive theology.
[67] See Lefebure 1993, 138–39.
[68] Chung 2008, 137–39, 345–48, 381–93.
[69] See May 2014, 64–70, 136–37.
[70] See Schmidt-Leukel 2006a, 36–37.

tianity, sin is characterized as a broken relationship, and it finds its central expression in the self's curving in on itself.[71] The *antithesis* in Buddhism and Christianity is therefore that the self must be saved or liberated from itself. Thus, while the thesis tends to affirm self-effort or self-redemption (one must do something oneself if one wishes to be saved), the antithesis tends to affirm grace or other-help. Since the self must be saved from itself, it cannot save itself. If, as Dharmapala puts it, selflessness is the "panacea" for attaining the happiness of nirvana,[72] then the self cannot achieve this by its own efforts but would only continue to affirm itself. In trying to save itself, the self remains focused and fixed on the self instead of becoming free from it. Those who wish to save themselves circle constantly around themselves. The essential help or power has to come from beyond the self.

Taken together, thesis and antithesis thus lead to a paradox. As the *Bodhicaryāvatāra* puts it, "If you have love of yourself, you must not love yourself. If your self must be protected, it should not be protected" (8:173).[73] Love and protection of the self in the sense of striving for one's own salvation thus paradoxically require the turning away from the self. This evokes associations with what is said in all four Gospels: "Whoever seeks to preserve his life will lose it, but whoever loses his life will keep it" (Luke 17:33).[74] It is true that the New Testament texts are speaking here within an apocalyptic context and in view of a situation where faith in Jesus could actually endanger one's own life. But the subsequent history of Christian piety has often understood this word as expressing an attitude of spiritual and moral selflessness or self-denial. As Volker Leppin comments, "Self-denial and thereby self-gain, that remains a basic concept . . . among the mystics."[75] This corresponds to the development (already explained in more detail) to transfer the attitude of nonattachment to the world, tied originally to the Second Coming, into a general inner spiritual attitude.[76]

The paradoxical tension of having to free oneself from the self out of concern for the self, and not being able to do so on account of this paradox—this drives attempts at a *synthesis*, i.e., a release of the tension that nevertheless retains both aspects and links them with each other. One such attempt that appears influential in both traditions consists in the idea of a "true" or "new self." On the one hand, this new or true self participates in ultimate reality, and thus in *that other power* that enables liberation from the ego-self; on the other hand, it also participates in the function of the

---

[71] See above, p. 137.
[72] See above, p. 172.
[73] Schmidt-Leukel 2019b, 403.
[74] See also the parallels in Luke 9:24; Matthew 10:39; 16:25; Mark 8:35; John 12:25.
[75] Leppin 2007, 19.
[76] See above, pp. 68–74.

ego-self—for it involves the individual person in need of redemption or liberation, insofar as the new self is also conceived as the true or new self *of that actual person*. The activity of the "true self" combines self-help and other-help.

In Buddhism, this synthesis is evident in the concept of the originally "pure" or "luminous" mind on the one hand, and in the related concept of Buddha nature on the other. The idea that the mind is originally pure does not refer to an origin in a temporal, chronological sense, but to the true nature of the mind. The defilements of the mind through greed, hate, and delusion therefore do not belong to the true nature of the mind. Even if they contaminate ("defile") the mind as always ("without beginning"), they are in a sense external to the mind, whereby their origin remains obscure. The complete and lasting elimination of the defilements comes along with the experience of nirvana in enlightenment. Hence there must be an inner relationship between the luminous nature of the mind and the transcendent reality of nirvana—a relationship that Peter Harvey has called "a kind of enlightenment-potential."[77] In this sense, Harvey says, the teaching of the primordially luminous mind "is also a part of the living tradition of meditation in Theravāda Buddhism."[78]

In Mahayana Buddhism, this teaching was combined with the belief in the embryonic Buddha nature of all beings.[79] This idea developed in India probably from around the first century CE onward. As Christopher Jones has recently shown, it does have different facets, but these being nevertheless variations of the one central idea of the "internalization of something supermundane."[80] The logic behind the idea is closely related to the Mahayana teaching that every being should and can reach Buddhahood one day, since, as Jones says, "If the deathless state enjoyed by a Buddha 'comes' from nowhere—that is, it is uncreated—some basis for this state should exist already, and must pertain to any sentient being who is capable of becoming a Buddha."[81] A number of Buddhist texts refer to this "basis" as the true or genuine self (*ātman*). According to the traditional Buddhist teaching of not-self (*anātman*), none of the constituent parts of the human being are to be considered as an eternal, immutable self. In contrast, texts such as the influential *Mahāparinirvāṇa-Mahāsūtra* state that there is a nondual relationship between not-self and true self. In other words, they are two sides of the same coin. Since they are contingent and mutable, the components of the human being that can be perceived do not constitute the

---

[77] Harvey 1995, 166–79, here 175.
[78] Ibid., 176.
[79] See Jones 2021, 214–18.
[80] Ibid., 251.
[81] Ibid., 244.

true self that participates in transcendent reality. Rather, they constitute as it were simply the external shell hiding the secret self, the reality of which is revealed in the texts of this particular tradition.[82]

The soteriological aspect of this teaching is obvious. At the center of the short and popular *Tathāgatagarbha-Sūtra* is a series of parables, all of which are suited to encouraging people in the pursuit of Buddhahood. It is precisely those who show increasing awareness of their own inadequacy (which means in Buddhism their own egocentrism) who are encouraged to continue in their religious practice with trust in their own hidden Buddha nature.[83] The encouragement to make one's own efforts is combined with the reliance on the power of a transcendent-immanent reality that will one day prevail despite one's own inadequacies.[84] Thus, while the synthesis maintains the tension between redemption by self-help and other-help, it also interprets one's own efforts as something sustained by the hidden immanent power of a reality external to the ego. Thus, the new or true self is neither identical to nor completely different from the ego-self.

A structurally similar synthesis can be seen in the motif of the inner Christ in Paul's theology (which I briefly mentioned in the previous chapter),[85] where the "Christ in me" takes the function of a true and new self, too. Paul understands Christ as the new Adam. The first Adam was created in the image of God. Distorted by Adam's sin, the human likeness to God is restored by the sinless Christ, the new Adam.[86] In this respect, the inner Christ is the true self, and at the same time the new self: the *true* self, insofar as our original likeness to God is renewed in Christ; the *new* self, insofar as the inner Christ replaces the sinful, egocentric self.[87] Paul also denotes the life of this true and new self as the life in the Spirit, since it is the Spirit of Christ that constitutes the inner self (see Romans 8:9–11). Life in the Spirit, however, is always in tension with life in the "flesh," a concept that, as already mentioned, has very strong parallels in Paul to that of defilements (*kleśas*) in Buddhism.[88]

As with the concept of Buddha nature, we can also say about the new self in Christ that it is neither identical to nor completely different from the old ego-self. This becomes quite clear when Paul says, "I have been crucified with Christ. It is no longer I who live, but Christ who lives in me. And the life I now live in the flesh I live by faith in the Son of God, who loved me and gave himself for me" (Galatians 2:20). Obviously, Paul speaks here of a

---

[82]See ibid., 59–62, 245–60.
[83]See also Zimmermann 2002, 76.
[84]See ibid., 62.
[85]See above, p. 160.
[86]See Dunn 2006, 199–204.
[87]In 2 Corinthians 5:17, Paul explicitly speaks of a "new creation" in this regard.
[88]See above, p. 71.

tense unity in difference. On the one hand, the old ego-self is crucified with Christ; it no longer lives, but is replaced by Christ. On the other, it continues to live "in the flesh," albeit in a new way, i.e., no longer according to the flesh alone,[89] but in faith in Christ, who as redeemer turns lovingly toward the ego-self. It becomes clear in the course of the passage that Paul is by no means speaking only of himself, but of all believers, since he wishes for all of them that Christ be "formed in you" (Galatians 4:19)—a motif that lives on in the later pseudo-Pauline letters (Colossians 1:27; Ephesians 3:17).

With a question that has now become well known, the Zen Buddhist philosopher Keiji Nishitani (1900–1990) showed that the tension between self and divine Other in the synthesis thus outlined is both preserved, and suspended and transcended: "'It is no longer I who live, but Christ who lives in me.' This makes immediate sense to me—only, may I ask, Who speaks these words actually?"[90] Nishitani turns Paul's phrase into a Zen-koan-like paradox. If we wanted to answer his question by saying that Paul is speaking here, then Christ apparently does not live in him after all. If, on the other hand, we wanted to say that it is Christ speaking, then the statement makes no sense. Taken by itself, neither the one nor the other is valid; rather, each of the two possible answers points beyond itself to the other, and thus to that higher synthetic level. In Paul's statement, the "I" can be identified completely neither with the ego-self nor with Christ. As "Christ in me," it participates instead in both realities—in "Christ" and "me"—and is therein the new and true self.[91] Referring explicitly to Nishitani, Samuel Vollenweider has acknowledged from an exegetical perspective clear "correspondences" here between Buddhist and Pauline motifs.[92] For Vollenweider, "Buddhism . . . and Paul . . . touch each other above all in grasping the breakthrough from the level of the ego to the level of the 'self' . . . as basic movements of being in general as it is brought to consciousness in religion."[93]

Chunyi Zhang (1871–1955), a scholar educated in the Chinese classics, apparently pursued a similar idea with his identification of Buddha nature and Holy Spirit. Zhang first turned to Christianity, and then later to Buddhism, but each phase saw him keen to integrate the insights from both traditions.[94] He was convinced that there were key similarities between

---

[89]Sanders (2015, 659) understands the statement "in the flesh" here as merely referring to bodily existence. In Dunn's (2006, 64, 68) view, this is less clear-cut.
[90]Fischer-Barnicol 1965/66, 210. On this, see also Ueda, S. 2001.
[91]Similarly, Hans-Martin Barth (2002, 176–77). Yet, unfortunately, Barth underestimates, at least here, the strong parallelism with the Buddha nature teaching. This is different with the Japanese New Testament scholar Seiichi Yagi (1988, 100), who explicitly emphasizes this parallelism.
[92]Vollenweider 1991, 365, 374.
[93]Ibid., 375.
[94]On Zhang's biography, see Feng 2018, 75–112, and Lai & So 2003, 53–56.

"authentic Christianity," which for him were the teachings of Jesus and Paul, and Mahayana Buddhism. He developed something like a Buddhist-Christian doctrine of the Spirit (pneumatology). For him, "The Holy Spirit is the awakening nature (*juexing* 覺性), which takes people out of evil into good, and enlightens them as regards the mystery of life and death as well. In the sense that the awakening nature is the human as well as the Buddha nature, we all have already possessed the Buddha nature and need not look for it from outside nor be afraid of losing it."[95] For Zhang, identifying Buddha nature and Holy Spirit is thus grounded in the fact that it on the one hand denotes a transcendent reality that makes salvation possible in the first place, and on the other is also so inherent in human nature that it inspires and motivates individuals to their own efforts and practice.

The dialectical structure, as it emerges in both Buddhism and Christianity when we analyze the self in terms of redemption, is presumably one of the reasons why a tension between an emphasis on self-help and other-help has developed and persisted in both traditions. A further reason might be found in how the two religions understand the value of human virtue.

The Nature of Virtue and the Problem of Evil

According to a canonical text of Theravada Buddhism (*Majjhima Nikāya* 78), the Buddha was once asked whether someone who does not commit evil deeds, does not speak evil words, does not have any evil intentions, and does not earn their livelihood in any evil way has perfected their virtue.[96] The Buddha replies in the negative, for otherwise "a young tender infant lying prone" and being nursed by its mother would also have to be seen as someone who is "perfected in what is wholesome." Only the kind of thought, mental effort, and practice that is specified by the Noble Eightfold Path could lead to spiritual and moral perfection. But, the Buddha continues, once perfection has been achieved, such a person's thoughts, words, and deeds no longer serve to improve their own karma. In such a case, a monk "is virtuous, but he does not identify with his virtue."[97] According to this text, then, virtue, on the one hand, does not consist merely in the absence of evil thoughts, words, and deeds, as in an infant, but rather implies insight, effort, and practice. On the other hand, though, its perfection consists in an attitude in which virtuous behavior is no longer ascribed to the ego-self.

Such an understanding of virtue has important implications with regard to the problem of evil. A paradisiacal world where everyone is in the situ-

---

[95] As summarized by Lai & So 2003, 65–66.
[96] See Ñāṇamoli & Bodhi 2001, 648–53.
[97] Ibid., 651.

ation of a well-cared-for infant would exclude virtue and spiritual growth, since there could be no virtue and no spiritual perfection in a world where no one is able to commit evil. Virtue and wisdom can be actively developed only in a world full of serious moral and spiritual challenges. The influential Mahayanist *Vimalakīrtinirdeśa-Sūtra* states explicitly a connection between this understanding of virtue and the problem of evil. Its tenth chapter describes how a great crowd of bodhisattvas from a faraway paradise visit the world of Gautama Buddha, the world of ancient India. They are horrified that there is "a buddha-field of such intense hardships" where the people are "wild and uncivilized." But the text then explains that all ten bodhisattva virtues can only be developed in such a world. The virtue of generosity presupposes that there is genuine need. The virtue of morality presupposes that there is the genuine possibility of evil behavior. The virtue of forbearance presupposes that there is hate that requires forbearance, and so on. "Those who engage in these ten virtuous practices do not exist in any other buddha-field."[98]

The problem of evil arises in theistic religions as a critical inquiry into the notion of a good and omnipotent creator. Parts of Buddhism, too, have repeatedly employed the problem of evil as an objection against belief in a divine creator.[99] But the problem also arises in nontheistic religions. In Buddhism, it appears as a question about the unexplained origin of defilements, if the mind is considered to be pure and luminous by nature. This problem gains special weight where Buddha nature is identified with the dharma body (*dharmakāya*), and the dharma body is understood as the ultimate ground of all reality. Peter Gregory has described the problem thus: "The Mind from which delusion arises is the intrinsically enlightened pure Mind and this Mind . . . is the fundamental ground of phenomenal reality. . . . How can delusion arise if the fundamental ground of phenomenal reality is the intrinsically enlightened Mind?"[100] If ultimate reality is characterized on the one hand as the pure and perfect mind, and on the other as the fundamental ground of the world, then why is there delusion and all the evils resulting from it?

The answer given in the *Vimalakīrtinirdeśa-Sūtra* is based on the value and nature of virtue. Against this background, a world full of suffering that nonetheless offers the possibility of developing those virtues that can combat evil is more valuable than a paradisiacal world where there is neither suffering nor virtue. This argument is very similar to the explanation of evil in terms of the human being's free will, the so-called free-will defense that we

---

[98]Thurman 1976, 82–83.
[99]See Schmidt-Leukel 2006b, 127–28; 2017b, 207–11; 2022b.
[100]Gregory 1986, 73.

know from theistic religions. Similarly, the Buddhist argument presupposes that there is a morally significant free will that can lead to both good and evil deeds. Alongside knowledge, free will is therefore the basis of virtue, and is of such great value that ultimately free will outweighs suffering.[101] If all beings were like robots, programmed to do only good, then their actions would not really be "good" in a moral sense. Robots function, but they are not virtuous. Realizing the value of virtue presupposes beings who are also free to behave in nonvirtuous ways.

This argument leads us back to the question of the importance of a person's own efforts in the process of salvation. On the one hand, we find in both Buddhism and Christianity the belief that the problem of evil can only be solved if special value is assigned to virtue and to a person's own efforts and responsibility associated with it. On the other, both traditions also include the widespread belief that a virtuous life involves overcoming deep-seated egocentrism, and that this is possible only through that "other-help" that comes from ultimate reality itself. Moreover, both traditions include the belief that only in this way can the unity of wisdom and compassion, or of knowledge/faith and love, be realized, i.e., that it only becomes concrete in a world as we know it, and as a good that ultimately comes from beyond the world, from its inconceivable ground. To depict this, Buddhism uses the image of the pure lotus blossom flourishing in the impure mud, while Christianity speaks of the light shining only in darkness.

---

[101] On the importance of the argument of free will within Christian theology, see the introductory overview in Loichinger & Kreiner 2010, 67–120, as well as Kreiner 2017.

8

Beyond the Horizon . . .

In her popular scientific work on the different ideas of afterlife that religions have, Catherine Wolff writes, from a Christian perspective, that in Hinduism and Buddhism "she encountered ways of reaching beyond this life that are essentially different from those offered by Western faiths."[1] Such an impression can indeed easily arise at first glance. But a closer look at Buddhism and Christianity shows that with regard to the issue of our final salvation the question is not simply about the differences between nirvana and kingdom of heaven. Rather, each of the two religions has developed its own variety of different ideas about the ultimate salvific destiny. Comparing these internal differences once more reveals fractal patterns: some forms of Christian concepts of salvation have parallels in Buddhism, and some features of Buddhist concepts of salvation have parallels in Christianity.

Before explaining this in more detail, I again look first and briefly at previous comparisons. However, I disregard those in which Christian authors have interpreted the Buddhist nirvana in terms of a nihilistic and complete extinction. As shown in chapter 4, this is largely a misinterpretation, and is based on the view that Buddhism does not believe in a transcendent, absolute reality.[2] To be sure, today both Buddhism and Christianity have secularized interpretations of their own teachings that do not accept the existence of an ultimate reality, thus reducing the goal of salvation of both religions to the realization of certain inner-worldly values.[3] However, this does not apply to traditional forms of both religions, which of course also continue to exist today.

8.1 BLISSFUL CESSATION OR BLISSFUL COMMUNION?

Since the beginnings of Western studies on Buddhism, Christian authors have had difficulty classifying the Buddhist goal of salvation. Those who

---
[1] Wolff 2021, 205.
[2] See above, pp. 85–91.
[3] See above, pp. 91–92.

rejected a nihilistic interpretation of nirvana saw the strongest parallels to Buddhist claims in the mystical forms of theistic religions and in an emphasis shaped by negative theology on the ineffability of ultimate reality.[4] However, there are few direct comparisons of the Buddhist and the Christian goal of salvation, and the few that there are often vacillate as far as Buddhism is concerned between a nihilistic and a mystical interpretation.

In his 1923 comparison, Joseph Estlin Carpenter argued that the Buddha had emphasized the inexpressibility and ineffability of nirvana because nirvana, free from death and suffering, belonged "to the transcendent order."[5] At the same time, though, the Buddha had also stressed that nirvana can be experienced. Carpenter related the Buddhist stages of so-called formless absorption to the Platonic mysticism found in Clement of Alexandria and Augustine.[6] According to Carpenter, it was especially the Christian mystics who had, like the Buddhist texts, emphasized the inconceivability and ineffability of ultimate reality.[7] Carpenter saw in the promise of salvation offered by Mahayana Buddhism, according to which all beings shall one day become Buddhas, an equivalent to the New Testament promise of one day becoming "partakers of the divine nature" (2 Peter 1:4).[8]

Eight years later, Hilko Wiardo Schomerus' comparison tended in the opposite direction. Like Carpenter, Schomerus cites the Buddhist position that nirvana can be described neither as being nor as not-being.[9] The Buddha, Schomerus concedes, did not understand nirvana as "salvation in an absolute nothingness."[10] However, nirvana, at least from a Western perspective, comes very close to a deathlike state.[11] For Schomerus, nirvana

> is the bliss of one who knows that he is beyond all sorrowful events, or does not know it anymore, to whom everything that otherwise causes suffering is no longer of any concern. This is a wonderful state of soul, which one might compare with a state beyond consciousness, e.g. with the state in narcosis. A permanent state of complete insensibility, in which there is no more sensation and perception, no imagination and thinking, no feeling, no striving, no desire, no wanting, in which one has only the feeling of absolute calmness and deepest peace, if such a feeling is still present at all, a state which cannot be described more precisely in positive terms.[12]

---

[4] See above, p. 88.
[5] See Carpenter 1923, 122–28, especially 127.
[6] Ibid., 142–45.
[7] Ibid., 264–71.
[8] Ibid., 231.
[9] Schomerus 1931, 55.
[10] Ibid., 57.
[11] Ibid., 58.
[12] Ibid., 56–57.

Schomerus contrasts this goal, which is "as similar to death ... as possible,"[13] with the Christian goal of eternal life, by which he understands a "life with God" that excludes "everything that is contrary to God," i.e., sin.[14] For Schomerus, this life already begins in this world for those who believe in Christ, but only finds its completion "in the world in which there is no more sin, in which God's will is the only law and the only power."[15] Schomerus sees the two goals of salvation as being diametrically opposed: "In Christ we have a guide from death to life, in Buddha from life to the death-like nirvana."[16]

Views like those held by Schomerus have been repeated until more recently, especially by Christian authors. Ulrich Luz, for example, writes in his 2002 comparison that the idea of salvation as the coming kingdom of God is linked in Jesus and early Christianity to the idea of "fulfillment" and "fullness of life." "How distant from this does appear to be, when described, as it must be, as liberation from life, the extinction of life."[17]

But Burnett Hillman Streeter provided a more nuanced picture in a comparative study that appeared at almost the same time as Schomerus' work. Streeter emphasizes that Buddhism has different conceptions of nirvana. While some currents teach a nirvana that actually comes very close to the idea of complete extinction, there is also the idea of a "liberation of the real and eternal self from the empirical self," whereby the real self is thought to be identical with the Absolute. Streeter describes this goal of salvation thus: "The storm is over; the tossed and troubled wave sinks back on the bosom of the unruffled ocean of Eternal Being."[18] In addition, Streeter noted the fact that Mahayana Buddhism had developed another idea: namely, the final liberation from the cycle of rebirths through rebirth in Amida's Pure Land.[19]

While it is true that Schomerus had also pointed out that some statements in the Buddhist texts give the impression that the goal of salvation consists in oneness with a transcendent reality, he, unlike Streeter, rejected this impression as misleading.[20] Similarly, Ninian Smart has in more recent times rejected the idea that the Buddha referred to any kind of absolute reality, arguing that this is not the case at least for the teachings of Theravada Buddhism.[21] Nevertheless, Smart does concede that even the canonical texts of Theravada Buddhism describe nirvana as "the supreme happiness, the

---

[13]Ibid., 58.
[14]Ibid., 60–61.
[15]Ibid., 62.
[16]Ibid., 64.
[17]Luz & Michaels 2006, 44 (= 2002, 58).
[18]Streeter 1932, 284.
[19]Ibid., 285.
[20]See Schomerus 1931, 56.
[21]Smart 1993, 18, 21–22.

permanent or deathless place, and the end of concern with the self or ego."[22] However, for Smart, the very idea of a loss of self in nirvana forbids seeing in this a similarity to the Christian faith, since Christianity is about the "full flowering of your gleaming personality which suffuses life with God in heaven."[23] Smart judges developments in Mahayana Buddhism differently, however, arguing that the figure of the Buddha Amida (= *Amitābha*) certainly shows traits of a theistic God. And the idea that all Buddhas are one in the highest dharma body (*dharmakāya*) is indeed reminiscent, Smart says, of certain forms of theistic mysticism, such as Meister Eckhart's idea of unity with the Godhead.[24]

Streeter sees the essential difference between the Buddhist and Christian goals of salvation in the latter's social dimension, arguing that the foretaste of eternal life in Christianity does not consist "chiefly, if at all, in the mystic rapture of the 'flight of the Alone to the Alone.'"[25] The kingdom of God consists not in the "everlasting calm of nirvana, as 'The Dewdrop slips into the shining Sea,'"[26] but in communion. "Love, it follows, is the essence of Eternal Life," which for Streeter applies both to the experience of the kingdom of God in the here and now, and to heaven. "On earth the Kingdom of God must be a society; in Heaven it will still be such—but instead of a kingdom it will be named a home."[27]

Hereby Streeter addresses a difference in the concepts of salvation that is emphasized in a number of comparisons. Both Schomerus and Luz stress the loving communion as a dimension of the kingdom of God proclaimed by Jesus.[28] According to Gustav Mensching, nirvana is "the extinction of all individuality and personality."[29] "As the streams flow into the ocean and lose their names and individual forms in it, but yet do not cease to exist in the great ocean, so it is with the redeemed in nirvana."[30] Like Schomerus, Mensching holds that the Buddhist goal of salvation is a "state of unconscious being,"[31] while the Christian goal of salvation is "a transformed world in which God's reign is fully realized."[32] "The kingdom of God," argues Mensching in an echo of Paul Tillich, "is a social, political and personalized

---

[22] Ibid., 47. Similarly ibid., 18.
[23] Ibid., 18.
[24] Ibid., 24.
[25] Streeter is taking up here a well-known formula of Plotinus, and is thus indirectly referring to the Neoplatonic influence in Christian mysticism.
[26] This is an unacknowledged quotation of the last line of *The Light of Asia*, an extraordinarily popular epic poem on the life of the Buddha that Edwin Arnold first published in 1879.
[27] All quotations Streeter 1932, 305.
[28] See Schomerus 1931, 62–63; Luz & Michaels 2006, 43–45 (2002, 57–59).
[29] Mensching 1978, 117.
[30] Ibid., 106.
[31] Ibid., 107.
[32] Ibid., 117.

symbol."[33] It is about realizing justice and peace, whereas nirvana is about overcoming finitude and suffering.[34]

Georg Siegmund takes a similar path in his comparison of the goals of salvation. Formally, he says, both are concerned with the striving for the absolute.[35] The Buddhist goal of salvation is freedom from suffering and transience,[36] "an entering into and being absorbed by the absolute substance, that is, an identification or fusion with the highest reality."[37] However, he argues, this presupposes that there is no other reality besides the absolute. Everything not-absolute is thought of as empty appearance, as deception, which does not allow the idea of the human being's own reality in the sense of a person different from the absolute. Therefore, unlike in Christianity, the goal of salvation cannot be understood for Siegmund as "a personal encounter with an absolute personal being," i.e., as a "union with the absolute in the sense of a personal communion of love with the personal Creator-God."[38] There is no room in Buddhism for "man's striving for infinity . . . as a loving desire."[39] However, according to Siegmund, the deepest striving of the human being consists precisely in such a desire for love and can find its fulfillment only in a "love-union" with a personal Absolute.[40]

Nevertheless, Siegmund claims, this inner human inclination has finally also broken through in Buddhism, despite its monistic underpinnings. The need for "love-union" is visible in Pure Land Buddhism, where the human being seeks "consolation and grace from the Buddha Amida." A bridge therefore appears here between East and West.[41] Ernest Valea, though, is much more skeptical in this regard, arguing that it would be "absurd to consider a Pure Land a place of perfect and everlasting communion with the Buddha." Hence it could not be deemed equivalent to the kingdom of God. For Valea, the Pure Land is only a transitional station from which nirvana is reached,[42] but there is no room for personhood in nirvana.[43] Valea's interpretation of nirvana is similar to its interpretation as final annihilation. While he admits that no self is annihilated in nirvana, since the self, according to Buddhism, is in any case only an illusion, nevertheless

---

[33]Ibid., 118. See Tillich's remarks on nirvana and the kingdom of God in his Bampton Lectures (Tillich 1964, 63–75). For a critique of Tillich's one-sided perception of Buddhism and his underestimation of the social dimension of the Buddhist idea of salvation, see Lai 2006b.
[34]See Mensching 1978, 118.
[35]Siegmund 1980, 126–51 (= Siegmund 1983, 215–52).
[36]Ibid., 128 (= 1983, 218).
[37]Ibid., 143 (= 1983, 241).
[38]Ibid., 143 (= 1983, 241–42).
[39]Ibid., 137 (= 1983, 232).
[40]"Liebes-Einung," following the German original here (= 1983, 245–46).
[41]Siegmund 1980, 148 (= 1983, 248–49).
[42]Valea 2008, 130.
[43]Ibid., 178.

all powers that produce existence find their final extinction here.[44] For a Buddhist, Valea says, the Christian idea of salvation can be nothing else than a continuation of illusion, an attachment to the craving for continued personal existence.[45]

Such conjectures, however, by no means represent the views of all Buddhists. The Buddhist religious studies scholar Hajime Nakamura has argued, for example, "that the Buddhist hope of *Nirvāṇa* has more in common with the Christian hope of heavenly, eternal Life than is sometimes supposed."[46] While dismissing the nihilistic interpretation of nirvana as a Western misinterpretation,[47] Nakamura does acknowledge that there have been quite different ideas of nirvana in Buddhism.[48] But, besides the fundamental belief in nirvana as that reality that brings release from suffering and death, it is, according to Nakamura, above all the ineffability of nirvana that is emphasized. At the same time, he points to the numerous poetic images and metaphors that highlight the desirable character of nirvana as supreme happiness: the "further shore," the "harbor of refuge," the "island amidst the floods," the "place of bliss," the "holy city," the "medicine for all evils," and so on. He attributes this to the fact that, according to Buddhism, nirvana can already be experienced in this life in the form of enlightenment. The peace and happiness of enlightenment are then, for Nakamura, thought of as something that outlasts death.[49] Nakamura sees parallels to Christian ideas of salvation above all in the fact that Christianity emphasizes the ineffability of eternal life on the one hand (he refers here to 1 Corinthians 2:9),[50] while also using many metaphors that are not dissimilar to Buddhist images on the other, these often also being about liberation from suffering and death.[51] Nakamura sees the social relevance of the Buddhist goal of salvation in the belief that enlightenment brings with it a charity that embraces all.[52]

The latter is something that Chai-Shin Yu has also emphasized in his comparison of early Buddhist and Christian communities. The image of rivers that lose their separate individuality when they flow into the great ocean (*Aṅguttara Nikāya* 8:19) finds its counterpart in the Buddhist ideal of a life in the monastic order where all are one because there is no more self-centered striving.[53] In early Christianity, Yu says, "The doctrine of the

---

[44]See ibid., 95–98.
[45]See ibid., 185.
[46]Nakamura 1986, 62.
[47]Ibid., 63.
[48]Ibid., 53.
[49]Ibid., 54–55.
[50]"No eye hath seen, nor ear heard nor the heart of man conceived, what God has prepared for those who love him." Ibid., 62.
[51]Ibid., 62.
[52]Ibid., 56–57.
[53]Yu, C.-S. 1981, 73.

Holy Spirit gave the members of the community a sense of unity in that they saw themselves as being led by one Spirit, who bound them into one body as the people of God in the New Covenant."[54]

Valea's assumption that the Christian hope for eternal life must appear to Buddhists as an attachment to the desire for continued individual existence touches on another aspect in the comparison of Christian and Buddhist notions of salvation: namely, the difference between belief in resurrection and belief in rebirth. What Valea only hints at is clearly expressed by Mensching:

> The Christian expectation of the end is connected with the belief in a resurrection as it lived in late Judaism, probably originated under Iranian influence. This is, of course, an idea that is impossible in Buddhism as an expectation of salvation; for constant rebirth is precisely the calamity and its termination is the salvation.[55]

While, like Valea, Mensching is suggesting here that from a Buddhist point of view resurrection cannot be considered salvific because it seems to be close to the idea of a continued existence, reminiscent of rebirth, Smart points out that Christianity "mostly" rejected the idea of rebirth or reincarnation in favor of the belief in the resurrection of the body and the immortality of the soul.[56] But neither Mensching's nor Smart's chosen point of comparison is without problems. How far can resurrection—or, better, being raised from death—be paralleled with that form of continued existence that Buddhism calls "rebirth"? And does the Buddhist belief in rebirth not also entail the possibility of a progressive purification, so that it could perhaps be related less to the belief in resurrection, and more to the Christian idea of purgatory, i.e., to the belief in a continuous purification of the human being in a postmortal form of existence?

8.2 INDIVIDUAL AND SOCIAL FACETS IN BUDDHIST CONCEPTS OF SALVATION

Attaining nirvana—this is the goal that Buddhist concepts of salvation revolve around. "Everywhere in Buddhism," says Steven Collins, nirvana is "symbolically central."[57] However, there are very different interpretations and understandings of this goal within the Buddhist tradition. I do not wish to repeat what I have already discussed in chapter 4 about nirvana as a tran-

---

[54]Ibid., 211.
[55]Mensching 1978, 117.
[56]Smart 1993, 17.
[57]Collins, S. 1998, 116.

scendent and ultimate reality, but focus here on the various forms and facets of the understanding of salvation/liberation associated with nirvana. Once again, I can only provide a cursory and selective overview: how far can we find among the different Buddhist concepts of salvation such differences that resemble the differences among the Christian concepts of salvation? As I have shown, there is an awareness in some previous comparisons that Buddhism does indeed contain different ideas of salvation. But rarely has the variety of ideas within Buddhism been compared with the variety within Christianity.

Salvation in and beyond the World

The texts of ancient Buddhism, as well as the authoritative sources of Theravada Buddhism, refer to both a this-worldly and a transcendent nirvana; or, as Steven Collins puts it, to a nirvana "in and out of time."[58] The first is the experience of nirvana in life, i.e., the experience of nirvana in enlightenment or awakening (*bodhi*); the second is the experience of nirvana at the death of the awakened person. These are not two different nirvanas; it is a distinction between two different forms of the nirvana experience. The Buddhist tradition often refers to this distinction as "nirvana with residue left" and "nirvana without residue left."[59] "Residue" (*upadhi*) here refers to the five "aggregates" (Pali: *khandha*, Sanskrit: *skandha*) or aspects of mental-physical existence: body, feelings, perceptions, mental formations (including will and karmic inclinations), and consciousness. The nonenlightened person clings to these "aggregates" by identifying with them as "I,"[60] whereas an enlightened person is no longer attached to them, but has not yet finally discarded them, this only happening with that person's ultimate death.[61] This corresponds to the similarly traditional distinction between the "nirvana of the defilements" and the "nirvana of the aggregates," i.e., between the final "extinction" (which is the literal meaning of *nirvāṇa*) in enlightenment of the "defilements" (greed, hate, and delusion), and the final extinction of the "aggregates" in the death of the enlightened person, so that there is no further rebirth and thus no further death.

But does this mean that an enlightened person no longer exists after entering transcendent nirvana, the nirvana out of time? The canonical texts

---

[58] See Collins, S. 1998, 147–77; 2010, 39–60.

[59] In Pali: *sa-upādi-sesa-nibbāna* and *an-upādi-sesa-nibbāna*. The distinction is found in the Pali canon, for example, in *Itivuttaka* 44 (my translation follows Ireland 1997, 181). See also Hwang 2006, whose study explores the dogmatic implications of this distinction in various non-Mahayana schools.

[60] See above, p. 181.

[61] According to early Buddhist beliefs, women can also attain enlightenment as women (i.e., without becoming male in a future life). However, the status of Buddhahood is tied to being male, so that women can only become a Buddha if they are first reborn as a man.

explicitly pose this question, and answer it with the well-known fourfold negation: it cannot be said of an enlightened person after death that they (1) exist, (2) not exist, (3) exist and not exist, (4) neither exist nor not exist.[62] This negation rejects all logically possible statements, the reason given for this being that the enlightened person can no longer be identified with the five aggregates.[63] Thus, according to the *Sutta Nipāta* (verse 1076),

> There is no measure of one who has gone out, ...
> There is no means by which they might speak of him.
> When all phenomena have been uprooted,
> all pathways of speech are also uprooted.[64]

A perfected one, it is said elsewhere, is "profound, immeasurable, unfathomable like the ocean."[65] And just as the Ganges flows toward the ocean and ends therein, so does the community of the Buddha, monastics and lay followers alike, flow toward the ocean of nirvana.[66] The image naturally evokes echoes of its use in the Upanishads, according to which the individual self is lost in the ocean of divine reality.[67] Steven Collins, however, has cautioned against attaching too much importance to such associations, arguing that this image, at least in the Pali canonical texts, is solely about the radical ineffability and untraceability of the enlightened person in postmortal nirvana.[68]

A formulation that is highly reminiscent of Upanishadic ideas is also used for the this-worldly nirvana, the nirvana in time. The one who has already become "nirvanized" and happy in enlightenment during their lifetime is often said in the Pali canonical texts to be "dwelling with a self that has become Brahma."[69] This phrase can be interpreted in such a way that it means only the completion of the human being during their lifetime (for example, in the sense of, "they have reached saintliness"), without implying an Upanishadic metaphysics in the sense of the unity of self (*ātman/atta*) and divine ground of the universe (*brahman*). However, the similarity to Upanishadic ideas is in some Indian Mahayana texts (namely, in those dealing with the Buddha nature of all beings) not just one of words, but also indisputably one of content—for the Buddha nature or the "Buddha

---

[62]See Collins, S. 1982, 131–32.
[63]As, for example, in *Majjhima Nikāya* 72 and *Saṃyutta Nikāya* 44.1.
[64]Bodhi 2017, 335.
[65]*Majjhima Nikāya* 72.20. Ñāṇamoli & Bodhi 2001, 594.
[66]*Majjhima Nikāya* 73.14. For further references, see Collins 1982, 260–61.
[67]See *Chāndogya Upaniṣad* 6.10; *Muṇḍaka Upaniṣad* 3.2.8.
[68]See Collins, S. 1982, 260–61; 1998, 221–22.
[69]Pali: *brahmabhūtena attanā vhiharati*. On this, see Pérez-Remón 1980, 113–18. He translates: "dwells with a self brahma-become."

seed" (*tathāgatagarbha*) is not only explicitly called the true *ātman* (self) here. Rather, as "Buddha seed," it also denotes a reality that is "permanent, indestructible, and superlatively valuable, and moreover points outside of oneself to the timeless, higher reality that is the Buddha."[70] The similarity to Upanishadic ideas becomes still greater where Buddha nature as the true self is also identified with the true nature of all reality.

Given such findings, two Japanese Buddhist scholars, Noriaki Hakamaya and Shiro Matsumoto, have argued that the doctrine of a universal Buddha nature is "not Buddhist"[71]—to which one of their teachers, Jikido Takasaki, responded,

> The idea that the *tathāgata-garbha* thought has much in common with the teachings of the mainstream of Indian thought as represented by the Upaniṣads and the Vedānta philosophy is a point I have often made myself and was hardly any cause for alarm. But it is quite another thing to conclude that such a way of thinking is "not Buddhist" simply because it is similar to the mainstream of Indian thought. Here I part company with them. . . . The problem, as I see it, is how one defines "Buddhism."[72]

With this remark, Takasaki implicitly refers to the inner diversity of the Buddhist tradition, since "Buddhism" cannot be defined by a single one of its manifestations. This diversity also comprises different concepts of salvation. And, while some have a strong tendency to keep their distance from any metaphysical description of the final state of salvation, others show certainly some proximity to metaphysical ideas of unity as found in the Upanishadic tradition.

As already pointed out in chapter 4, the "incomprehensible ocean" is by no means the only image for nirvana.[73] On the contrary, the canonical and noncanonical texts use an enormous range of images and metaphors, with images such as those of the safe island or the happy city expressing above all liberation from suffering and death. Yet, as Nakamura has argued, it is precisely in their figurative character that they refer back to the experience of nirvana during a person's lifetime: to enlightenment. For only from this experience can that hope be expressed (if only in the form of allegorical images) that is associated with the final attainment of the transcendent goal of salvation, the nirvana out of time.[74] The experience of those enlightened

---

[70] Jones 2021, 251.
[71] See Hubbard & Swanson 1997.
[72] Takasaki 1997, 314.
[73] See above, p. 95.
[74] See again Nakamura 1986, 54–55. See also above, p. 194.

is also referred to by the hope of those who trust their message, as the *Milindapañha* (3.4.8) says: "It is by hearing the glad words of those who have seen Nirvāṇa, that they who have not received it know how happy a state it is."[75]

Although there are texts in the Pali canon that speak of a sudden and unexpected onset of the experience of enlightenment, enlightenment is usually associated with meditation—or, more specifically, with the attainment of certain meditative states of mind. Another revealing distinction emerges here: some texts associate the experience of enlightenment with the highest level of so-called form-based absorption, i.e., with a state of equanimous mindfulness, free from pleasure and pain. It was in this state that Siddhartha Gautama attained enlightenment and the insight associated with it.[76] Other texts, though, associate the experience of nirvana with the highest level of "formless" absorption, which is described as the "cessation of perception and sensation."[77] This quite clearly presupposes that the experience of nirvana, and especially its experience as "happiness," is of a very different nature from all experiences associated with the usual forms of perception and sensation.[78]

This has important implications for how the postmortal experience of nirvana is understood, since the question arises here, too, of how far transcendent nirvana can be denoted as "highest happiness," if it also means the extinction of the five aggregates and thus the extinction of perception, sensation, and consciousness. According to Collins, the Pali canonical texts can be summarized as follows: "nirvana is the cessation of the consciousness aggregate, but that is not equivalent to becoming non-existent: nirvana is beyond designation." In other words, "A nirvanized consciousness is not non-existent."[79]

The same is true for happiness. The happiness of nirvana is not identical with a contingent and thus transient feeling of happiness. Rather, happiness lies in the permanent liberation from the world of the contingent and transient.[80] Nevertheless, temporary experiences of liberation are considered a kind of foretaste of nirvana. Form-based absorption involves a temporary overcoming of those mental "hindrances," including greed and hate, which are permanently overcome in enlightenment. The temporary liberation from these obstacles produces a happy joy that the canonical texts often

---

[75]Rhys Davids 1890, 108.

[76]This state of absorption relates both to his nirvana within time (see *Majjhima Nikāya* 36), i.e., his enlightenment, and to his entry into nirvana out of time at the time of his death (*Dīgha Nikāya* 16).

[77]For example, *Aṅguttara Nikāya* 6.46; 9.51; 10.29. On this, see also Schmidt-Leukel 1993b, especially 384–91; 2006a: 57–60. See also Collins, S. 1998, 156–61, and the literature mentioned there.

[78]As, for example, in *Aṅguttara Nikāya* 10.6.

[79]Collins, S. 1998, 205.

[80]See ibid., 207–13.

compare with the joy of liberation from financial hardships, recovery from serious illness, release from prison or enslavement, or of arriving safely after a perilous journey. The message is clear: liberation will be happy and complete in nirvana.[81]

Social Aspects of Salvation

According to Steven Collins, Buddhist thought, at least in Indian culture, "is individualist."[82] A person reaches nirvana as an individual, even if individuality is lost in nirvana. And even when comparing the postmortal nirvana to a city, the ancient texts do not portray this "city" as an otherworldly society. But this does not mean that the Buddhist understanding of salvation completely lacks a social dimension. The further development of Buddhism could even lead in its later forms (as I soon discuss in more detail) to the identification of nirvana with the "Pure Land" as a well-populated world.

The lasting liberation from greed and hate in enlightenment, i.e., nirvana in time, is not only connected with the personal experience of happiness. Rather, according to the early Buddhist texts, this experience also has important social implications. Thus, the *Dhammapada* (197–199), probably the most popular collection of sayings in ancient Buddhism, states,

> We live happily indeed, not hating among the hateful!
> Among men who hate we dwell free from hate!
> We live happily indeed, free from ailments among the ailing!
> Among men who are ailing let us dwell free from ailments!
> We live happily indeed, free from greed among the greedy!
> Among men who are greedy let us dwell free from greed![83]

Not returning hatred and being without greed is positively expressed in the social qualities of loving-kindness, compassion, and sympathetic joy. No less popular than the *Dhammapada* is the *Metta Sutta*.[84] It characterizes loving-kindness (*metta*) as the wish for the happiness of all beings:

> May all beings be happy and secure;
> may they be inwardly happy!
> No one should deceive another,
> nor despise anyone anywhere.
> Because of anger and thoughts of aversion
> no one should wish suffering for another.

---

[81] See Schmidt-Leukel 2006a, 60–61.
[82] Collins, S. 1988, 50.
[83] Translation modified from Müller 2000, 24.
[84] See above, p. 81.

> Just as a mother would protect her son,
> her only son, with her own life,
> so one should develop toward all beings
> a state of mind without boundaries.
> And toward the whole world
> one should develop loving-kindness
> a state of mind without boundaries—
> above, below, and across—
> unconfined, without enmity, without adversaries.[85]

There is a form of meditation in Buddhism that serves to develop this inner attitude of loving-kindness. The *Visuddhimagga*, one of the most important classical manuals in Theravada Buddhism, says that the person in this meditation should relate to all beings "just as to oneself, . . . without making the distinction 'This is another being.'"[86] Such an inner attitude naturally also influences practical action. The ideal in the monastic order is for people to serve one another openly and silently with loving deeds, words, and thoughts, and to live as if they had different bodies but only one will.[87] In this context, the Upanishadic image of rivers that lose their identity in the ocean and become one is related explicitly to cohabitation in the order, since here the different caste affiliations disappear and are no longer allowed to play a role.[88] In addition, the order is also an important help on the Buddhist path of salvation, which is why every Buddhist, whether lay follower or member of the order, declares their refuge not only to the Buddha and the dharma, but also to the sangha, the community.

Refuge to the Buddha is reflected generally in ritual forms of his veneration. At times, such veneration can take on a deeply emotional form in parts of the Buddhist tradition. One text in the Pali canon compares the pursuit of enlightenment to the intimate longing of the lover for their beloved.[89] In a popular Sri Lankan text from the thirteenth century, the author Sri Ramacandra Bharati explicitly transfers this love to the veneration of the Buddha. All his senses, he says, dwell constantly with the Buddha: "As the thoughts of the young men always dwell with the virgin."[90] But he also praises the Buddha as mother and as father,[91] and confesses in glowing terms his desire to sink into the Buddha alone, that "sea of love for all."[92]

Such forms of inner devotion (*bhakti*) were obviously supported by

---

[85] Bodhi 2017, 179–80.
[86] *Visuddhimagga* 9.47. Ñāṇamoli 1999, 301.
[87] *Majjhima Nikāya* 31.
[88] *Aṅguttara Nikāya* 8.19.
[89] *Dīgha Nikāya* 21.5.11–12.
[90] *Bhaktiśataka* 89. Otto 1917, 156.
[91] *Bhaktiśataka* 28 and 90.
[92] *Bhaktiśataka* 25.

the idea that the Buddha, despite his entrance into nirvana, is still accessible, with the Buddhist cult of relics gaining a special role here. For the widespread belief is that the Buddha is still physically present in his relics, even if this—strictly speaking—contradicts the doctrine that the Buddha cannot be identified with his five aggregates (including the body). It was not uncommon for Buddha statues and especially for the stupas, widespread throughout the Buddhist world, to serve as containers for his relics and thus as objects for his ritual veneration.[93] But how can there be so many Buddha relics? The prevalent belief is that what distinguishes his relics is precisely the fact that they can multiply miraculously.[94]

However, the cult of relics remained only a weak substitute for the lost physical presence of the Buddha, this cult therefore also expressing the longing for the Buddha. The poems of Matrceta (second century CE) achieved great popularity in Buddhist India. "Without you," he wrote in one of his hymns to the Buddha, "the world has greatly changed, O Lord, as the sky emptied of the moon on a starlit night. Without you, the beauty of this preaching is not the same."[95] According to the *Lotus-Sūtra*, which originated in India and became immensely influential especially in East Asia, the Buddha's intention was to evoke such a longing for his proximity. The message of this text is that the Buddha only feigned his extinction so that people would venerate his relics and develop love and longing. Then, when they desire "wholeheartedly to meet the Buddha, . . . I will declare this to sentient beings. . . . I am always here without extinction."[96] According to this text, the Buddha thus remains present and accessible to the believer even beyond his appearance in human form.

The idea that a Buddha does not in fact expire in nirvana heralds a significant change in the understanding of nirvana that then became widely accepted in Mahayana Buddhism. This says that a person who follows the bodhisattva path and thus aspires to Buddhahood continues to strive for nirvana in the sense of the "extinction of defilements," but does not aspire to leave samsara.[97] Rather, compassion leads the person to remain in the cycle of rebirth in order to liberate all beings from suffering. To denote this, Mahayana Buddhism coined the term "dynamic" or "non-abiding" nirvana (*apratiṣṭita nirvāṇa*).[98] According to an early systematic exposition of Mahayana doctrines, this idea constitutes a central difference from

---

[93] See Collins, S. 1998, 246–48, and Strong 2004.
[94] See Strong 2004, 157.
[95] *Varṇārhavarṇa Stotra* 12.12–13. Bailey 1951, 1002.
[96] *Saddharmapuṇḍarīka-Sūtra* 16 (in the Kumārajīva version). Kubo & Yuyama 2007, 228. See also above, pp. 97–98.
[97] *Mahāyānasaṃgraha* 9.1. Keenan 2003, 99.
[98] See Williams 1989, 52–54, 181–84; Nagao 1991, 23–34.

non-Mahayana schools,[99] the same text arguing that this understanding of nirvana is possible because Mahayana Buddhism understood that there is in truth no difference between nirvana and samsara.[100] If the latter is only a veil that shrouds the true and ultimate reality, then this-worldly and otherworldly nirvana are in a nondualistic relationship, with nirvana out of time being realized within time.

Celestial Worlds, Chiliastic Hopes, and Pure Lands

There have repeatedly been disputes in Buddhism about whether enlightenment is a sudden event or the culmination of a gradual development. The view prevailed in ancient Buddhism that enlightenment will be approached through a longer process of development, with the person gaining the right mental disposition for awakening, while the event itself occurs suddenly.[101] Such texts describe the person's development from an unenlightened "worldling," through the stage of "stream-entry" to the attainment of "arhatship" (enlightened perfection) as a gradual and growing act of overcoming the ten "fetters" (Pali: *saṃyojana*), these being different variants of the three "defilements" (greed, hate, delusion). This process of inner development can extend over several, even countless, lives.[102] Regarding the goal of Buddhahood, ancient texts already assume that numerous lives are necessary to develop the respective mental and spiritual qualities. This belief gained central importance in Mahayana Buddhism in connection with the bodhisattva ideal: each bodhisattva develops the individual bodhisattva virtues over many world ages and countless rebirths.

The cycle of rebirths therefore takes on an ambivalent character. On the one hand, it can be an aimless roaming about, driven by the respective karmic impulses that can lead the being sometimes to a worse rebirth as animal, ghost, or denizen of hell, and sometimes to a better rebirth as human being or celestial deity. On the other, it also offers the person the chance to develop gradually through the different experiences of various existences toward the goal of enlightenment or even Buddhahood. Thus, inherent in samsara is the potential of a spiritual purification process,[103] this giving every Buddhist believer hope that they can attain the ultimate salvation of nirvana—if not in this, then at some point in a future life.

A more immediate interim goal is rebirth in a heavenly world. Like ex-

---

[99]See *Mahāyānasaṃgraha* 3.15; 8.22.
[100]*Mahāyānasaṃgraha* 9.3. Keenan 2003, 101. See also above, pp. 101–02.
[101]See *Aṅguttara Nikāya* 8.19.
[102]On this, see Schmidt-Leukel 1996.
[103]For an early testimony of such purification across multiple births (from hell to human existence), see *Therīgāthā* 400–27.

istence in the different hells, life as a deity in the heavenly worlds is very long, but is considered to be extraordinarily happy. While this happiness in the lower celestial worlds takes the form of cultivated sensual pleasures in a divine ethereal body, it corresponds in higher celestial worlds to the more abstract but blissful states experienced in the more intense forms of Buddhist absorption.[104] Life in the heavenly worlds does not, however, offer too-good conditions for attaining enlightenment, precisely because it is too happy to understand the fundamentally unsatisfactory character of samsara.[105] Buddhist texts therefore often extol human existence as the ideal mode to attain enlightenment and thus salvation. However, it is deemed possible for a person to attain such a high degree of spiritual perfection in their last human rebirth (the spiritual level of a "non-returner") that there is then only one further rebirth in a heavenly world, from where the person directly enters final nirvana.[106] There are also tendencies, especially in narrative Buddhist texts, to suggest an even greater continuity between celestial worlds and the "city of nirvana" than the doctrinal presuppositions mentioned above would allow.[107]

While the individual can move toward their personal end or "eschaton" in nirvana, Buddhism knows the idea of something like a collective "end of the world" only for individual world systems, but not for the totality of all worlds; for every perished world is followed by a new world, which emerges from the karmic tendencies of the beings of the preceding world, and, in addition, there are also countless parallel world systems or chains of successive worlds.[108] Nevertheless, some Buddhist texts assume that there are also developmental processes in collective entities such as states and societies, both for the better and for the worse. According to a traditional idea, such collective developments take place in very long cyclical periods of time. For example, a widespread belief is that the coming of the future Buddha, Maitreya, will be preceded by a long period of collective decadence, which then gradually turns for the better. After another very long period of time, Buddha Maitreya will finally appear. The expectation of Maitreya is widespread, and he is revered in all currents of Buddhism.[109] The state of the world at the time of his coming is portrayed not as a heavenly world, but rather as a perfect earthly paradise, since the land will

> be prosperous, . . . free from thieves and robbers, without (any) grasping at (Wrong) Views, blazing with royal cities, . . . replete with all treasures,

---

[104]See Gethin 1998, 112–32; Collins, S. 1998, 297–316.
[105]See Schlingloff 1963, 43.
[106]See Schmidt-Leukel 1996, 43–51.
[107]See Collins, S. 1998, 290–92.
[108]See above, p. 116.
[109]However, the various Buddhist sources are anything but uniform concerning the chronological scenarios. On the Maitreya cult, see the contributions in Sponberg & Hardacre 1988.

happy, with abundant alms-food and at peace, replete with great amounts of food and drink, . . . husbands and wives will enjoy the pleasures of the five senses without arguments or anger; farmers, traders, and the like will live happily without (needing to) work; men and women will not (need to) spin thread or weave the loom, (but) will wear celestial clothes. Men will be content with their wives, and women with their husbands; restrained, men will not commit adultery nor women make another man their husband, (but) they will be loving and pleasant to one another. No one will stir up quarrels because of villages, towns, wealth, crops, fields, property or soil; all human beings will be handsome, with beautiful bodies, (and will be) loving and pleasant to each other. Crows will become friends with owls, cats with mice, deer with lions, mongooses with snakes, lions with deer, and so on: in this way all animals which are (usually) enemies will be friendly to each other.[110]

The hope to be eventually reborn in this paradisiacal world and to experience the coming of Maitreya himself became a popular motif of religious life in parts of Buddhism. What crowned this hope was the promise that a person could easily reach enlightenment and thus enter into permanent liberation in Maitreya's future world. According to the general Buddhist belief, the future Buddha Maitreya currently resides as a bodhisattva in Tushita heaven waiting there for his appearance on earth. Some Buddhist texts speak of the possibility, by acquiring an appropriately good karma, to be reborn before Maitreya's advent in Tushita heaven, and being close to him there. Also mentioned is the possibility of using meditative techniques to gain visionary glimpses of Maitreya's heaven and thereby communing with him in one's current life.[111] In some cases, especially in China, the expectation of Maitreya's coming was also tied to revolutionary, quasi-apocalyptic movements,[112] with people believing that the advent of Maitreya would not take place in the distant future, but was instead imminent. It would be preceded by a decisive battle between the forces of good and evil, being also a fight between the true believers and those "sinners" who oppose Maitreya.[113] Only after the victory of the good would there be a renewal of the earth and its transformation into an ideal world. Hence there were uprisings against what people perceived to be unbearable and unjust social conditions, where those fighting saw themselves and their struggle as part of the events preceding Maitreya's coming.[114] "Convinced that the future Buddha was about to arrive, they proceeded to try to install their own leader

---

[110]From the *Māleyyadevattheravatthu*, quoted in Collins, S. 1998, 623.
[111]See Nattier 1988 and Collins, S. 1998, 355–78.
[112]See Overmyer 1988, 113–15, and the extensive treatment in Overmyer 1976.
[113]See Zürcher 1982, 39.
[114]See ibid., 43.

as a new, pious emperor who would prepare for the messiah's coming."[115]

What became even more popular than the expectation of the future Buddha Maitreya was especially but by no means only in East Asia the hope of being reborn in a Buddha land, with Sukhavati, the land of Buddha Amitabha ("Immeasurable Light") / Amitayus ("Immeasurable Life") (Amida in Japanese) being the most popular of all Buddha lands. In China, it was later called the "Pure Land."[116] Buddha lands are not located in a distant future, but rather in the present, albeit in a distant place. They are also paradisiacal worlds, but ones that resemble an idealized Buddhist heavenly world rather than the utopian vision of a perfect earthly world. For example, in Abhirati, the far eastern land of Buddha Akshobya, there are still women and men with beautiful bodies, but sexual desire, if it occurs at all, instantly transforms into meditative happiness. Pregnancies, with painless childbirth, occur in this Buddha land solely through the radiance of the partners.[117] In contrast, in Amitabha's far western land of Sukhavati, there are no women at all. Its inhabitants are born as bodhisattvas in lotus flowers,[118] and they will be like gods. The palaces, lotus ponds, and even the plants are made of precious materials such as silver, gold, pearls, and jewels. They are all overwhelmingly beautiful and suffused with supernatural light. There is no physical or spiritual suffering in this world, and no possessiveness of any kind. Heavenly music resounds and brings about a bodily experience of the presence of Buddha, dharma, and sangha. Even the chirping of birds conveys the sound of dharma, but these birds are magical creatures, since there are no lower forms of existence such as animals, ghosts, or denizens of hell. Every morning, the inhabitants of Sukhavati visit a hundred thousand million Buddhas in other Buddha lands, whom they venerate, and then return to their own blissful world, where they pay homage to Amitabha. Their lives finally culminate in perfect enlightenment, so that they either enter nirvana or return to the world of samsara to help other beings. Whoever hears the name of the Buddha Amitabha/Amitayus in the present world and keeps it mindfully in their heart will at their death be personally guided by this Buddha to rebirth in the Pure Land.[119] This "best and highest of all Buddha

---

[115]Overmyer 1976, 4. For an intercultural comparison, with among others the Anabaptist kingdom of Münster, see ibid., 62–72, 157–61.

[116]Originating in Indian Mahayana Buddhism well before the second century CE, this form of Buddhism thus belongs to the early forms of Mahayana.

[117]See Williams, P. 2009, 231–34.

[118]The longer *Sukhāvatīvyūha-Sūtra*, however, still introduces a lower form of birth into the Pure Land. Those who have doubted the message are born in enclosed lotus blossoms, where they spend five hundred years until they, too, are finally perfected. See Gomez 1996, 104–6.

[119]This is the condition for rebirth into the Pure Land as described in the shorter *Sukhāvatīvyūha-Sūtra*. The longer *Sukhāvatīvyūha-Sūtra* describes the condition in a more detailed and narrow way: it is about the hearing of the name, its trustful representation (via invocation), and the wish for rebirth in the Pure Land. Excluded, however, are those who have committed the "five grave offenses" and have been

lands" was created by Amitabha from the power of his all-encompassing compassion and from the vows that he had taken once in an unimaginable past as Bodhisattva Dharmakara.[120]

Such a different Buddhist idea of salvation also changes and relativizes belief in reincarnation. While not disappearing, it concerns more the person's own past than the future, which is now only about this one rebirth in the Pure Land. And even for those who return as bodhisattvas from the Pure Land to the world of rebirths, it is no longer their own salvation that matters, but the salvation of all others. However, by no means all forms of Buddhism interpreted the Pure Land as a quasi-otherworldly, salvific parallel world that a person can enter after death. For China, for example, there is evidence that the idea of the Pure Land merged with the heavenly world of Maitreya, but also with his future earthly paradise.[121] Typical for the latter are some doctrines within the White Lotus School, which were behind the rebellions linked to this particular strand of Pure Land Buddhism in the fourteenth and sixteenth to nineteenth centuries.[122]

But the Pure Land was understood not only as a spatially or temporally remote world. Parts of Chinese Ch'an (= Zen Buddhism), as well as some prominent Chinese patriarchs of Pure Land Buddhism, identify the Pure Land with the original purity of mind, and with the Buddha nature or dharma body. From this perspective, entering the Pure Land means to regain this purity of mind, and the invocation of Amitabha (Chinese: Amituo) is considered a way to realize the universal emptiness of all things.[123] For Tan-luan (T'an-luan) (sixth century CE), birth into the Pure Land is synonymous with attaining nirvana in the sense of Mahayana Buddhism. According to Robert Sharf, for Tan-luan, "the Pure Land is the realm of *saṃsāra* seen from the vantage point of the awakened."[124]

A very similar view can be found in the medieval Japanese master Shinran, who was strongly influenced by Tan-luan. Shinran also refers to the teaching that there is no difference between samsara and nirvana, and identifies birth into the Pure Land with the attainment of nirvana.[125] According to Shinran, rebirth in the Pure Land already takes place to some extent in the here and now: in the act of entrusting oneself to the compassion of Amida and the confidence that Amida will lead especially the sinner, en-

---

slanderers of the dharma. What the "five grave offenses" are is interpreted differently in Buddhist texts.

[120] I summarize here the descriptions from the shorter and the longer *Sukhāvatīvyūha-Sūtra*. In the latter, these are considerably more detailed. See the Indian and Chinese variants of both texts in Gomez 1996.

[121] See Mochizuki 2016, 74–75, 140, 239.

[122] Lai, P.-C. 2006a, 12–13.

[123] See also the numerous examples in Sharf 2002, e.g., 303–4, 313–14, 316–17. See also Tanaka 2007.

[124] Sharf 2002, 318. On T'an-luan, see also Corless 1996.

[125] *Yuishinshō mon'i*. Hirota 1997, 460–61.

tangled in the defilements, to salvation. For Shinran, however, the idea that rebirth in the Pure Land is already happening now by no means erases the hope for future salvation as an event after death. Rather, we find in him the paradox that salvation already becomes reality in faithful trust, precisely in being confidently hoped for as a future event. Shinran is also able to understand the patriarchs of Pure Land Buddhism, and especially his own teacher Honen, as people who, as bodhisattvas, lived in the mode of return to the world of samsara—which they did out of Amida's power.[126] Thus, we again encounter in Shinran the ancient Upanishadic image of rivers that are lost in the ocean. In a hymn to Tan-luan, Shinran writes that, in entrusting oneself to Amida, "the myriad rivers" of bad karma are lost in the ocean of his great compassion, and "on entering it, become one in taste with the ocean water" of virtue and wisdom.[127]

Modern Buddhism has often perceived traditional ideas of celestial worlds, future paradises, and Buddha lands as problematic, and reinterpreted them accordingly. In Japan at the beginning of the twentieth century, the religious studies scholar and Jodo Shinshu priest Naotaro Nonomura spoke out against interpreting the Pure Land in realistic terms, thereby drawing on arguments from Western criticism of religion: on the one hand, he argues, there is no proof that such a paradisiacal world exists, while on the other the hope for it would prevent people from improving life in this world.[128] Nonomura's Chinese contemporary Taixu sought to reinterpret the hope for the Pure Land or for the future world of Maitreya as a political ideal, arguing that it is important to bring this world closer to the future ideal in a gradual process of improving karma collectively, which for him means by collective social effort.[129] Thich Nhat Hanh's teachings are based on the ancient Ch'an tradition, which says that the Pure Land is to be understood as the true nature of the mind:

> The notion that the Pure Land is an exterior reality, a place to be found far away in the western direction, is just for beginners. If we deepen our practice, the Buddha and the Buddha's land become a reality in our mind. Our ancestral teachers have always said this.[130]

But this true nature of the mind also contains for Thich Nhat Hanh a potential whose realization yields a social dimension as an ideal community:

---

[126] On Shinran, see Ueda & Hirota 1989; Schmidt-Leukel 1992, 605–54.
[127] *Kōsō wasan* 41–42. Hirota 1997, 371.
[128] See Kigoshi 2004.
[129] See Ritzinger 2013.
[130] Hanh 2003, 23.

As human beings, our deepest desire is to find a secure environment where there is love and understanding. The Buddhas and the bodhisattvas understood that all of us want to live in such an environment. We all imagine establishing a place where we can nourish ourselves and other people. In such a place, we have the right conditions to develop our understanding and love, to transform our own suffering and that of others. This place is called a Pure Land. . . . We . . . want to establish a place where we . . . benefit from the presence of solidarity, freedom, love and peace.[131]

In his commentary on the shorter *Sukhāvatīvyūha-Sūtra*, Thich Nhat Hanh shows throughout that he sees in a Pure Land interpreted in this way primarily the ideal model for a modern organization of the sangha, a model that guides the community of Plum Village that he founded.[132]

Manshi Kiyozawa, who, like Nonomura, was also a Jodo-Shinshu cleric, and who strongly influenced many Japanese scholars of the twentieth century, put forward a more existential interpretation of the Pure Land. He, too, was concerned with focusing on the present, in terms of a Mahayana-Buddhist spirituality with a strong interreligious dimension.[133] For him, Amida and the Pure Land are not eternal realities, but historically contingent symbols. However, through them, as well as through the beliefs of other religions, an absolute reality manifests itself. A Buddhist, according to Kiyozawa, ideally lives simultaneously in two worlds, the world of oneness and the absolute, and the world of diversity and the relative. But he clings to neither of the two worlds,[134] which enables him to combine transcendent wisdom with compassion in the world. Kiyozawa, too, argues that such a spirituality "encourages and promotes the welfare of the people and the nation through peaceful cooperation."[135] But does the Pure Land still have meaning beyond death for modern Pure Land Buddhist "theologians"? Another Jodo Shinshu scholar, John S. Yokota, has argued against abandoning the possibility of transformation beyond death, among else by invoking Shinran's version of the image of the rivers of sin being transformed as they enter the ocean of Amida's goodness. Yokota points out that it is difficult to assert Amida's ultimate compassion and wisdom if there is no lasting resolution of "the evil we are and do and the evil that is and is done in the world."[136]

---
[131] Ibid., 22–23.
[132] See ibid., especially 86–95, 130–31, and passim. For further examples of a this-worldly reinterpretation of the Pure Land among contemporary Buddhists, see Lai, P.-C. 2006b, 196–203.
[133] See Johnston 2007.
[134] Kiyozawa 2014, 60–61.
[135] Ibid., 16.
[136] Yokota 2000, 97.

210   The Celestial Web

We must live as if this time is our only chance, and yet in the hope that the wrongs and evils of this time will be transformed in the processes of the ever becoming reality of ourselves and God/Amida. . . . The Pure Land must have this power finally to transform these evils of life, or what is the use of it? This power to transform has been the lure of the Pure Land tradition for ages and needs to be rearticulated so that the tradition can . . . again impart hope to those whose lives are filled with despair.[137]

8.3 SALVATION AS UNION WITH GOD AND AS PERFECTED SOCIETY IN CHRISTIANITY

Ideas of our final state of salvation are anything but uniform in Christianity, either. In their extensive cultural history of Christian heaven, Bernhard Lang and Colleen McDannell speak of "endless heavenly speculations," a "diversity, richness and complexity of centuries of thought."[138] But they also discern two ever recurring and varying ideas: final salvation or "heaven" as a state in which people lose themselves in communion with God, and heaven as a perfected society.[139] Another distinction concerns the location of the final goal of salvation in terms of space and time. On the one hand, the "kingdom of heaven" or "eternal life" can designate a dimension that is beyond the spatiotemporal world with which we are familiar, that the person is able to enter after death (with or without a period of preparation), and that some people already glimpse in visions before death. On the other hand, it can also mean the transformation of our world into a paradise, a process that will find its completion only in the future, but that can already be experienced rudimentarily in the here and now. Both variants can be found in Christianity, sometimes combining with each other, and sometimes existing just side by side.

Salvation in and beyond the World: New Testament Foundations

The New Testament contains a variety of ideas about salvation and the afterlife, which reflect the different Jewish ideas as they can be found

---

[137]Ibid.
[138]Lang & McDannell 2001, 353; 1990, 471. Lang & McDannell 1990 is a revised and partly enlarged German translation of Lang & McDannell 1988. The latter I quoted here from its second edition of 2001.
[139]Lang & McDannell (2001, 353–58; 1990, 471–77) speak of a "theocentric" and an "anthropocentric model"; or, according to the preface to the second English edition, of a "God-oriented" and a "people-oriented heaven" (McDannell & Lang 2001, xiv). The latter model is primarily concerned with the social dimension.

before and around the New Testament texts. In the 1960s and 1970s, New Testament scholars such as Oscar Cullmann and Krister Stendahl, and then systematic theologians such as Jürgen Moltmann, argued that the idea of an immortal soul is alien to the Jewish conception of the human being. From this, they drew the wide-ranging implication that the Christian hope for salvation is based not on the immediate survival of the soul after death, but exclusively on the belief in the resurrection/raising from the dead, or in the re-creation of the human being at the end of time. While conceding that the idea of a soul surviving the death of the body has been enormously influential throughout the history of Christianity, they nonetheless argue that this idea was originally neither Jewish nor Christian, but had its origins in Greek, and especially Platonic, thought. However, more recent research has corrected the image of a more or less homogeneous conception of the human being in Jewish and early Christian thought.[140] It is uncontested that Greek ideas had a lasting influence on Christianity, but this influence can already be seen in pre–New Testament Judaism. Moreover, there were some ideas in Judaism that resembled Greek ideas without descending directly from them, such as regarding the realm of the dead,[141] and a soul that was essentially distinct from the body.[142] According to James Barr, the Judaism of the last two centuries before Christ comprised many different notions of life after death: "immortality of the soul, resurrection of some few, general resurrection, no resurrection at all, 'eternal life' earned and enjoyed here and now, and other eschatological schemes."[143] And neither was the idea of reincarnation completely alien to Judaism at that time.[144]

In their early beginnings, however, Jewish ideas of salvation had focused only on this world, since existence in Sheol, that is, in the shadowy realm of the dead, was by no means regarded as a state of salvation, but rather the opposite. The broad belief was that the reward for faithfulness to the covenant with God consisted in well-being in this world: in health, offspring, good harvests, prosperity, and peace. The experience that this reward by no means always materialized, neither for individual God-fearing people nor for

---

[140]"In previous scholarship, the resurrection of the dead and the immortality of the soul have often been understood as opposing beliefs, the first one assigned to 'Hebrew' thinking, the latter to 'Greek.' This dichotomy does not stand up to closer scrutiny. Both ideas and their many conflations existed side by side in early Judaism." Lehtipuu 2015, 66. For a summary of the main objections to Cullmann's position, see Nickelsburg 2006, 219–23.

[141]For example, Barr 1992, 30–31, refers to the parallels between Hades and Sheol.

[142]On those aspects of *nephesh* and *ruah* that resemble Greek notions of the soul, see ibid., 36–47. However, Barr sees a difference to the Platonic notion of the soul in the fact that the Bible does not understand the soul as being eternal in the sense of having no beginning (ibid., 107).

[143]Barr 1992, 113–14; see also ibid., 23. George Nickelsburg (2006, 222) makes a similar point, arguing that, in this period, "there was no single Jewish orthodoxy on the time, mode, and place of the resurrection, immortality, and eternal life."

[144]See Barr 1992, 107; Lang & McDannell 2001, 17–18.

the people of Israel as a whole, may have been a key reason for why there developed expectations of salvation in the other-world or in the future. "It was only then under social, economic, and political oppression that pious Jews looked beyond their bitter disappointment with this world to a future beyond the grave when virtue would receive its due reward and vice its befitting punishment."[145] There is broad agreement among biblical scholars that a central role was played here by the first experience of martyrdom and persecution for religious reasons under the Seleucid rulers (second century BCE),[146] since those martyred suffered their torments and an often cruel death despite—or, indeed, precisely because of—their faithfulness to God. Thus, it was hoped that God would one day restore their martyred bodies or that their souls would pass immediately into a happy, heavenly existence after death.[147] The impetus for the slow but steady spread of belief in the resurrection of at least individual believers is likely to have come from Zoroastrianism in Iran.[148] In Jewish apocalyptic literature, the hope for a physical restoration of individual believers was also partly combined with the expectation of death and resurrection in a collective sense, i.e., with the expectation of the end of the present world followed by a glorious new world order in which nothing would obstruct God's reign.[149] In contrast to the current creation, this future creation will be a world where "the earth will be filled with the knowledge of the Lord as the waters cover the sea," and where no person will do evil and all creatures will have peace. The "wolf will live with the lamb, and the leopard will lie down with the goat . . . and the lion will eat straw like the ox. The infant will play near the cobra's den" (Isaiah 11:6–9). Such hopes were often linked to the anticipation of a messianic figure.

All of this already indicates some essential elements of New Testament ideas of salvation,[150] at the center of which is the belief that God raised Jesus after his agonizing and ignominious death on the cross. The early belief was that by doing so, God himself had vindicated Jesus as his messenger in the face of his rejection from the people and the religious authorities.[151] At the same time, early Christianity saw in Jesus' resurrection the beginning of those cosmic events that would bring about the new world of God, whose imminent coming was already at the center of Jesus' own message.

---

[145]Cohn-Sherbok 1987, 24. See also the detailed studies in Nickelsburg 2006, 138–40.
[146]See Barr 1992, 53–54, 114; Lang & McDannell 2001, 11–14.
[147]The former in 2 Maccabees 7, and the latter in 4 Maccabees. See Nickelsburg 2006, 138–40.
[148]See Lang & McDannell 2001, 11–14; Plöger 1978, 85. Citing 1 Enoch 22, Nickelsburg (2006, 5–6, 168–71) sees the beginnings of the belief in resurrection in the context of the belief in a universal judgment. However, here it is a resurrection of the spirits of the deceased, not of their bodies.
[149]See Plöger 1978, 85.
[150]See the summaries in Nickelsburg 2006, 227–47, and in Lang & McDannell 2001, 23–46.
[151]Especially in Acts (e.g., Acts 2:23–24; 3:13; 4:10; 5:30–31, etc.).

The future resurrection of all the righteous and believers in Christ would also enable those who had already died to participate in this final world of salvation. According to Matthew (27:52–53), Jesus' resurrection had already been accompanied by the resurrection of "many saints" from their tombs and their appearing to the people.

Some New Testament texts limit resurrection only to the righteous and the faithful, so that resurrection is synonymous with entry into final salvation (Luke 20:35),[152] while others speak of a general resurrection of all the dead that is tied to the Last Judgment (1 Corinthians 15:22; John 5:28–29; Matthew 25:31–46).[153] According to Paul, those believers still alive at what was believed to be the imminent end[154] "will be caught up together with" the resurrected believers in Christ "in the clouds to meet the Lord in the air" (1 Thessalonians 4:17), with the bodies of the enraptured, like those of the resurrected (1 Corinthians 15:51–53), being transformed into new "imperishable" and "spiritual" bodies (1 Corinthians 15:35–55). According to Jesus, those raised from the dead will be "equal to angels," having become "sons of God." They will no longer be concerned with earthly matters such as marriage (Luke 20:27–40; Matthew 22:30; Mark 12:24–25).

However, the New Testament texts also testify in some places to the idea that a person can enter a world of salvation before a general or partial resurrection in the future. For example, Jesus promises one of the two criminals crucified with him, "Today you will be with me in Paradise" (Luke 23:43). This presupposes for Jesus as well as for the person addressed that entry into the heavenly world already takes place before or independent from a resurrection of the body, i.e., it obviously concerns only the "soul" of the human being. Something similar can be seen in the story of the rich man and the poor Lazarus (Luke 16:19–31). Here, too, Lazarus finds himself in a heavenly world immediately after his death and the rich man in an infernal world, while his relatives still live on earth. Paul also seems to assume in his letter to the Philippians that he will be "with Christ" even before the resurrection of the faithful, immediately after his death (Philippians 1:21–25). In the Second Letter to the Corinthians (12:1–5), he speaks of his own experience of having once been caught up into the paradise of the "third heaven."

According to Paul, the salvation promised to the faithful, whether in the hereafter or following resurrection in a future world, exceeds any human

---

[152]See also Lehtipuu 2015, 24: "Resurrection is sometimes understood as the privilege of the righteous, while the punishment is that they will not be resurrected."

[153]The Book of Revelation combines both ideas by mentioning a "first resurrection" involving all Christian martyrs, and a second, general resurrection of all the dead at the Last Judgment (see Revelation 20).

[154]See above, pp. 70–71.

imagination: "What no eye has seen, what no ear has heard, and what no human mind has conceived—the things God has prepared for those who love him" (1 Corinthians 2:9). Nevertheless, the New Testament texts, too, could not refrain from using metaphors as well as concrete depictions of the state of salvation, and in this the New Testament again takes up older Jewish models. Here, the two fundamental motifs of the Christian concept of salvation already emerge: the image of salvation as a great heavenly banquet or wedding feast (Matthew 8:11; 22:2; Luke 14:15) is close to the communal aspect of Christian salvation, whereas the image of the heavenly Jerusalem, the city of God among the people, stands for the aspect of complete concentration on God. The description of the heavenly Jerusalem in the Book of Revelation is based on the temple visions of the prophet Ezekiel (Ezekiel 40–48). It resembles the holy of holies of the Jerusalem temple, and is filled completely with the eternal praise of God. Regarding the heavenly feast, Matthew says, as already in Isaiah (25:6–7), that all nations will participate in it, and it is God himself who invites them. But not only the many peoples are united peacefully here; according to Luke, it is precisely those who have spent their lives on the margins of society who will also join in this meal: "the poor and crippled" (Luke 14:21). The words of Isaiah saying that at this feast God will "swallow up death forever" and "wipe away tears from all faces" (Isaiah 25:8) are taken up in the description of the heavenly Jerusalem, where God will "wipe every tear from their eyes. There will be no more death or mourning or crying or pain" (Revelation 21:4). The heavenly Jerusalem is made of pure gold, as pure as glass, its walls built of precious stones and each of its twelve gates made of a pearl. It is crossed by a stream with the "water of life," its banks populated by the "trees of life" that bear fruit every month and whose leaves are used for healing. The city is illuminated by the splendor of God. The nations will enter into this light and behold God's face (see Revelation 21–22).

The Book of Revelation combines future and other-worldly expectations of salvation in two ways. First, in the new world, the heavenly Jerusalem, the transcendent place of God, will descend from heaven to the "new" (!) earth and will become the dwelling place of God among people (Revelation 21:1–3). Second, this new world will be preceded on the old earth by a messianic kingdom lasting one millennium in which Christ will rule the world together with the resurrected martyrs (Revelation 20:1–6).

According to the testimony of New Testament texts, salvation is not only a future or transcendent reality, but is already dawning in that people follow and rely on Christ. For, according to the message of Jesus, whoever loves God and their neighbor fulfills the highest commandment of God and has thus already submitted themselves to God's reign.[155] According

---

[155]See above, pp. 68–70.

to Paul, believers will one day see "face to face." But already in the here and now there is an incomplete knowledge, a seeing "in a mirror dimly" (1 Corinthians 13:12). For Paul, the Spirit of God is already given to believers in Christ as a "deposit" of the future celestial glory (2 Corinthians 5:1–10), the very Spirit through whom Christ was raised from the dead and who thus also guarantees the resurrection of the faithful (Romans 8:11). Some New Testament authors, such as the authors of the Epistle to the Ephesians and the Epistle to the Colossians, even claim that the resurrection with Christ has already happened in faith (Ephesians 2:1–8; Colossians 3:1–4), whereas the Second Epistle to Timothy warns against such a claim (2 Timothy 2:16–18). The idea that the faithful already possess "eternal life" in the here and now, and thus the kind of community with God that death can no longer touch, is most pronounced in the Gospel of John. Whoever trusts in God and follows Jesus' words "has eternal life" and "has crossed over from death to life" (John 5:24; similarly, 3:36; 6:47). But at the same time John also holds on to the expectation of resurrection in terms of a future event (5:25–29; 6:39–40). In essence, salvation is already there, but it will only be completed in the beyond or in the future.

"For some," writes Outi Lehtipuu in her summary of early Christian ideas, "resurrection was first and foremost an event in the future that would take place when Christ returns to judge the world. For others, it meant an ascent to heaven at the moment of death. For yet others still, it denoted a spiritual experience in this life."[156] All these different concepts continued to influence Christian ideas of salvation, but took on much more concrete forms and sometimes developed surprising variants.

The Goal of Salvation as the Vision of God

The belief that the fulfillment and perfection of the human being consists in the "beatific vision of God" (*visio dei beatifica*) developed into a central motif of Christian ideas of salvation, with Augustine (354–430) being the first to deal with this in more detail. This "vision" is a spiritual recognition of God that is connected with love and praise. This recognition is made possible by the participation of the soul in the light of God; it is actually "enraptured" into the divine light. It is a participation in the eternal being of God, where there is neither past nor future.[157] But it was above all Thomas Aquinas (1225–1274) who elevated the vision of God to the essence of Christian salvation. According to Thomas, the happiness that every human being strives for is nothing other than God himself. In all the happiness

---
[156]Lehtipuu 2015, 200.
[157]See Ruh 2001, 103–12.

that people seek, they are unconsciously seeking God,[158] and they can therefore find their lasting fulfillment in God alone. Even if the soul of a person receives a new body at resurrection, says Thomas, the vision of God is nevertheless of a purely spiritual or contemplative nature and free from all activity.[159] But in the eternal vision of God the spirit of the human being remains finite. The finite person is therefore not able to grasp the infinity of God, so that God remains inconceivable even in this highest and ultimate experience of God.[160] In addition, the extent of the vision of God and the happiness that accompanies it is not the same for all people. Rather, there are different levels of realization that correspond to the different degrees of people's love of God.[161]

Whereas in Thomas, despite all the immediacy of the vision of God, the finite spirit of the human being remains distinguished from the infinity of God with regard to the final goal of salvation, this boundary becomes fluid in some Christian mystics, among whom there is even the idea of an experience of unity (*unio mystica*).[162] This idea covers a range of "God-human symbiosis" that stretches "from the fusion leaving no more room for individuality to the personal union of love."[163] The notion of *unio mystica* obviously goes back to Pseudo-Dionysius the Areopagite,[164] a fifth- to sixth-century scholar who was strongly influenced by Neoplatonism and who was mistakenly thought to be a disciple of Paul. His treatises had a significant influence on large sections of Christian theology and mysticism. In unifying with God, the person reaches, argues Dionysius, "a 'de-restriction' of himself which is, in the proper sense, a dissolution of limitations: a being retained and rescinded in his primordial ground," a "return to his origin from which he was never really separated."[165] Thus, final salvation consists in a state that overcomes the illusion of apparent separation from the divine ground and arrives at the abiding experience of true unity.

Such a concept appears even more clearly in Meister Eckhart (d. 1328), who argued that the highest form of the experience of union is a breakthrough into the "Gottesgrund," the ground of God, i.e., a transcendence of all duality between God and creation. This is a level, which Eckhart also calls "Godhead," being prior to the distinction between God and creature. It is at this level that both God and "I" lose their identity, an identity that is determined by their difference from one another:

---

[158]*Summa theologiae* I.2.1 ad 1. See also Davies 1993, 227–30.
[159]*Summa theologiae* I-II.3.5.
[160]*Summa theologiae* I.12.7, as well as *Super Evangelium S. Joannis Lectura. Caput I, Lectio XI.*
[161]Lang & McDannell 2001, 90.
[162]See the summary in McGinn 2016.
[163]Haas 1998, 2.
[164]Ibid., 7–8.
[165]Leppin 2007, 34.

Everything that is in the Godhead is one, and of that there is nothing to be said.... When I enter the ground, the bottom, the river and fount of the Godhead, none will ask me whence I came or where I have been. No one missed me, for there God *unbecomes*.[166]

When I flowed forth from God, all creatures declared, "There is a God;" but *this* cannot make me blessed, for with this I acknowledge myself as a creature. But in my breaking-through, . . . *then* I am . . . neither God nor creature, but I am that which I was and shall remain for evermore. . . . For this breaking-through guarantees to me that I and God are one. *Then* I am what I was, then I neither wax nor wane, for then I am an unmoved cause that moves all things.[167]

The Neoplatonic context becomes especially tangible in such ideas. The ground of God, which is beyond all conceptual distinctions, corresponds here to the *hen* (the "One") in Plotinus' philosophy. The One is beyond conceptual understanding, but gives rise to the world of multiplicity, a world that finds its redemption in returning to this original unity. Alluding to the preparation of the gifts offertory in the Catholic Church's Mass liturgy, Meister Eckhart also describes the unity with God as the soul losing herself in God "just as if you were to pour a drop of water into a butt of wine,"[168] which is almost a Catholic version of the Upanishadic image of the rivers losing themselves in the ocean.[169]

Christian mystics, however, could also express the union with God in very personal images, preferring to draw here on the union of the beloved with her lover. This so-called bridal mysticism has a long tradition stretching back to Origen, but it is particularly prominent in Bernard of Clairvaux (d. 1153). Theologians did not rely solely on the Pauline idea of the church as the bride of Christ, but interpreted the Song of Songs in the Hebrew Bible as an allegory of the love between God and the soul. Although speaking of a spiritual love, they use the imagery of erotic and indeed physical love. In Bernard, the kiss of the bridegroom on the mouth of his bride functions as the highest image of union with God.[170] The Beguine mystic Mechthild

---

[166] *Sermon 26* (Quint) = *Sermon 56* (Pfeiffer). Walshe 2009, 294; Quint 1979, 273.

[167] *Sermon 32* (Quint) = *Sermon 87* (Pfeiffer). Walshe 2009, 424; Quint 1979, 308–9.

[168] Sermon 54 (Quint) = *Sermon 62* (Pfeiffer). Walshe 2009, 316; Quint 1979, 407. The same image is also used by Bernhard von Clairvaux in *De diligendo Deo*, although he emphasizes that the soul is not absorbed in God. See Lerner 1971, 97–98.

[169] In *Sermon 55* (Quint) = Sermon 97 (Pfeiffer), Eckhart uses the image of a drop of water being poured into the sea. When he emphasizes here that the soul thereby loses its name and its power, but not its will and its being (see Walshe 2009, 456; Quint 1979, 410), this should be understood in the sense that there is no longer a difference in the divinity between being and will, and that the soul is now in its actual being. A different interpretation is provided by Lerner 1971, 402–3.

[170] See Leppin 2007, 61, 64–65.

of Magdeburg (d. 1282) goes much further, describing in one of her many visions the love of Christ for the soul thus:

> He kisses her passionately with his divine mouth.
> You are happy, more than happy in this most glorious hour.
> He caresses her, as well he can, on the bed of love.
> Then she rises to the heights of bliss
> and to the most exquisite pain
> when she becomes truly intimate with him.[171]

In formulations such as, "He gives himself to her, and she gives herself to him,"[172] and "I am in you, you are in me,"[173] Mechthild shows that she transfers in her images "the worldly idea of the act of love making to her mystical 'unification.'"[174]

In their explanations of unity with God, mystics refer not only to biblical, theological, and philosophical sources, but also often to their own religious experiences. This is especially true, as here with Mechthild, for the various descriptions of the ultimate goal of salvation. They conceive their contemplative or visionary experiences of mystical unity as a selective "anticipation of something that is actually reserved for the hereafter."[175] This is already the case with Augustine in his well-known description of the so-called Ostia experience in the *Confessions*: when he and his mother ask themselves shortly before her death "what the eternal life of the saints will be like," they experience—or, as Augustine describes it, "touch"—in a brief moment the eternal wisdom of God and reach "the land of inexhaustible abundance."[176] But in Christianity this "land" was not only understood as the soul's losing itself in the timeless vision of God and mystical union. It also often took the form of very concrete ideas about a perfect heavenly society where the messianic expectations of a collective state of salvation continue to exert their effect.

---

[171]*Das fließende Licht der Gottheit* II.23. Translation by F. Tobin in Mechthild of Magdeburg 1998, 88–89. See also Driller 2005, 155.

[172]*Das fließende Licht der Gottheit* I.44. Translation following Driller 2005, 154.

[173]*Das fließende Licht der Gottheit* III.5. Translation following Driller 2005, 155.

[174]Driller 2005, 154. See also the words of Meister Eckhart: "God must really become I and I must really become God, so fully one that this 'he' and 'I' become and are one 'is.'" *Sermon 42* (Quint) = *Sermon 99* (Pfeiffer). Walshe 2009, 464; Quint 1979, 354. As recent research has revealed, Eckhart was influenced by the mysticism of the Beguines, especially by Marguerite Porete (d. 1310). See McGinn 2016, 74–75; Leppin 2007, 96.

[175]Leppin 2007, 23.

[176]Augustine, *Confessiones* 9.10.

The Goal of Salvation as Perfected Society

Be it in the world beyond or in the world to come, will we see only God or also meet again those loved ones from whom death has separated us? Ambrose of Milan (d. 397), Augustine's teacher, answered this question in the affirmative. Augustine himself also admitted this possibility in his late work, arguing that there will continue to be true love among the resurrected, as among angels: without any desire and without the typical earthly bonds of friendship, marriage, or domestic community.[177] "All special attachments will be absorbed into one comprehensive and undifferentiated community of love."[178]

In the Middle Ages, the social dimension of eternal life took a back seat to the idea of contemplation of and union with God. Heaven is populated, but the souls of the saints as well as the righteous among the resurrected enter the pure world of light of the empyrean ("place of fire"). Even though Dante (d. 1321) in his *Divine Comedy* sees his early love Beatrice again in heaven and incorporates numerous well-known persons into his descriptions, the saints are also in the higher spheres of heaven as transfigured lights completely turned toward the divine source of all light.[179] It is true that the Middle Ages also had more material conceptions of heaven, such as the idea of heaven as the restored paradise where people live together in paradisiacal nakedness and, simultaneously, paradisiacal innocence. Or the idea of the heavenly Jerusalem as an idealized city with magnificent houses, palaces, and castles, where people wear precious costumes and ornaments, and where there are feasts as well as a hierarchical order and a celestial court.[180] However, such ideas "made only tentative entrance in religious thought."[181]

The Renaissance, however, saw a clear intensification of social ideas of salvation, this reaching its pinnacle in the nineteenth century. At first, ancient Greco-Roman ideas of heaven began to influence Christianity.[182] In heaven, there is not only a reunion with loved ones, but also realms of sensual pleasures with celestial nymphs. Heaven sometimes developed into a place of supernaturally enhanced, but thoroughly earthly, enjoyments. In artistic representations, the world beyond encompasses both the heavenly city and the garden of paradise, with the garden in particular often being

---

[177]Lang & McDannell 2001, 59–66.
[178]Lang & McDannell 2001, 64.
[179]See ibid., 80–88.
[180]See ibid., 70–80.
[181]Ibid., 109.
[182]See ibid., 111–44.

a place of pleasures enjoyed by humans and angels together. According to Lang and McDannell, this combination of the heavenly city and the garden of paradise, while retaining their difference, is symbolic: Besides the beatitude of the entire orientation toward the divine as symbolized by the heavenly city, what also receives a place in final salvation is nature as a human habitat in the form of its paradisiacal transfiguration. In heaven, "Nature is domesticated.... People touch, play, listen to music, and pass eternity in pleasure.... Martyrs can chat with virgins, teachers sing to merchants, and couples stroll hand-in-hand."[183]

The Reformation rejected such sensual ideas as unbiblical, seeing eternal life primarily as the blissful closeness to God granted by divine grace. It tended to be skeptical of the mystical interpretation of this closeness as unity with God, although Calvin in his early writing *Psychopannychia* defined real salvation as "oneness with God."[184] The Reformation rejected the medieval doctrine of a graded vision of God that depended on human merit.[185] All in all, the confessional writings of the Reformation are comparatively silent about what constitutes "heaven." As Luther writes in his *Large Catechism*, it is salvation from the earthly "vale of tears," an end in which God wants to "preserve" the redeemed from "sin and shame," and "from everything that may hurt or injure us."[186] There are also statements in Luther that continue the idea of a restored and at the same time supernaturally transfigured paradise, with the heavenly world of God and the renewed paradise forming a unity.[187] According to Luther and Calvin, there will no longer be a hierarchy of estates in the new world.[188] In the radical branches of the Reformation, such as the Anabaptist movement, there was sometimes an intensive revival of chiliastic expectations. The belief in the imminent return of Christ and in the beginning of the millennial messianic kingdom was often combined with a radical social critique of the existing social conditions, which the coming kingdom would vanquish completely.[189]

Social relations became increasingly important in the concepts of heaven of the eighteenth and nineteenth centuries. Influenced not least by the extensive writings of Emanuel Swedenborg (1688–1772), the blissful vision of God was no longer the sole focus of eternal life, but was supplemented by

---

[183] Ibid., 142–43.
[184] "non aliud esse, quam illam cum deum unionem." Calvin, *Vivere apud Christum*, https://www.e-rara.ch/gep_r/content/zoom/21791216. See also Lang & McDannell 2001, 205.
[185] Lang & McDannell 2001, 150.
[186] *Large Catechism*, The Lord's Prayer 118.
[187] See Lang & McDannell 2001, 152–54.
[188] See ibid., 154.
[189] See van Dülmen 1979. While the chiliastic orientation of Thomas Müntzer is contested (see McLaughlin 2004), it is beyond dispute for the Dutch and Westphalian Anabaptists who played a central role in the Anabaptist kingdom of Münster.

the relations between the people dwelling in heaven: "God is loved not only directly but also through the love and charity shown to others in heaven."[190] In Swedenborg's visions (and he was by no means alone), heaven, despite all its emphasized spirituality, becomes a quite concrete, though far more pleasant, reflection of this world, full of spiritual and sensual experiences. Swedenborg interprets this "materiality" of heaven in a quasi-idealistic manner: "The sensual world of heaven directly reflects the spiritual state of its inhabitants."[191] Other authors, such as the Lutheran Philipp Nicolai (1556–1608), the Catholic Martin of Cochem (1634–1712), and the Calvinist Johann Caspar Lavater (1741–1801) fully understand heaven as a material reality, and thus conflate the idea of heaven as a present reality beyond this world with the idea of a new and future creation.[192]

Moreover, there was now also the growing assumption that there is progress even in the heavenly world, and by no means only in spiritual terms.[193] The saints in heaven can share their new insights with each other and actively serve one another. There was disagreement about how far social relations in heaven include sexuality. While a number of theologians explicitly rejected this and considered only "Platonic love" to be possible, Swedenborg held that marriage and sexuality also exist in heaven. Swedenborg argued that, unlike the earthly reality, marriage in heaven is a pure expression of true love. In heaven, the enjoyment of love is an indescribable and indefatigable bliss. However, there is no procreation, with the children in heaven being those who had died as children.[194]

Swedenborg's ideas were fiercely rejected, but also positively accepted and further developed, especially under the influence of the increasingly popular spiritualist movement. The nineteenth century saw numerous books deal with life in heaven, and in this devoting increasing attention to romantic love.[195] In art, this is reflected in the works of William Blake (1757–1827) and others.[196] Like Swedenborg, the influential Anglican theologian Charles Kingsley (1819–1875) claimed that sexuality will be even more incomparably perfect in heaven than on earth.[197] In the nineteenth century, as Lang and McDannell summarize,

> A wide variety of preachers, theologians, poets, and popular writers depicted heaven as a social community where the saints meet their

---

[190] Lang & McDannell 2001, 183.
[191] Ibid., 193.
[192] See ibid., 194–99.
[193] See ibid., 209, 276–87.
[194] See ibid., 210–23.
[195] See ibid., 228–29.
[196] See ibid., 234–47.
[197] See ibid., 261–64.

relatives and friends. The union of God and the soul after death gave way to the union of the lover and the beloved. Ideas of productive work, spiritual development, and technological progress contributed to the completeness of the other-worldly society.[198]

It was this kind of imagining of heaven that prevailed in Christianity when Christians first began to study Buddhist texts and to strive for an understanding of the Buddhist nirvana.[199] Given such an enlivened heaven, nirvana must have seemed to them like a sepulchral peace, which only permitted a comparison with the atheistic nihilism of the nineteenth century or with the by then largely shelved mystical ideas of the Middle Ages. It is precisely the latter, though, that are today enjoying a revival of interest going hand in hand with the Western interest in Buddhism.[200]

The overall situation is ambivalent in the twentieth century.[201] On the one hand, the graphic ideas of heaven of the nineteenth century continue, enriched with new forms of chiliastic eschatology among Christian groupings such as the Mormons[202] or Jehovah's Witnesses,[203] but also in charismatic and Pentecostal movements[204] that now make up a large proportion of contemporary global Christianity. On the other, the theology of the traditional churches presents "a heaven of minimal description" that is satisfied for the most part with the idea of an encounter with God that cannot be defined further.[205]

In a speculative and daring synthesis, John Hick sought to combine both sides in his 1976 work *Death and Eternal Life*. He proposes a two-stage eschatology—a postmortal process (calling it "pareschatology") and a final ultimate state—while leaving chiliastic ideas aside.[206] For Hick, resurrection is, as was often the case in nineteenth-century scenarios, identical with entry into a new world, and follows the individual death after only a short intermediate "bardo" state. According to Hick, the new world, located in another dimension, resembles the earthly world in many respects and contains its own moral challenges, since its very purpose is to enable the

---

[198]Ibid., 356.
[199]See Collins, S. 1998, 98–101.
[200]See, for example, the various contributions in Lengsfeld 2005.
[201]Lang & McDannell 2001, 308.
[202]See Lang & McDannell 2001, 313–22.
[203]See Elliott 2006. Jehovah's Witnesses, however, make a clear distinction between heaven as God's real dwelling place, where only a few chosen ones will enter, and the paradisiacal earth as the place of resurrection of the righteous, who live here eternally under God's rule.
[204]See Whalen 2006.
[205]Lang & McDannell 2001, 354–55. See also ibid., 326–32.
[206]For a brief summary of his eschatology, see the Ingersoll Lecture on Immortality that Hick gave at Harvard University in 1977 (Hick 1988, 129–45).

unfinished human maturation process ("soul-making" or "person-making"), i.e., "sanctification" or *theosis* (divinization), to continue. According to Hick, this continuation is only conceivable if life in the new world is also finite, ending with death, followed by a brief intermediate state and a further resurrection in another world, and so on. The process only comes to an end when the person has completely overcome their natural self-centeredness, and finally leads to a state beyond materiality and time that Hick designates both as a joint (communal) vision of God and as a kind of nirvana.[207]

This conception tries to integrate not only different ideas of salvation from the Christian tradition, but also ideas from Asian religions. In his idea that the person develops progressively in a series of successive existences in ever higher worlds, Hick explicitly draws on some features of Asian ideas of reincarnation. In his later writings, Hick no longer rejects (which he did before) the possibility that a progressive spiritual development might also happen across several lives on earth.[208] Apart from this, Hick's assumption of postmortal development also falls within the tradition of Christian ideas of postmortal purification, which I now turn to briefly.

Purgatory, Journeys of the Soul, and Reincarnation

The diversity of Christian ideas of salvation is of course only a part of the even greater diversity of ideas of the afterlife. For, besides heaven, people also believed in the existence of one or more (and very different sorts of) hells,[209] as well as in the far more pleasant limbo (*limbus*), the "periphery" of hell, which according to a widespread belief is the place (in most cases thought to be permanent) where unbaptized children and righteous "heathens" reside after death.[210] The idea of postmortal purification was often associated with so-called purgatory, a place of purification (*purgatorium*) for all those deceased Christians who still needed purification from sinful inclinations before they were ready to enter heaven.[211] But, even without assuming such a special place, parts of the Christian tradition reckoned with the possibility that the souls of the deceased could undergo a further development toward spiritual perfection in a kind of "journey." Clement of Alexandria and Origen already assumed the idea of a divine pedagogy

---

[207]See Hick 1990, 464; Hick 1988, 144.

[208]See Hick 1999, 244–49; 2010, 151–58.

[209]See the overviews in Vorgrimmler 1994 and Minois 2000. On Buddhist conceptions of hell, see Van Put 2015; for a brief comparison of Buddhist and Christian hells, see Schmidt-Leukel 2019b, 331–45.

[210]At the same time, part of the tradition assumed that the righteous of the Old Covenant stayed in limbo until they were led to heaven by Christ in his "descent into hell" after the crucifixion. Hence for them, limbo was not permanent.

[211]See Le Goff 1990.

that could continue beyond death.[212] For Origen, moreover, hell was not an eternal state either, but also served purification. For Augustine, at least part of hell had that temporary pedagogical function.[213] Such beginnings gave rise finally to the idea of a temporary place of punishment in the hereafter for the purification of souls.

Whereas the Western church elevated the doctrine of purgatory to a dogma in the thirteenth century, the Eastern church took a less rigid position. While also assuming the possibility of progressive development after death, it did not want to limit this to a particular place.[214] Eastern Orthodoxy is familiar with a tradition of postmortal trials that are designed to reveal the soul's true orientation, partly depicting this as a journey of the soul with demons and angels fighting for her.[215] According to Carol Zaleski, medieval literature sometimes assumes that, after leaving the body, the soul "must face a bewildering variety of obstacles and ordeals," all of which are different kinds of "tests."[216] Death becomes a "journey" during which "the soul must prove itself worthy to proceed to happier realms."[217] According to Zaleski, "interest in purgatorial experience was strong throughout the Middle Ages."[218] Despite rejecting the Catholic doctrine of purgatory, Calvin still held that there is a progression of the soul in the afterlife between death and resurrection, this, though, having nothing to do with a necessary purification, but representing instead a divine gift of grace.[219]

The idea of purification through reincarnation was also not completely foreign to Christianity. While it can already be found in parts of Christian gnosis,[220] it reappears most notably in the Renaissance and Enlightenment. Especially in the work of Gotthold Ephraim Lessing (1729–1781), the idea of gradual perfection through reincarnation is at least taken as a serious hypothesis, and it influenced a number of other thinkers from then onward, often being linked to the idea of other-worldly journeys of the soul.[221] In the twentieth century, no less a figure than Karl Rahner played with the idea of translating the traditional doctrine of purgatory today into ideas such as that of reincarnation.[222]

---

[212] See ibid., 52–53.
[213] See ibid., 69.
[214] See ibid., 280–84.
[215] See Cattoi 2021, 365–68.
[216] Zaleski 1987, 61.
[217] Ibid., 62.
[218] Ibid., 57.
[219] See Lang & McDannell 2001, 204–5.
[220] See above, p. 73.
[221] See Bischofberger 1996, 34–47.
[222] See Rahner 1978, 441–42; 1982, 126–27.

8.4 ON THE COMPLEMENTARITY OF ESCHATOLOGICAL IMAGES

Fractal Contrasts

As shown, previous comparisons of Buddhist and Christian ideas of salvation tend to repeat similar contrasts. Both religions, it is said, are concerned with among other things overcoming death. While Christianity represents this overcoming as an eternal life no longer threatened by death in all its fullness, so the story goes, the Buddhist goal of salvation tends to equal a deathlike state in which there is no further death. Whereas the resurrection of the dead expected in Christianity is the entrance into a new life, the entrance into nirvana expected in Buddhism means liberation from any further new life in the form of further rebirths. The contrast between eternal life and eternal quasi-death is tied to the thesis that eternal life should be characterized primarily as an experience of community (community with God and community with all the redeemed), whereas Buddhism is not about community, but about the dissolution of the self or of the illusion of a substantial, immutable self in a greater transcendent reality. This contrast then corresponds to the idea that the Christian goal of salvation also includes the expectation of a future world community that is just and peaceful, whereas the Buddhist expectation is individualistic and aims at overcoming a person's own suffering.

However, previous comparisons at times also showed, to some extent, some differentiations that contradict such overly schematic contrasts and point toward a fractal perspective. Looking more closely at the different ideas of salvation within each of the two traditions reveals that the said contrasts occur in modified forms within both Buddhism and Christianity. This means in concrete terms that Christianity also harbors ideas of salvation that interpret eternal life less as a communion but more as an absorption of the "I" in God, as a merging with the divine ground, or as an experience of an original unity that, as in the case, say, of Meister Eckhart, was never broken but merely obscured by the false idea of a separate individuality. Despite all differences, we can discern in this a structural analogy to Buddhist ideas. Conversely, ideas of salvation bearing communal traits are by no means alien to Buddhism. For example, Buddhist forms of *bhakti*, the loving worship of the Buddha, and in fact of an eternal and ever-present Buddha, have certain similarities to the Christian love of God. Indeed, they become even more similar to the Christian idea of a blissful contemplation of God in heaven where the worship of the Buddha is considered the essential feature of existence in a Buddha land that the person hopes to enter after death. With regard to the community among people, we can also refer to the Buddha lands (which are certainly conceived as communities), but also to the typically Mahayana idea of the dynamic nirvana, i.e., of an experience of nirvana that consists in the eternal activity of the enlightened bodhisattva for the benefit of all beings.

Both Buddhist and Christian ideas of salvation take in some parts more other-worldly and in other parts more this-worldly forms. It is true that rebirth in Buddhist heavenly worlds is "other-worldly" only from the point of view of earthly life, since the heavenly worlds are still regarded doctrinally as part of the unredeemed reality of samsara. However, the idea of a direct entry into nirvana from a heavenly world makes the difference between the two spheres fluid. This is even more clearly the case where rebirth in a Pure Buddha Land replaces heavenly rebirth, or where the Pure Land is even explicitly identified with nirvana, as is the case in parts of Pure Land Buddhism. In addition, Buddhism, especially in the form of the Maitreya expectation, is also familiar with chiliastic or apocalyptic forms of hope for salvation that anticipate some kind of perfected and happy communal life for a future phase in the development of the world. This is structurally somewhat similar to what we find in Christianity: While the this-worldly but future-oriented apocalyptic expectation of salvation was originally dominant, there is already in the New Testament also the idea of a present but other-worldly realm of salvation that the righteous or those trusting in Christ enter immediately after death. Likewise, both religions have ideas of salvation that are neither future nor other-worldly, but are present-oriented and this-worldly. As the Gospel of John teaches in particular, eternal life already begins here and now in the life of faith, and nirvana can already be experienced here and now in the awakening, even if it then still remains connected with the "residues" of earthly life and is an experience only possible for a few. In Pure Land Buddhism we find the idea that rebirth in the Pure Land already happens to some extent here and now in the act of faith.

The idea that a further mental development toward a perfected state of salvation is possible also beyond death is present not only in Buddhism, but in Christianity, too. While this idea is guaranteed in Buddhism by the belief that people are able to perfect themselves over numerous rebirths, it is also found to some extent in Christian doctrines of postmortal purification, be it in purgatory or in heavenly worlds, and also in certain forms of belief in rebirth that are found at least occasionally in Christianity. Moreover, both religions are familiar with and attach importance to the idea of compensatory and postmortal justice in the form of reward or punishment.

Complementarities

Thus, there are ideas of salvation in both Buddhism and Christianity that have in diverse variants a more transcendent or a more social character.

Moreover, ideas of salvation in both religions can be either more otherworldly or more this-worldly, and the primarily this-worldly orientation can refer both to the here and now in the sense of a "realized eschatology," or else to an apocalyptic and chiliastic future. There are sometimes fluid transitions, so that precisely the future salvation can appear as the irruption or anticipation of an other-worldly salvation. Do such fractal patterns in the different ideas of salvation point to a complementarity between the said contrasts?

When it comes to Christian ideas of salvation, Bernhard Lang and Colleen McDannell have argued strongly that there is indeed such a complementarity (albeit a tense one) between the transcendent and the social, i.e., between what they call theocentric and anthropocentric models in the various ideas of heaven:[223]

> Although the two models often co-exist, one of them can generally be considered the dominant view for a given time and place. But the leading position, whether occupied by the theocentric or the anthropocentric view cannot be firmly established in the long run. . . . Since human love and longing cannot be utterly suppressed, even the most rigorous theocentric theology retains a human element. . . . Likewise, when the human dimension threatens to weaken or supplant the divine, the pendulum again swings to the other side. Like human passion, the love of God can never be suppressed or forgotten.[224]

According to Lang and McDannell, this complementary tension is not only reflected in the different ideas of the afterlife. Rather, it is also expressed in different attitudes toward the world: namely, the world-renouncing focus on the divine in the case of the ascetic, in contrast to the more optimistic view of the world in the case of those "who do not feel separated or alienated from the world."[225] Ultimately, according to Lang and McDannell, this underlying tension is already "foreshadowed" in Jesus' "injunction to love both God and neighbor."[226] Thus, Lang and McDannell suggest that the two contrasting poles are indispensable for reasons not only anthropological but also theological. For, if love of God and love of neighbor are inseparable and form in this cohesion the underlying structure of the Christian understanding of salvation, then ultimately neither of the two poles is redundant, with regard not only to this-worldly and present salvation, but also to otherworldly and future salvation.

---

[223]See above, p. 210.
[224]Lang & McDannell 2001, 357.
[225]Ibid. See also ibid., 355.
[226]Ibid., 357.

In Buddhism, too, the cohesive tension between the transcendent and the social in concepts of salvation is discernable in the idea, already present in its beginnings, that an awakened person is perfect in both wisdom and compassion. The perfection of wisdom is rooted in the experience of nirvana, i.e., in the experience of a transcendent reality in this world. This experience, in turn, includes the perfection of compassion. Liberation from egocentric self-attachment substantiates the wish that all beings may be freed from suffering. As in Christianity, so in Buddhism are ideas of salvation sometimes dominated by the transcendent, i.e., salvation as an entry into an other-worldly nirvana where there are no more individuals, and sometimes by the social. The latter is particularly the case where, for example, compassion for all beings and devotion to their liberation is declared to be the "dynamic nirvana," and thus the real goal of salvation.

Differences in the relationship to the world are reflected in the different ideas of salvation not only in Christianity, but also in Buddhism. As already explained in the comparison of Buddhist and Christian attitudes toward the world with which I began my comparative analysis, such differences can develop into harsh opposites, but they do not have to. It can be justified, at least with regard to the relationship to the world, that an attitude of non-attachment may be combined meaningfully with a positive commitment to the world.[227] In itself, of course, this does not yet say anything about the nature of ultimate salvation—if indeed it really exists. Does it consist in the cessation and absorption of the individual in ultimate reality or in the participation in a perfect society? Or in a variant that, as Hick speculates, combines the two? But it does explain at least to some extent why such parallel differences have developed in both religions: the roots for the different ideas about the beyond lie in this world.

According to Hick, the different ideas of salvation of the great religious traditions are varieties of an underlying common structure: salvation or liberation consists in the transformation of the human being from self-centeredness to a centeredness on ultimate, transcendent reality ("the Real"), "a transformation which shows itself, within the conditions of this world, in compassion (*karuṇā*) or love (*agape*)."[228] This formula covers both the Christian idea of the unity of love of God and love of neighbor, and the Buddhist idea of the unity of wisdom and compassion. It draws on experiences of salvation in this world; but these can be taken as starting points from where we can understand basic features of salvation concepts related to the beyond and to the future in both religions. This is presumably supported by the idea that the experience of salvation in the present is a foretaste of salva-

---

[227]See above, pp. 76–84.
[228]Hick 1989, 164. See also ibid., 299–342.

tion in the hereafter and the future. In addition, there is also the hope in both religions that the injustice so often experienced in the here and now will be transformed into a compensatory justice in the hereafter and/or in the future. In parts of both religions, this is also connected to the continuing hope that love and compassion for those who commit injustice will ultimately be even stronger than compensatory justice, thereby allowing healing to take place.

If such a processual dynamic can indeed be discerned in how both religions understand salvation, it will not be surprising that in both traditions people also believe in the possible continuation of the process of salvific transformation beyond death. Christian ideas of postmortal purification have a structural equivalent in the Buddhist belief that the cycle of rebirth also includes the possibility of progressive development toward awakening. The Buddhist idea that residence in the hells is never eternal finds a counterpart at least among some Christian thinkers in their interpretation of hell as purification. But the idea widespread in Christianity of an irreversible eternity of hell has hardly any counterpart in Buddhism—unless we include here the view held in parts of Mahayana Buddhism that some beings, the so-called *icchantikas*, either cannot unfold or simply lack the Buddha nature (and thus the potential for salvation).[229] In Christianity, the idea of eternal damnation was long dominant, and the idea of salvation for all human beings tended to be a minority position. It was the other way round in Buddhism. Here, the hope dominated that there can be liberation for all from the bonds of samsara, while only a minority of Buddhist masters held the view that some beings were irredeemably bound to samsara.

The Clouded View

"For we know in part," writes Paul in the First Letter to the Corinthians (1 Corinthians 13:9). Especially with regard to the end, he compares our knowledge with looking into a dark mirror through which we can see only "in enigmas" (*en ainigmati*) (1 Corinthians 13:12). As much as Christianity has always speculated and pontificated about the end, it has also been aware that we have no clear knowledge about it, but instead only pictures that allow us to know "in enigmas." As for the ultimate goal of salvation, both Christianity and Buddhism have their magnificent depictions on the one hand, and their awareness of impenetrable mystery on the other. But, rather than appreciate the fact of this tension in both traditions, people have at times tried to make apologetic capital out of it.

---

[229]Ming-Wood Liu has therefore compared this interpretation of the *icchantikas* with the doctrine of eternal damnation (see Liu 1984, 67). As Liu also shows, however, other parts of Mahayana Buddhism have denied that such beings actually exist, or that the *icchantikas* were indeed irredeemable. See also Lai, W. 1982.

During the Christian-Buddhist encounter in the Japan of the sixteenth and seventeenth centuries, for example, Allessandro Valignano (1539–1606), the superior of the Jesuit mission, criticized the Buddhist idea of the Pure Land as foolish because it was described in concrete material images that pleased the senses.[230] Valignano countered this with the idea of Christian heaven as a purely spiritual place whose "splendors . . . cannot be captured by the senses and cannot be thought of by the mind."[231] At the same time, Habian Fukansai (or Fabian Fucan) (d. 1621), a Japanese convert to Christianity, was able to reproach Buddhism for precisely the opposite reason. He argued that the Pure Land did not in truth denote any form of eternal life or eternal bliss, but rather only symbolized the state of enlightenment, which in turn implied that the person was dissolved into nothingness.[232] Habian presents the Christian heaven on the other hand as a concrete other-worldly reality, which he describes by borrowing from the traditional representations of the Pure Land.[233] This inverse polemic—which sees one Christian reproach Buddhism for treating its sensual and therefore unsuitable images as real, and the other criticize Buddhism for *not* treating its images as real—is only possible because both traditions do actually contain both: namely, a realistic interpretation of the pictorial description of the beyond, as well as the conviction that any pictorial description is insufficient.

In the context of contemporary dialogue between Christianity and Japanese Buddhism, Christiane Langer-Kaneko has favored interpreting the Pure Land only as a symbol "of a reality" that "has dawned with the awakening of faith."[234] "What happens after death, human beings cannot know. What is important is the concrete here and now."[235] According to Langer-Kaneko, this also applies to Jesus' proclamation of the kingdom of God.[236] For Paul Knitter, too, all talk about the beyond, be it Christian or Buddhist, should be understood only in a symbolic sense, since on "this side of the grave" things concerning the other side "cannot be known neatly and clearly."[237] As for Langer-Kaneko, this symbolism also points for Knitter to experience in the here and now, without, in principle, denying the possibility of an afterlife: "By being fully in the present moment, we will no longer have any worries about the next moment, and that includes the moment we die and the moments that come after our death."[238]

---

[230]See Baskind 2018, 244–49.
[231]Ibid., 249.
[232]See ibid., 252–57.
[233]See ibid., 260.
[234]Langer-Kaneko 1986, 148.
[235]Ibid., 149.
[236]See ibid., 150.
[237]See Knitter 2009, 74–91, here 75.
[238]Ibid., 79.

Lang and McDannell conclude their extensive cultural history of Christian heaven by observing that a number of Christian thinkers have ceased to concern themselves today with the question of life after death.[239] As indicated above, there are similar tendencies among contemporary Buddhist thinkers, too, this pertaining above all to an other-worldly, final salvation. *One*, though probably not the only, reason is the issue of the indescribability or inconceivability of a final state of salvation. Understanding eternal life as a literally unceasing, everlasting continuation of life suggests the idea of an endless repetition that, as Steven Collins sets forth with reference to the Buddhist idea of the cycle of rebirths, would correspond more to hell than heaven. If, on the other hand, we understand eternal life as a timeless state where it is not even clear how far it can be a conscious state at all, then it remains questionable how this can differ from an eternal death.[240] According to Collins, the idea of eternal (whether everlasting or timeless) bliss cannot be translated into a coherent concept that allows itself to be spelled out clearly.[241]

However, the limits of what for us can be conceived and described do not necessarily mark the limits of what is possible. If, as all major religious traditions affirm, ultimate reality (be it God, nirvana, dharma body, etc.) is itself inconceivable and indescribable, then it should not be too surprising that this also applies to the possibility of an ultimate unity with ultimate reality. We cannot see clearly what lies beyond the horizon; we cannot say for certain that things continue beyond the horizon. And how things might continue we can neither conceive nor describe—at least if we mean here a final deathlessness or eternity, one that is "bliss" and not simply annihilation. Whether there is such a "beyond the horizon" depends presumably on whether there is an ultimate reality that is not constrained by the limits of space and time.

---

[239] See Lang & McDannell 2001, 358.
[240] See Collins, S. 1998, 126–33.
[241] See ibid., 133.

9

Buddhism and Christianity

A New Understanding—A New Relationship

> Buddhism is not Buddhism and Christianity is not Christianity. There are many forms of Buddhism and many ways of understanding Buddhism. There are many ways of understanding Christianity. Therefore, let us forget the idea that Christianity must be like this, and that Buddhism can only be like that.[1]

Thich Nhat Hanh's simple statement can no longer be doubted today. This has also been the focus of this book: the diversity of forms of Buddhism and Christianity, something to which discussions about both religions are still paying far too little attention. What does it imply for the relationship between religious traditions if we no longer treat them as more or less homogeneous blocks? Thich Nhat Hanh himself hints at *one* implication: It may well be the case that how a particular Christian understands and lives their faith is much closer to Thich Nhat Hanh's idea of Buddhism than to that of another Buddhist.[2] And, we may add, that the other Buddhist may also be closer to another form of Christianity than to Thich Nhat Hanh's version of Buddhism. In other words, there is always a piece of Christianity in Buddhism, and a piece of Buddhism in Christianity.

The question of differences and similarities in the relationship between the two religions therefore requires a new and much more nuanced perspective. Such generalizations as "Buddhists think differently than Christians"[3] are unacceptable. This is not to deny differences; however, they exist not only *between* the religions, but also *within* them. And it is only because there are strong parallels between the *inter*religious and *intra*religious differences

---

[1] Hanh 1999, 16.
[2] See ibid.
[3] Radaj 2011, 9 and 20.

that a certain phenomenon from one tradition can be more similar to a phenomenon from the other tradition than to another phenomenon from one's own religion. It is thus the recognition of fractal patterns within religious diversity that facilitates—indeed, demands—not only a new understanding of, but also a new perspective on the relationship between Buddhism and Christianity. And this of course applies not only to this particular relationship, but to the relationship between all major religious traditions.

9.1 IN THE EYE OF THE BEHOLDER?

Given the age and breadth of both Buddhism and Christianity, what I have presented and compared in terms of differences within the traditions is still a comparatively small and selective sample. There are major gaps, for example, with regard to tantric forms of Buddhism and diverse local forms in Southeast Asia, and to Eastern Christianity and the numerous Free Church and Pentecostal forms of Christianity. But even the few highlights that I have focused on should suffice to confirm the basic thesis that *within* both religions are such differences that are equal or similar to those that have often been and often still are cited as the central differences *between* the two traditions.

Did perhaps the mistake in understanding the relationship between the two religions derive, from the outset, from the very attempt to define something such as key differences? Did scholars perhaps pick out certain aspects more or less at random from the abundance of different individual phenomena, which they then claimed to be characteristic or even normative for the entire tradition—in the case of Buddhism, for example, the Theravada tradition considered to be "original"; in the case of Christianity, its late-antique Latin or its later Reformation form? Did scholars perhaps simply project the characteristics of the religious other from their own tradition onto the foreign tradition as a whole? Do the intrareligious differences possibly constitute the real starting point for the mistaken construction of the interreligious difference? Is thus the impression that there are fractal patterns perhaps due merely to a mistaken perception of interreligious diversity—a perception that wrongly believes it can recognize in the foreign religion the familiar features of the religious other within one's own tradition? Is the similarity only imagined? Or is it perhaps indeed a reality that actually constitutes a structural feature of religious differences and thus of religious diversity?

Such questions lead to the suspicion already raised by Jonathan Z. Smith in 1982 that religious comparisons might have more in common with magic than with science, since they transfer to objective reality a purely subjective link between two different things.[4] Put simply, is the fractal pattern that emerges in the comparison only in the eye of the beholder?[5] We can perhaps answer this question with the help of Couliano's historical approach.[6] Religious traditions develop over the course of time, a fact that apparently does not reside only in the eye of the beholder. But this observation implies that religious traditions with a certain nameable identity also have something like a beginning. Not necessarily only one single beginning, but—much more likely—several beginnings running side by side and into each other; in other words, they have something like a network of roots that is itself fractal. There are points or sequences where the roots drive their shoots upward, and thus become visible and identifiable. Even if their emergence is processual and diffuse, we can still speak at some point of something like "Buddhism" or "Christianity." Moreover, large religious traditions continue to grow, becoming broader and more complex as they branch out. In doing so, they absorb new influences, and thus draw on additional roots.

My strong suspicion is that comparing different religious traditions in terms of their original roots, their first shoots, and their first larger formations, will reveal different emphases and different constellations in the connection between those manifold factors that are within the religions from the very beginning, and often already within their roots. Comparing religions historically can draw on relevant data to show that such differences between the religions are real and not just a figment of the imagination. Since such differences also remain somehow present throughout their subsequent development, it seems justified to a certain extent to speak of typological differences between religious traditions as a whole. But this should not obscure the fact that such differences are based on typical focal points, each of which emerges within a complex structure of several different characteristics, some of which are already present at the beginning (and even before that in the very "roots"). Such typological focal points may well remain discernible for a longer time. But, as the complexity of the structure increases within the further development of individual religious traditions, so may, in a sense, "regional" changes in the characteristic typological features also occur at different places and at different times. All this is not only a theoretical possibility, but a process that the study of religious history has actually observed and often confirmed.

Thus, in my opinion, fractal patterns exist and emerge in religious history. These patterns are not due to a false impression that is created by projecting individual features from the intrareligious diversity of one's own tradition

---

[4] See Smith, J. Z. 1982, 21–22.
[5] See Sullivan 2000, 218.
[6] See above, pp. 32–33.

onto another religion. Christianity and Buddhism do indeed differ in certain salient features, even if these features do not emerge as dominant in all their manifestations and at all times. This is possible precisely because the typological differences between the two traditions are also inherent within each of them. We do not do wrong to them if we state that both comprise world-renouncing *and* world-affirming tendencies, with the former being more prominent in Buddhism and the latter in Christianity—even if this does not *always* apply and does not apply to *all* of their manifestations. The same can be said about the other typological distinctions discussed: in Buddhism, impersonal representations of ultimate reality dominate, while in Christianity it is personal representations that prevail, even if both forms coexist alongside and with each other, and the dominance cannot be found always and everywhere. And this is also true for the understanding of the dark side of human existence as delusion or sin, of the bearer of hope as enlightened teacher or incarnated savior, of the path of salvation as path of liberation by self-power or other-power, and of the hope of salvation as blissful absorption in the Absolute or as perfection in a blissful community.

To corroborate the thesis that such macro level typological differences in interreligious diversity are replicated not only at the meso level of intrareligious diversity, but also at the micro level of the individual subject would of course require a much larger body of research in the psychology of religion than has been available to date. The synchronicity of these differences among those who claim for themselves a dual Christian-Buddhist identity is by its very nature easy to demonstrate, including the fact, as Rose Drew puts it, that such persons often "oscillate" between the differences in their individual spirituality.[7] Aloysius Pieris goes much further in his assertion that every Christian and every Buddhist always to some extent combines both religions.[8] This remark relates to the fundamental connection between liberating knowledge and liberating love, and is therefore not meant empirically. But such a view could certainly motivate respective investigations and studies in the psychology of religion. This is also true with regard to the assumption that the presence of different forms of religion and religiosity in the religious individual can be not only synchronic, but above all diachronic. In other words, the assumption that individual believers from both traditions pass through phases during their lives that are, as it were, sometimes more "Buddhist" and sometimes more "Christian." In this respect, future research on religious biographies would be helpful.

The heart of a fractal interpretation of the relationship between Buddhism

---

[7] Drew 2011, 224–27.

[8] "Deep within each one of us there is a Buddhist and a Christian engaged in a profound encounter." Pieris 1988, 113.

and Christianity consists of course in the demonstration, as attempted here, that the said differences between the two religions can also be found within each one of them, i.e., at the meso level. If this is indeed the case, we will have to ask why this is so and whether this mutual presence of similar differences might point to a complementarity of what at first sight seems to be contradictory. Thus, the question of why fractal patterns exist would be at least partly answered by the fact that in each case of these differences one side is incomplete and therefore triggers the other side to emerge—from, as it were, an inner dynamic that strives for completeness. However, we should also be prepared to see that by no means all differences between and within religions turn out to be complementary. Irreconcilable opposites are certainly possible. But the irreconcilability might depend in many cases on a special interpretation of the differences, i.e., on an interpretation that may often not be the only one possible.

In my preceding reflections on the possible complementarities between the differences mentioned in this book, I have consistently adhered to the idea of locating such complementarities on the human, existential side. This approach is more or less self-evident when it comes to the question of a complementarity between nonattachment to the world and loving commitment to it, or the question of identifying the human predicament as delusion or sin. However, I have also used the same approach where the relationship of the human being to transcendent reality raises the question of how this reality is conceived. This concerns primarily the differences between personal and impersonal notions of transcendence, but indirectly also the ideas concerning the role and nature of the central bearers of hope in both religions, as well as the definition of the path of salvation and the ultimate goal of salvation. My approach differs here from other current attempts to understand religious differences as complementary. Theologians such as John Cobb, Mark Heim, and John Thatamanil see the reason for possible complementarities in the complex nature of divine reality itself.[9] However, if we take seriously the inconceivability and ineffability of transcendence as affirmed in all major religious traditions, then such attempts are leading us astray. Against their own intention, they remain at the level of images and therefore tell us something about different aspects of human experience of transcendence and about different forms of human relation to transcendence. But they tell us nothing about the nature of transcendent reality in itself.[10]

As mentioned in the beginning of this study,[11] my human-focused ap-

---

[9] See the conclusion from the comparative study of religions undertaken by Holmes Rolston (1985, 136): "The comprehensive ultimate is, almost analytically, incomprehensible. Comprehended by it, we cannot comprehend it." Rolston refers in this context to Augustine, al-Ghazali, Shankara, and Nagarjuna.

[10] See above, pp. 34–38.

[11] See above, pp, 9–10, 38–40, 113–14.

proach can be extended and supported by reflections from transcendental philosophy, but also by further empirical investigations on the part of cognitive science and the psychology of religion. As also mentioned,[12] my approach to interpreting fractal patterns in religious diversity can therefore by no means exclude a purely naturalistic, nonreligious reading. Those who deny the existence of an ultimate reality that transcends space and time will interpret the fractal patterns as recurring forms of human illusion and self-deception. But the human-focused approach is also open to a religious interpretation assuming that there is an ultimate, transcendent reality. Then the religious traditions of the world articulate different experiences of this reality, as well as the significance of this reality for understanding human existence, in such a way that fractal patterns emerge that recur across religious diversity. In that sense, a more detailed analysis of these patterns, and in particular the exploration of the complementary differences that they contain, offer an immense opportunity for interreligious learning and interreligious theology, and thus for a new relationship between religions.

9.2 FRACTAL STRUCTURES AS A BASIS FOR INTERRELIGIOUS LEARNING

More recently, Catherine Cornille in particular has done much to flesh out the idea of interreligious learning.[13] She distinguishes six different learning processes. First, *intensification*, by which is meant that the discovery of significant correspondences with similar ideas in other religions strengthens the conviction that certain beliefs in one's own tradition are true. Second, *rectification*, which is a matter of correcting reciprocal distortions and overcoming misunderstandings. Third, *recovery*, by which is meant that encountering other religions makes one aware of neglected, marginalized, or ostracized elements from one's own tradition, which one then might see in a different and more positive light. Fourth, *reinterpretation*, where the influence of another religious tradition leads one to reinterpret certain aspects of one's own tradition, or even leads the tradition as a whole to understand itself differently. Fifth, there can be an *appropriation* or adoption of elements and insights of other religions into one's own. And, sixth, there can be a *reaffirmation* of one's own faith, which, unlike intensification, involves a kind of self-reassurance through demarcation, i.e., there is a "reaffirmation

---

[12]See above, p. 47.
[13]See Cornille 2020, 115–47. Cornille had previously developed five of these six forms by analyzing learning processes in Christian-Hindu dialogue (see Cornille 2016). On the following, see also Schmidt-Leukel 2024.

of one's own beliefs and practices in light of alternate religious views."[14]

The existence of fractal structures explains why the learning processes mentioned by Cornille are real possibilities. Intensification and recovery can occur in many ways between Christians and Buddhists. Precisely because the otherness of the other tradition corresponds to the otherness of the other within one's own tradition, it is possible not only to rediscover the other in our own tradition, but also to gain a new, more positive evaluation of this other. This is exactly what has happened on the Christian side in the *recovery* and reevaluation of mysticism, initiated not least by its encounter with Buddhism.[15] And so-called socially engaged Buddhism is a prime example on the Buddhist side, since their encounter with Christianity has led Buddhists to recover and revitalize socioethically significant manifestations and aspects of their own tradition.[16] There are also examples of the process of *intensification*, such as the intensified awareness on both sides of the problems of a self-centered life and the importance of love and compassion.

Somewhat contiguous to recovery is the *appropriation* of practices and insights from other religions. Thus, the Christian recovery of mysticism was accompanied by the adoption of Buddhist meditation practices, this taking place in the awareness that Buddhist meditation could not only enliven, but also greatly enrich, Christian contemplation. Conversely, one may point to the appropriation of elements of Christian worship in some more recent forms of Buddhist cultic practice,[17] or the adaptation of structures of Christian social works in Buddhism,[18] as an example of the renewed appreciation of the social dimension of Buddhist practice. But all this may be only the beginning of much deeper processes of appropriation. For example, John Yokota suggests seeing Jesus as a manifestation or incarnation of Amida, and therefore equates the Gospels and the Pauline scriptures with the classical Buddhist manuals and commentaries in a new and transformed form of Pure Land Buddhism.[19] This sounds like a pipe dream, but it is in fact already common practice among a number of Buddhist thinkers and some

---

[14]Cornille 2020, 141.

[15]See above, p. 222.

[16]See above, pp. 57–58, 66.

[17]See, for example, the introduction of a "Buddhist catechism" by "Colonel" Henry Steel Olcott in Sri Lanka in 1881—with the approval of Buddhist authorities. Ernst Benz mentions, as examples, Buddhist communities in the United States using the harmonium and adapting Christian hymns "in which the name of Jesus is replaced by the name of the Buddha." Benz 1970, 192.

[18]A well-known example of this is the YMBA (Young Men's Buddhist Association), which was founded in Sri Lanka in 1998. Modeled on the YMCA (Young Men's Christian Association), it has since spread to many parts of the Buddhist world (see Gombrich 2006, 185, 194–95). In China, Taixu raised the almost programmatic demand to learn from Christianity with regard to how to organize and motivate individual believers. See Pittman 2001, 248–50.

[19]See Yokota 2005, 100.

Christian theologians, who have long since ceased to draw only on the sources of their own tradition.[20]

Rectification of misinterpretations and mutual distortions occurs above all when people perceive more clearly the diversity of the other tradition as well as of their own, since one of the main sources of distortion is precisely the one-sided and homogenizing view of other religions. A wide field of learning opens up here for many Buddhists and Christians, and this may strongly influence their relationship to one another. Christian ideas of Buddhism as an atheistic religion of self-redemption based on the pessimistic philosophy of Gautama with a life-denying, even nihilistic, objective—these need to be corrected by the facts: namely, the personal features in the conception of the absolute, the incarnational features in the understanding of the Buddha, the awareness of sin and dependence on external help as they are found also in Buddhism, and a goal of salvation that is no less multifaceted than its counterparts in Christianity. For their part, Buddhists can correct their own negative perceptions of Christianity by seeing its rich diversity more clearly and by recognizing there those elements that they particularly value in their own tradition: namely, nonattachment to the transient, silence in the face of ultimate reality, the importance of knowledge and the role of Jesus as teacher, the involvement of the self in the process of overcoming the self, and the manifold symbolism in the hope of ultimate salvation.

Corrections in mutual perception combined with a better understanding of both the other and one's own tradition can sometimes lead to far-reaching *reinterpretations* in self-understanding. Reinterpretation can be combined with the creative appropriation or adoption of the once foreign perspective. Cornille describes this form of interreligious learning as the attempt to understand anew one's own tradition or some of its elements "through the categories or philosophical framework of another" tradition. As she points out, this is something that already happened when early Christianity not only reinterpreted but virtually reconstructed its Jewish heritage in the light of the strongly religious Greek philosophy.[21] Such processes can be repeated today with regard to the categories and philosophies of other religions. One explicit attempt to reinterpret Christian teachings within the framework of Mahayanist philosophies is the works of John Keenan.[22] Another example of this form of learning are the attempts already mentioned to reinterpret Jesus in the context of the bodhisattva ideal.[23] Even more far-reaching,

---

[20] There are now also in Pentecostal churches theologians who take Buddhist sources seriously, and who even, like Amos Yong, integrate them into their own theological reflections in a constructive way. See Yong 2012a & 2012b.
[21] Cornille 2020, 129.
[22] See Keenan 1989; 1995; 2005; Kenan & Keenan 2011.
[23] See above, pp. 160–66. See also Schneider 2023.

though, is the attempt to reinterpret the conventional self-understanding of one's own tradition. In practical terms, this means no longer understanding its claim to show the human being a path to salvation as if it alone could point out such a path, or as if it alone could do so in a way superior to all other religions. Attempts on the part of Christians and Buddhists no longer to think of their own religion as the only true religion, nor as the objectively best religion, but to take seriously the idea of a plurality of equally valid paths of salvation, are undoubtedly a particularly significant result of processes of interreligious learning.[24] Such attempts are not due, as some critics have claimed, to a purely theoretical construction that misses the reality of religions. Rather, it can be demonstrated that several pioneers of pluralist theologies of religion were initially motivated by actual encounters with people of other religions and the processes of dialogical learning that these encounters entailed.[25]

Contrasting with reinterpretation is Cornille's possible learning outcome of *reaffirmation* of the claims of one's own tradition. Such a classification as a form of interreligious learning seems surprising, since, as Cornille herself notes, "reaffirmation may seem reminiscent of traditional apologetics."[26] In my view, this impression is reinforced rather than mitigated when Cornille points as an example of this kind of learning to Paul Williams' reflections on his reconversion from Buddhism to Christianity.[27] She justifies this by arguing that, in Williams' case, the reaffirmation of Christian beliefs is "informed by the Buddhist teachings against which they are reaffirmed."[28] One can certainly agree with Cornille's point that the encounter with the religious other can lead to a reaffirmation of one's own faith. When in a foreign land, one often learns to appreciate anew what is familiar. And yet there is a great difference between reaffirming one's own faith in a way that is confrontational toward the other, and adopting a kind of ecumenical attitude that appreciates and reaffirms one's faith as part of a more comprehensive whole. Cornille is right that both may be the result of learning processes, but the difference is that the first variant entails no significant change. Rather, the older negative attitudes toward other faiths are for whatever reason reconfirmed. Especially in the case of Paul Williams, however, it is questionable how far one can speak of a reaffirmation in the sense mentioned, since the Christianity to which he converted is not the same as the Christianity of his youth.[29] One should therefore perhaps see

---

[24]See Schmidt-Leukel 2019a, 39–61, 118–44.
[25]See ibid., 188–90.
[26]Cornille 2020, 138.
[27]See Williams, P. 2002.
[28]Cornille 2002, 139.
[29]Paul Williams grew up as an Anglican and, after turning away from Buddhism, joined the Roman Catholic Church, or more precisely a rather conservative form of Catholicism. But it was only this step

his "reconversion" as a conversion to a resolute Christianity that took a detour via Buddhism. Williams himself notes that he never stopped being a Christian emotionally.[30] This, however, would be a completely different learning process, one in which the person does not reaffirm their own faith, but accepts it in an altered form.

My remarks on Cornille's category of "reaffirmation" in no way exclude the fact that religious traditions contain not only good but also evil. The dark aspects of religion may also form parts of fractal patterns that recur in modified but similar form in different traditions. I also do not exclude the possibility that there are real and irreconcilable differences between and within religions. The question is rather whether what initially emerges just as a difference must really be interpreted *only* as an irreconcilable contradiction, or whether it can also be understood as a compatible and even complementary difference.

In this last respect, the learning processes of ecumenical theology are instructive. In twentieth-century Christianity, theologians of different denominations invested serious effort into studying the question of whether what for long appeared to the divided churches as irreconcilable opposites cannot also be understood in terms of a compatible and "reconciled" diversity. If, according to a fractal perspective, we can expect substantive correspondences between the macro and meso levels of religious diversity, then ecumenical efforts for a better understanding of *intra*religious diversity are at the same time of great importance for the understanding of *inter*religious diversity.[31]

The Reformation doctrine of justification by faith alone and the Catholic doctrine of justification by faith and works, as well as all other variants of these positions, were understood for centuries as irreconcilable opposites in the wake of the Reformation. Moreover, this difference was also employed interreligiously: the Reformation side imputed to Jews and Muslims a quasi-"Catholic" works righteousness, while the Catholic Jesuit missionaries in Japan accused Pure Land Buddhism of propagating the same devil-inspired heresy as Luther.[32] The negative judgment of the *intra*religious other was transferred to the *inter*religious other. However, the ecumenical efforts of the twentieth century finally led to the signing of the *Joint Declaration on the Doctrine of Justification* (1999), which saw Lutherans and Catholics affirm the legitimacy and fundamental value of each side's doctrine of justification, notwithstanding the differences in how each expressed this.

---

that obviously constituted for him a more or less clear decision for embracing Christian faith.

[30] See Williams 2002, 7: "I strongly suspect that many Western Buddhists are deep down still Christians. I was. I was a lapsed Christian perhaps, but still a Christian."

[31] See Schmidt-Leukel 2020d.

[32] See above, pp. 45, 178.

Reciprocal condemnations of the other side's doctrines are here confined to extreme and one-sided expressions of the respective doctrines. "The Lutheran and the Catholic explications of justification are in their difference open to one another and do not destroy the consensus regarding the basic truths" (paragraph 40). What was long considered an irreconcilable opposition is understood here as a difference that can be legitimately interpreted as a complementary difference. This interpretation was by no means a merely verbal formulaic compromise, but the result of many years of in-depth studies of the controversies from the Reformation period.[33] If similarly intensive hermeneutical efforts are also made at the level of interreligious dialogue, then similar results can be expected from the thesis of a fractal correspondence of meso and macro levels. Catholics, for example, can be open and sympathetic to Pure Land Buddhism's doctrine of salvation by other power alone, and Protestants can see that the emphasis on righteous works in Judaism and Islam is embedded in a fundamental trust in divine grace and mercy.

The learning process behind the *Joint Declaration* undoubtedly led to a *reaffirmation* of faith on the part of Lutherans and Catholics—but a reaffirmation that no longer affirmed the old and purely negative judgments, but that was now part of a larger and all-encompassing consensus. Very much behind this was the learning process that Cornille calls "rectification," i.e., the overcoming of reciprocal distortions and misunderstandings. Fractal patterns within religious diversity can explain why both are possible in principle: the reaffirmation of confrontative antagonisms, as well as the reaffirmation of differences as part of a larger consensus. The reaffirmation of antagonisms, however, is excluded if the differences that make up the fractal structure are understood as being complementary.

The examples of Swami Vivekananda and Bhikkhu Buddhadasa mentioned at the beginning show that, from the perspective of other religions, too, the ecumenical effort to understand *intra*religious diversity correlates with the *inter*religious level. Both reformers drew on schemata from their own traditions that allowed them to transfer a positive evaluation of *intra*religious diversity to the *inter*religious level.[34] And both understood the differences on both levels as essentially complementary. If serious interreligious studies can lead to a situation where religions understand themselves as being, like other religions, extremely diverse entities internally, and if this diversity can be interpreted as largely complementary, then the ecumenical spirit is transferred to a larger, i.e., interreligious, ecumenism. As indicated, this is likely to be the culmination of processes of rectification

---

[33] See Lehmann & Pannenberg 1988.
[34] See above, pp. 40–43.

and reinterpretation, since the improved understanding of the other also leads to "a new understanding of one's own tradition in relation to the other."[35]

Regarding the discovery of fractal structures in religious diversity, the theologian, historian, and cultural anthropologist Stanislaw Obirek has written,

> From now on it will be impossible to see particular religions as separate entities which should be by their natures in constant conflict. The opposite is true: thanks to the Fractal Interpretation of Religious Diversity we are able to see all of them as part of a greater divine design.[36]

Using the ancient Hindu-Buddhist image, one can describe this design as Indra's (God's) net: as the celestial web.

---

[35] Cornille 2020, 121.
[36] Obirek 2020, 101.

References

Abe, Masao, 1985. "A Dynamic Unity in Religious Pluralism: A Proposal from the Buddhist Point of View." In *The Experience of Religious Diversity*, ed. by J. Hick; H. Askari, 163–90. Aldershot: Gower Publishing.

Amaladass, Anand; Löwner, Gudrun, 2012. *Christian Themes in Indian Art*. New Delhi: Manohar.

Anderson, Carol S.; Cattoi, Thomas (eds.), *The Routledge Handbook of Buddhist-Christian Studies*. New York: Routledge.

Anderson, Gary A., 2009. *Sin: A History*. New Haven, CT: Yale University Press.

Augustine, 1977. *Bekenntnisse*. Intro. and trans. by Wilhelm Thimme. Stuttgart: Reclam.

Bailey, D. R. Shackleton, 1951. "The Varṇārhavarṇa Stotra of Mātṛceṭa (II)." *Bulletin of the School of Oriental and African Studies* 13:4, 947–1003.

Barr, James, 1992. *The Garden of Eden and the Hope of Immortality*. London: SCM Press.

Barth, Hans-Martin, 2002. "'Ich lebe, aber nicht mehr ich . . .' Christlicher Glaube und personale Identität." *Neue Zeitschrift für Systematische Theologie* 44, 174–88.

Barthes, Roland, 1974. *S/Z*. Trans. by Richard Miller. New York: Hill and Wang. [French original 1970.]

———. 1992. *Empire of Signs*. 10th reprint. New York: Hill and Wang. [French original 1970.]

Basham, Arthur L., 1997. "The Evolution of the Concept of the Bodhisattva." In *The Bodhisattva Doctrine in Buddhism*, ed. by L. S. Kawamura, 19–59. Delhi: Sri Satguru Publications.

Baskind, James Matthew, 2018. "The Pure Land Is No Heaven: Habian's *Myōtei Dialogues*, Valignano's *Japanese Catechism*, and Discourses on the Afterlife during Japan's Christian Century." *History of Religions* 57:3, 229–69.

Batchelor, Stephen, 1998. *Buddhism without Beliefs: A Contemporary Guide to Awakening*. London: Bloomsbury.

———. 2011. *Confessions of a Buddhist Atheist*. New York: Spiegel & Grau.

Bauks, Michaela, 2011. "Monotheismus." *Wissenschaftliches Bibellexikon im Internet*. http://www.bibelwissenschaft.de/stichwort/27997.

Bechert, Heinz, 1992. "Buddha-Field and Transfer of Merit in a Theravāda Source." *Indo-Iranian Journal* 35:2/3, 95–108.

Belsey, Catherine, 2002. *Poststructuralism: A Very Short Introduction*. Oxford: Oxford University Press.
Bendall, Cecil; Rouse, W. H. D., 1922. *Śikshā-Samuccaya: A Compendium of Buddhist Doctrine*. Comp. by Śāntideva. London: John Murray.
Benz, Ernst, 1970. "Buddhismus in der westlichen Welt." In *Buddhismus der Gegenwart*, ed. by H. Dumoulin, 191–204. Freiburg i.Br.: Herder.
Berger, Peter, 2014. *The Many Altars of Modernity: Toward a Paradigm for Religion in a Pluralist Age*. Boston: De Gruyter.
Bergunder, Michael, 2011. "Was ist Religion? Kulturwissenschaftliche Überlegungen zum Gegenstand der Religionswissenschaft." *Zeitschrift für Religionswissenschaft* 19:1/2, 3–55.
———. 2016. "Comparison in the Maelstrom of Historicity: A Postcolonial Perspective on Comparative Religion." In *Interreligious Comparisons in Religious Studies and Theology. Comparison Revisited*, ed. by P. Schmidt-Leukel; A. Nehring, 34–52. London: Bloomsbury Academic.
Bernhardt, Reinhold, 2005. *Ende des Dialogs? Die Begegnung der Religionen und ihre Reflexion?* Zürich: Theologischer Verlag Zürich.
———. 2019a. *Inter-Religio. Das Christentum in Beziehung zu anderen Religionen*. Zürich: Theologischer Verlag Zürich.
———. 2019b. "'Theologie der Religionen'—Streit um eine Formel." *Zeitschrift für Missions- und Religionswissenschaft* 103:3–4, 191–204.
———. 2021. *Jesus Christus—Repräsentant Gottes. Christologie im Kontext der Religionstheologie*. Zürich: Theologischer Verlag Zürich.
Bernhardt, Reinhold; Schmidt-Leukel, Perry (eds.), 2008. *Multiple religiöse Identität. Aus verschiedenen religiösen Traditionen schöpfen*. Zürich: Theologischer Verlag Zürich.
———. 2019. *Interreligiöse Theologie. Chancen und Probleme*. Zürich: Theologischer Verlag Zürich.
Bernhardt, Reinhold; von Stosch, Klaus (eds.), 2009. *Komparative Theologie. Interreligiöse Vergleiche als Weg der Religionstheologie*. Zürich: Theologischer Verlag Zürich.
Berry, Thomas Sterling, 1890. *Christianity and Buddhism: A Comparison and a Contrast*. London: SPCK.
Bertelsmann Stiftung, 2007. *Religionsmonitor 2008*. Gütersloh: Gütersloher Verlagshaus.
Bertholet, Alfred, 1909. *Buddhismus und Christentum*. 2nd rev. ed. Tübingen: J. C. B. Mohr.
Bidwell, Duane R., 2018. *When One Religion Isn't Enough: The Lives of Spiritually Fluid People*. Boston: Beacon Press.
Billmann-Mahecha, Elfriede, 2003. "Entwicklung von Moralität und Religiosität." In *Einführung in die Religionspsychologie*, ed. by C. Henning; S. Murken; E. Nestler, 118–37. Paderborn: Schöningh.
Bischofberger, Norbert, 1996. *Werden wir wiederkommen? Der Reinkarnationsgedanke im Westen und die Sicht der christlichen Eschatologie*. Mainz:

Matthias-Grünewald Verlag; Kampen: Kok Pharos Publishing House.
Blée, Fabrice, 2011. *The Third Desert: The Story of Monastic Interreligious Dialogue*. Collegeville, MN: Liturgical Press.
Bleeker, C. Jouco, 1972. "The Contribution of the Phenomenology of Religion to the Study of the History of Religions." In *Problems and Methods of the History of Religions*, ed. by U. Bianchi; C. J. Bleeker; A. Bausani, 35–54. Leiden: E. J. Brill.
Bodhi, Bhikkhu, 1995. "Replies to Questions from 'SOURCE.'" *Dialogue (NS)* 22, 20–28.
———. 2000. *The Connected Discourses of the Buddha: A Translation of the Saṃyutta Nikāya*. Boston: Wisdom Publications.
———. 2012. *The Numerical Discourses of the Buddha: A Translation of the Aṅguttara Nikāya*. Boston: Wisdom Publications.
———. 2017. *The Suttanipāta: An Ancient Collection of the Buddha's Discourses. Together with Its Commentaries*. Boston: Wisdom Publications.
Bosch, Gabriele, 2015. "Luther und der augustinische 'homo incurvatus.'" In *Das in sich verkrümmte Herz. Anamnesen, Diagnosen und Perspektiven menschlichen Seins im 21. Jahrhundert*, ed. by H. Speier, 41–60. Marburg: Tectum Verlag.
Boyarin, Daniel, 2004. *Border Lines: The Partition of Judaeo-Christianity*. Divinations: Rereading Late Ancient Religion 3. Philadelphia: University of Pennsylvania Press.
Brox, Norbert, 1989. *Erleuchtung und Wiedergeburt. Aktualität der Gnosis*. München: Kösel.
Bubolz, Georg, 2019. *Ohne Taube und Kamel. Die vier Evangelien des Neuen Testatemts aus der aramäischen Peschittā*. Frankfurt a.M.: Verlag Hans-Jürgen Maurer.
Buddhadāsa, Bhikkhu Indapañño, 1967. *Christianity and Buddhism*. Sinclaire Thompson Memorial Lecture. Fifth Series. Bangkok: Sublime Life Mission.
Burckhardt, Titus, 2008. *Introduction to Sufi Doctrine*. Bloomington, IN: World Wisdom.
Büttner, Gerhard; Dietrich, Veit-Jacobus (eds.), 2000. *Die religiöse Entwicklung des Menschen. Ein Grundkurs*. Stuttgart: Calwer.
Cabezón, José I., 1999. "A Buddhist Response to John Paul II." In *John Paul II and Interreligious Dialogue*, ed. by B. L. Sherwin; H. Kasimow, 113–22. Maryknoll, NY: Orbis Books.
———. 2000. "A God but Not a Savior." In *Buddhists Talk about Jesus, Christians Talk about the Buddha*, ed. by R. Gross; T. Muck, 17–31. New York: Continuum.
———. 2016. "Three Buddhist Views of the Doctrines of Creation and Creator." In *Buddhism, Christianity and the Question of Creation*, 2nd ed., ed. by P. Schmidt-Leukel, 33–45. London: Routledge.
Carpenter, Joseph Estlin, 1923. *Buddhism and Christianity: A Contrast and a Parallel*. London: Hodder & Stoughton.

Carus, Paul, 1897. *Buddhism and Its Christian Critics*. Chicago: The Open Court.

Cattoi, Thomas, 2021. "Demons, Toll Houses, and the *Bardo*: Patristic and Tibetan Reflections on Individual Destiny after Death." In *A Visionary Approach: Lynn A. de Silva and the Prospects for Buddhist-Christian Encounter*, ed. by J. Harris; P. Schmidt-Leukel, 357–78. St. Ottilien: EOS Editions.

Ceming, Katharina, 2004. *Einheit im Nichts. Die mystische Theologie des Christentums, des Hinduismus und des Buddhismus im Vergleich*. Augsburg: Edition Verstehen.

Chandrkaew, Chinda, 1982. *Nibbāna: The Ultimate Truth of Buddhism*. Bangkok: Mahachula Buddhist University.

Chung, Paul S., 2008. *Martin Luther and Buddhism: Aesthetics of Suffering*. Cambridge: James Clarke & Co.

Clark, Anthony E., 2018. *Catholicism and Buddhism: The Contrasting Lives and Teachings of Jesus and Buddha*. Eugene, OR: Cascade Books.

Cleary, Thomas, 1983. *Entry into the Inconceivable. An Introduction to Hua-Yen Buddhism*. Honolulu: University of Hawai'i Press.

———. 1993. *The Flower Ornament Scripture: Translation of the Avatamsaka Sutra*. Boston: Shambhala.

Clooney, Francis X., 2010a. *Comparative Theology: Deep Learning across Religious Borders*. Chichester: Wiley-Blackwell.

———. 2010b. "Response." In *The New Comparative Theology: Interreligious Insights from the Next Generation*, ed. by F. X. Clooney, 191–200. London: T&T Clark International.

Clooney, Francis X.; Berthrong, John (eds.), 2014. *European Perspectives on the New Comparative Theology*. Basel: MDPI.

Clooney, Francis X.; von Stosch, Klaus (eds.), 2018. *How to Do Comparative Theology*. New York: Fordham University Press.

Cobb, John B., 1999. *Transforming Christianity and the World: A Way beyond Absolutism and Relativism*, ed. and intro. by Paul Knitter. Maryknoll, NY: Orbis Books.

Cohn-Sherbok, Daniel, 1987. "Death and Immortality in the Jewish Tradition." In *Death and Immortality in the Religions of the World*, ed. by P. Badham; L. Badham, 24–36. New York: Paragon House.

Cole, Alan, 1998. *Mothers and Sons in Chinese Buddhism*. Stanford, CA: Stanford University Press.

Collins, John J., 2016. *The Apocalyptic Imagination: An Introduction to Jewish Apocalyptic Literature*. 3rd ed. Grand Rapids: Eerdmans.

Collins, Steven, 1982. *Selfless Persons: Imagery and Thought in Theravāda Buddhism*. Cambridge: Cambridge University Press.

———. 1998. *Nirvana and Other Buddhist Felicities*. Cambridge: Cambridge University Press.

———. 2010. *Nirvana: Concept, Imagery, Narrative*. Cambridge: Cambridge University Press.

Colpe, Carsten, 1990. "Erlösungsreligion." In *Handbuch religionswissenschaftlicher Grundbegriffe*, vol. 2, ed. by H. Cancik; B. Gladigow; M. Laubscher, 323–29. Stuttgart: Kohlhammer.
Conze, Edward, 1966. "Buddhism and Gnosis." In *Le origini dello gnosticismo. Colloquio di Messina, 13–18 Aprile 1966. Testi e discussioni*, ed. by U. Bianchi, 651–67. Leiden: Brill.
———. 1984. *Eine kurze Geschichte des Buddhismus*. Frankfurt a.M.: Insel Verlag.
Corless, Roger J., 1996. "T'an-luan: The First Systematizer of Pure Land Buddhism." In *The Pure Land Tradition: History and Development*, ed. by J. Foard; M. Solomon; R. K. Payne, 107–37. Berkeley: The Regents of the University of California.
Cornille, Catherine (ed.), 2002. *Many Mansions? Multiple Religious Belonging and Christian Identity*. Maryknoll, NY: Orbis Books.
——— (ed.), 2013. *The Wiley-Blackwell Companion to Inter-religious Dialogue*. Chichester: Wiley-Blackwell.
———. 2016. "Discipleship in Hindu-Christian Comparative Theology." *Theological Studies* 77, 869–885.
———. 2020. *Meaning and Method in Comparative Theology*. Chichester: Wiley-Blackwell.
Couliano, Ioan P., 1992. *The Tree of Gnosis: Gnostic Mythology from Early Christianity to Modern Nihilism*. New York: HarperCollins.
Coward, Harold, 2003. *Sin and Salvation in the World Religions: A Short Introduction*. Oxford: Oneworld.
Cowell, E. B., 1894. "The Buddhacarita of Asvaghosha." In *Buddhist Mahāyāna Texts*, ed. by E. B. Cowell, vi–x, 1–206. SBE 49. Oxford: Clarendon Press.
Cunningham, Lawrence S., 1999. *Thomas Merton and the Monastic Vision*. Grand Rapids: Eerdmans.
Cupitt, Don, 2003. *The Sea of Faith*. New ed. London: SCM Press.
Dalai Lama, 2002. *The Good Heart*, ed. by Robert Kiely. London: Ryder.
———. 2005. *Practicing Wisdom: The Perfection of Shantideva's Bodhisattva Way*. Boston: Wisdom Publications.
Danz, Christian, 2020. *Jesus von Nazareth zwischen Judentum und Christentum. Eine christologische und religionstheologische Skizze*. Tübingen: Mohr Siebeck.
Davies, Brian, 1993. *The Thought of Thomas Aquinas*. Oxford: Clarendon Press.
Dayal, Har, 1932. *The Bodhisattva Doctrine in Buddhist Sanskrit Literature*. London: Routledge.
D'Costa, Gavin; Thompson, Ross (eds.), 2016. *Buddhist-Christian Dual Belonging: Affirmations, Objections, Explorations*. Farnham: Ashgate.
Dehn, Ulrich, 2019. *Geschichte des interreligiösen Dialogs*. Berlin: EB-Verlag.
Dehn, Ulrich; Caspar-Seeger, Ulrike; Bernstorff, Freya (eds.). *Handbuch Theologie der Religionen. Texte zur religiösen Vielfalt und zum interreligiösen Dialog*. Freiburg i. Br.: Herder.

Deitrick, James E., 2003. "Engaged Buddhists Ethics: Mistaking the Boat for the Shore." In *Action Dharma: New Studies in Engaged Buddhism*, ed. by C. S. Queen; C. Prebish; D. Keown, 252–69. London: RoutledgeCurzon.

Deleuze, Gilles; Guattari, Félix, 2006. "Rhizome." In *A Thousand Plateaus: Capitalism and Schizophrenia*. Trans. by Brian Massumi, 3–25. 11th printing. Minneapolis: University of Minnesota Press.

Demacopoulos, George E.; Papanikolaou, Aristotle, 2008. "Augustine and the Orthodox: 'The West' in the East." In *Orthodox Readings of Augustine*, ed. by G. E. Demacopoulos; A. Papanikolaou, 11–40. Crestwood, NY: St. Vladimir's Seminary Press.

Desideri, Ippolito, SJ, 2010. *Mission to Tibet. The Extraordinary Eighteenth-Century Account of Father Ippolito Desideri, S.J.* Trans. by Michael J. Sweet; ed. by Leonard Zwilling. Boston: Wisdom Publications.

De Silva, Lynn A., 1982. "Buddhism and Christianity Relativised." *Dialogue* N.S. 9, 43–72.

———. 1998. *Mit Buddha und Christus auf dem Weg*. Theologie der Dritten Welt 24. Freiburg i. Br.: Herder.

DeVido, Elise Anne, 2019. "Thích Nhất Hạnh's Propagation of Mindfulness in the West." In *Meditation in Buddhist-Christian Encounter: A Critical Analysis*, ed. by E. Harri; J. O'Grady, 217–52. St. Ottilien: EOS-Editions.

Dharmasiri, Gunapala, 1974. *A Buddhist Critique of the Christian Concept of God*. Colombo: Lake House.

———. 1976. "Comments on Responses to a Buddhist Critique." *Dialogue* N.S. 3:1, 20–21.

———. 1988. *A Buddhist Critique of the Christian Concept of God*. 2nd enlarged ed. Antioch, CA: Golden Leaves.

Diller, Jeanine, 2013. "Epilogue." In *Models of God and Alternative Ultimate Realities*, ed. by J. Diller; A. Kasher, 1025–29. Dordrecht: Springer.

———. 2016. "Global and Local Atheisms." *International Journal for Philosophy of Religion* 79, 7–18.

Diller, Jeanine; Kasher, Asa (eds.), 2013. *Models of God and Alternative Ultimate Realities*. Dordrecht: Springer.

Doering, Lutz, 2020. "Bilderverbot und Götzendienst. Zum Verständnis des 'Bilderverbots' in Texten des hellenistisch-frühromischen und des rabbinischen Judentums, mit einem Blick auf den archäologischen Befund." In *Bilder, Heilige und Religquien. Beiträge zur Christentumsgeschichte und zur Religionsgeschichte*, ed. by M. Delgado; V. Leppin, 21–48. Basel: Schwabe Verlag; Stuttgart: Kohlhammer.

Drew, Rose, 2011. *Buddhist and Christian? An Exploration of Dual Belonging*. London: Routledge.

Driller, Josephine, 2005. *"O du gießender Gott in deiner Gabe!" Gaben und Gegengaben im Werk der Mechthild von Magdeburg*. Inaugural-Dissertation Universität Paderborn, https://d-nb.info/978189612/34.

Dunn, James D. G. 1989. *Christology in the Making: A New Testament Inquiry*

into the Origins of the Doctrine of the Incarnation. 2nd ed. London: SCM Press.
———. 2006. *The Theology of Paul the Apostle.* Pbk. ed. Grand Rapids: Eerdmans.
Eckel, Malcolm David, 1997. "Is There a Buddhist Philosophy of Nature?" In *Buddhism and Ecology: The Interconnection of Dharma and Deeds*, ed. by M. E. Tucker; D. R. Williams, 327–49. Cambridge, MA: Harvard University Press.
Eliade, Mircea, 1996. *Patterns in Comparative Religion.* Lincoln: University of Nebraska Press.
Elinor, Robert, 2000. *Buddha and Christ: Images of Wholeness.* New York: Weatherhill.
Elison, George, 1991. *Deus Destroyed: The Image of Christianity in Early Modern Japan.* Cambridge, MA: Harvard University Press.
Elliott, Joel, 2006. "Jehova's Witnesses." In *Encyclopedia of Millennialism and Millennial Movements*, ed. by R. A. Landes, 358–65. New York: Routledge.
Emmerick, R. E., 1970. *The Sūtra of Golden Light: Being a Translation of the Suvarṇaprabhāsottamasūtra.* London: Luzac.
Englert, Winfried Phillip, 1898. *Christus und Buddha in ihrem himmlischen Vorleben.* Wien: Verlag von Mayer.
Faber, Roland, 2019. *The Ocean of God: On the Transreligious Future of Religions.* London: Anthem Press.
Faure, Bernard, 2009. *Unmasking Buddhism.* Oxford: Wiley-Blackwell.
Feng, Jinxueh, 2018. *Die chinesisch-christliche Rezeption des Mozi am Beispiel von Zhang Chunyi (1871–1955).* St. Ottilien: EOS-Verlag.
Ferraro, Guiseppe, 2013. "A Criticism of M. Siderits and J. L. Garfield's 'Semantic Interpretation' of Nāgārjuna's Theory of Two Truths." *Journal of Indian Philosophy* 41:2, 195–219.
Feulner, Rüdiger, 2016. *Christus Magister. Gnoseologisch-didaktische Erlösungsparadigmen in der Kirchengeschichte der Frühzeit und des Mittelalters bis zum Beginn der Reformation mit einem theologiegeschichtlichen Ausblick in die Neuzeit.* Wien: LIT Verlag.
Fischer-Barnicol, Hans, 1965/66. "Fragen aus Fernost. Eine Begegnung mit dem japanischen Philosophen Nishitani." *Hochland* 58, 205–18.
Fitzgerald, Timothy, 2000. *The Ideology of Religious Studies.* Oxford: Oxford University Press.
Flasch, Kurt, 1990. *Logik des Schreckens. Augustinus von Hippo. De diversis quaestionibus ad Simplicianum I 2.* Deutsche Erstübersetzung von Walter Schäfer, ed. and comm. by Kurt Flasch. Mainz: Diederichs.
———. 1994. *Augustin. Einführung in sein Denken.* 2nd rev. ed. Stuttgart: Reclam.
Ford, James L., 2016. *The Divine Quest, East and West: A Comparative Study of Ultimate Realities.* Albany: State University of New York Press.
Fredericks, James L., 1995. "A Universal Religious Experience? Comparative

Theology as an Alternative to a Theology of Religions." *Horizons* 22:1, 67–87.

———. 1999. *Faith among Faiths. Christian Theology and Non-Christian Religions.* New York: Paulist Press.

———. 2003. "Masao Abe: A Spiritual Friendship." *Spiritus: A Journal of Christian Spirituality* 3, 219–30.

———. 2015. "Dem Politischen entsagen. Vom Gottesstaat und die Aśokāvadāna." In *Buddhismus und Komparative Theologie*, ed. by K. von Stosch; H.-J. Röllicke; D. Rumel, 57–89. Paderborn: Ferdinand Schöningh.

Fredriksen, Paula, 2012. *Sin: The Early History of an Idea.* Princeton, NJ: Princeton University Press.

Freiberger, Oliver, 2019. *Considering Comparison: A Method for Religious Studies.* New York: Oxford University Press.

Freiberger, Oliver; Kleine, Christoph, 2011. *Buddhismus. Handbuch und kritische Einführung.* Göttingen: Vandenhoeck & Ruprecht.

Fu, Charles Wie-hsun; Spiegler, Gerhard E. (eds.), 1989. *Religious Issues and Interreligious Dialogue: An Analysis and Sourcebook of Developments since 1945.* New York: Greenwood Press.

Garfield, Jay L., 2002. *Empty Words: Buddhist Philosophy and Cross-Cultural Interpretation.* New York: Oxford University Press.

Geis, Lioba, 2007. "Das 'Siegel der Ewigkeit' als Universalsymbol." In *Vom Bild zur Erkenntnis. Visualisierungskonzepte in den Wissenschaften*, ed. by D. Gross; S. Westermann, 131–47. Kassel: Kassel University Press.

Gemeinsame Erklärung zur Rechtfertigungslehre, 1999. In *Texte aus der VELKD* 87, 1–19.

Gethin, Rupert, 1998. *The Foundations of Buddhism.* Oxford: Oxford University Press.

Gladigow, Burkhard, 1988. "Gegenstände und wissenschaftlicher Kontext von Religionswissenschaft." In *Handbuch religionswissenschaftlicher Grundbegriffe.* Vol. 1, ed. by H. Cancik; B. Gladigow; M. Laubscher, 26–38. Stuttgart: Kohlhammer.

Gombrich, Richard F., 2006. *Theravāda Buddhism: A Social History from Ancient Benares to Modern Volombo.* 2nd ed. London: Routledge.

Gōmez, Luis O., 1996. *The Land of Bliss: The Paradise of the Buddha of Measureless Light. Sanskrit and Chinese Versions of the Sukhāvativyūha Sutras.* Intro. and English trans. by Luis O. Gōmez. Honolulu: University of Hawai'i Press.

Goosen, Gideon, 2011. *Hyphenated Christians: Towards a Better Understanding of Dual Religious Belonging.* Frankfurt a.M.: Peter Lang.

Gowans, Christopher W., 2003. *Philosophy of the Buddha.* London: Routledge.

Granoff, Phyllis, 2012. "After Sinning: Some Thoughts on Remorse, Responsibility, and the Remedies for Sin in Indian Religious Traditions." In *Sin and Sinners: Perspectives from Asian Religions*, ed. by P. Granoff; K. Shinohara, 175–215. Leiden: Brill.

Gregory, Peter N., 1986. "The Problem of Theodicy in the 'Awakening of Faith.'" *Religious Studies* 22:1, 63–78.
Griffin, David Ray, 2005. "John Cobb's Whiteheadian Complementary Pluralism." In *Deep Religious Pluralism*, ed. by D. R. Griffin, 39–66. Louisville, KY: Westminster John Knox Press.
Griffiths, Paul J., 1994. *On Being Buddha: The Classical Doctrine of Buddhahood*. Albany, NY: SUNY Press.
Grimm, Georg, 1928. *Buddha und Christus*. Leipzig: Neuer Geist Verlag.
Groner, Paul, 2012. "The Role of Confession in Chinese and Japanese Tiantai/Tendai Bodhisattva Ordinations." In *Sin and Sinners: Perspectives from Asian Religions*, ed. by P. Granoff; K. Shinohara, 216–42. Leiden: Brill.
Gross, Rita; Muck, Terry (eds.), 1999. *Buddhists Talk about Jesus, Christians Talk about the Buddha*. New York: Continuum.
Guardini, Romano, 1997 [1937]. *Der Herr. Betrachtungen über die Person und das Leben Jesu Christi*. Mainz: Matthias-Grünewald; Paderborn: Shöningh.
Guruge, Ananda (ed.), 1965. *Return to Righteousness: A Collection of Speeches, Essays and Letters of the Anagarika Dharmapala*. Colombo: The Government Press.
Gupta, Satish, 2005. *I Am the Dewdrop, I Am the Ocean . . . : Zen Stories, Haikus and Reflections*. New Delhi: Popular Prakashan.
Gustafson, Hans (ed.), 2020. *Interreligious Studies: Dispatches from an Emerging Field*. Waco, TX: Baylor University Press.
Gwynne, Paul, 2014. *Buddha, Jesus and Muhammad. A Comparative Study*. Oxford: Wiley Blackwell.
Haas, Alois M., 1998. "Unio mystica. Hinweise zur Geschichte des Begriffs." In *Erkennen und Erinnern in Kunst und Literatur: Kolloquium Reisensburg, 4.–7. Januar 1996*, in Verbindung mit W. Frühwald, ed. by D. Peil; M. Schilling; P. Strohschneider, 1–17. Tübingen: Max Niemeyer Verlag.
Haight, Roger; Knitter, Paul, 2015. *Jesus and Buddha: Friends in Conversation*. Maryknoll, NY: Orbis Books.
Hanh, Thich Nhat, 1996. *Living Buddha, Living Christ*. London: Rider.
———. 1999. *Going Home: Jesus and Buddha as Brothers*. New York: Riverhead Books.
———. 2003. *Finding Our True Home: Living in the Pure Land Here and Now*. Berkeley, CA: Parallax Press.
———. 2005. "Jesus and Buddha as Brothers." In *Jesus in the World's Faiths: Leading Thinkers from Five Religions Reflect on His Meaning*, ed. by G. A. Barker. Maryknoll, NY: Orbis Books, 38–45.
———. 2010. *Together We Are One: Honoring Our Diversity, Celebrating Our Connection*. Berkeley, CA: Parallax Press.
Hardy, Edmund, 1919. *Der Buddhismus nach älteren Pāli-Werken*. Neue Ausgabe besorgt von Richard Schmidt. Münster: Aschendorff.
Harris, Elizabeth J., 1997. *Detachment and Compassion in Early Buddhism*. Bodhi Leaves 141. Kandy: Buddhist Publication Society.

———. 2000. "My Unfinished Business with the Buddha." In *Buddhists Talk about Jesus, Christians Talk about the Buddha*, ed. by R. Gross; T. Muck, 89–94. New York: Continuum.

———. 2006. *Theravāda Buddhism and the British Encounter: Religious, Missionary and Colonial Experience in Nineteenth-Century Sri Lanka*. London: Routledge.

———. 2021. "May Dialogue Change Our Understanding of Ultimate Reality? A Case Study of Lynn de Silva, Aloysius Pieris and One of Their Pupils." In *A Visionary Approach: Lynn A. de Silva and the Prospects of Buddhist-Christian Encounter*, ed. by E. Harris; P. Schmidt-Leukel, 193–215. St. Ottilien: EOS Editions.

Harris, Elizabeth; Schmidt-Leukel, Perry (eds.), 2021. *A Visionary Approach: Lynn A. de Silva and the Prospects of Buddhist-Christian Encounter*. St. Ottilien: EOS Editions.

Harris, Ian, 1995. "Buddhist Environmental Ethics and Detraditionalization: The Case of EcoBuddhism." *Religion* 25, 199–211.

———. 2000. "Buddhism and Ecology." In *Contemporary Buddhist Ethics*, ed. by D. Keown, 113–35. London: RoutledgeCurzon.

Hartmann, Heiko, 2011. "Die geblendete Welt: Zur Übertragung und Auslegung der Blindenheilung (Joh 9) im Evangelienbuch Otfrids von Weißenburg." *Mediaevistik* 24, 15–36.

Harvey, Peter, 1995. *The Selfless Mind: Personality, Consciousness and Nirvāṇa in Early Buddhism*. London: RoutledgeCurzon.

———. 2000. *An Introduction to Buddhist Ethics: Foundations, Values and Issues*, Cambridge: Cambridge University Press.

———. 2019. *Buddhism and Monotheism*. Cambridge: Cambridge University Press.

Hasenhüttl, Gotthold, 1979. *Kritische Dogmatik*. Graz: Styria Verlag.

Haußig, Hans-Michael, 1999. *Der Religionsbegriff in den Religionen. Studien zum Selbst- und Religionsverständnis in Hinduismus, Buddhismus, Judentum und Islam*. Berlin: Philo Verlag.

Hazra, Kanai Lal, 1995. *The Rise and Decline of Buddhism in India*. New Delhi: Munshiram Manoharial.

Hedges, Paul, 2010. *Controversies in Interreligious Dialogue and the Theology of Religions*. London: SCM Press.

Heiler, Friedrich, [1919] 1921. *Das Gebet. Eine religionsgeschichtliche und religionspsychologische Untersuchung*. 3rd ed. München: Ernst Reinhardt Verlag.

Heim, S. Mark, 2003. "The Depth of the Riches: Trinity and Religious Ends." In *Theology and the Religions: A Dialogue*, ed. by V. Mortensen, 387–402. Grand Rapids: Eerdmans.

Heyer, Friedrich, 1977. "Orthodoxe Theologie." In *Konfessionskunde*, ed. by F. Heyer, 132–201. Berlin: De Gruyter.

Hick, John H., 1988. *Problems of Religious Pluralism*. Reprint. Basingstoke: Macmillan.

———. 1989. *An Interpretation of Religion: Human Responses to the Transcendent*. Basingstoke: MacMillan.

———. [1976] 1990. *Death and Eternal Life*. Basingstoke: Macmillan.

———. 1993. *Disputed Questions in Theology and Philosophy of Religion*. Basingstoke: Macmillan.

———. 1995. *The Rainbow of Faiths: Critical Dialogues on Religious Pluralism*. London: SCM Press.

———. 1999. *The Fifth Dimension: An Exploration of the Spiritual Realm*. Oxford: Oneworld.

———. 2004. *An Interpretation of Religion: Human Responses to the Transcendent*. 2nd ed. Basingstoke: Palgrave Macmillan.

———. 2006. *The New Frontier of Religion and Science: Religious Experience, Neuroscience and the Transcendent*. Basingstoke: Palgrave Macmillan.

———. 2010. *Between Faith and Doubt: Dialogues on Religion and Reason*. Basingstoke: Palgrave Macmillan.

Hirota, Dennis (ed.), 1997. *The Collected Works of Shinran*. Volume 1: *The Writings*. Trans., with intro., glossaries, and reading aids by Denis Hirota (head translator); Hisao Inagaki; Michio Tokunaga; Ryunshin Uryuzu. Kyoto: Jōdo Shinshū Hongwanji-ha.

Hock, Klaus, 2006. *Einführung in die Religionswissenschaft*. 2nd rev. ed. Darmstadt: Wissenschaftliche Buchgesellschaft.

Hoheisel, Karl, 1984/85. "Das frühe Christentum und die Seelenwanderung." *Jahrbuch für Antike und Christentum* 27/28, 24–46.

Holenstein, Elmar, 1985. *Menschliches Selbstverständnis. Ichbewußtsein—Intersubjektive Verantwortung—Interkulturelle Verständigung*. Frankfurt a.M.: Suhrkamp.

———. 2003. "A Dozen Rules of Thumb for Avoiding Intercultural Misunderstandings." *Polylog*. https://them.polylog.org/4/ahe-en.htm.

Hubbard, Jamie; Swanson, Paul L., 1997. *Pruning the Bodhi Tree: The Storm over Critical Buddhism*. Honolulu: University of Hawai'i Press.

Hübner, Reinhard M., 1996. "Εἰς θεὸς 'Ιησοῦς Χριστός:. Zum christlichen Gottesglauben im 2. Jahrhundert—ein Versuch." *Münchener Theologische Zeitschrift* 47, 325–44.

Hühn, Helmuth, 2001. "Verblendung; Verblendungszusammenhang." In *Historisches Wörterbuch der Philosophie*, ed. by J. Ritter; K. Gründer; G. Gabriel. Basel: Schwabe Verlag. DOI: 10.24894/HWPh.4538.

Hume, David, 1748 [1777]. *An Enquiry concerning Human Understanding*. https://davidhume.org/texts/e/.

———. 1757 [1777]. *The Natural History of Religion*. https://davidhume.org/texts/n/.

———. 1779. *Dialogues concerning Natural Religion*. https://davidhume.org/texts/d/.

Hutchison, John A., 1991. *Paths of Faith*. 4th ed. Boston: McGraw-Hill.

Hwang, Soonil, 2006. *Metaphor and Literalism in Buddhism: The Doctrinal History of Nirvana*. London: Routledge.

Ingram, Paul O., 1988. *The Modern Buddhist-Christian Dialogue: Two Universalistic Religions in Transformation.* Lewiston, ME: Edwin Mellen Press.

———. 2009. *The Process of Buddhist-Christian Dialogue.* Eugene, OR: Cascade Books.

Ireland, John D. (trans.), 1997. *The Udāna. Inspired Utterances of the Buddha & the Itivuttaka: The Buddha's Sayings.* Translated from the Pāli. Kandy: Buddhist Publication Society.

Izutsu, Toshihiko, 2008. *The Structure of Oriental Philosophy: Collected Papers of the Eranos Conference.* Vol. 2. Tokyo: Keio University Press.

Jackson, Carl T., 1968. "The Meeting of East and West: The Case of Paul Carus." In *Journal of the History of Ideas* 29, 73–92.

Jackson, Roger, 1999. "Atheology and Buddhalogy in Dharmakīrti' Pramāṇavārttika." *Faith and Philosophy* 16:4, 472–505.

Jackson, William J., 2004. *Heaven's Fractal Net: Retrieving Lost Visions in the Humanities.* Bloomington: Indiana University Press.

James, William, (1902) 1990. *The Varieties of Religious Experience: A Study in Human Nature.* New York: Vintage Books.

Jenson, Matt, 2006. *The Gravity of Sin: Augustine, Luther and Barth on homo incurvatus in se.* London: T&T Clark.

Johnston, Gilbert L., 2007. "The Theme of Subjectivity in Kiyozawa Manshi's *Seishinshugi.*" In *Shin Buddhism: Historical, Textual, and Interpretative Studies*, ed. by R. K. Payne, 303–19. Berkeley, CA: Institute of Buddhist Studies and Numata Center for Buddhist Translation and Research.

Jones, Christopher Victor, 2021. *The Buddhist Self: On Tathāgatagarbha and Ātman.* Honolulu: University of Hawai'i Press.

Junginger, Horst, 2021. "Etsi deus non daretur: die Säkularität von Religionswissenschaft." In *Religion in Culture—Culture in Religion: Burkhard Gladigow's Contribution to Shifting Paradigms in the Study of Religion*, ed. by C. Auffarth; A. Grieser; A. Koch, 119–39. Tübingen: Tübingen University Press.

Kaelber, Walter O., 2007. "Āśrama." In *The Hindu World*, ed. by S. Mittal; G. Thursby, 383–403. New York: Routledge.

Kak, Subhash, 2008–2009. "The Great Goddess Lalitā and the Śrī Cakra." *Brahmavidyā: The Adyar Library Bulletin* 72–73, 155–72. http://ikashmir.net/subhashkak/docs/SriChakra.pdf.

Karunadasa, Yakupitiyage, 2007. "The Unanswered Questions: Why Were They Unanswered? A Re-examination of the Textual Data." *Pacific World* 3rd Series 9, 3–31.

Kaza, Stephanie; Kraft, Kenneth (eds.), 2000. *Dharma Rain: Sources of Buddhist Environmentalism.* Boulder, CO: Shambhala.

Keel, Hee-Sung, 1995. *Understanding Shinran: A Dialogical Approach.* Freemont: Asia Humanities Press.

———. 1996. "Jesus the Bodhisattva: Christology from a Buddhist Perspective." *Buddhist Christian Studies* 16, 169–85.

Keenan, John P., 1989. *The Meaning of Christ: A Mahāyāna Theology*. Maryknoll, NY: Orbis Books.
———. 1995. *The Gospel of Mark: A Mahāyāna Reading*. Eugene, OR: Wipf & Stock.
———. 2003. *The Summary of the Great Vehicle by Bodhisattva Asaṅga*. Translated from the Chinese of Paramārtha by John P. Keenan. Rev. 2nd ed. Berkeley, CA: Numata Center for Buddhist Translation and Research.
———. 2005. *The Wisdom of James: Parallels with Mahāyāna Buddhism*. New York: Newman Press.
———. 2015. *The Emptied Christ of Philippians: Mahāyāna Meditations*, Eugene, OR: Wipf & Stock.
Keenan, John P.; Keenan, Linda K., 2011. *I Am / No Self. A Christian Commentary on the Heart* Sūtra, Leuven: Peeters; Grand Rapids: Eerdmans.
Kehl-Bodrogi, Krisztina, 1988. *Die Kızılbaş-Aleviten. Untersuchungen über eine esoterische Glaubensgemeinschaft in Anatolien*. Berlin: Klaus Schwarz Verlag.
Kelly, J. N. D. 1977. *Early Christian Doctrines*. 5th rev. ed. London: Adam & Charles Black.
Kenntner, Karl, 1939. *Die Wandlungen des Lebensbegriffs im Urbuddhismus und im Urchristentum*. Bonn: Köllen Verlag.
Kenkel, N. C.; Walker, D. J., 1996. "Fractals in the Biological Sciences." *Coenoses* 11:2, 77–100.
Kern, Hendrik, 1884. *Saddharma-Puṇḍarīka or The Lotus of the True Law*. SBE 21. Oxford: Clarendon Press.
Kern, Iso, 1984/5. "Matteo Riccis Verhältnis zum Buddhismus." *Monumenta Serica* 36, 65–126.
———. 2001. "Buddhist Perceptions of Jesus and Christianity in the Early Buddhist-Christian Controversies in China during the 17th Century." In *Buddhist Perceptions of Jesus*, ed. by P. Schmidt-Leukel with J. Götz; G. Köberlin, 32–41. St. Ottilien: EOS-Editions.
Khorchide, Mouhanad; von Stosch, Klaus (eds.), 2016. *Streit um Jesus. Muslimische und christliche Annäherungen*. Paderborn: Ferdinand Schöningh.
———. 2018. *Der andere Prophet. Jesus im Koran*. Freiburg i.Br.: Herder.
Kiblinger, Kristin Beise, 2010. "Relating Theology of Religions and Comparative Theology." In *The New Comparative Theology: Interreligious Insights from the Next Generation*, ed. by F. X. Clooney, 21–42. London: T&T Clark International.
Kiefer, Jörn, 2017. "Sünder / Sünder (AT)." *Wissenschaftliches Bibellexikon im Internet*. http://www.bibelwissenschaft.de/stichwort/31970/.
Kigoshi, Yasushi, 2004. "Shin Buddhist Doctrinal Studies and Modernization: A Dispute over the Understanding of the Pure Land." In *Buddhismus und Christentum vor der Herausforderung der Säkularisierung*, ed. by H.-M. Barth; K. Kadowaki; E. Minoura; M. Pye, 89–101. Schenefeld: EB-Verlag.
King, Sallie, 2003. "The Mommy and the Yogi." In *Beside Still Waters: Jews,*

Christians, and the Way of the Buddha, ed. by H. Kasimow; J. P. Keenan; L. Klepinger Keenan, 157–70, 261f. Boston: Wisdom Publications.

———. 2009. *Socially Engaged Buddhism.* Honolulu: University of Hawai'i Press.

King, Winston, 1963. *Buddhism and Christianity: Some Bridges of Understanding.* London: Allen and Unwin.

Kiyozawa, Manshi, 2014. *December Fan: The Buddhist Essays of Manshi Kiyozawa.* 2nd ed. Los Angeles: Shinshu Center of America.

Klimkeit, Hans-Joachim, 1986. *Die Begegnung von Christentum, Gnosis und Buddhismus an der Seidenstraße.* Oplande: Westdeutscher Verlag.

Knitter, Paul, 1997. "Five Theses on the Uniqueness of Jesus." In *The Uniqueness of Jesus: A Dialogue with Paul F. Knitter*, ed. by L. Swidler; P. Mojzes, 3–16. Maryknoll, NY: Orbis Books.

———. 2009. *Without Buddha I Could Not Be a Christian.* Oxford: Oneworld.

Knitter, Paul; Schmidt-Leukel, Perry, 2020. "Seeking Buddhist-Christian Understanding: Friends in Dialogue." *Buddhist-Christian Studies* 41, 338–50.

Koch, Klaus; Schmidt, Johann Michael (eds.), 1982. *Apokalyptik.* Darmstadt: Wissenschaftliche Buchgesellschaft.

Kreinath, Jens, 2012. "Naven, Moebius Strip, and Random Fractal Dynamics: Reframing Bateson's Play Frame." *Journal of Ritual Studies* 26:2, 39–64.

———. 2020. "Playing with Frames of Reference in Veneration Rituals: Fractal Dynamics in Encounters with a Muslim Saint." *Anthropological Theory* 20:2, 221–50.

Kreiner, Armin, 2019. "Gottes Güte und das Leid in der Welt." In *Handbuch für Analytische Theologie*, ed. by G. Gasser; L. Jaskolla; T. Schärtl, 429–52. Münster: Aschendorff.

Kretser, Bryan de, 1954. *Man in Buddhism and Christianity.* Calcutta: Y.M.C.A. Publishing House.

Krishna, Daya, 1996. *The Problematic and Conceptual Structure of Classical Indian Thought about Man, Society and Polity.* Delhi: Oxford University Press.

Kubo, Tsugunari; Yuyama, Akira, 2007. *The Lotus Sutra: Translated from the Chinese of Kumārajīva.* BDK English Tripiṭaka Series. Berkeley, CA: Numata Center for Buddhist Translation and Research.

Küng, Hans, 1994. *Das Christentum. Wesen und Geschichte.* 2nd ed. München: Piper.

Küng, Hans; Ching, Julia, 1989. *Christianity and Chinese Religions.* New York: Doubleday.

Küng, Hans; Ess, Josef van; Stietencron, Heinrich von; Bechert, Heinz, 1984. *Christentum und Weltreligionen. Hinführung zum Dialog mit Islam, Hinduismus und Buddhismus.* München: Piper.

———. 1986. *Christianity and the World Religions: Paths of Dialogue with Islam, Hinduism, and Buddhism.* London: SCM Press.

Lai, Pan-chiu, 2006a. "Eschatological Faith in the Coming Kingdom, East and

West: Mao Tzu-yüan and the Four Pure Lands." *Ching Feng* New Series 7:1–2, 11–29.

———. 2006b. "The Kingdom of God and the Pure Land: A Dialogical Study of Eschatology and Praxis." *Ching Feng* New Series 7:1–2, 183–210.

———. 2009. "Buddhist-Christian Studies in a Scientific Age: A Case Study of Burnett Hillman Streeter (1874–1937)." *Studies in Interreligious Dialogue* 19:1, 34–49.

Lai, Pan-chiu; So, Yuen-tai, 2003. "Zhang Chunyi's Chinese Buddhist-Christian Pneumatology." *Ching Feng* New Series 4:1, 51–77.

———. 2007. "Mahāyāna Interpretation of Christianity: A Case Study of Zhang Chunyi (1871–1955)." *Journal of Buddhist-Christian Studies* 27, 67–87.

Lai, Whalen, 1982. "Sinitic Speculations on Buddha-Nature: The Nirvāṇa School (420–589)." *Philosophy East and West* 32:2, 135–49.

———. 1992. "Chinese Buddhist and Christian Charities: A Comparative History." *Buddhist-Christian Studies* 12, 5–33.

———. 2010. "Political Authority: The Two Wheels of the Dharma." *Buddhist-Christian Studies* 30, 171–86.

Lampe, G. W. H., 1977. *God as Spirit: The Bampton Lectures, 1976*. Oxford: Clarendon Press.

Lanczkowski, Günter, 1978. *Einführung in die Religionsphänomenologie*. Darmstadt: Wissenschaftlche Buchgesellschaft.

———. 1980. *Einführung in die Religionswissenschaft*. Darmstadt: Wissenschaftliche Buchgesellschaft.

Lande, Aasulv (ed.), 2002. "Special Issue on Christian Perceptions of the Buddha." *Swedish Missiological Themes (SMT)* 90:1.

Lang, Bernhard; McDannell, Colleen, 1990. *Der Himmel. Eine Kulturgeschichte des ewigen Lebens*. Frankfurt a.M.: Suhrkamp.

———. 2001. *Heaven. A History*. 2nd ed. New Haven, CT: Yale University Press. [1st ed., 1988.]

Langer-Kaneko, Christiane, 1986. *Das Reine Land. Zur Begegnung von Amida-Buddhismus und Christentum*. Leiden: E. J. Brill.

Lefebure, Leo, 1993. *The Buddha and the Christ: Explorations in Buddhist and Christian Dialogue*. Maryknoll, NY: Orbis Books.

Lefebure, Leo; Feldmeier, Peter, 2011. *The Path of Wisdom: A Christian Commentary on the* Dhammapada. Leuven: Peeters; Grand Rapids: Eerdmans.

Le Goff, Jacques, 1990. *The Birth of Purgatory*. Aldershot: Scholar Press.

Lehmann, Karl; Pannenberg, Wolfhart (eds.), 1988. *Lehrverurteilungen—kirchentrennend? I. Rechtfertigung, Sakramente und Amt im Zeitalter der Reformation und heute*. 3rd ed. Freiburg i. Br.: Herder; Göttingen: Vandenhoeck & Ruprecht.

Lehtipuu, Outi, 2015. *Debates over the Resurrection of the Dead: Constructing Early Christian Identity*. Oxford: Oxford University Press.

Leirvik, Oddbjørn, 2015. *Interreligious Studies: A Relational Approach to Religious Activism and the Study of Religion*. London: Bloomsbury Academic.

Lengsfeld, Peter (ed.), 2005. *Mystik—Spiritualität der Zukunft. Erfahrung des Ewigen. Festschrift P. Willigis Jäger, OSB.* Freiburg i. Bf.: Herder.

Leppin, Volker, 2007. *Die christliche Mystik.* München: C. H. Beck.

Lerner, Robert E., 1971. "The Image of Mixed Liquids in Late Medieval Mystical Thought." *Church History* 40, 397–411.

Liu, Ming-Wood, 1984. "The Problem of the *Icchantiha* in the Mahāyāna *Mahāparinirvāṇa Sūtra.*" *The Journal of the International Association of Buddhist Studies* 7:1, 57–81.

Löhr, Gebhard (ed.), 2000. *Die Identität der Religionswissenschaft. Beiträge zum Verständnis einer unbekannten Disziplin.* Frankfurt a.M.: Peter Land.

Löhr, Winrich, 2007. "Exkurs: Das Verhältnis zwischen Pelagius und Augustin und das theologische Anliegen des Pelagius." In *Augustin Handbuch*, ed. by Volker Henning Drecoll, 190–97. Tübingen: Mohr Siebeck.

Loichinger, Alexander; Kreiner, Armin (eds.), 2010. *Theodizee in den Weltreligionen. Ein Studienbuch.* Paderborn: Schöningh.

Lopez, Donald S.; Rockefeller, Steven C. (eds.), 1987. *The Christ and the Bodhisattva.* Albany, NY: SUNY Press.

Lovin, Robin W., 1992. "Ethics, Wealth, and Eschatology: Buddhist and Christian Strategies for Change." In *Ethics, Wealth, and Salvation: A Study in Buddhist Social Ethics*, ed. by R. F. Sizemore; D. K. Swearer, 190–208, 271f. Columbia: University of South Carolina Press.

Luz, Ulrich; Michaels, Axel, 2002. *Jesus oder Buddha. Leben und Lehre im Vergleich.* München: C. H. Beck.

———. 2006. *Encountering Jesus and Buddha: Their Lives and Teachings.* Trans. by Linda M. Maloney. Minneapolis: Fortress Press.

Magliola, Robert, 2014. *Facing Up to Real Doctrinal Difference.* Kettering: Angelico Press.

Majrashi, A.; Bin Bakar, B.; Moneruzzaman Khandaker, M.; Nasrulhaq Boyce, A.; Muniandy, S. V., 2013. "Fractal Analysis of Rhizome Growth Patterns of *Scirpus grossus* L. on Peat and Paddy Soils." *Bulgarian Journal of Agricultural Science* 19:6, 1319–26.

Maharaj, Ayon, 2019. "'Infinite Paths, Infinite Doctrines': Perry Schmidt-Leukel's Fractal Approach to Religious Diversity from the Standpoint of the Ramakrishna-Vivekananda Tradition." In *New Paths for Interreligious Theology: Perry Schmidt-Leukel's Fractal Interpretation of Religious Diversity*, ed. by A. Race; P. Knitter, 100–114. Maryknoll, NY: Orbis Books.

Makransky, John, 2005. "Buddhist Analogues of Sin and Grace: A Dialogue with Augustine." *Studies in Interreligious Dialogue* 15:1, 5–15.

Malinar, Angelika, 2007. *The Bhagavadgītā: Doctrines and Contexts.* Cambridge: Cambridge University Press.

Mall, Ram Adhar, 2000. *Intercultural Philosophy.* Lanham, MD: Rowman & Littlefield.

Mandelbrot, Benoît B., 1983. *The Fractal Geometry of Nature.* Updated and augmented. New York: W. H. Freeman and Company. [First ed. 1977.]

Mann, Ulrich (ed.), 1973. *Theologie und Religionswissenschaft. Der gegenwärtige Stand ihrer Forschungsergebnisse und Aufgaben im Hinblick auf ihr gegenseitiges Verhältnis.* Darmstadt: Wissenschaftliche Buchgesellschaft.

Masefield, Peter, 1986. *Divine Revelation in Pali Buddhism.* London: Allen & Unwin.

Masutani, Fumio. 1967. *A Comparative Study of Buddhism and Christianity.* 8th ed. Tokyo: Young East Association.

Masuzawa, Tomoko, 2003. "Our Master's Voice: F. Max Müller after a Hundred Years of Solitude." *Method & Theory in the Study of Religion* 15:4, 305–28.

———. 2005. *The Invention of World Religions: Or, How European Universalism Was Preserved in the Language of Pluralism.* Chicago: University of Chicago Press.

Matsunaga, Daigan; Matsunaga, Alicia, 1972. *The Buddhist Concept of Hell.* New York: Philosophical Library.

May, John D'Arcy, 2014. *Buddhologie und Christologie. Unterwegs zu einer kollaborativen Theologie.* Innsbruck: Tyrolia Verlag.

———. 2019. *Pluralism and Peace: The Religions in Global Civil Society.* Bayswater, Victoria: Coventry Press.

———. 2020. "From Comparative to Interreligious Theology: Perry Schmidt-Leukel's 'Fractal' Version of Pluralism." *Journal of Religious History* 44:3, 376–79.

McCutcheon, Russell T., 1997. *Manufacturing Religion.* Oxford: Oxford University Press.

——— (ed.), 1999. *The Insider/Outsider Problem in the Study of Religion: A Reader.* London: Continuum International Publishing.

McDannell, Colleen; Lang, Bernhard, 2001. *Heaven: A History.* 2nd ed. New Haven, CT: Yale University Press.

McGinn, Bernard, 2016. "Love, Knowledge and Unio mystica in the Western Christian Tradition." In *Mystical Union in Judaism, Christianity and Islam: An Ecumenical Dialogue*, ed. by M. Idel; B. McGinn, 59–86. London: Bloomsbury Academic.

McLaughlin, Robert E., 2004. "Apocalypticism and Thomas Müntzer." *Archiv für Reformationsgeschichte* 95, 98–131.

Mechthild of Magdeburg, 1998. *The Flowing Light of the Godhead.* Trans. and intro. by Frank Tobin. New York: Paulist Press.

Meier-Staubach, Christel, 2003. "Die Quadratur des Kreises." *Die Bildwelt der Diagramme Joachims von Fiore*, ed. by Alexander Patschovsky, 23–53. Ostfildern: Jan Thorbecke Verlag.

Mensching, Gustav, 1978. *Buddha und Christus—ein Vergleich.* Stuttgart: Deutsche Verlags-Anstalt.

Mercadante, Linda, 2020. "Theology without Walls: Is a Theology for SNBRs Possible?" In *Theology without Walls: The Transreligious Imperative*, ed. by J. L. Martin, 189–200. London: Routledge.

Metzner, Rainer, 2000. *Das Verständnis der Sünde im Johannesevangelium*. Tübingen: Mohr-Siebeck.

Minois, Georges, 2000. *Hölle. Kleine Kulturgeschichte der Unterwelt*. Freiburg i.Br.: Herder.

Mochizuki, Shinkō, 2016. *Pure Land Buddhism in China: A Doctrinal History*. Volume 1: *Translation*, ed. by R. K. Payne; N. E. F. Quli. Moraga: Institute of Buddhist Studies and BDK America.

Mommaers, Paul; Van Bragt, Jan, 1995. *Mysticism Buddhist and Christian: Encounters with Jan van Ruusbroec*. New York: Crossroad.

Monier-Williams, Monier, 1889. *Buddhism, in Its Connection with Brāhmanism and Hindūism and in Its Contrast with Christianity*. London: John Murray.

Moyaert, Marianne, 2013. "Interreligious Dialogue." In *Understanding Interreligious Relations*, ed. by D. Cheetham; D. Pratt; D. Thomas, 193–217. Oxford: Oxford University Press.

———. 2020. "Komparative Theologie zwischen Text und Ritual." In *Gemeinsam Christsein*, ed. by R. A. Klein, 245–66. Tübingen: Mohr Siebeck.

Müller, Friedrich Max, 1868. *Chips from a German Workshop*. Vol. 1: *Essays on the Science of Religion*. 2nd ed. London: Longmans, Green, and Co.

———. 1874. *Einleitung in die vergleichende Religionswissenschaft*. Straßburg: Verlag Karl J. Trübner.

———. 2000. *Wisdom of the Buddha: The Unabridged Dhammapada*. Trans. and ed. by F. Max Müller. Mineola, NY: Dover Publications.

Nagao, Gadjin M., 1991. *Mādhyamika und Yogācāra: A Study of Mahāyāna Philosophies*. Albany, NY: SUNY Press.

Nakamura, Hajime, 1986. *Buddhism in Comparative Light*. 2nd rev. ed. Delhi: Motilal Banarsidass.

———. 1992. *A Comparative History of Ideas*. Pbk. of 2nd rev. ed. London: Kegan Paul International.

Ñāṇamoli, Bhikkhu, 1999. *The Path of Purification (Visuddhimagga)* by Bhadantācariya Bhuddhaghosa. Trans. from the Pali. Seattle: BPS Pariyatti Editions.

Ñāṇamoli, Bhikkhu; Bodhi, Bhikkhu, 2001. *The Middle Length Discourses of the Buddha: A Translation of the Majjhima Nikāya*. 2nd ed. Boston: Wisdom Publications.

Nash, Jonathan David; Newberg, Andrew; Awasthi, Bhuvanesh, 2013. "Toward a Unifying Taxonomy and Definition for Meditation." *Frontiers in Psychology* 4, 1–18.

Nattier, Jan, 1988. "The Meaning of the Maitreya Myth: A Typological Analysis." In *Maitreya, the Future Buddha*, ed. by A. Sponberg; H. Hardacre, 23–47. Cambridge: Cambridge University Press.

———. 2003. *A Few Good Men: The Bodhisattva Path according to* The Inquiry or Ugra (Ugraparipṛcchā). Honolulu: University of Hawai'i Press.

Neumaier, Eva K., 2016. "Buddhist Forms of Belief in Creation." In *Buddhism, Christianity and the Question of Creation*, ed. by P. Schmidt-Leukel, 47–60. 2nd ed. London: Routledge.

Neumaier-Dargyay, Eva K., 1992. *The Sovereign All-Creating Mind: The Motherly Buddha*. A Translation of the *Kun byed rgyal po'i mdo*. Albany, NY: SUNY Press.
Neville, Robert Cummings (ed.), 2001a. *The Human Condition: A Volume in the Comparative Religious Ideas Project*. Albany: State University of New York Press.
——— (ed.), 2001b. *Ultimate Realities: A Volume in the Comparative Religious Ideas Project*. Albany: State University of New York Press.
——— (ed.), 2001c. *Religious Truth: A Volume in the Comparative Religious Ideas Project*. Albany: State University of New York Press.
Nicholson, Hugh, 2009. "The Reunification of Theology and Comparison in the New Comparative Theology." *Journal of the American Academy of Religion* 77:3, 609–46.
Nickelsburg, George W. E., 2006. *Resurrection, Immortality, and Eternal Life in Intertestamental Judaism and Early Christianity*. Expanded ed. Cambridge, MA: Harvard University Press.
Niculescu, Mira, 2012. "I the Jew. I the Buddhist: Multi-religious Belonging as Inner Dialogue." *Crosscurrents* 62:3, 350–59.
Nishitani, Keiji, 1983. *Religion and Nothingness*. Pbk. ed. Berkeley: University of California Press.
Nisker, Wes; Gates, Barbara; Macy, Joanna, 2000. "The Third Turning of the Wheel: A Conversation with Joanna Macy." In *Dharma Rain: Sources of Buddhist Environmentalism*, ed. by S. Kaza; K. Kraft, 150–60. Boulder, CO: Shambhala.
Nitsche, Bernhard, 2017. "Formen des menschlichen Transzendenzbezuges (1. Teil): Hypothese." In *Gott—jenseits von Monismus und Theismus?*, ed. by B. Nitsche; K. von Stosch; M. Tatari, 25–61. Paderborn: Ferdinand Schöningh.
———. 2018a. "Formen des menschlichen Transzendenzbezuges (2. Teil): Phänomene und Reflexionen." In *Dimensionen des Menschseins—Wege der Transzendenz?*, ed. by B. Nitsche; F. Baab, 31–87. Paderborn: Ferdinand Schöningh.
———. 2018b. "Lerngewinne." In *Dimensionen des Menschseins—Wege der Transzendenz?*, ed. by B. Nitsche; F. Baab, 369–405. Paderborn: Ferdinand Schöningh.
———. 2023a. "Dimensions of Human Existence as Dimensions of the Hermeneutics of Transcendence." In *God or the Divine? Religious Transcendence beyond Monism and Theism, between Personality and Impersonality*, ed. by B. Nitsche; M. Schmücker, 5–8. Berlin: De Gruyter.
———. 2023b. "God or the Divine?" In *God or the Divine? Religious Transcendence beyond Monism and Theism, between Personality and Impersonality*, ed. by B. Nitsche; M. Schmücker, 9–40. Berlin: De Gruyter.
Notz, Klaus-Josef, 1984. *Der Buddhismus in Deutschland in seinen Selbstdarstellungen*. Frankfurt a.M.: Peter-Lang Verlag.
Obirek, Stanislaw, 2020. "Review: New Paths for Interreligious Theology. Eds.

Alan Race and Paul Knitter." *Interreligious Insight: A Journal of Dialogue and Engagement* 18:2, 100–102.

O'Grady, John, 2010. *Beyond Immanence: A Buddhological Observing of Grace.* Trinity College Dublin Irish School of Economics (unpublished dissertation).

Oguro, Tatsuo, 1985. *Der Rettungsgedanke bei Shinran und Luther.* Hildesheim: Georg Olms Verlag.

Ohlig, Karl-Heinz 1999. *Ein Gott in drei Personen? Vom Vater Jesu zum "Mysterium" der Trinität.* Mainz: Matthias-Grünewald Verlag; Luzern: Edition Exodus.

Ohnuma, Reiko, 2007. *Head, Eyes, Flesh, and Blood: Giving Away the Body in Indian Buddhist Literature.* New York: Columbia University Press.

Okochi, Ryogi; Otte, Klaus, 1979. *Tan-ni-sho. Die Gunst des Reinen Landes. Begegnung zwischen Buddhismus und Christentum.* Bern: Orgio Verlag.

Orzech, Charles D., 1998. *Politics and Transcendent Wisdom: The "Scripture for Humane Kings" in the Creation of Chinese Buddhism.* University Park: Pennsylvania State University Press.

Otto, Rudolf, 1917. *Siddhānta des Rāmānuja. Texte zur indischen Gottesmystik II.* Jena: Eugen Diederichs.

———. 1923. *Vischnu-Nārāyana. Texte zur indischen Gottesmystik.* Jena: Eugen Diederichs.

———. 1936. *The Idea of the Holy.* Trans. by John W. Harvey. Oxford: Oxford University Press.

———. 1987. *Das Heilige. Über das Irrationale in der Idee des Göttlichen und sein Verhältnis zum Rationalen.* München: C. H. Beck [first edition 1917].

Overmyer, Daniel L., 1976. *Folk Buddhist Religion: Dissenting Sects in Late Traditional China.* Cambridge, MA: Harvard University Press.

———. 1988. "Messenger, Savior, and Revolutionary: Maitreya in Chinese Popular Religious Literature of the Sixteenth and Seventeenth Centuries." In *Maitreya, the Future Buddha*, ed. by A. Sponberg; H. Hardacre, 110–34. Cambridge: Cambridge University Press.

Paden, William E., 2000. "Patterns of a New Comparativism." In *A Magic Still Dwells: Comparative Religion in the Postmodern Age,* ed. by K. C. Patton; B. C. Ray, 182–92. Berkeley: University of California Press.

Pagels, Elaine, 1996. "Introduction." In Thich Nhat Hanh, *Living Buddha, Living Christ.* London: Rider, xix–xxvii.

Palihawadana; Mahinda, 1978. "Is There a Theravada Buddhist Idea of Grace?" In *Christian Faith in a Religiously Plural World*, ed. by D. G. Dawe; J. B. Carman. Maryknoll, NY: Orbis Books, 181–95.

Pande, Govind Chandra, 1999. *Studies in the Origins of Buddhism.* Reprint of the 4th ed. Delhi: Motilal Banarsidass.

Pandi, Moti Lal, 1993. *Being as Becoming: Studies in Early Buddhism.* New Delhi: Intercultural Publications.

Panikkar, Raimundo, 1981. *The Unknown Christ of Hinduism.* Completely rev. and enlarged ed. Maryknoll, NY: Orbis Books.

───── , 1989. *Den Mönch in sich entdecken.* München: Kösel. [The English version is now found in Raimon Panikkar, *Mysticism and Spirituality: Spirituality, the Way of Life,* ed. by Milena Carrara Pavan (Opera Omnia, vol. I.2.). Maryknoll, NY: Orbis Books, 2014.]

Pannenberg, Wolfhart, 1987. *Wissenschaftstheorie und Theologie.* Frankfurt a.M.: Suhrkamp.

─────. 1991. *Systematische Theologie.* Vol. 2. Göttingen: Vandenhoeck & Ruprecht.

─────. 1994. *Systematic Theology.* Vol. 2. Grand Rapids: Eerdmans.

Patel, Eboo; Peace, Jennifer Howe; Silverman, Noah J., (eds.), 2018. *Interreligious/Interfaith Studies: Defining a New Field.* Boston: Beacon Press.

Patton, Kimberley C.; Ray, Benjamin C. (eds.), 2000. *A Magic Still Dwells: Comparative Religion in the Postmodern Age.* Berkeley: University of California Press.

Pérez-Remón, Joaquín, 1980. *Self and Non-self in Early Buddhism.* The Hague: Mouton Publishers.

Pieris, Aloysius, 1988. *Love Meets Wisdom: A Christian Experience of Buddhism.* Maryknoll, NY: Orbis Books.

Pitre, Brant James, 2001. "Blessing the Barren and Warning the Fecund: Jesus' Message for Women concerning Pregnancy and Childbirth." *Journal for the Study of the New Testament* 81, 59–80.

Pittman, Don A., 2001. *Toward a Modern Chinese Buddhism: Taixu's Reforms.* Honolulu: University of Hawai'i Press.

Plöger, Otto, 1978. "Tod und Jenseits im Alten Testament." In *Tod und Jenseits im Glauben der Völker*, ed. by J. Klimkeit, 77–85. Wiesbaden: Harrassowitz.

Pollack, Detlef; Rosta, Gergely, 2015. *Religion in der Moderne. Ein internationaler Vergleich.* Frankfurt: Campus Verlag.

Pruden, Leo M., 1991. *Abhidharmakośabhāṣyam of Vasubandhu.* Vol. 1. Berkeley, CA: Asia Humanities Press.

Queen, Christopher S., 1996. "Introduction: The Shapes and Sources of Engaged Buddhism." In *Engaged Buddhism: Buddhist Liberation Movements in Asia*, ed. by C. S. Queen; S. B. King, 1–44. Albany: State University Press of New York.

Queen, Christopher S.; King, Sallie B. (eds.), 1996. *Engaged Buddhism: Buddhist Liberation Movements in Asia.* Albany: State University Press of New York.

Queen, Christopher S.; Prebish, Charles; Keown, Damien (eds.), 2003. *Action Dharma: New Studies in Engaged Buddhism.* London: RoutledgeCurzon.

Quint, Josef (ed.), 1979. *Meister Eckehart, Deutsche Predigten und Traktate.* Ed. and trans. by Josef Quint. Zürich: Diogenes.

Race, Alan, 2019. "The Fractal Proposal and Its Place in the Christian Theology of Religions." In *New Paths for Interreligious Theology: Perry Schmidt-Leukel's Fractal Interpretation of Religious Diversity*, ed. by A. Race; P. Knitter, 145–61. Maryknoll, NY: Orbis Books.

Race, Alan; Knitter, Paul (eds.), 2019. *New Paths for Interreligious Theology: Perry Schmidt-Leukel's Fractal Interpretation of Religious Diversity*. Maryknoll, NY: Orbis Books.

Radaj, Dieter, 2011. *Buddhisten denken anders. Schulen und Denkwege des traditionellen und neuzeitlichen Buddhismus*. München: Iudicium.

Raddatz, Alfred, 2006. "Christliche Kunst—auch ein Spiegel des Verhältnisses von Christen und Juden." https://www.christenundjuden.org/index_files/96 7d00bda0c33e8061c8b4c008b8d16a-131.html.

Rahner, Karl, 1964. "Das Christentum und die nichtchristlichen Religionen." In *Schriften zur Theologie*, vol. 5, 136–58. Zürich: Benziger Verlag.

———. 1977. *Grundkurs des Glaubens*. 9th ed. Freiburg i. Br.: Herder.

———. 1978. *Foundations of Christian Faith*. Trans. by Wiliam v. Dych. New York: Seabury Press.

———. 1982. "Das christliche Verständnis der Erlösung." In *Erlösung in Christentum und Buddhismus*, ed. by A. Bsteh, 112–27. Mödling: St. Gabriel.

———. 2001. "Christianity and the Non-Christian Religions." In *Christianity and Other Religions: Selected Readings*. Rev. ed., ed. by John Hick; Brian Hebblethwaite, 19–38. Oxford: Oneworld.

Rahula, Walpola, 1974. *What the Buddha Taught*. 2nd ed. New York: Grove Press.

Religionswissenschaft–Theologie. Erkundungen einer strittigen Zuordnung (Themenheft). *Berliner Theologische Zeitschrift* 29:1.

Rhys Davids, T. W., 1890. *The Questions of King Milinda*, Part 1. SBE 35. Oxford: Clarendon Press.

———. 1894. *The Questions of King Milinda*, Part 2. SBE 36. Oxford: Clarendon Press.

Rhys Davids, T. W.; Oldenberg, H., 1881. *Vinaya Texts: Part I—The Pātimokkha, The Mahāvagga I–IV*. SBE 13. Oxford: Clarendon Press.

Riches, John, 2008. *Galatians through the Centuries*. Oxford: Blackwell.

Ritzinger, Justin R., 2013. "If We Build It, He Will Come: Eschatology, Hope, and the Reinvention of Maitreya in Modern China." In *Hope: A Form of Delusion? Buddhist and Christian Perspectives*, ed. by E. Harris, 207–27. St. Ottilien: EOS Editions.

Robson, James, 2012. "Sin, Sinification, Sinology: On the Notion of Sin in Buddhism and Chinese Religions." In *Sin and Sinners: Perspectives from Asian Religions*, ed. by P. Granoff; K. Shinohara, 73–92. Leiden: Brill.

Rolston, Holmes, III, 1985. *Religious Inquiry—Participation and Detachment*. New York: Philosophical Library.

Römer, Thomas, 2018. *Die Erfindung Gottes. Eine Reise zu den Quellen des Monotheismus*. Darmstadt: Wissenschaftliche Buchgesellschaft.

Rose, Kenneth, 2016. *Yoga, Meditation, and Mysticism: Contemplative Uni-*

versals and Meditative Landmarks. London: Bloomsbury Academics.

———. 2019. "Perry Schmidt-Leukel's Incarnated Prophets and Awakeners: Beyond Stalemates in the Theology of Religions and Comparative Theology." In *New Paths for Interreligious Theology: Perry Schmidt-Leukel's Fractal Interpretation of Religious Diversity*, ed. by A. Race; P. Knitter, 25–38. Maryknoll, NY: Orbis Books.

Rubenstein, Richard L., 1995. "Holocaust, Sunyata, and Holy Nothingness: An Essay in Interreligious Dialogue." In *Divine Emptiness and Historical Fullness: A Buddhist-Jewish-Christian Conversation with Masao Abe*, ed. by C. Ives, 93–112. Valley Forge, PA: Trinity Press International.

Ruh, Kurt, 2001. *Geschichte der abendländischen Mystik*. Vol. 1: *Die Grundlegung durch die Kirchenväter und die Mönchstheologie des 12. Jahrhunderts*. 2nd ed. München: C. H. Beck.

Sabbatucci, Dario, 1988. "Kultur und Religion." In *Handbuch religionswissenschaftlicher Grundbegriffe*. Vol. 1, ed. by H. Cancik; B. Gladigow; M. Laubscher, 43–58. Stuttgart: Kohlhammer.

Saler, Benson, [1993] 2000. *Conceptualizing Religion: Immanent Anthropologists, Transcendent Natives, and Unbounded Categories*. New York: Berghahn Books.

Sanders, E. P., 1995. *The Historical Figure of Jesus*. London: Penguin Books.

———. 2015. *Paul: The Apostle's Life, Letters and Thought*. Minneapolis: Fortress Press.

Sawicki, Bernard, OSB (ed.), 2020. *Thomas Merton: Prophecy and Renewal*. Acts of the International Symposium. Rome, June 12–15, 2018. St. Ottilien: EOS Editions.

Schalk, Peter; Deeg, Max; Freiberger, Oliver; Kleine, Christoph; Nahl, Astrid van (eds.), 2013. *Religion in Asien? Studien zur Anwendbarkeit des Religionsbegriffs*. Uppsala: Uppsala Universitet.

Schleiermacher, Friedrich, 1960 [1830]. *Der christliche Glaube*. 2 vols., 7th ed. Berlin: De Gruyter.

Schlieter, Jens (ed.), 2010. *Was ist Religion? Texte von Cicero bis Luhmann*. Stuttgart: Reclam.

———. 2013. "Checking the Heavenly 'Bank Account of Karma': Cognitive Metaphors for Karma in Western Perception and Early Theravāda Buddhism." *Religion* 43, 463–86.

Schlingloff, Dieter, 1963. *Die Religion des Buddhismus*. II. *Der Heilsweg für die Welt*. Berlin: De Gruyter.

Schmidt-Leukel, Perry, 1984. *Die Bedeutung des Todes für das menschliche Selbstverständnis im Pali-Buddhismus*. St. Ottilien: EOS-Verlag.

———. 1992. *"Den Löwen brüllen hören"—Zur Hermeneutik eines christlichen Verständnisses der buddhistischen Heilsbotschaft*. Paderborn: Schöningh.

———. 1993a. "Christliche Buddhismus-Interpretation und die Gottesfrage." *Münchener Theologische Zeitschrift* 44, 349–58.

———. 1993b. "Mystische Erfahrung und logische Kritik bei Nāgārjuna. Zum

Verhältnis von meditativer, begrifflicher und existentieller Welttranszendenz im Buddhismus." In *Religiöse Erfahrung und theologische Reflexion. Festschrift für Heinrich Döring*, ed. by A. Kreiner; P. Schmidt-Leukel, 371–93. Paderborn: Bonifatius.

———. 1996. "Reinkarnation und spiritueller Fortschritt im traditionellen Buddhismus." In *Die Idee der Reinkarnation in Ost und West*, ed. by P. Schmidt-Leukel, 29–56, 205–12. München: Eugen Diederichs Verlag.

———. 1997. *Theologie der Religionen. Probleme, Optionen, Argumente.* Neuried: Ars Una.

———. 1998 (ed.). *Wer ist Buddha? Eine Gestalt und ihre Bedeutung für die Menschheit.* München: Eugen Diederichs Verlag.

———. 2001 (ed.). *Buddhist Perceptions of Jesus.* St. Ottilien: EOS Verlag.

———. 2005. *Gott ohne Grenzen. Eine christliche und pluralistische Theologie der Religionen.* Gütersloh: Gütersloher Verlagshaus.

———. 2006a. *Understanding Buddhism.* Edinburgh: Dunedin Academic Press.

———. 2006b. "The Unbridgeable Gulf? Towards a Buddhist-Christian Theology of Creation." In *Buddhism, Christianity and the Question of Creation: Karmic or Divine?* ed. by P. Schmidt-Leukel, 109–78. Aldershot: Ashgate.

———. 2012. "Der methodologische Agnostizismus und das Verhältnis der Religionswissenschaft zur wissenschaftlichen Theologie." *Berliner Theologische Zeitschrift* 29:1, 48–72.

———. 2013. "Eine Verteidigung des Synkretismus." In *Gott–Götter–Götzen. XIV. Europäischer Kongress für Theologie (11.–15. September 2011 in Zürich)*, ed. by C. Schwöbel, 728–49. Leipzig: Evangelische Verlagsanstalt.

———. 2016a. "Christ as Bodhisattva: A Case of Reciprocal Illumination." In *Interreligious Comparisons in Religious Studies and Theology: Comparison Revisited*, ed. by P. Schmidt-Leukel; A. Nehring, 204–19. London: Bloomsbury Academic.

———. 2016b. "Gotterede im Kontext interreligiöser Theologie." In *Glauben denken. Zur philosophischen Durchdringung der Gottesrede im 21. Jahrhundert*, ed. by K. Viertbauer; H. Schmidinger, 355–76. Darmstadt: Wissenschaftliche Buchgesellschaft.

———. 2016c. "Nirvāṇa as 'Unconditioned' (*asaṃskṛta*) and 'Transcendent' (*lokottara*) Reality." *The Japan Mission Journal* 70:3, 170–79.

———. 2017a. *God beyond Boundaries: A Christian and Pluralist Theology of Religions.* Münster: Waxman.

———. 2017b. *Religious Pluralism and Interreligious Theology: The Gifford Lectures—An Extended Edition.* Maryknoll, NY: Orbis Books.

———. 2018. "Zur Einheit von Transzendenz und Immanenz in Śāntidevas Bodhicaryāvatāra." In *Dimensionen des Menschseins—Wege der Transzendenz?*, ed. by B. Nitsche; F. Baab, 183–98. Paderborn: Ferdinand Schöningh.

———. 2019a. *Wahrheit in Vielfalt. Vom religiösen Pluralismus zum interreligiösen Dialog.* Gütersloh: Gütersloher Verlagshaus.

———. 2019b. *Buddha Mind—Christ Mind: A Christian Commentary on the Bodhicaryāvatāra.* Leuven: Peeters.

———. 2019c. Yi hua yi shi jie. fen xing li lun shi jiao xia de fo ye dui hua (一花一世界:分形理论视角下的佛耶对话) (= *To See a World in a Flower: A Fractal Interpretation of the Relation between Buddhism and Christianity*). Beijing: Zong jiao wen hua chu ban she (Religious Culture Publishing House).

———. 2020a. *Buddhismus verstehen. Geschichte und Ideenwelt einer ungewöhnlichen Religion*. 2nd ed. Gütersloh: Gütersloher Verlagshaus.

———. 2020b. "Interreligious Theology and Truth Seeking." In *Interreligious Studies: Dispatches from an Emerging Field*, ed. by H. Gustafson, 141–46. Waco, TX: Baylor University Press.

———. 2020c. "'Jesus, der Christus'—von der Lehrformel zur Leerformel. Eine kritische Replik auf Christian Danz." *Theologische Rundschau* 85, 393–415.

———. 2020d. "Fraktale und Ökumene. Eine Theorie religiöser Vielfalt." In *Gemeinsam Christsein. Potenziale und Ressourcen einer Theologie der Ökumene für das 21. Jahrhundert*, ed. by R. Klein, 227–43. Tübingen: Mohr-Siebeck.

———. 2020e. "Buddhistische Schöpfungsmythen und das Problem des Übels." In *In der Schöpfung Heimat finden. Asiatische Schöpfungsspiritualitäten im Dialog*, ed. by I. Ibrahim; S. G. Kochuthara; K. Vellguth, 121–34. Ostfildern: Matthias Grünewald Verlag.

———. 2020f. "Begehren und Loslassen." In *Menschliches—Allzumenschliches. Phänomene des Menschseins in den Horizonten theologischer Lebensdeutung*, ed. by M. Beintker; H.-P. Großhans, 49–63. Leipzig: Evangelische Verlagsanstalt.

———. 2020g. "Simul Bodhisattva et Icchantika: A Christian Reflection on Jinen." *The Japan Mission Journal* 74:1, 16–26.

———. 2021. "From Translation to Reciprocal Relativisation. Inter-Faith Dialogue and de Silva's Theological Development." In *A Visionary Approach: Lynn A. de Silva and the Prospects of Buddhist-Christian Encounter*, ed. by E. Harris; P. Schmidt-Leukel, 99–119. St. Ottilien: EOS Editions.

———. 2022a. "The Demonization of the Other through the Narrative of Māra's Defeat (*māravijaya*)." In *Buddhism and Its Religious Others: Historical Encounters and Representations*. Proceedings of the British Academy, ed. by C. Jones, 155–84. Oxford: Oxford University Press.

———. 2022b. "Buddhist Creation Myths and the Problem of Evil." In *Finding a Home in Creation: Asian Spiritualities of Creation in Dialogue*, ed. by I. Ibrahim; S. G. Kochuthara; K. Vellguth, 52–69. Bengaluru: Dharmaram Publications.

———. 2023. "Religious Pluralism and Critical Realism." In *John Hick's Religious Pluralism in Global Perspective*, ed. by S. Sugirtharajah, 67–89. London: Palgrave.

———. 2024. "Reciprocal Illumination and the Discovery of Fractal Patterns in Religious Diversity." *International Journal of Hindu Studies* 28:1, 49–62.

Schmidt-Leukel, Perry; Nehring, Andreas (eds.), 2016. *Interreligious Compari-*

sons in *Religious Studies and Theology: Comparison Revisited*. London: Bloomsbury Academic.

Schmithausen, Lambert, 2010. "The Early Buddhist Tradition and Ecological Ethics." In *How Much Is Enough? Buddhism, Consumerism and the Human Environment*, ed. by R. K. Payne, 171–222. Boston: Wisdom Publications.

Schneider, Mathias, 2023. *Buddhistische Interpretationen Jesu. Eine religionshistorische und theologische Studie*. Zürich: Theologischer Verlag Zürich.

Schomerus, Hilko Wiardo, 1931. *Buddha und Christus*. Halle-Saale: Buchhandlung des Waisenhauses Frankesche Stiftungen.

———. 1932. *Parallelen zum Christentum als religionsgeschichtliches und theologisches Problem*. Gütersloh: Bertelsmann.

Schopen, Gregory, 1997. *Bones, Stones, and Buddhist Monks: Collected Papers on the Archaeology, Epigraphy, and Texts of Monastic Buddhism in India*. Honolulu: University of Hawai'i Press.

Schrage, Wolfgang, 1964. "Die Stellung zur Welt bei Paulus, Epiktet und in der Apokalyptik: Ein Beitrag zu 1 Kor 7, 29–31." *Zeitschrift für Theologie und Kirche* 61:2, 125–54.

Schreiber, Stefan, 2015. *Die Anfänge der Christologie. Deutungen Jesus im Neuen Testament*. Neukirchen-Vluyn: Neukirchner Theologie.

Scott, Archibald, 1890. *Buddhism and Christianity: A Parallel and a Contrast*. Edinburgh: David Douglas.

Sebastian, C. D., 2016. *The Cloud of Nothingness: The Negative Way in Nāgārjuna and John of the Cross*. Sophia Studies in Cross-Cultural Philosophy of Traditions and Cultures 19. New Delhi: Springer India.

Seiwert, Hubert, 2020. "Theory of Religion and Historical Research: A Critical Realist Perspective on the Study of Religion as an Empirical Discipline." *Zeitschrift für Religionswissenschaft* 28:2, 207–36.

Sell, Alan P. F., 1977. "Augustine *versus* Pelagius: A Cautionary Tale of Perennial Importance." *Calvin Theological Journal* 12:2, 117–43.

Shah-Kazemi, Reza, 2010. *Common Ground between Islam and Buddhism*. Louisville, KY: Fons Vitae.

Sharf, Robert H., 2002. "On Pure Land Buddhism and Ch'an / Pure Land Syncretism in Medieval China." *T'oung Pao* 3rd Series 88:4–5, 282–331.

Sharma, Arvind, 2005. *Religious Studies and Comparative Methodology: The Case for Reciprocal Illumination*. Albany, NY: SUNY Press.

Sharpe, Eric, 1974. "The Goals of Inter-Religious Dialogue." In *Truth and Dialogue. The Relationship between World Religions*, ed. by J. Hick, 77–95. London: Sheldon Press.

Sherwin, Byron L.; Kasimow, Harold (eds.), 1999. *John Paul II and Interreligious Dialogue*. Maryknoll, NY: Orbis Books.

Shuyin; Queen, Christopher, 2016. "Exploring Engaged Buddhism with Professor Christopher Queen." *Global Buddhistdoor*, December 16, https://www2.buddhistdoor.net/features/exploring-engaged-buddhism-with-professor-christopher-queen.

Siderits, Mark, 2007. *Buddhism as Philosophy*. Aldershot: Ashgate Publishing.
Siegmund, Georg, 1980. *Buddhism and Christianity: A Preface to Dialogue*. Trans. by Sister Mary Frances McCarthy. Tuscaloosa: University of Alabama Press.
———. 1983. *Buddhismus und Christentum. Vorbereitung eines Dialogs*. 2nd ed. Sankt Augustin: Steyler Verlag.
Sigalow, Emily, 2019. *American JewBu: Jews, Buddhists, and Religious Change*. Princeton, NJ: Princeton University Press.
Slone, D. Jason, 2005. *Theological Incorrectness: Why Religious People Believe What They Shouldn't*. Oxford: Oxford University Press.
Smart, Ninian, 1993. *Buddhism and Christianity: Rivals and Allies*. Basingstoke: Macmillan.
———. 1996. *Dimensions of the Sacred: An Anatomy of the World's Beliefs*. Berkeley: University of California Press.
Smith, Jonathan Z., 1982. *Imagining Religion: From Babylon to Jonestown*. Chicago: University of Chicago Press.
Smith, Steven G., 2021. "What Is Merit, That It Can Be Transferred?" *International Journal for Philosophy of Religion*, https://doi.org/10.1007/s11153-021-09798-8.
Smith, Wilfred Cantwell, [1963] 1978. *The Meaning and End of Religion*. San Francisco: Harper & Row.
———. 1979. *Faith and Belief*. Princeton, NJ: Princeton University Press.
———. 1993. *What Is Scripture? A Comparative Approach*. London: SCM Press.
Snellgrove, David, 1971. *The Hevajra Tantra: A Critical Study*. Part I: *Introduction and Translation*. Reprint. London: Oxford University Press.
Snellgrove, David; Richardson, Hugh, 1986. *A Cultural History of Tibet*. Boston: Shambhala.
So, Yuen-tai, 2017. "Buddhist-Christian Relations in China: An Overview." In *Buddhist-Christian Relations in Asia*, ed. by P. Schmidt-Leukel, 355–73. St. Ottilien: EOS Editions.
Spae, Joseph J., 1980. *Buddhist-Christian Empathy*. Chicago: Chicago Institute of Theology and Culture; Tokyo: Oriens Institute for Religious Research.
Spence Hardy, Robert, 1874. *Christianity and Buddhism Compared*. Colombo: Wesleyan Mission Press.
Spiro, Melford, 1982. *Buddhism and Society: A Great Tradition and Its Burmese Vicissitudes*. 2nd exp. ed. Berkeley: University of California Press.
Sponberg, Alan; Hardacre, Helen (eds.), 1988. *Maitreya, the Future Buddha*. Cambridge: Cambridge University Press.
Steinberg, Julius, 2010. "Fels." *Wissenschaftliches Bibellexikon im Internet*, http://www.bibelwissenschaft.de/stichwort/18257/.
Steineck, Christian, 2000. *Grundstrukturen mystischen Denkens*. Würzburg: Königshausen und Neumann.
Stimpfle, Alois, 1996. "'Ihr seid schon rein durch das Wort' (Joh 15,3a). Her-

meneutische und methodische Überlegungen zur Frage nach 'Sünde' und 'Vergebung' im Johannesevangelium." In *Sünde und Erlösung im Neuen Testament*, ed. by H. Frankemölle, 108–22. QD 161. Freiburg: Herder.

Streeter, Burnett Hillman, 1932. *The Buddha and the Christ: An Exploration of the Meaning of the Universe and of the Purpose of Human Life*. London: Macmillan and Co.

Strong, John S., 2004. *Relics of the Buddha*. Princeton, NJ: Princeton University Press.

———. 2016a. *The Legend of King Aśoka. A Study and Translation of the Aśokāvadāna*. Delhi: Motilal Banarsidass.

———. 2016b. "The Buddha, Fact and Fiction: A Kaleidoscopic History of Western Views of the Buddha." In *History as a Challenge to Buddhism and Christianity*, ed. by E. Harris; J. O'Grady, 139–65. St. Ottilien: EOS-Editions.

Studholme, Alexander, 2002. *The Origins of Oṃ Maṇipadme Hūṃ: A Study of the Kāraṇḍavyūha Sūtra*. Albany: State University Press of New York.

Sullivan, Lawrence, 2000. "The Net of Indra: Comparison and the Contribution of Perception." In *A Magic Still Dwells: Comparative Religion in the Postmodern Age,* ed. by K. C. Patton; B. C. Ray, 206–34. Berkeley: University of California Press.

Suwanbubbha, Parichart 1994. *Grace and Karma: A Case Study of Religio-Cultural Encounters in Protestant and Buddhist Communities in Bangkok and Its Relevant Environs, Thailand*. Chicago: Lutheran School of Theology (unpublished dissertation).

Suzuki, Daisetz Teitaro, 1965. "Review of: *A History of Zen Buddhism* by Heinrich Dumoulin." *The Eastern Buddhist* New Series 1:1, 123–26.

———. 1973a. *Collected Writings on Shin Buddhism*, ed. by the Eastern Buddhist Society. Kyoto: Shinshū Ōtaniha.

———. 1973b. *Zen and Japanese Culture*. 3rd ed. Princeton, NJ: Princeton University Press [1959].

———. 1977. *Outlines of Mahayana Buddhism*. New York: Schocken Books. [First ed. London: Luzac, 1907.]

———. 1980. *Der westliche und der östliche Weg. Essays über christliche und buddhistische Mystik*. Frankfurt a.M.: Ullstein.

———. 2007. *Mysticism: Christian and Buddhist*. London: Routledge Classics. [First ed. London: Allen & Unwin, 1957.]

Swearer, Donald K., 1989. *Me and Mine: Selected Essays of Bhikkhu Buddhdāsa*. Albany: State University of New York Press.

———. 2006. "An Assessment of Buddhist Eco-Philosophy." *The Harvard Theological Review* 99:2, 123–37.

Swidler, Leonard, 1990. *After the Absolute: The Dialogical Future of Religious Reflection*. Minneapolis: Fortress Press.

Takacs, Axel M. Oaks; Kimmel, Joseph L. (eds.), 2024. *The Wiley Blackwell*

Companion to Comparative Theology. A Festschrift in Honor of Francis X. Clooney, SJ. Hoboken, NJ: Wiley-Blackwell.

Takasaki, Jikidō, 1997. "Thoughts on Dhātu-vāda and Recent Trends in Buddhist Studies." In *Pruning the Bodhi Tree: The Storm over Critical Buddhism*, ed. by J. Hubbard; P. L. Swanson, 314–20. Honolulu: University of Hawai'i Press.

Tambiah, Stanley J., 2007. *World Conqueror and World Renouncer: A Study of Buddhism and Polity in Thailand against a Historical Background*. Cambridge: Cambridge University Press. [Reissue of the 1977 edition.]

Tanaka, Kenneth K., 1990. *The Dawn of Chinese Pure Land Buddhism*. Albany, NY: SUNY Press.

———. 2007. "Where Is the Pure Land? Controversy in Chinese Buddhism on the Nature of the Pure Land." In *Shin Buddhism: Historical, Textual, and Interpretative Studies*, ed. by R. K. Payne, 99–113. Berkeley, CA: Institute of Buddhist Studies and Numata Center for Buddhist Translation and Research.

Taves, Anne, 2009. *Religious Experience Reconsidered: A Building-Block Approach to the Study of Religion and Other Special Things*. Princeton, NJ: Princeton University Press.

Teiser, Stephen F., 1994. *The Scripture of the Ten Kings and the Making of Purgatory in Medieval Chinese Buddhism*. Honolulu: University of Hawai'i Press.

Thatamanil, John J., 2017. "Learning from (and Not Just about) Our Religious Neighbors: Comparative Theology and the Future of *Nostra Aetate*." In *The Future of Interreligious Dialogue: A Multireligious Conversation on Nostra Aetate*, ed. by C. L. Cohen; P. F. Knitter; U. Rosenhagen, 289–301. Maryknoll, NY: Orbis Books.

———. 2020. *Circling the Elephant: A Comparative Theology of Religious Diversity*. New York: Fordham University Press.

Thomas à Kempis, 2012. *The Imitation of Christ*. Translated from the Latin into modern English. Originally published by the Bruce Publishing Company, Milwaukee. Republished by B. C. Okonkwo.

Thompson, Ross, 2010. *Buddhist Christianity: A Passionate Openness*. Winchester: O-Books.

Thurman, Robert A. F., 1976. *The Holy Teaching of Vimalakīrti: A Mahāyāna Scripture*. University Park: Pennsylvania State University Press.

Thurston, Bonnie Bowman (ed.), 2007. *Merton and Buddhism: Wisdom, Emptiness, and Everyday Mind*. Louisville, KY: Fons Vitae.

Tiefenauer, Marc, 2017. *Les enfers indiens. Histoire multiple d'un lieu commun*, Boston: Brill.

Tilakaratne, Asanga, 2016. "The Ultimate Buddhist Religious Goal: Nirvana and Its Implications for Buddhist-Christian Dual Belonging." In *Buddhist-Christian Dual Belonging: Affirmations, Objections, Explorations*, ed. by G. D'Costa; R. Thompson, 89–106. Farnham: Ashgate.

Tillich, Paul, 1964. *Christianity and the Encounter of the World Religions.* New York: Columbia University Press.
———. 1987. "In der Tiefe ist Wahrheit." In *Religiöse Reden*, 3–173. Berlin: De Gruyter.
———. 2015. *Der Mut zum Sein.* Mit einem Vorwort von Christian Danz. 2nd ed. Berlin: De Gruyter.
Turner, Steve, 2009. *Amazing Grace: The Story of America's Most Beloved Song.* New York: HarperCollins.
Tweed, Thomas A., 2006. *Crossing and Dwelling: A Theory of Religion.* Cambridge, MA: Harvard University Press.
Tworuschka, Udo, 2015. *Einführung in die Geschichte der Religionswissenschaft.* Darmstadt: Wissenschaftliche Buchgesellschaft.
Ueda, Shizuteru, 2001. "Jesus in Contemporary Japanese Zen: With Special Regard to Keiji Nishitani." In *Buddhist Perceptions of Jesus*, ed. by P. Schmidt-Leukel, 42–58. St. Ottilien: EOS Verlag.
Ueda, Yoshifumi; Hirota, Dennis, 1989. *Shinran: An Introduction to His Thought.* Kyoto: Hongwanji International Center.
Usarski, Frank, 2001. "The Perception of Jesus and Christianity among Early German Buddhists." In *Buddhist Perceptions of Jesus*, ed. by P. Schmidt-Leukel; with J. Götz and G. Köberlin, 106–29. St. Ottilien: EOS-Editions.
Valea, Ernest, 2008. *The Buddha and the Christ: Reciprocal Views.* Eigenverlag durch BookSearch.
Valignano, Alessandro, SJ, 1944. *Historia del Principio y Progresso de la Compañía de Jesús en las Indias Orientales (1542–64).* Ed. and commentary by Josef Wicki, SJ. Roma: Institutum Historicum SI.
Valkenber, Pim (ed.), 2022. *A Companion to Comparative Theology*, ed. by Pim Valkenberg; with Marianne Moyaert; Kristin Johnston Largen; James Fredericks; Bede Benjamin Bidlack. Leiden: Brill.
Van Dülmen, Richard, 1979. "Das Täufertum als sozialreligiöse Bewegung: Ein Versuch." *Zeitschrift für Historische Forschung* 6:2, 185–97.
Van Put, Ineke, 2015. *Buddhist Hells: The Northern Tradition.* Mumbai: Somaiya Publications.
Veer, Peter van der, 1994. "Syncretism, Multiculturalism, and the Discourse of Tolerance." In *Syncretism/Anti-syncretism: The Politics of Religious Synthesis*, ed. by C. Stewart; R. Shaw, 196–211. London: Routledge.
Vermes, Geza, 1981. *The Gospel of Jesus the Jew.* The Riddell Memorial Lectures. Newcastle upon Tyne: University of Newcastle upon Tyne.
———. 1993. *Jesus der Jude. Ein Historiker liest die Evangelien.* Neukirchen-Vluyn: Neukirchner Verlag.
———. 2001. *The Changing Faces of Jesus.* London: Penguin Books.
Vivekananda, Swami, 1994. *The Complete Works of Swami Vivekananda.* Mayavati Memorial Edition. 8 vols. Calcutta: Advaita Ashrama.
Völker, Fabian, 2016. "On All-Embracing Mental Structures: Towards a Transcendental Hermeneutics of Religion." In *Interreligious Comparisons in*

Religious Studies and Theology: Comparison Revisited, ed. by P. Schmidt-Leukel; A. Nehring, 142–60. London: Bloomsbury.
———. 2018a. "Transzendentale Subjektivität und Geistmetaphysik. Zur noomorphen Grundlegung des anthropologischen Transzendenzbezuges im Advaita- und Viśiṣṭādvaita-Vedānta." In *Dimensionen des Menschseins—Wege der Transzendenz?*, ed. by B. Nitsche; F. Baab, 199–223. Paderborn: Ferdinand Schöningh.
———. 2018b. "'Die tiefste unlösbare Verlegenheit des abstrakten Monismus': Śaṅkara und Schelling über den Ursprung der endlichen Erscheinungswelt." In *Schelling Studien. Internationale Zeitschrift zur klassischen deutschen Philosophie*. Vol. 6, 79–100. Freiburg: Karl Alber.
———. 2019. "Transzendentalphilosophie und transkulturelle Religionsphilosophie. Zur Lehre des Absoluten bei Śaṅkara und Fichte." In *Philosophie der Zukunft–Zukunft der Philosophie. Zu den Perspektiven der Philosophie als Grundlagenwissenschaft*, ed. by K. Gregor, 184–242. Freiburg: Karl Alber 2019.
———. 2020. "Methodologie und Mystik. Plädoyer für eine integrale Religionswissenschaft." In *Wissen um Religion: Erkenntnis—Interesse. Epistemologie und Episteme in Religionswissenschaft und Interkultureller Theologie*, ed. by K. Hock, 339–62. Leipzig: Evangelische Verlagsanstalt.
Vollenweider, Samuel, 1991. "Großer Tod und Großes Leben. Ein Beitrag zum buddhistisch-christlichen Gespräch im Blick auf die Mystik des Paulus." *Evangelische Theologie* 51, 365–82.
———. 2014. "Weltdistanz und Weltzuwendung im Urchristentum." In *Der Mensch zwischen Weltflucht und Weltverantwortung. Lebensmodelle der paganen und der jüdisch-christlichen Antike*, ed. by H.-G. Nesselrath; M. Rühl, 127–45. Tübingen: Mohr Siebeck.
Von Borsig, Margareta, 1992. *Lotos-Sūtra. Sūtra von der Lotosblume des wunderbaren Gesetzes*. Nach dem chinesischen Text von Kumārajīva ins Deutsche übersetzt und eingeleitet von Margareta von Borsig. Gerlingen: Lambert Schneider.
Von Brück, Michael, 1999. *Religion und Politik im Tibetischen Buddhismus*. München: Kösel Verlag.
Von Brück, Michael; Lai, Whalen, 1997. *Buddhismus und Christentum. Geschichte, Konfrontation, Dialog*. München: C. H. Beck Verlag.
Von Glasenapp, Helmuth, 1966. *Der Buddhismus—eine atheistische Religion.* Mit einer Auswahl buddhistischer Texte, zusammengestellt von Heinz Bechert. München: Szczesny Verlag.
———. 1970. *Buddhism—A Non-theistic Religion*. With a selection from Buddhist Scriptures, ed. by Heinz Bechert. New York: George Braziller.
Von Harnack, Adolf, 1904. "Die Aufgabe der theologischen Fakultäten und die allgemeine Religionsgeschichte (1901)." In Adolf von Harnack, *Reden und Aufsätze*. Vol. 2:1, 159–87. Gießen: Töppelmann.
Von Stosch, Klaus, 2002. "Komparative Theologie—ein Ausweg aus dem

Grunddilemma jeder Theologie der Religionen?" *Zeitschrift für katholische Theologie* 124, 294–311.

———. 2012. *Komparative Theologie als Wegweiser in der Welt der Religionen.* Paderborn: Ferdinand Schöningh.

———. 2028. "Reflecting on Approaches to Jesus in the Qur'ān from the Perspective of Comparative Theology." In *How to Do Comparative Theology*, ed. by F. C. Clooney; K. von Stosch, 37–58. New York: Fordham University Press.

Vorgrimmler, Herbert, 1993. *Geschichte der Hölle.* München: Wilhelm Fink Verlag.

Voss Roberts, Michele (ed.), 2016. *Comparing Faithfully: Insights from Systematic Theological Reflection.* New York: Fordham University Press.

Waardenburg, Jacques, 2003. *Muslims and Others: Relations in Context.* Berlin: de Gruyter.

Wach, Joachim, [1924] 2001. *Religionswissenschaft. Prolegomena zu ihrer wissenschaftstheoretischen Grundlegung.* Neu herausgegeben und eingeleitet von Christoffer H. Grundmann. Waltrop: Hartmut Spenner.

———. 1988. *Introduction to the History of Religions*, ed. by Joseph M. Kitagawa; Gregory D. Alles, with the collaboration of Karl W. Lickert. New York: Macmillan.

Waldenfels, Bernhard, 1995. "Verschränkung von Heimwelt und Fremdwelt." In *Philosophische Grundlagen der Interkulturalität*, ed. by R. A. Mall; D. Lohmar, 55–65. Amsterdam: Rodopi.

Walshe, Maurice O'Connell, 1982. "Buddhism and Christianity: A Positive Approach." *Dialogue* N.S. 9, 3–39.

———. 1995. *The Long Discourses of the Buddha: A Translation of the Dīgha Nikāya. Translated from the Pāli.* Boston: Wisdom Publications.

———. 2009. *The Complete Mystical Works of Meister Eckhart.* Trans. and ed. by Maurice O'C. Walshe. Rev. with a foreword by Bernard McGinn. Reissue of the three-volume *Meister Eckhart: Sermons and Treatises*, trans. and ed. by M. O'C. Walshe. New York: Crossroad.

Ward, Keith, 1987. *Images of Eternity: Concepts of God in Five Religious Traditions.* London: Darton, Longman and Todd.

———. 1994. *Religion and Revelation: A Theology of Revelation in the World's Religions.* Oxford: Clarendon Press.

———. 1996. *Religion and Creation.* Oxford: Clarendon Press.

———. 1998. *Religion and Human Nature.* Oxford: Clarendon Press.

———. 2000. *Religion and Community.* Oxford: Clarendon Press.

Weber, Claudia, 1994. *Wesen und Eigenschaften des Buddha in der Tradition des Hīnayāna-Buddhismus.* Wiesbaden: Harrassowitz Verlag.

———. 1998. "Der Buddha nach der Lehre des Theravāda." In *Wer ist Buddha? Eine Gestalt und ihre Bedeutung für die Menschheit*, ed. by P. Schmidt-Leukel, 35–49. München: Eugen Diederichs Verlag.

Wecker, Otto, 1908. *Christus und Buddha.* Münster: Aschendorff.

Wecker, Otto; Koch, Wilhelm, 1910. *Christentum und Weltreligionen*. 2nd rev. ed. Rottenburg a.N.: Wilhelm Bader.
Weinrich, Friedrich. 1935. *Die Liebe im Buddhismus und im Christentum*. Berlin: Alfred Töpelmann.
Welbon, Guy Richard, 1968. *The Buddhist Nirvāṇa and Its Western Interpreters*. Chicago: University of Chicago Press.
Whalen, Robert K., 2006. "Pentecostalism." In *Encyclopedia of Millennialism and Millennial Movements*, ed. by R. A. Landes, 534–40. New York: Routledge.
Whaling, Frank, 1986. *Christian Theology and World Religions: A Global Approach*. Basingstoke: Marshall Pickering.
White, Lynn, 1967. "The Historical Roots of Our Ecological Crisis." *Science* 155, 1203–7.
Wiebe, Donald, 2020. *The Learned Practice of Religion in the Modern University*. London: Bloomsbury Academic.
Wildman, Wesley J., 2017. *In Our Own Image: Anthropomorphism, Apophaticism, and Ultimacy*. Oxford: Oxford University Press.
Wilke, Alexa, 2016. "Licht / Dunkelheit (AT)." *Wissenschaftliches Bibellexikon im Internet*. http://www.bibelwissenschaft.de/stichwort/24979/.
Williams, Janett P., 2000. *Denying Divinity: Apophasis in the Patristic Christian and Soto Zen Buddhist Traditions*. Oxford: Oxford University Press.
Williams, Paul, 2002. *The Unexpected Way: On Converting from Buddhism to Catholicism*. Edinburgh: T&T Clark.
———. 2006a. *Buddhism from a Catholic Perspective*. London: Catholic Truth Society.
———. 2006b. *Mein Weg zu Buddha und zurück: Warum ich wieder Christ bin*. München: Pattloch.
———. 2009. *Mahāyāna Buddhism: The Doctrinal Foundations*. 2nd rev. ed. London: Routledge.
———. 2011. "Catholicism and Buddhism." In *The Catholic Church and the World Religions: A Theological and Phenomenological Account*, ed. by G. D'Costa, 141–77. London: T&T Clark International.
Winkler, Ulrich, 2013. *Wege der Religionstheologie. Von der Erwählung zur komparativen Theologie*. Innsbruck: Tyrolia.
Winter, Franz, 2008. *Das Frühchristliche Mönchtum und der Buddhismus. Religionsgeschichtliche Studien*. Frankfurt am Main: Peter Lang.
Wittgenstein, Ludwig, 1986. *Philosophical Investigations*. Trans. by G. E. M. Anscombe. 3rd ed. Oxford: Basil Blackwell. [1st ed. 1958.]
Wolff, Catherine, 2021. *Beyond: How Humankind Thinks about Heaven*. New York: Riverhead Books.
Yagi, Seiichi, 1988. *Die Front-Struktur als Brücke vom buddhistischen zum christlichen Denken*. München: Christian Kaiser Verlag.
Yandell, Keith; Netland, Harold, 2009. *Buddhism: A Christian Exploration and Appraisal*. Downers Grove, IL: IVP Academic.

Yokota, John Shunji, 2000. "Understanding Amida Buddha and the Pure Land: A Process Approach." In *Toward a Contemporary Understanding of Pure Land Buddhism: Creating a Shin Buddhist Theology in a Religiously Plural World*, ed. by D. Hirota, 73–100. Albany, NY: SUNY Press.

———. 2005. "Where beyond Dialogue? Reconsiderations of a Buddhist Pluralist." In *Deep Religious Pluralism*, ed. by David Ray Griffin, 91–107. Louisville, KY: Westminster John Knox Press.

Yong, Amos, 2012a. *Pneumatology and the Christian-Buddhist Dialogue: Does the Spirit Blow through the Middle Way?* Leiden: Brill.

———. 2012b. *The Cosmic Breath: Spirit and Nature in the Christianity-Buddhism-Science Trialogue*. Leiden: Brill.

Young, Frances M., 1983. *From Nicaea to Chalcedon: A Guide to the Literature and Its Background*. London: SCM Press.

Young, R. F.; Senanayaka, G. S. B., 1998. *The Carpenter-Heretic: A Collection of Buddhist Stories about Christianity from 18th-Century Sri Lanka*. Colombo: Karunaratne & Sons.

Yu, Chai-Shin, 1981. *Early Buddhism and Christianity: A Comparative Study of the Founders' Authority, the Community and the Discipline*. Delhi: Motilal Banarsidass.

Yu, Xue, 2003. "Buddhist-Christian Encounter in Modern China: Taixu's Perspective on Christianity." *Ching Feng* New Series 4:2, 157–201.

Zaleski, Carol, 1987. *Otherworld Journeys: Accounts of Near-Death Experience in Medieval and Modern Times*. New York: Oxford University Press.

Zimmermann, Michael, 2002. *A Buddha within the Tathâgatagarbhasūtra: The Earliest Exposition of the Buddha-Nature Teaching in India*. Tokyo: International Research Institute for Advanced Buddhology, Soka University.

Zin, Monika; Schlingloff, Dieter, 2007. *Saṃsāracakra. Das Rad der Wiedergeburten in der indischen Übderlieferung*. Düsseldorf: EKŌ-Haus.

Zürcher, Erik, 1982. "'Prince Moonlight': Messianism and Eschatology in Early Medieval Chinese Buddhism." *T'oung Pao* Second Series 68, 1–3, 1–75.

———. 2007. *The Buddhist Conquest of China: The Spread and Adaptation of Buddhism in Early Medieval China*. 3rd ed. Leiden: Brill.

Index of Names

Abe, Masao, 161, 164
Amaladass, Anand, 164
Alighieri, Dante, 219
Anderson, Carol S., 21
Anderson, Gary A., 132, 133
Ambedkar, Bhimrao Ramji, 58
Ambrose of Milan, 219
Aquinas, Thomas, 103, 105, 115, 137, 215
Ariaratne, Ahangamage Tudor, 58
Ashoka, 54, 82–83
Ashvaghosha, 143–44
Augustine of Hippo, 40, 44, 72, 82–83, 103, 135–37, 152, 179–80, 190, 215, 218–19, 224, 236
Awasthi, Bhuvanesh, 114

Bailey, D. R. Shackleton, 202
Barr, James, 77, 211–12
Barth, Hans-Martin, 185
Barth, Karl, 48, 170
Barthélemy Saint-Hilaire, Jules, 87–88
Barthes, Roland, 24–25
Basham, Arthur L., 127
Baskind, James Matthew, 230
Batchelor, Stephen, 88
Bauks, Michaela, 102
Bechert, Heinz, 176
Belsey, Catherine, 24
Bendall, Cecil, 127, 129
Benedict of Nursia, 75
Benz, Ernst, 238
Berger, Peter, 11
Bergunder, Michael, 7, 12
Bernard of Clairvaux, 217
Bernhardt, Reinhold, 10, 16, 18–19, 21, 49
Bernstorff, Freya, 17
Berrigan, Daniel, 80
Berry, Thomas Sterling, 52–53, 144, 170
Bertholet, Alfred, 52, 87

Berthrong John, 16
Bhavaviveka. *See* Bhaviveka
Bhaviveka, 129
Bhavya. *See* Bhaviveka
Bidwell, Duane R., 10
Billmann-Mahecha, Elfriede, 10
Bischofberger, Norbert, 224
Blake, William, 221
Blée, Fabrice, 75
Bleeker, C. Jouco, 24
Bodhi, Bhikkhu, 52, 55, 60, 62, 77, 79, 88, 96, 116, 152, 175, 186, 197, 201
Bosch, Gabriele, 137
Boyarin, Daniel, 68
Brox, Norbert, 73
Bubolz, Georg, 132
Buddha. See Gautama, Siddhartha
Buddhadasa, Bhikkhu Indapañño, 41–42, 58, 161, 242
Buddhaghosa, 117
Burckhardt, Titus, 44
Büttner, Gerhard, 10

Cabezón, José I., 55, 118, 158
Calvin, John, 180, 220, 224
Carpenter, Joseph Estlin, 55, 142, 149, 190
Carus, Paul, 144–45, 147
Casadio, Giovanni, 31
Caspar-Seeger, Ulrike, 17
Cattoi, Thomas, 21, 224
Ceming, Katharina, 91
Chandrkaew, Chinda, 95
Ching, Julia, 33–34
Chung, Paul, 181
Clark, Anthony E., 145
Cleary, Thomas, xiii, xiv, 177
Clement of Alexandria, 115, 190, 223
Clooney, Francis X., 16, 20
Cobb, John B., 34–38, 40, 107, 236,
Cohn-Sherbok, Daniel, 212

280 The Celestial Web

Cole, Alan, 124, 126
Collins, John, 69–70
Collins, Steven, 91–93, 95, 114–15, 195–97, 199–200, 202, 204, 205, 222, 231
Colpe, Carsten, 120
Conze, Edward, 67, 75
Corless, Roger J., 207
Cornille, Catherine, 10, 16–17, 19, 237–43
Couliano, Ioan P., 31–33, 73, 76, 149, 234
Coward, Harold, 122
Cowell, E. B, 143
Culiano, Ioan P. *See* Couliano, Ioan P.
Cullmann, Oscar, 211
Cunningham, Lawrence S., 75
Cupitt, Don, 92

D'Costa, Gavin, 10
Dalai Lama. *See* Gyatso, Tenzin
Dante. *See* Alighieri, Dante
Danz, Christian, 18
Davies, Brian, 216
Dayal, Har, 127, 176
Dehn, Ulrich, 17
Deitrick, James E., 57–58
Deleuze, Gilles, 24–25
Demacopoulos, George E., 180
Desideri, Ippolito, 86
De Silva, Lynn A., 112–13, 164–65
Dharmapala, Anagarika, 2, 56, 89, 172, 182
Dharmasiri, Gunapala, 89, 172
Dietrich, Veit-Jacobus, 10
Diller, Jeanine, 91, 92, 119
Doering, Lutz, x, 103
Dogen Zenji, 91
Drew, Rose, 10, 81, 235
Driller, Josephine, 218
Dunn, James D. G., 133, 148, 184, 185
Dushun, xiii

Eckel, Malcolm David, 100
Eckhart, Meister, 90–91, 105, 113, 192, 216–18, 225
Eliade, Mircea, 35, 155
Elinor, Robert, 151
Elison, George, 158
Elliott, Joel, 222
Emmerick, R. E., 127
Englert, Winfried Philipp, 146
Evagrius Ponticus, 75

Fa-shun. *See* Dushun
Faber, Roland, 33
Faure, Bernard, 150
Feldmeier, Peter, 75
Feng, Jinxueh, 185
Ferraro, Guiseppe, 88
Feuerbach, Ludwig, 92
Feulner, Rüdiger, 151, 152
Fischer-Barnicol, Hans, 185
Fitzgerald, Timothy, 7
Flasch, Kurt, 136, 152, 179,
Ford, James L., 32–33
Franck, Adolphe, 88
Fredericks, James L., 82–84, 164
Fredriksen, Paula, 135–37
Freiberger, Oliver, xv, 12–15, 65, 150,
Fucan, Fabian. *See* Fukansai, Habian
Fukansai, Habian, 230

Garfield, Jay L., 88, 94, 108
Garnier, Adolphe, 88
Gates, Barbara, 57, 60
Geis, Lioba, 44
Gethin, Rupert, 204
Gautama, Siddhartha, 2, 51–53, 61, 65, 99, 142–45, 147–49, 151–55, 161, 172, 175, 187, 199, 239
Gladigow, Burkhard, 6
Gogerly, Daniel, 86–87
Gombrich, Richard F., 57, 238
Gōmez, Luis O., 206, 207
Goosen, Gideon, 10
Gowans, Christopher W., 93, 114
Granoff, Phyllis, 124, 127
Gregory, Peter N., 187
Griffin, David Ray, 34, 35, 107
Griffiths, Paul J., 151, 154
Grimm, Georg, 2, 142
Groner, Paul, 127
Guardini, Romano, 145–46
Guattari, Félix, 24–25
Gupta, Satish, 164–65
Guruge, Ananda, 3, 56, 89, 172
Gustafson, Hans, 21
Gwynne, Paul, 14
Gyatso, Tenzin, 161, 164

Haas, Alois M., 216
Haight, Roger, 138–40, 154, 160
Hakamaya, Noriaki, 198
Hanh, Thich Nhat, 58, 79–81, 140, 158, 208–09, 232

Index of Names

Hardacre, Helen, 204
Hardy, Edmund, 54
Harris, Elizabeth J., 62, 87, 112, 160, 161
Harris, Ian, 57
Hartmann, Heiko, 134
Harvey, Peter, 93, 100, 114, 128, 183
Hasenhüttl, Gotthold, 92
Haußig, Hans-Michael, 7
Hazra, Kanai Lal, 83
Hedges, Paul, 19
Heiler, Friedrich, 2, 5, 33, 88
Heim, S. Mark, 35–38, 40, 107, 236
Heymericus de Campo, 44
Hick, John H., 8, 20, 88, 107–11, 113, 222–23, 228
Hirota, Dennis, 99, 101, 131, 132, 178, 207, 208,
Hock, Klaus, 5
Hoheisel, Karl, 73
Holenstein, Elmar, 28–30
Honen Shonin, 140, 208
Hubbard, Jamie, 198
Hübner, Reinhard M., 150
Hühn, Helmuth, 137
Hume, David, 2, 47
Hutchison, John A., 35
Hwang, Soonil, 196

Ikeda, Daisaku, 58
Ingram, Paul O., 21
Izutsu, Toshihiko, 156

Jackson, Carl T., 144
Jackson, Roger, 119
Jackson, William J., xv–xvi, 27, 30, 44
James, William, 9
Jenson, Matt, 136, 137
Jesus of Nazareth, 31, 48–49, 53, 56, 68–71, 102, 104, 133–35, 142–56, 158–61, 163, 171–72, 179, 191–92, 212–14, 238–39
John Cassian, 75
John Paul II, 55
Johnston, Gilbert L., 209
Jones, Christopher Victor, 64, 183, 198
Junginger, Horst, 15

Kaelber, Walter O., 63
Kak, Subhash, 44
Karunadasa, Yakupitiyage, 116
Kasher, Asa, 119
Kaza, Stephanie, 60

Keel, Hee-Sung, 159, 163
Keenan, John P., 202, 203, 239
Keenan, Linda K., 239
Kehl-Bodrogi, Kriztina, 156
Kelly, J. N. D., 102, 104, 151
Kenkel, N. C., 27
Kenntner, Karl, 54, 120
Keown, Damien, 57
Kern, Hendrik, 86, 98, 118
Kern, Iso, 158
Khorchide, Mouhanad, 21
Kiblinger, Kristin Beise, 19
Kiefer, Jörn, 133
Kigoshi, Yasushi, 208
Kimmel, Joseph L., 16
king, 55
King, Martin Luther, Jr., 80
King, Sallie B., 57, 81–82
King, Winston, 54–55
Kingsley, Charles, 221
Kiyozawa, Manshi, 209
Kleine, Christoph, 65, 150
Klimkeit, Hans-Joachim, 78
Knitter, Paul, xi, 10, 33, 113, 138–41, 154, 159–60, 230
Koch, Klaus, 69
Koch, Wilhelm, 87
Kraemer, Hendrik, 170
Kraft, Kenneth, 60
Kreinath, Jens, 33
Kreiner, Armin, 188
Kretser, Bryan de, 54, 170
Krishna, Daya, 60, 61, 63
Küng, Hans, 34, 68, 75, 148

Lai, Pan-chiu, 148, 163, 185, 186, 193, 207, 209
Lai, Whalen, 21, 66–67, 80, 91, 229
Lampe, G.W.H., 153
Lanczkowski, Günter, 5, 24, 44
Lang, Bernhard, 210, 211, 212, 216, 219–22, 224 227, 230–31
Langer-Kaneko, Christiane, 230
Lavater, Johann Caspar, 221
Le Goff, Jacques, 223
Lefebure, Leo, 75 142, 181
Lehmann, Karl, 242
Lehtipuu, Outi, 211, 213, 215
Leirvik, Oddbjørn, 21
Lengsfeld, Peter, 222
Leppin, Volker, 182, 216, 217, 218
Lerner, Robert E., 217

Lessing, Gotthold Ephraim, 224
Liu, Ming-Wood, 229
Löhr, Gebhard, 13
Löhr, Winrich, 180
Loichinger, Alexander, 188
Lopez, Donald S., 164
Lovin, Robin W., 84
Löwner, Gudrun, 164
Luther, Martin, 45, 104, 121, 137, 152, 178, 180–81, 220, 241
Luz, Ulrich, 142, 153–54, 191–92

Macy, Joanna, 57, 60n57
Magliola, Robert, 171
Maharaj, Ayon, 40
Majrashi, A., 25
Makransky, John, 130
Malinar, Angelika, 63
Mall, Ram Adhar, 28
Mandelbrot, Benoît, xv, 25–26, 29–31
Mani, 73–74
Mann, Ulrich, 13
Marcion, 73–74
Martin of Cochem, 221
Masefield, Peter, 153
Masutani, Fumio, 58, 140, 173
Masuzawa, Tomoko, 2, 7
Matrceta, 202
Matsumoto, Shiro, 198
Matsunaga, Alicia, 125
Matsunaga, Daigan, 125
Maximus Confessor, 91
May, John D'Arcy, 21, 33, 47, 164, 181
McCutcheon, Russell T., 7, 13
McDannell, Colleen, 210–12, 216, 219–22, 224, 227, 231
McGinn, Bernard, 216, 218
McLaughlin, Robert E., 220
Mechthild of Magdeburg, 217–18
Medhananda, Swami. *See* Maharaj, Ayon
Meier-Staubach, Christel, 44
Mensching, Gustav, 54, 88, 121, 142, 169, 192, 193, 195
Mercadante, Linda, 16
Merton, Thomas, 75, 80
Metzner, Rainer, 134
Michaels, Axel, 142, 153–154, 191–92
Minois, Georges, 223
Mochizuki, Shinkō, 207
Mohl, Jules, 88
Moltmann, Jürgen, 211
Mommaers, Paul, 91

Monier-Williams, Monier, 54, 87, 144–45, 168–70
Moyaert, Marianne, 17, 19
Muhammad, 155–56
Müller, Friedrich Max, 1–2, 45–46, 200
Müntzer, Thomas, 220

Nagao, Gadjin M., 202
Nagarjuna, 88, 92, 100–101, 107–08, 236
Nakamura, Hajime, 58, 123, 125, 138, 173, 194, 198
Ñāṇamoli, Bhikkhu, 60, 77, 79, 152, 175, 186, 197, 201
Nash, Jonathan David, 114
Nattier, Jan, 127, 205
Nehring, Andreas, 12,13
Netland, Harold, 92, 122, 145, 170–71
Neumaier, Eva K., 118–19
Neville, Robert Cummings, 16
Newberg, Andrew, 114
Newton, John Henry, 132
Nicholson, Hugh, 2, 16, 19
Nickelsburg, George W.E., 211, 212
Nicolai, Philipp, 221
Niculescu, Mira, 10
Nietzsche, Friedrich, 29
Nishitani, Keiji, 90–91, 114, 160, 164, 166, 185
Nisker, Wes, 57, 60
Nitsche, Bernhard, 38–40, 113
Nonomura, Naotaro, 208
Notz, Klaus-Josef, 143

O'Grady, John, 181
Obirek, Stanislaw, 243
Oguro, Tatsuo, 181
Ohlig, Karl-Heinz, 150
Ohnuma, Reiko, 78
Olcott, Henry Steel, 238
Oldenberg, Hermann, 175
Origen, 135, 217, 223–24
Orzech, Charles D., 67
Otto, Rudolf, 2, 38, 48, 88, 128, 201
Ouyang Jingwu, 89
Overmyer, Daniel L., 205–06

Paden, William E., 26, 43
Pagels, Elaine, 75
Palihawadana, Mahinda, 174
Pallis, Marco, 113
Pande, Govind Chandra, 92
Pandit, Moti Lal, 92

Index of Names

Panikkar, Raimon, 20, 81–82
Pannenberg, Wolfhart, 13, 115, 148, 242
Papanikolaou, Aristotle, 180
Patel, Eboo, 21
Patton, Kimberley C., 12
Paul (Apostle), 70–71, 77, 133–34, 139, 160, 165, 173, 179, 184–86, 213, 215–16
Peace, Jennifer Howe, 21
Pelagius, 179–80
Pérez-Remón, Joaquín, 197
Pfeiffer, Franz, 217–18
Philo of Alexandria, 103
Pieris, Aloysius, 159, 235
Pitre, Bran James, 70
Pittman, Don A., 3, 89, 90, 172, 238
Plöger, Otto, 212
Plotinus, 102, 192, 217
Pollack, Detlef, 106
Porete, Marguerite, 218
Prebish, Charles, 57
Pruden, Leo M., 127 174
Pseudo-Dionysus the Areopagite, 91

Queen, Christopher S., 57–58
Quint, Josef, 217–18

Race, Alan, 47
Radaj, Dieter, 232
Raddatz, Alfred, 134
Rahner, Karl, 103, 105, 159–60, 224
Rahula, Walpola, 123
Ray, Benjamin C., 12
Rhys Davids, T.W., 157, 175, 199
Ricci, Mateo, 86
Richardson, Hugh, 67
Riches, John, 160
Ritzinger, Justin R., 208
Robson, James, 124–25, 127
Rockefeller, Steven C., 164
Rolston, Holmes, III, 236
Römer, Thomas, 102–03
Rose, Kenneth, 9, 46–47, 114
Rosta, Gergely, 106
Rouse, W. H. D., 127, 129
Rubenstein, Richard L., 114
Ruh, Kurt, 215

Sabbatucci, Dario, 6
Saler, Benson, 8
Sanders, Ed Parish, 133, 153, 185
Sawicki, Bernard, OSB, 75

Schalk, Peter, 7
Schleiermacher, Friedrich, 164
Schlieter, Jens, 7, 127
Schlingloff, Dieter, 120, 129, 204
Schmidt-Leukel, Perry, ix, x, xiii, xv, 3, 8, 10, 12–15, 18–21, 40, 42, 45–47, 51–53, 61, 63, 64, 67, 71–73, 77–79, 92, 97, 107, 109, 112, 114, 116, 117, 119–22, 126–31, 139, 143, 147, 148, 154, 155, 157, 159, 161–64, 177, 178, 181, 182, 187, 199, 200, 203, 204, 208, 223, 237, 240, 241
Schmithausen, Lambert, 60
Schomerus, Hilko Wiardo, 30–31, 40, 51–52, 87, 142, 190–92
Schopen, Gregory, 176
Schrage, Wolfgang, 68, 71
Schreiber, Stefan, 150
Schweitzer, Albert, 29
Scott, Archibald, 142, 144, 168–70
Sebastian, C.D., 94, 107–08
Seiwert, Hubert, 7
Sell, Alan P.F., 180
Senanayaka, G.S.B, 147
Shantideva, 126, 128–31, 139
Sharf, Robert H., 207
Sharma, Arvind, 153
Sharpe, Eric, 17
Shuyin, 58
Shinran Shonin, 99, 101, 131–32, 140, 171, 178, 181, 207–09
Siderits, Mark, 88, 94, 108
Siegmund, Georg, 142, 193
Sigalow, Emily, 10
Silverman, Noah J., 21
Sivaraksa, Sulak, 58
Slone, D. Jason, 9
Smart, Ninian, 8, 145, 191–92, 195
Smith, Jonathan Z., 7, 233–34
Smith, Steven G., 176
Smith, Wilfred Cantwell, 6, 20, 145
Snellgrove, David, 67, 118
So, Yuen-tai, 163, 172, 185, 186
Socrates, 146, 158
Söderblom, Nathan, 2, 33
Spae, Joseph J., 21
Spence Hardy, Robert, 87, 142
Spiegler, Gerhard E., 17
Spiro, Melford, 54–55, 67
Sri Ramacandra Bharati, 128, 201
Steinberg, Julius, 104
Steineck, Christian, 91

Stendahl, Krister, 211
Stimpfle, Alois, 135
Streeter, Burnett Hillman, 142, 148–50, 191–92
Strong, John S., 83, 150, 202
Studholme, Alexander, 99, 118
Sullivan, Lawrence, 25, 234
Suwanbubbha, Parichart, 181
Suzuki, Daisetz Teitaro, 57, 90, 131, 158, 161
Swanson, Paul L., 198
Swearer, Donald K., 42, 57
Swedenborg, Emanuel, 220–21
Swidler, Leonard, 17

T'ai-hsü. *See* Taixu
Taixu, 3, 89–90, 171–72, 208, 238
Takacs, Axel M. Oaks, 16
Takasaki, Jikidō, 198
Tambiah, Stanley J., 66, 67
Tanaka, Kenneth K., 177, 207
Tan-luan, 99, 207–08
Taves, Anne, 9
Thatamanil, John J., 20, 37–38, 40, 107, 236
Thomas à Kempis, 79
Thompson, Ross, 10, 161
Thurman, Robert A.F., 118, 187
Thurston, Bonnie Bowman, 75
Tiefenauer, Marc, 125
Tilakaratne, Asanga, 88
Tillich, Paul, 105, 192–93
Tweed, Thomas A., 9
Tworuschka, Udo, 1
Tu-shun. *See* Dushun

Ueda, Shizuteru, 160, 185
Ueda, Yoshifumi, 208n126

Valea, Ernest, 122, 193–95
Valignano, Allesandro, 178, 230
Van Bragt, Jan, 91
Van Dülmen, Richard, 220
Van Put, Ineke, 125, 126, 180, 223
Vermes, Geza, 70, 148, 150, 153
Vivekananda, Swami, 40–42, 242
Völker, Fabian, 113
Vollenweider, Samuel, 68, 185

Von Brück, Michael, 21, 67, 80, 91
Von Glasenapp, Helmuth, 85
Von Harnack, Adolf, 45–46
Von Stosch, Klaus, 16, 19–21
Vorgrimmler, Herbert, 223
Voss Roberts, Michele, 16

Waardenburg, Jacques, 45
Wach, Joachim, 4
Waldenfels, Bernhard, 28
Walker, D. J., 27
Walshe, Maurice O'Connell, 113, 175, 217, 218
Ward, Keith, 16
Weber, Claudia, 148, 151, 154
Wecker, Otto, 87, 142
Weeraratna, Senaka, 147
Weinrich, Friedrich, 169
Welbon, Guy Richard, 87–88
Whalen, Robert K., 66, 222
Whaling, Frank, 7–8
White, Lynn, 56–57
Wildman, Wesley J., 87, 106, 107, 111, 114
Wilke, Alexa, 104
Williams, Janett P., 91
Williams, Paul, 92, 98, 127, 163–64, 206, 240–41
Winkler, Ulrich, 19
Winter, Franz, xv, 73, 75, 76
Wittgenstein, Ludwig, 8
Wolff, Catherine, 189

Yagi, Seiichi, 185
Yandell, Keith, 92, 122, 145, 170, 171
Yokota, John Shunji, 161, 209, 238
Yong, Amos, 239
Young, Frances M., 148
Young, R. F., 147
Yu, Chai-Shin, 58, 194
Yu, Xue, 90, 172

Zaleski, Carol, 224
Zhang, Chunyi, 163, 185–86
Zimmermann, Michael, 184
Zin, Monika, 120, 129
Zürcher, Erik, 67, 205